HERO × DAISUKE HAGIWARA

Translation: Taylor Engel
Lettering: Alexis Eckerman

HORIMIYA vol. 4
© HERO • OOZ
© 2013 Daisuke Hagiwara / SQUARE ENIX CO., LTD. First published in Japan in 2013 by SQUARE ENIX CO., LTD. English translation rights arranged with SQUARE ENIX CO., LTD. and Yen Press, LLC through Tuttle-Mori Agency, Inc.

English translation © 2016 by SQUARE ENIX CO., LTD.

Yen Press
1290 Avenue of the Americas
New York, NY 10104

Visit us at yenpress.com • facebook.com/yenpress •
twitter.com/yenpress • yenpress.tumblr.com

First Yen Press Edition: July 2016

Yen Press is an imprint of Yen Press, LLC.
The Yen Press name and logo are trademarks
of Yen Press, LLC.

The publisher is not responsible for websites
(or their content) that are not owned by the
publisher.

Library of Congress Control Number:
2015960115

ISBNs: 978-0-316-27011-3 (paperback)
978-0-316-35664-0 (ebook)
978-0-316-35665-7 (app)

10 9 8 7 6 5

WOR

Printed in the United States of America

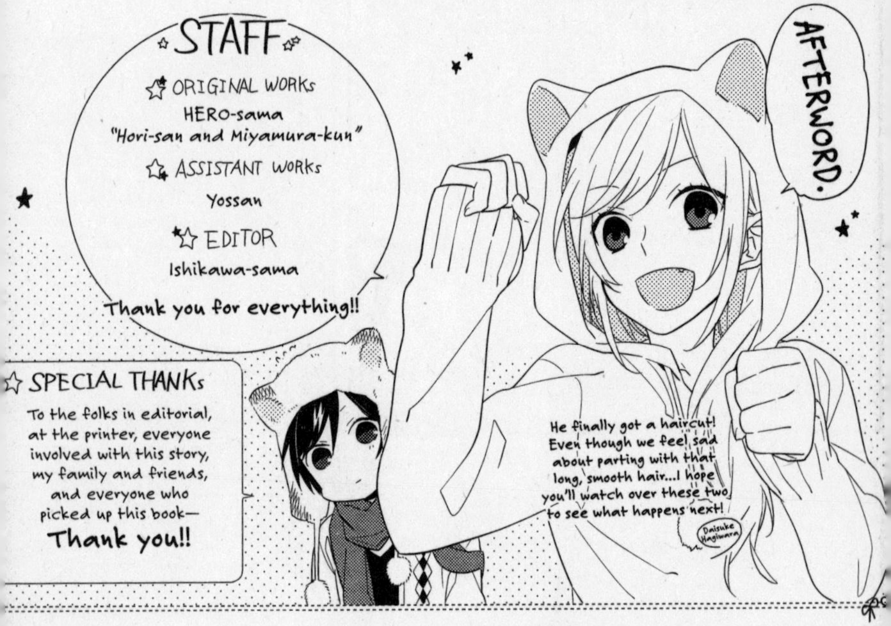
AFTERWORD.
He finally got a haircut! Even though we feel sad about parting with that long, smooth hair...I hope you'll watch over these two to see what happens next!
Daisuke Hagiwara
STAFF
ORIGINAL WORKs
HERO-sama
"Hori-san and Miyamura-kun"
ASSISTANT WORKs
Yossan
EDITOR
Ishikawa-sama
Thank you for everything!!
SPECIAL THANKs
To the folks in editorial, at the printer, everyone involved with this story, my family and friends, and everyone who picked up this book—
Thank you!!

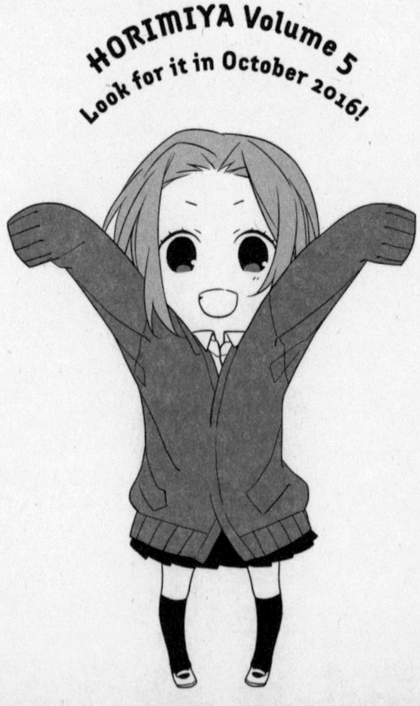
HORIMIYA Volume 5
Look for it in October 2016!

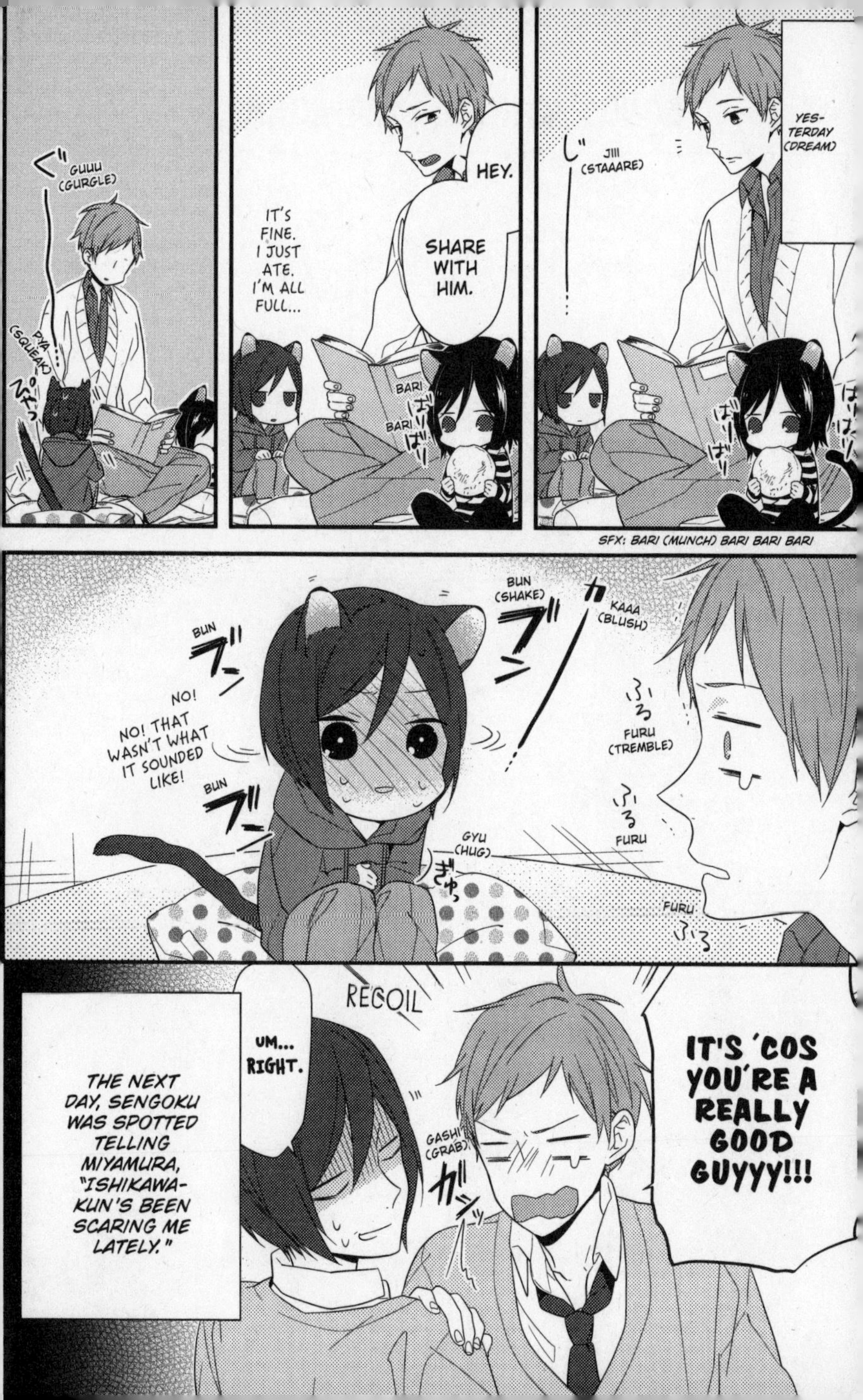
YES-TERDAY (DREAM)
JIII (STAARE)
HEY.
SHARE WITH HIM.
IT'S FINE. I JUST ATE. I'M ALL FULL...
BARI
BARI
GUUU (GURGLE)
PYA (SQUEAK)
SFX: BARI (MUNCH) BARI BARI BARI
KAAA (BLUSH)
BUN (SHAKE)
FURU (TREMBLE)
BUN
NO! NO! THAT WASN'T WHAT IT SOUNDED LIKE!
BUN
FURU
GYU (HUG)
FURU
IT'S 'COS YOU'RE A REALLY GOOD GUYYY!!!
RECOIL
UM... RIGHT.
GASHI (GRAB)
THE NEXT DAY, SENGOKU WAS SPOTTED TELLING MIYAMURA, "ISHIKAWA-KUN'S BEEN SCARING ME LATELY."

BONUS MANGA: MYAMURA ③

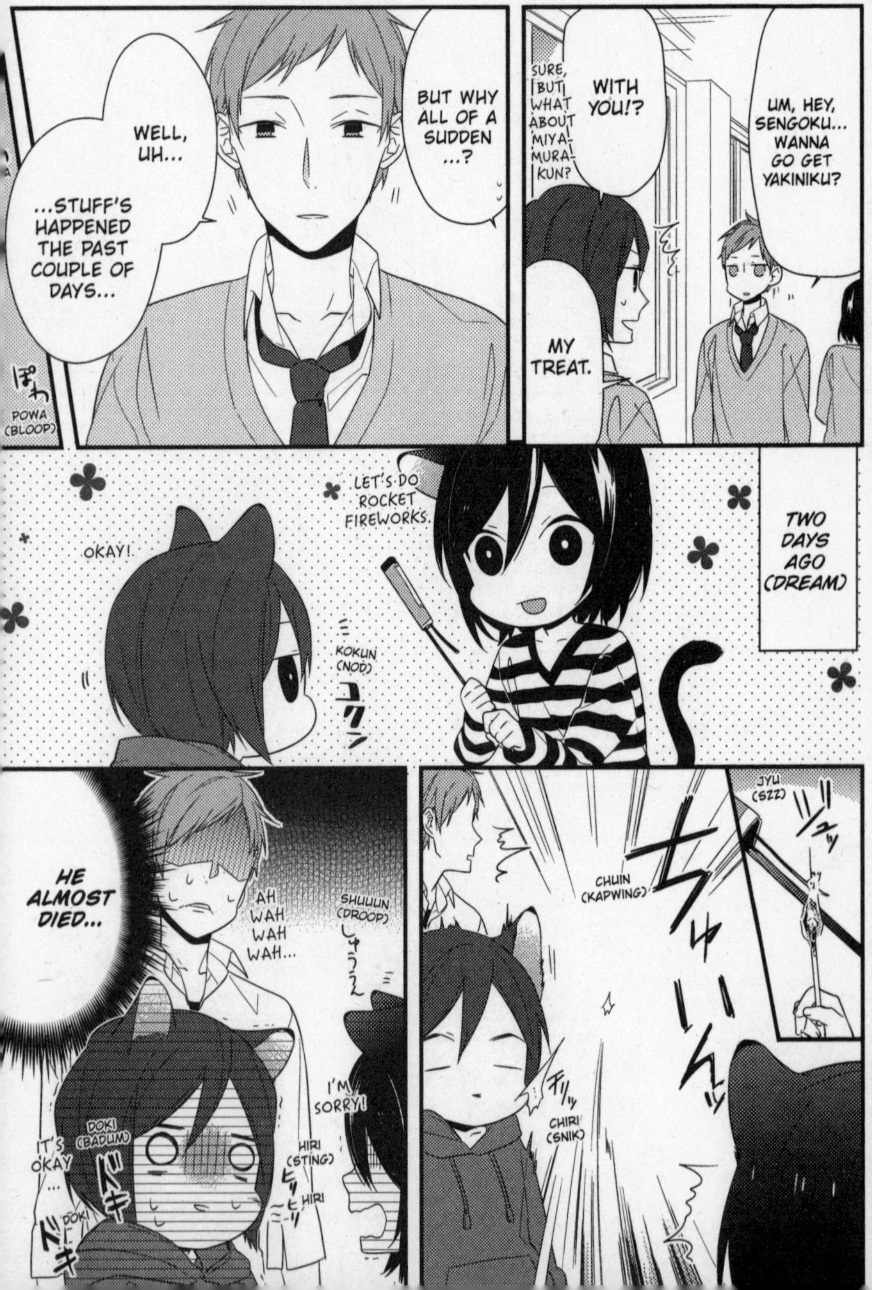
UM, HEY, SENGOKU... WANNA GO GET YAKINIKU?
WITH YOU!?
SURE, BUT WHAT ABOUT MIYA-MURA-KUN?
MY TREAT.
BUT WHY ALL OF A SUDDEN ...?
WELL, UH...
...STUFF'S HAPPENED THE PAST COUPLE OF DAYS...
ぽわ
POWA (BLOOP)
TWO DAYS AGO (DREAM)
LET'S DO ROCKET FIREWORKS.
OKAY!
KOKUN (NOD)
コクン
JYU (SZZ)
CHUIN (KAPWING)
CHIRI (SNIK)
HE ALMOST DIED...
AH WAH WAH WAH...
SHUUUN (DROOP)
I'M SORRY!
HIRI (STING)
HIRI
DOKI (BADUM)
DOKI
IT'S OKAY ...

Translation Notes

Page 129 – Ukyou
Ukyou is a neighborhood in Kyoto, but the character used for *-kyou* is in both Kyousuke's and Kyouko's names.

Page 130 – Sumika
Sumika is written with the characters for "clear/limpid" and "flower." *Sumi* is also the second character in Miyamura's first name.

Page 132 – Izumi
The surname of Souta's friend and Miyamura's given name are both Izumi but written with different characters.

Page 134 – Worm/warm
In the original, Miyamura is having trouble pronouncing Japanese words that can be easy to stumble over. In the original, he says *atatakai* ("warm") as "akkatai," *katatataki* ("shoulder massage") as "kakatataki," *yamabuki-iro* ("bright yellow") as "mamabuki-iro," and *zashiki warashi*—a childlike guardian spirit that lives in old, large houses and is said to ensure the fortunes of the house, provided the family takes care of it—as "washiki zarashi."

Page 136 – Tongue twisters
The original tongue twisters are:
Takeyabu ni take tatekaketa no ha takeyabu ni take tatekaketakatta kara takeyabu ni taketatekaketa.
("I almost stood up bamboo in the bamboo grove because I wanted to almost stand up bamboo in the bamboo grove, which is why I almost stood up bamboo in the bamboo grove.")
Bouzu ga byoubu ni jouzu ni bouzu no e wo kaita.
("The monk drew a good picture of a monk on the standing screen.")
Aka pajama ao pajama ki pajama.
("Red pajamas, blue pajamas, yellow pajamas.")

Page 152 – *Gestaltzerfall*
German for "shape decomposition," this is the term for what happens when you look at a word or complex shape for so long that you can't be conscious of it as itself anymore. It seems to lose meaning and come apart as individual letters or pieces.

Page 153 – Bathing with Hori's dad
Culturally, it isn't that weird to bathe with adults of the same gender in Japan, although it usually happens in public baths. Bathing with your girlfriend's dad at her house in a regular bathtub is still about as awkward as you'd expect.

Page 163 – "You say 'I'll see you later.'"
Miyamura is saying good-bye as if he was a guest, but Yuriko is telling him to say good-bye as if he's family.

To Be Continued...

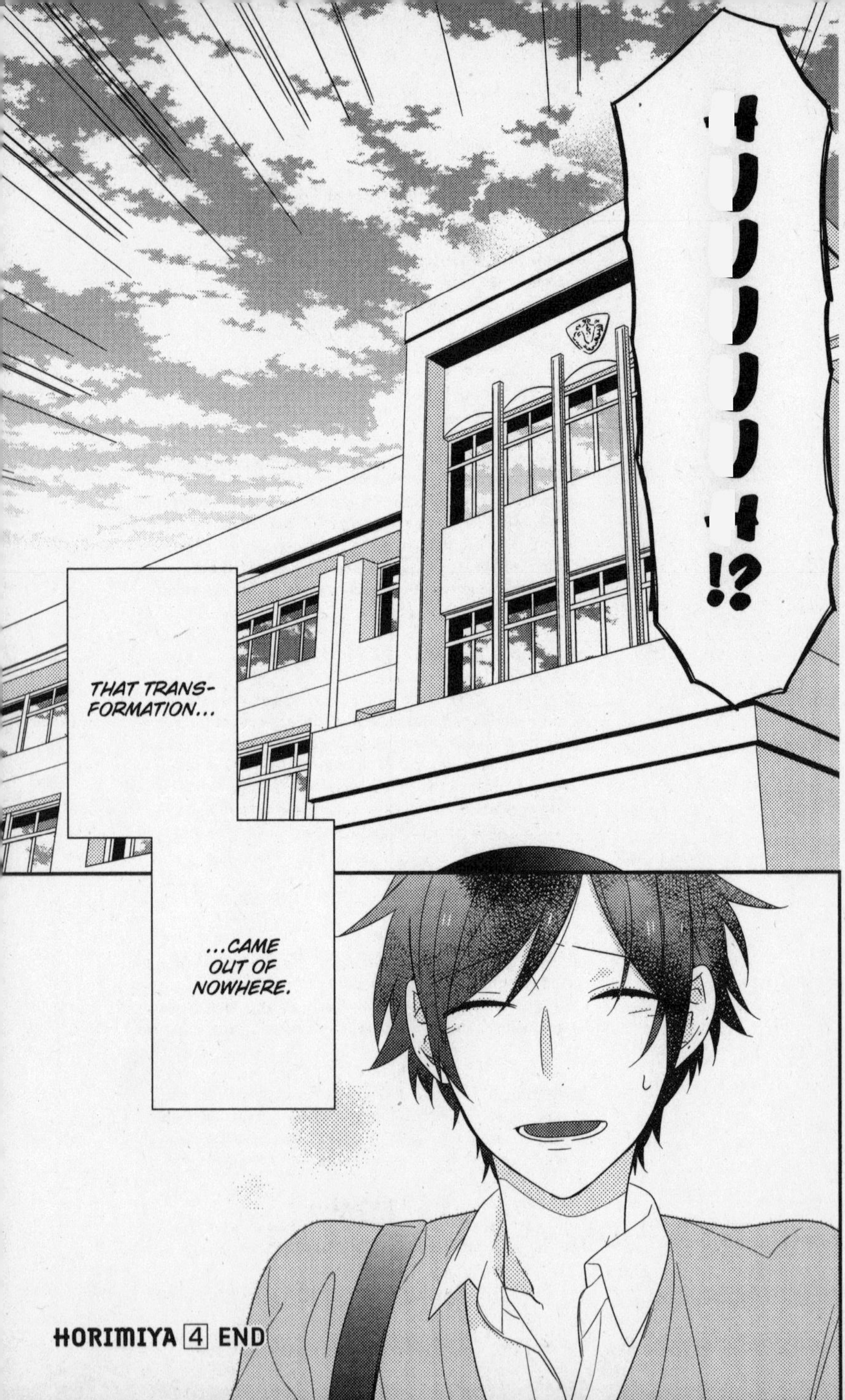
!?
THAT TRANS-FORMATION...
...CAME OUT OF NOWHERE.
HORIMIYA 4 END

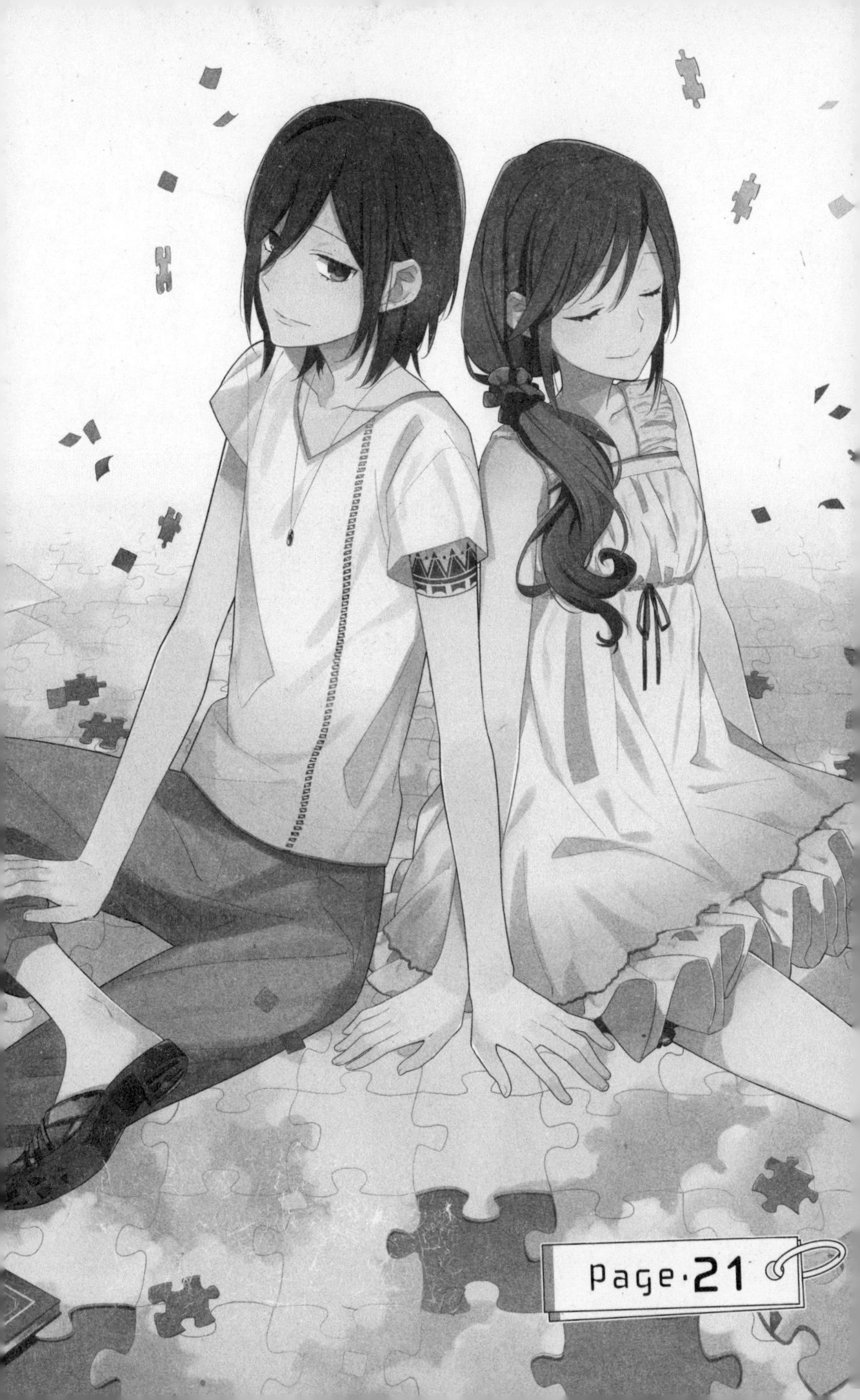
page·21

HORIMIYA

"I LIKE YOU."

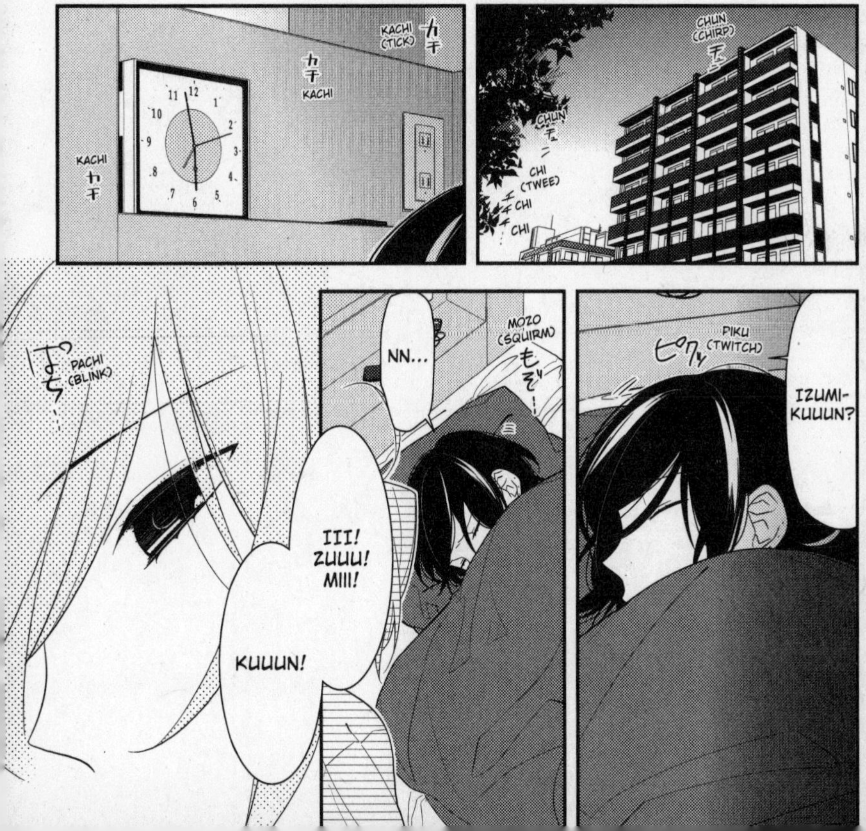
CHUN (CHIRP)
CHUN
CHI (TWEE)
CHI
CHI
KACHI (TICK)
KACHI
KACHI
PIKU (TWITCH)
IZUMI-KUUUN?
MOZO (SQUIRM)
NN...
III! ZUUU! MIII!
KUUUN!
PACHI (BLINK)

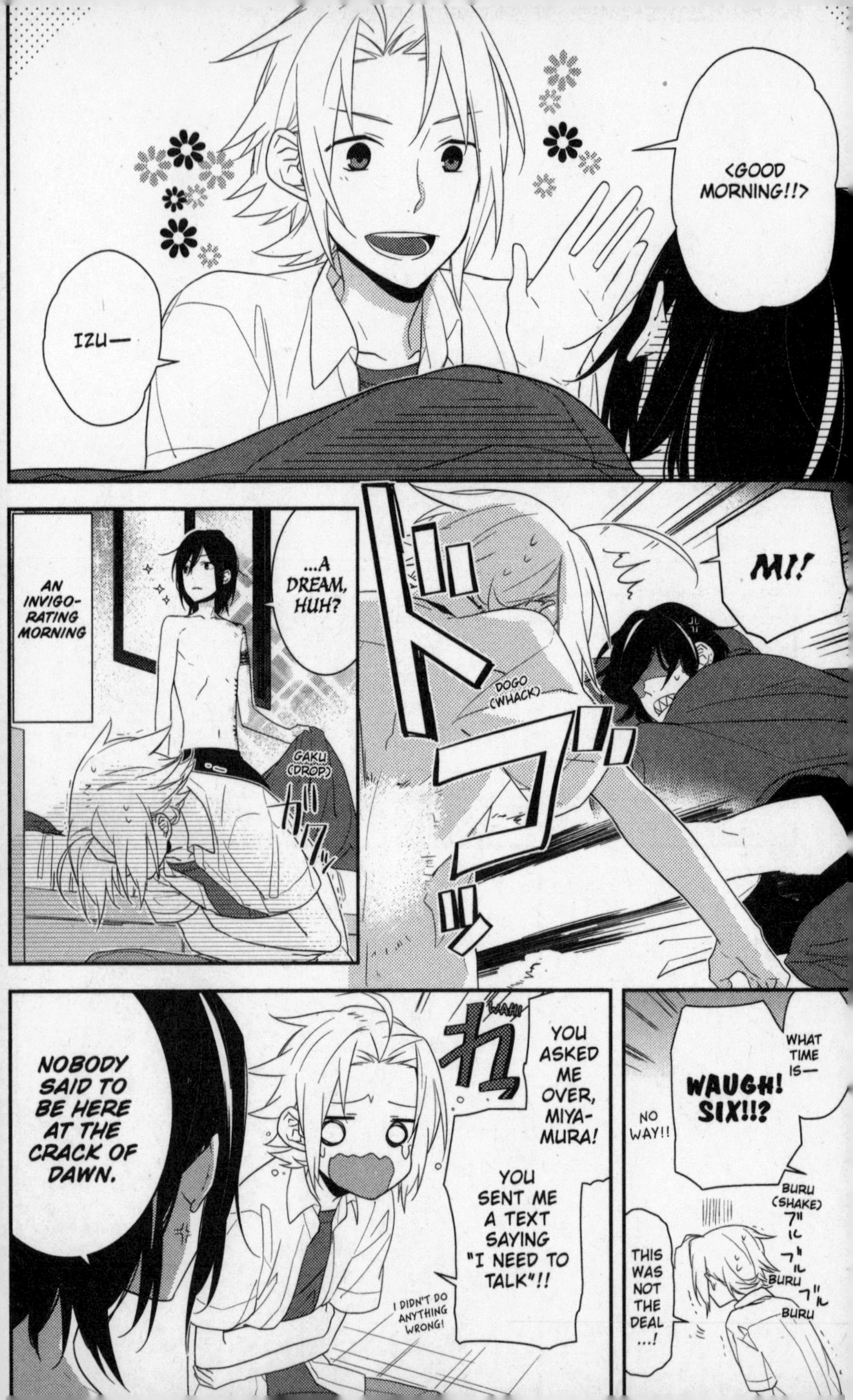
<GOOD MORNING!!>
IZU—
MI!
DOGO (WHACK)
...A DREAM, HUH?
AN INVIGO-RATING MORNING
GAKU (DROP)
WHAT TIME IS—
WAUGH! SIX!!?
NO WAY!!
BURU (SHAKE)
THIS WAS NOT THE DEAL...!
BURU
BURU
WAH!
YOU ASKED ME OVER, MIYAMURA!
YOU SENT ME A TEXT SAYING "I NEED TO TALK"!!
I DIDN'T DO ANYTHING WRONG!
NOBODY SAID TO BE HERE AT THE CRACK OF DAWN.

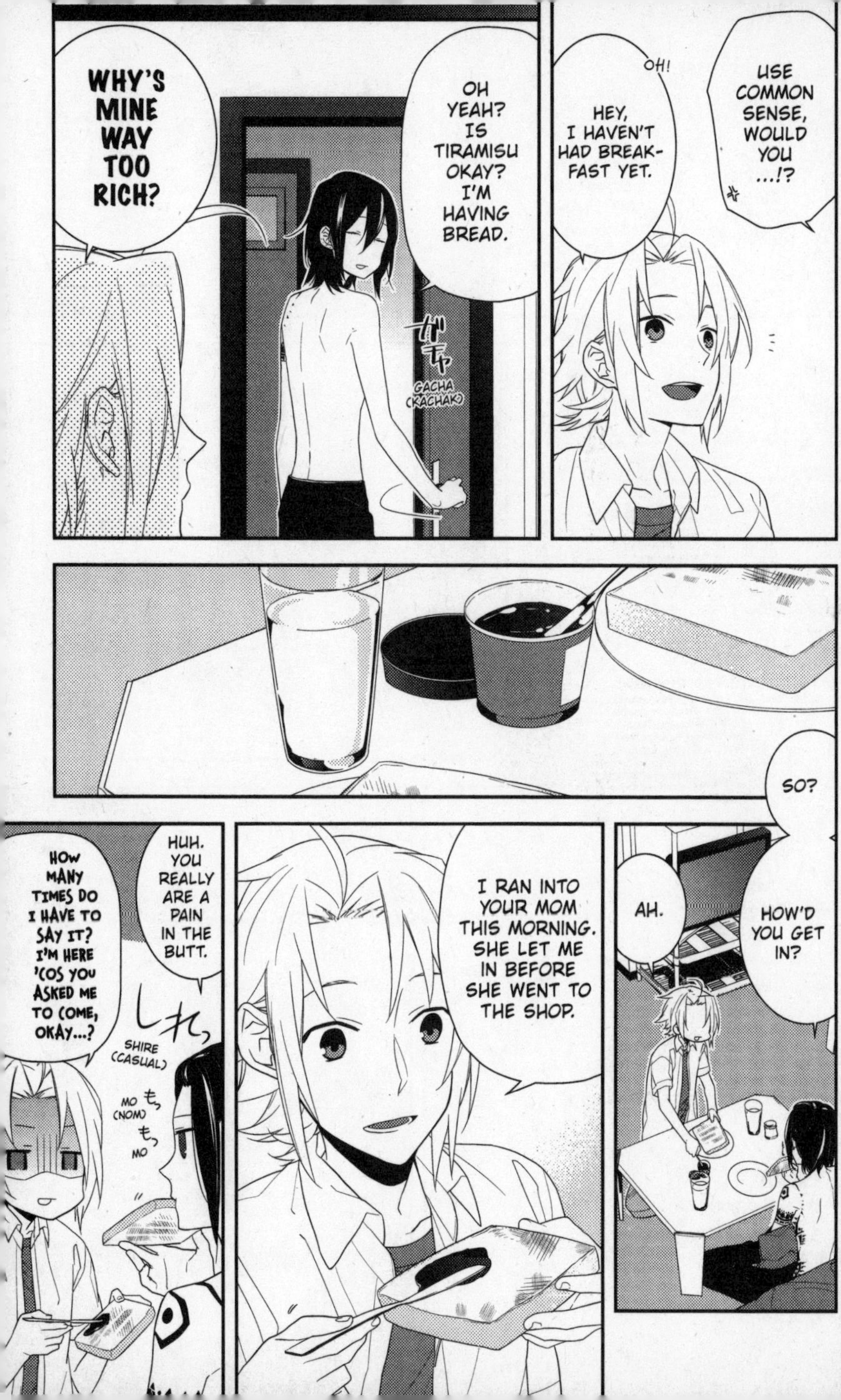

USE COMMON SENSE, WOULD YOU ...!?
OH!
HEY, I HAVEN'T HAD BREAK-FAST YET.
OH YEAH? IS TIRAMISU OKAY? I'M HAVING BREAD.
ガチャ
GACHA (KACHAK)
WHY'S MINE WAY TOO RICH?
SO?
HOW'D YOU GET IN?
AH.
I RAN INTO YOUR MOM THIS MORNING. SHE LET ME IN BEFORE SHE WENT TO THE SHOP.
HUH. YOU REALLY ARE A PAIN IN THE BUTT.
しれっ
SHIRE (CASUAL)
HOW MANY TIMES DO I HAVE TO SAY IT? I'M HERE 'COS YOU ASKED ME TO COME, OKAY...?
もっ MO (NOM)
もっ MO

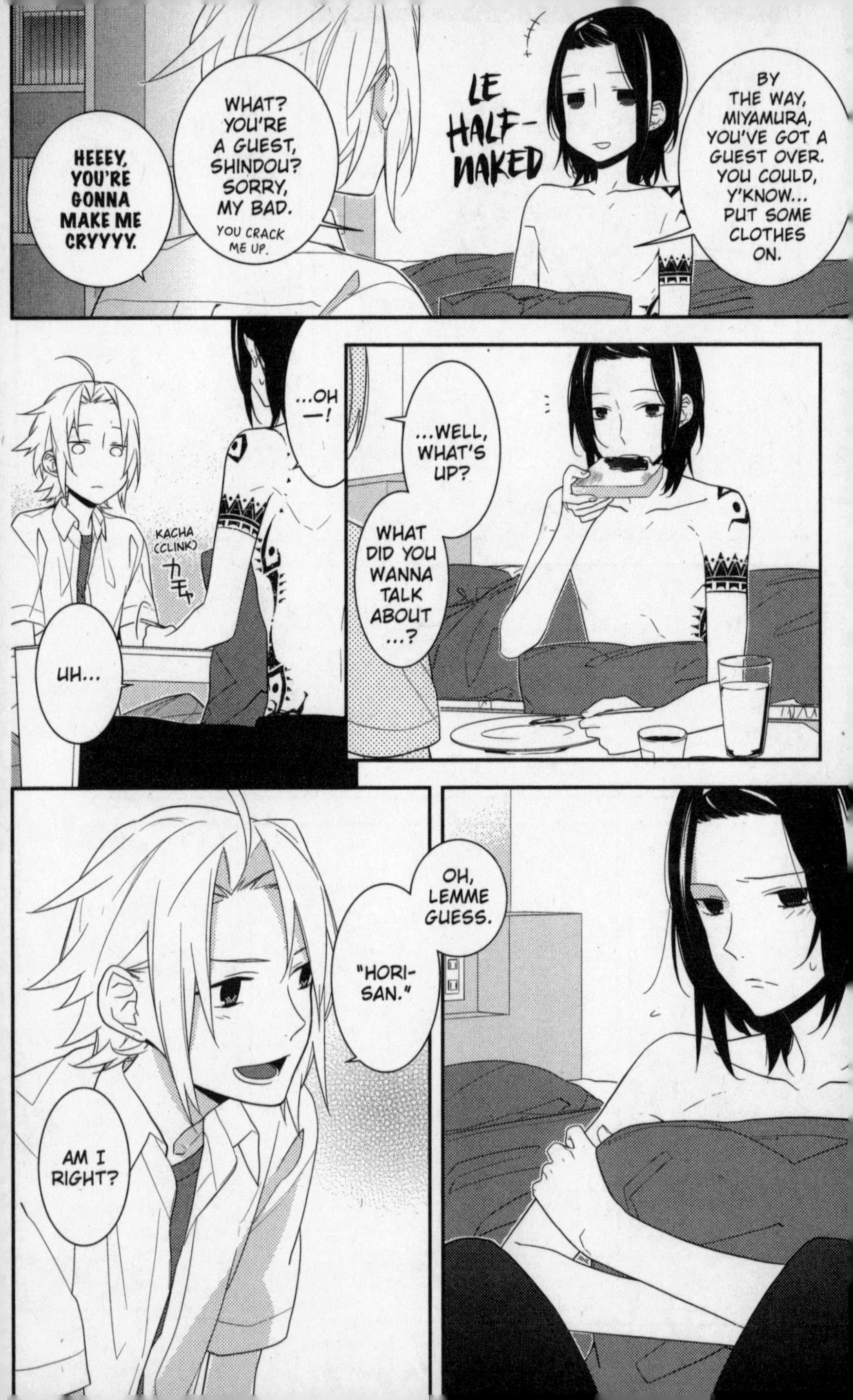
BY THE WAY, MIYAMURA, YOU'VE GOT A GUEST OVER. YOU COULD, Y'KNOW... PUT SOME CLOTHES ON.
LE HALF-NAKED
WHAT? YOU'RE A GUEST, SHINDOU? SORRY, MY BAD.
YOU CRACK ME UP.
HEEEY, YOU'RE GONNA MAKE ME CRYYYY.
...WELL, WHAT'S UP?
WHAT DID YOU WANNA TALK ABOUT ...?
...OH —!
KACHA (CLINK)
UH...
OH, LEMME GUESS.
"HORI-SAN."
AM I RIGHT?

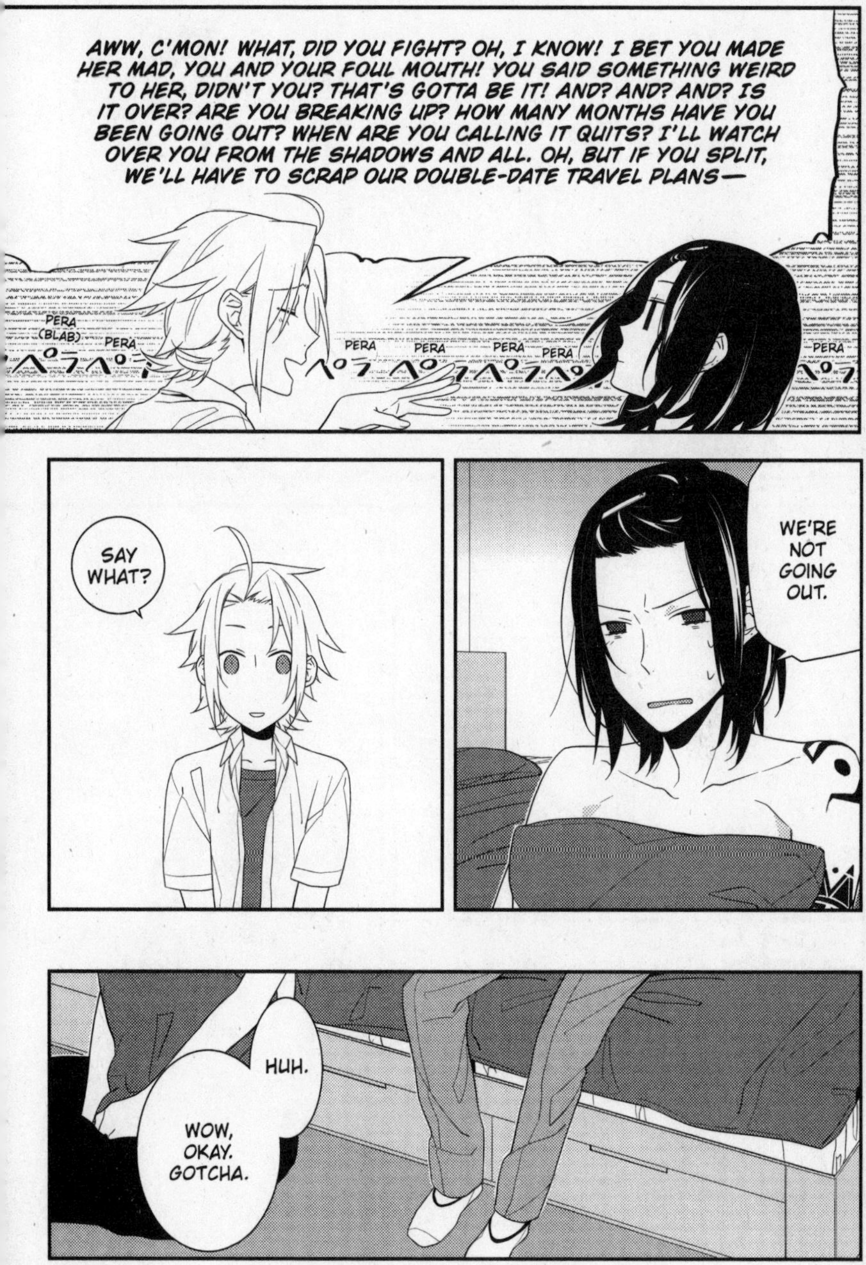
AWW, C'MON! WHAT, DID YOU FIGHT? OH, I KNOW! I BET YOU MADE HER MAD, YOU AND YOUR FOUL MOUTH! YOU SAID SOMETHING WEIRD TO HER, DIDN'T YOU? THAT'S GOTTA BE IT! AND? AND? AND? IS IT OVER? ARE YOU BREAKING UP? HOW MANY MONTHS HAVE YOU BEEN GOING OUT? WHEN ARE YOU CALLING IT QUITS? I'LL WATCH OVER YOU FROM THE SHADOWS AND ALL. OH, BUT IF YOU SPLIT, WE'LL HAVE TO SCRAP OUR DOUBLE-DATE TRAVEL PLANS—
PERA PERA PERA PERA PERA PERA
PERA (BLAB)
WE'RE NOT GOING OUT.
SAY WHAT?
HUH.
WOW, OKAY. GOTCHA.

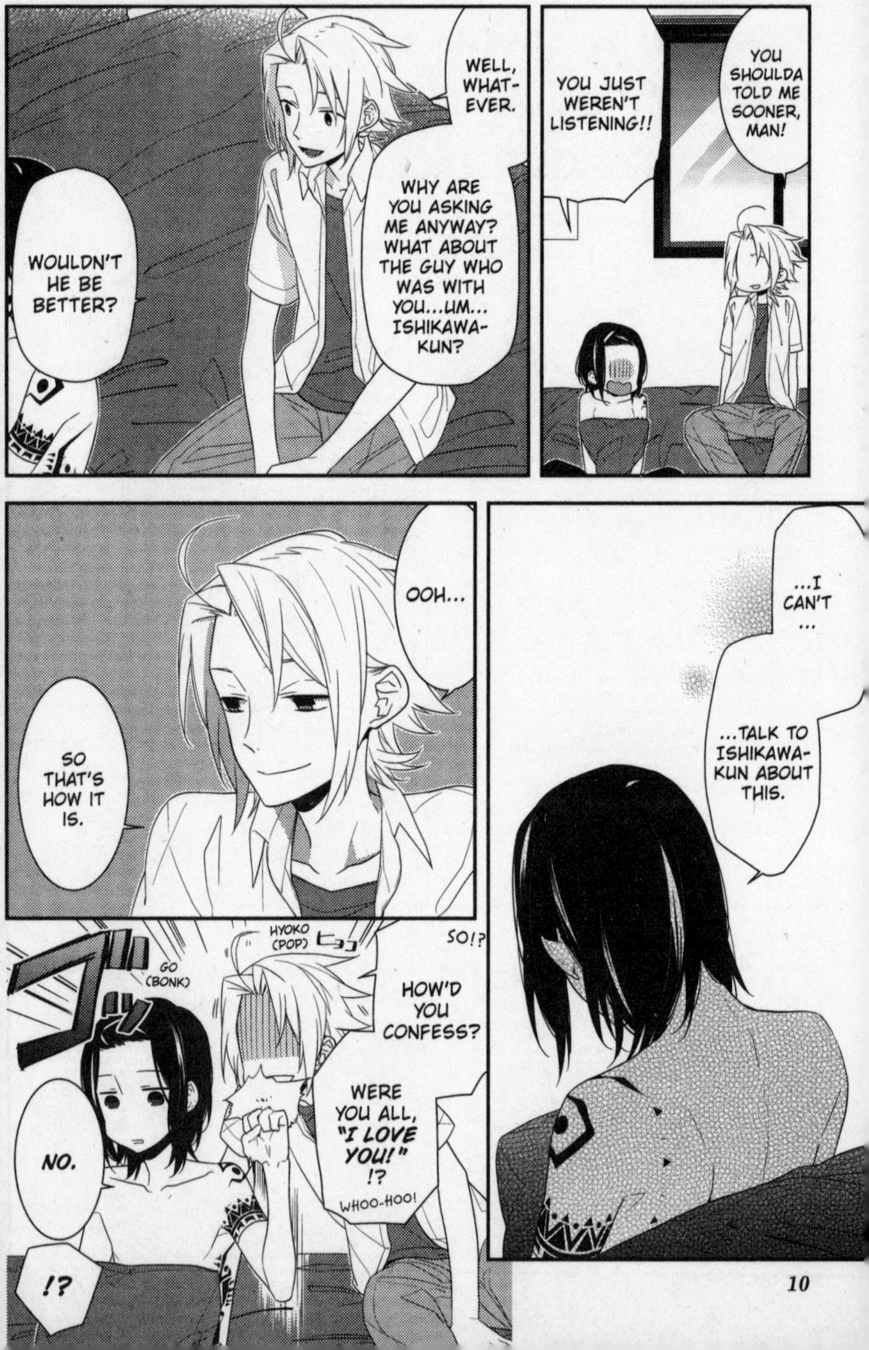
YOU SHOULDA TOLD ME SOONER, MAN!
YOU JUST WEREN'T LISTENING!!
WELL, WHAT-EVER.
WHY ARE YOU ASKING ME ANYWAY? WHAT ABOUT THE GUY WHO WAS WITH YOU...UM... ISHIKAWA-KUN?
WOULDN'T HE BE BETTER?
...I CAN'T ...
...TALK TO ISHIKAWA-KUN ABOUT THIS.
OOH...
SO THAT'S HOW IT IS.
HYOKO (POP)
SO!?
HOW'D YOU CONFESS?
WERE YOU ALL, "I LOVE YOU!" !?
WHOO-HOO!
GO (BONK)
NO.
!?

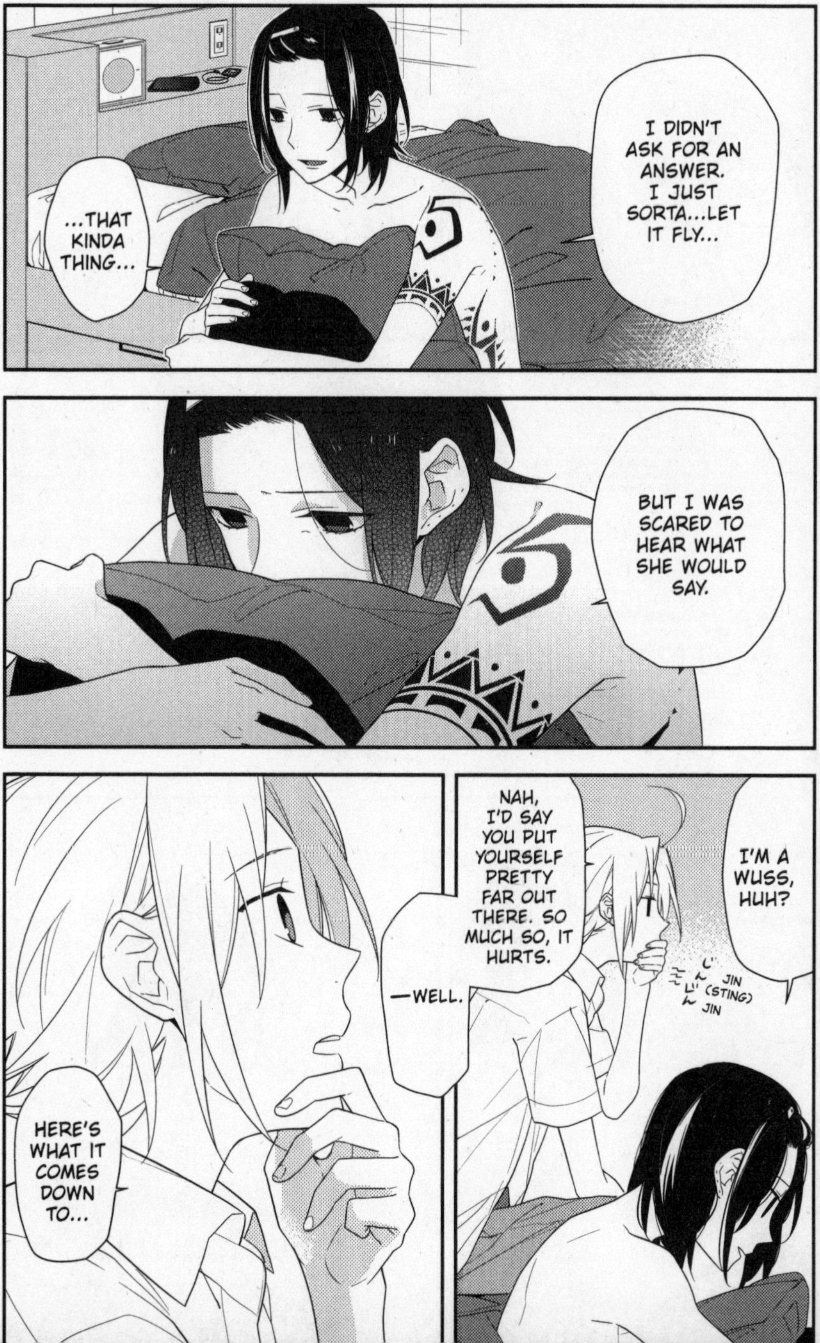
I DIDN'T ASK FOR AN ANSWER. I JUST SORTA...LET IT FLY...
...THAT KINDA THING...
BUT I WAS SCARED TO HEAR WHAT SHE WOULD SAY.
I'M A WUSS, HUH?
JIN (STING) JIN
NAH, I'D SAY YOU PUT YOURSELF PRETTY FAR OUT THERE. SO MUCH SO, IT HURTS.
—WELL.
HERE'S WHAT IT COMES DOWN TO...

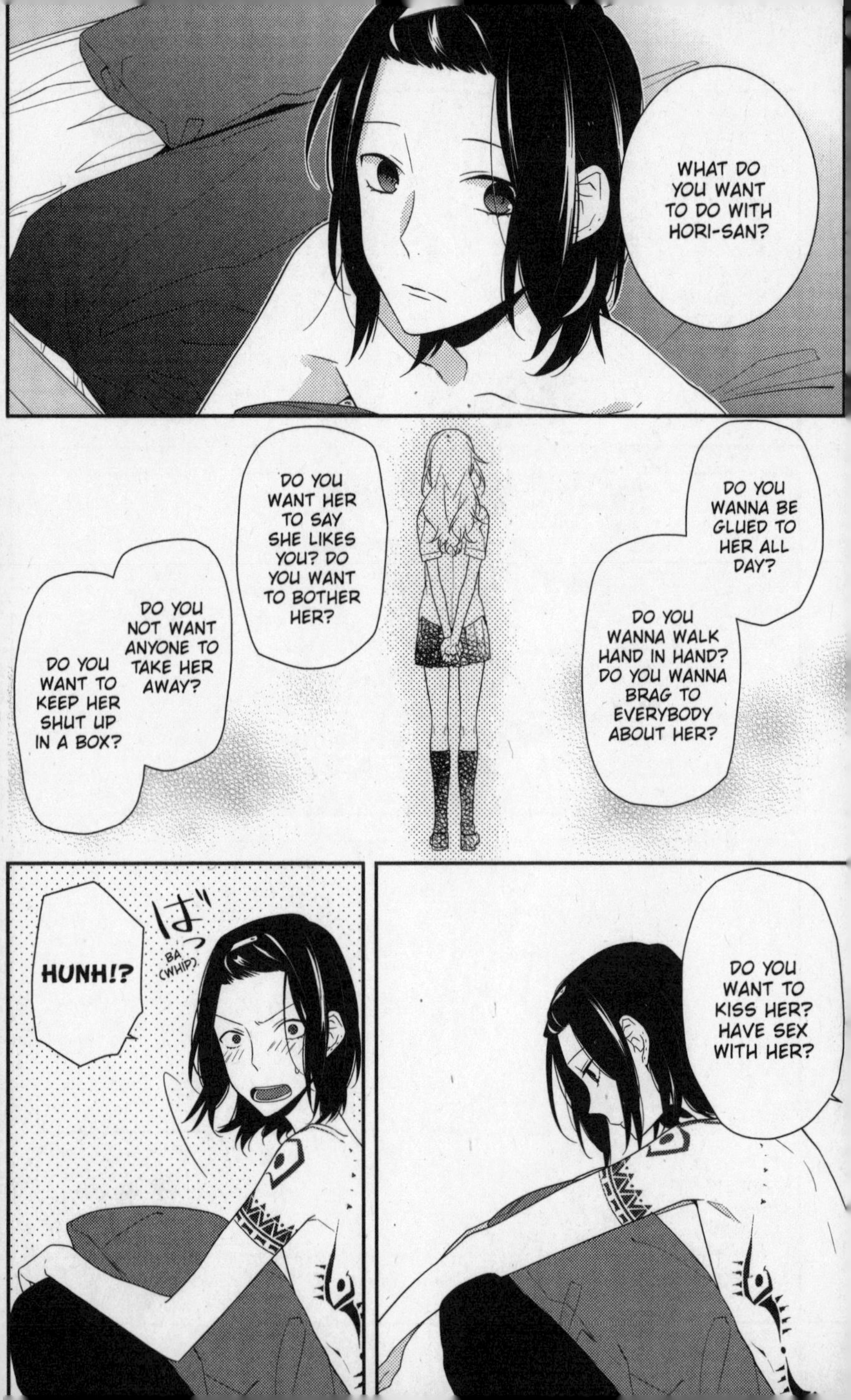
WHAT DO YOU WANT TO DO WITH HORI-SAN?
DO YOU WANNA BE GLUED TO HER ALL DAY?
DO YOU WANNA WALK HAND IN HAND? DO YOU WANNA BRAG TO EVERYBODY ABOUT HER?
DO YOU WANT HER TO SAY SHE LIKES YOU? DO YOU WANT TO BOTHER HER?
DO YOU NOT WANT ANYONE TO TAKE HER AWAY?
DO YOU WANT TO KEEP HER SHUT UP IN A BOX?
DO YOU WANT TO KISS HER? HAVE SEX WITH HER?
ばっ
BA (WHIP)
HUNH!?

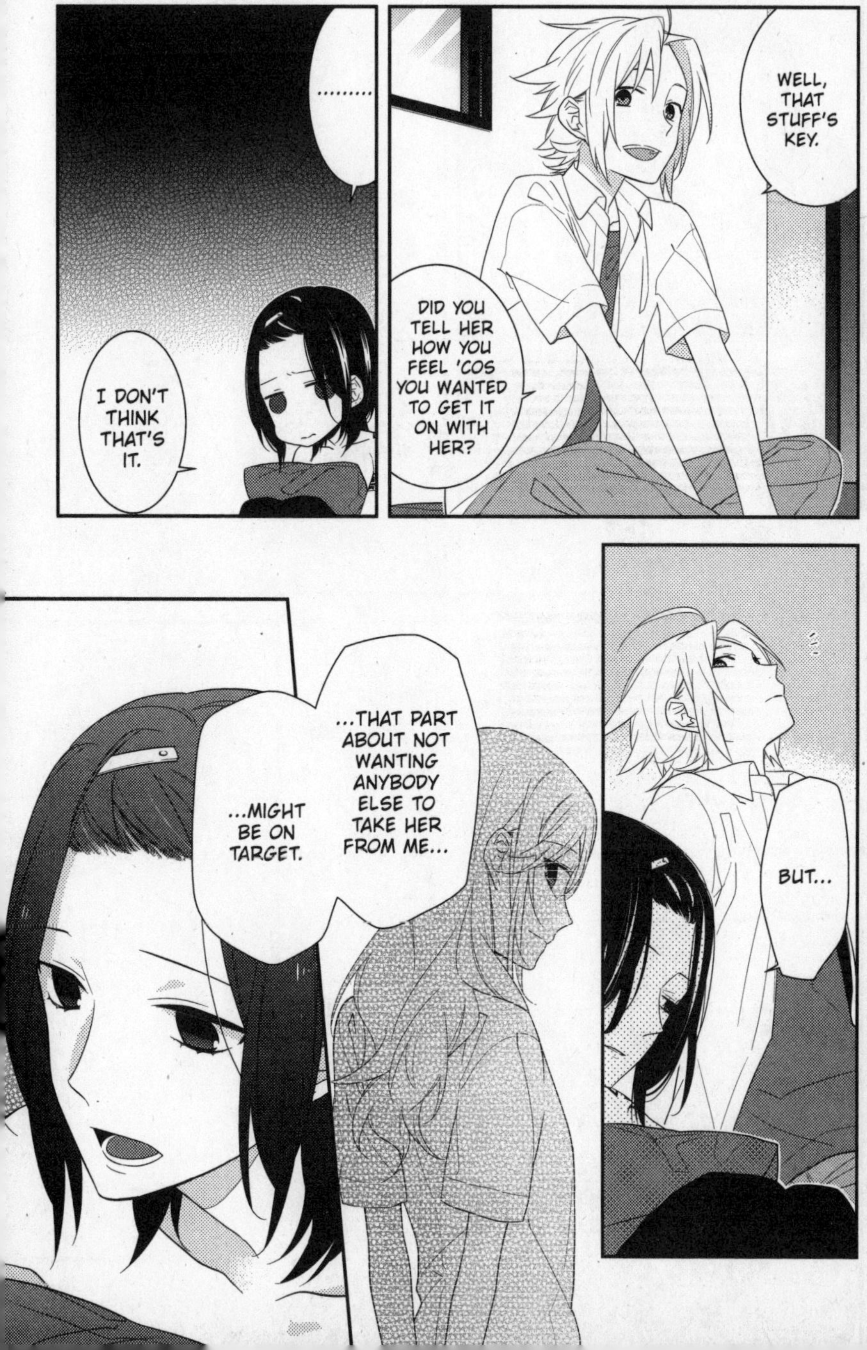
WELL, THAT STUFF'S KEY.
DID YOU TELL HER HOW YOU FEEL 'COS YOU WANTED TO GET IT ON WITH HER?
....
I DON'T THINK THAT'S IT.
BUT...
...THAT PART ABOUT NOT WANTING ANYBODY ELSE TO TAKE HER FROM ME...
...MIGHT BE ON TARGET.

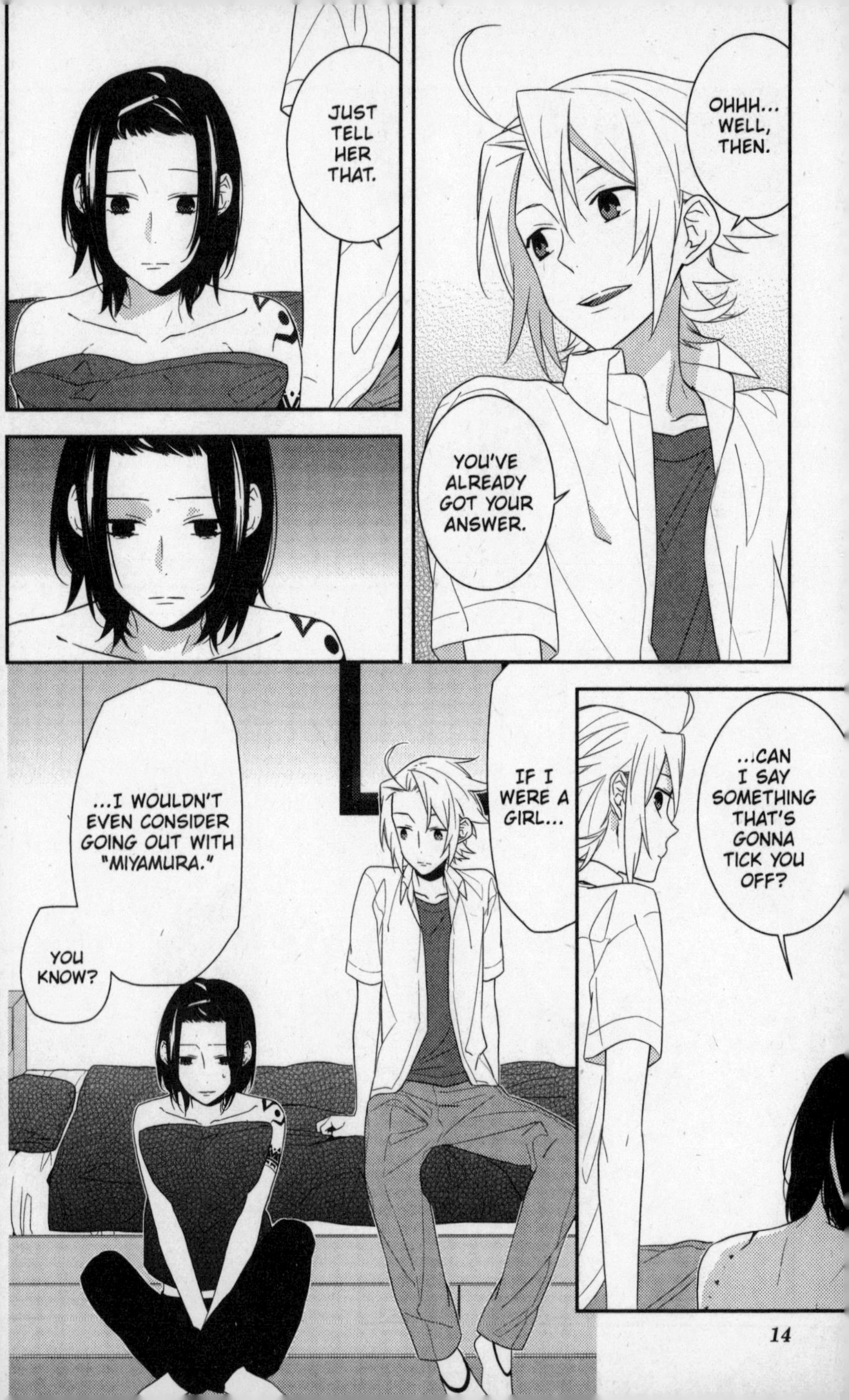
OHHH... WELL, THEN.
YOU'VE ALREADY GOT YOUR ANSWER.
JUST TELL HER THAT.
...CAN I SAY SOMETHING THAT'S GONNA TICK YOU OFF?
IF I WERE A GIRL...
...I WOULDN'T EVEN CONSIDER GOING OUT WITH "MIYAMURA."
YOU KNOW?

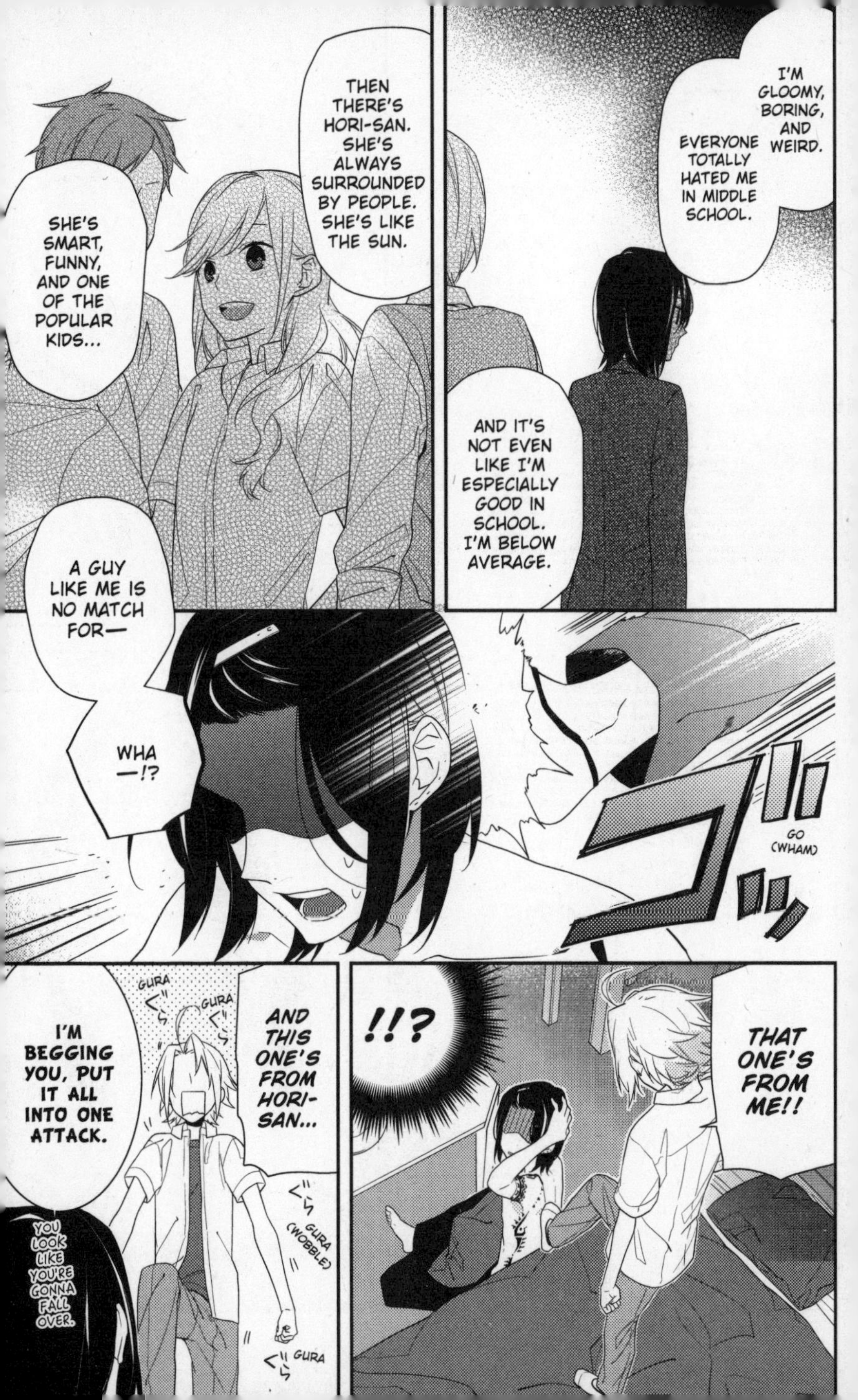
I'M GLOOMY, BORING, AND WEIRD.
EVERYONE TOTALLY HATED ME IN MIDDLE SCHOOL.
AND IT'S NOT EVEN LIKE I'M ESPECIALLY GOOD IN SCHOOL. I'M BELOW AVERAGE.
THEN THERE'S HORI-SAN. SHE'S ALWAYS SURROUNDED BY PEOPLE. SHE'S LIKE THE SUN.
SHE'S SMART, FUNNY, AND ONE OF THE POPULAR KIDS...
A GUY LIKE ME IS NO MATCH FOR—
GO (WHAM)
WHA—!?
THAT ONE'S FROM ME!!
!!?
AND THIS ONE'S FROM HORI-SAN...
GURA
GURA
I'M BEGGING YOU, PUT IT ALL INTO ONE ATTACK.
GURA (WOBBLE)
GURA
YOU LOOK LIKE YOU'RE GONNA FALL OVER.

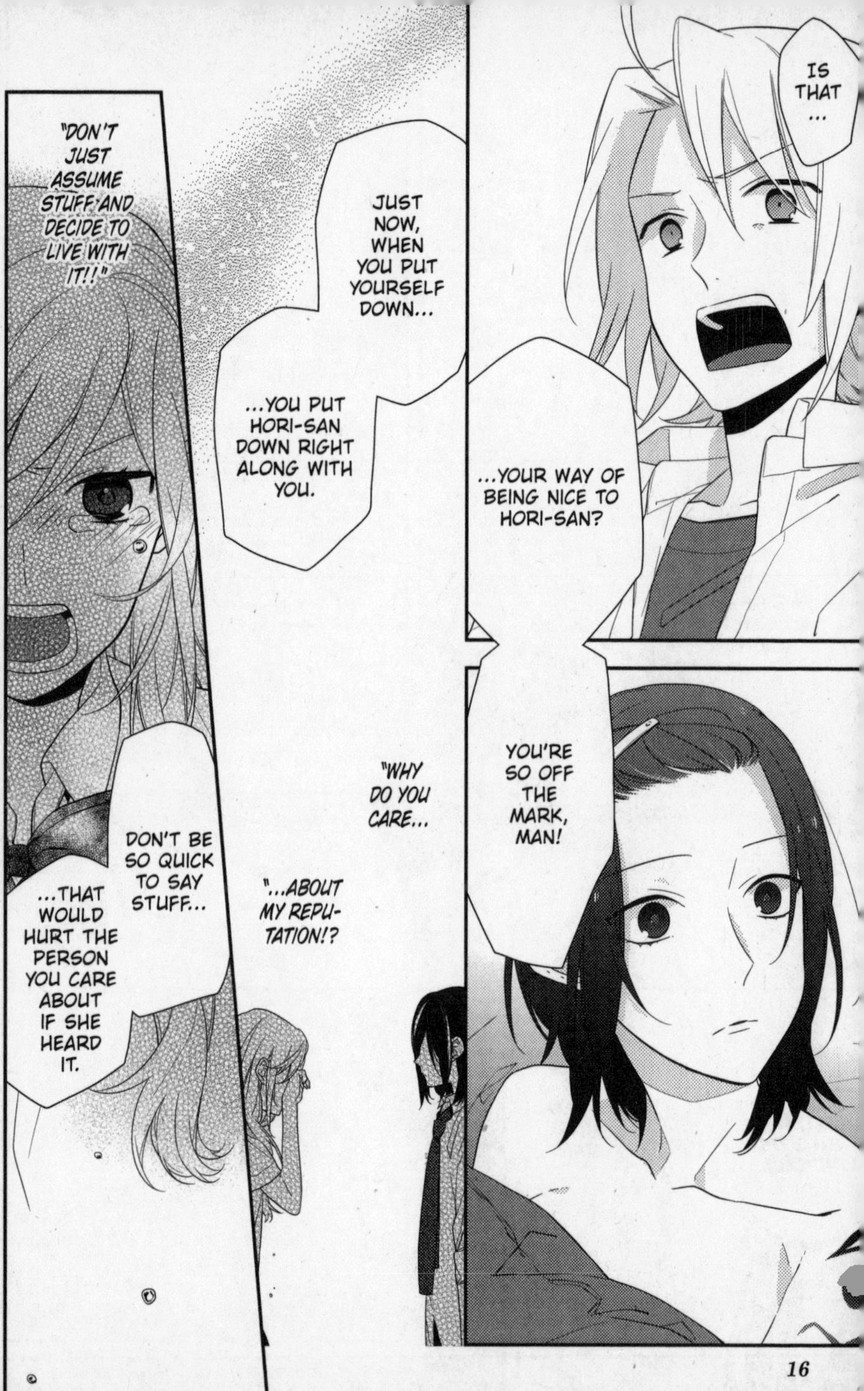
IS THAT ...
...YOUR WAY OF BEING NICE TO HORI-SAN?
YOU'RE SO OFF THE MARK, MAN!
JUST NOW, WHEN YOU PUT YOURSELF DOWN...
...YOU PUT HORI-SAN DOWN RIGHT ALONG WITH YOU.
"DON'T JUST ASSUME STUFF AND DECIDE TO LIVE WITH IT!!"
"WHY DO YOU CARE...
"...ABOUT MY REPUTATION!?
DON'T BE SO QUICK TO SAY STUFF...
...THAT WOULD HURT THE PERSON YOU CARE ABOUT IF SHE HEARD IT.

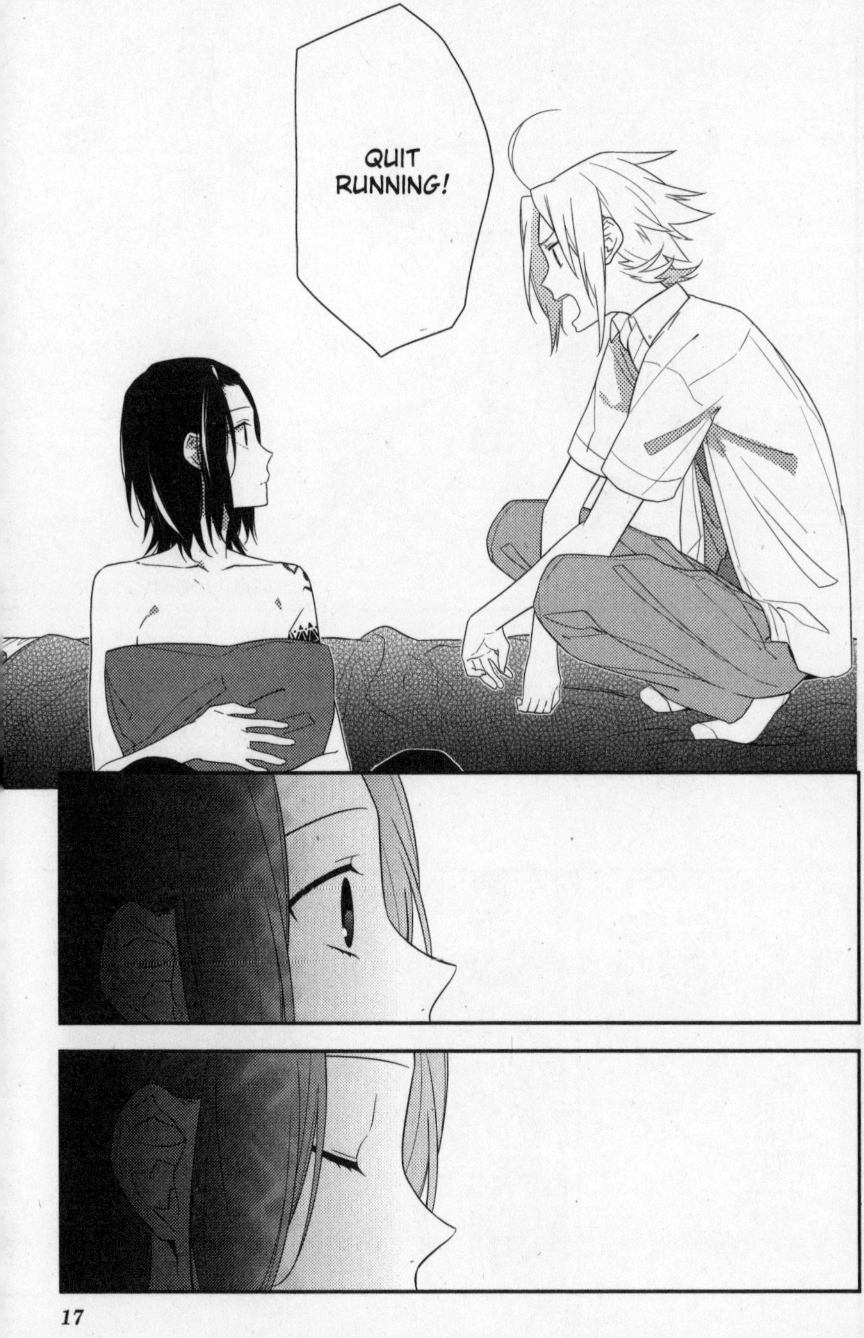
QUIT RUNNING!

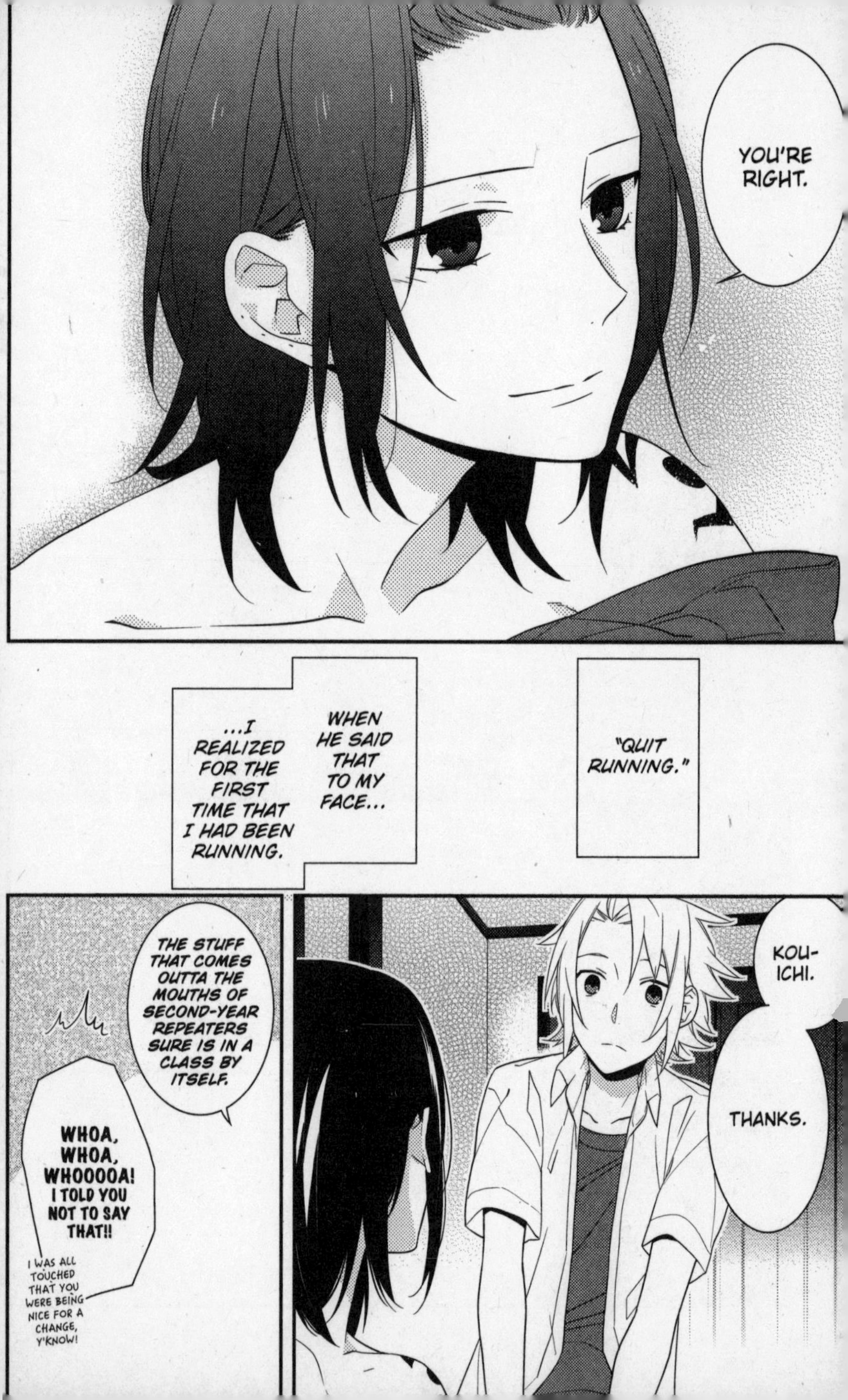
YOU'RE RIGHT.
"QUIT RUNNING."
WHEN HE SAID THAT TO MY FACE...
...I REALIZED FOR THE FIRST TIME THAT I HAD BEEN RUNNING.
KOU-ICHI.
THANKS.
THE STUFF THAT COMES OUTTA THE MOUTHS OF SECOND-YEAR REPEATERS SURE IS IN A CLASS BY ITSELF.
WHOA, WHOA, WHOOOOA! I TOLD YOU NOT TO SAY THAT!!
I WAS ALL TOUCHED THAT YOU WERE BEING NICE FOR A CHANGE, Y'KNOW!

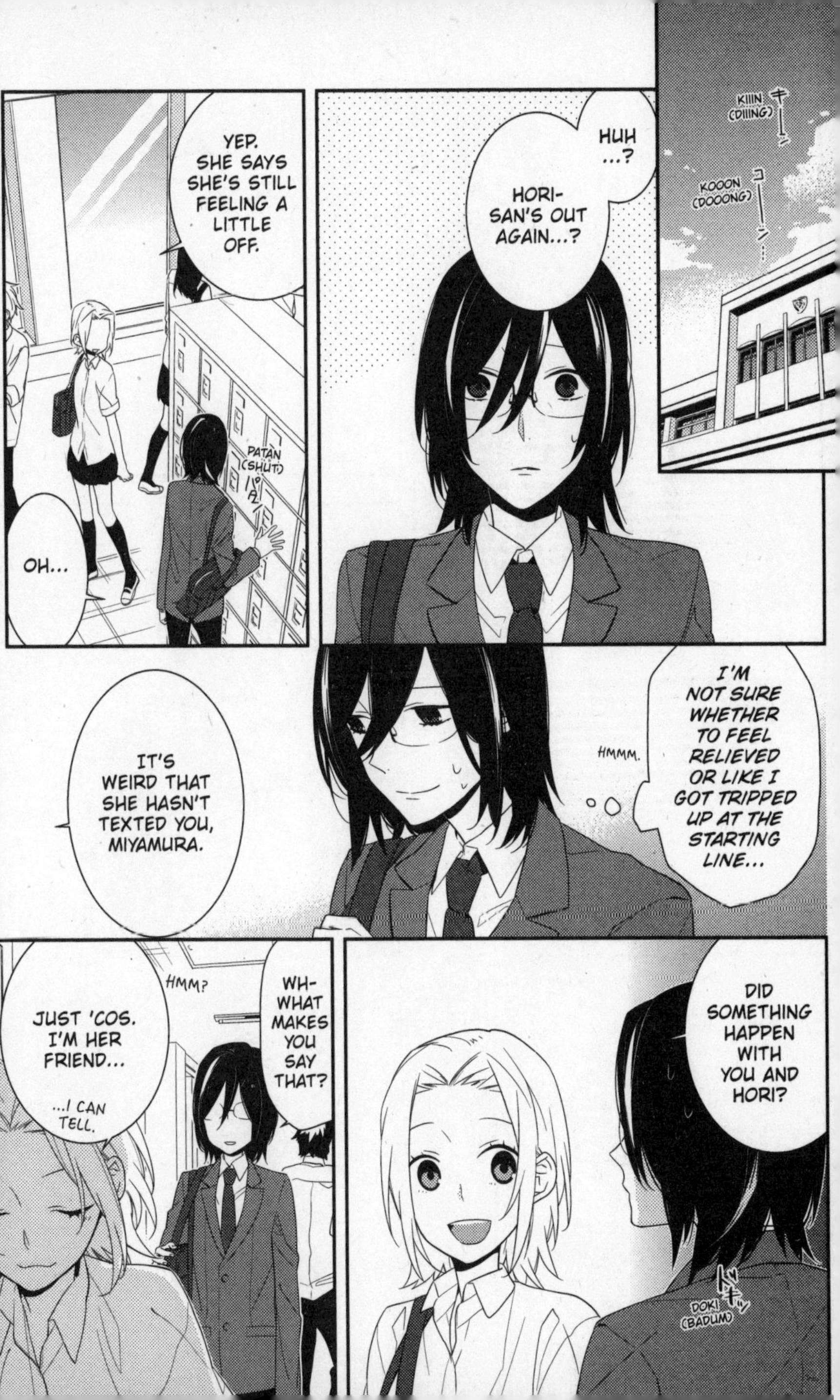
KIIN (DIIING)
KOOON (DOOONG)
HUH ...?
HORI-SAN'S OUT AGAIN...?
YEP. SHE SAYS SHE'S STILL FEELING A LITTLE OFF.
PATAN (SHUT)
OH...
I'M NOT SURE WHETHER TO FEEL RELIEVED OR LIKE I GOT TRIPPED UP AT THE STARTING LINE...
HMMM.
IT'S WEIRD THAT SHE HASN'T TEXTED YOU, MIYAMURA.
DID SOMETHING HAPPEN WITH YOU AND HORI?
DOKI (BADUM)
WH- WHAT MAKES YOU SAY THAT?
HMM?
JUST 'COS. I'M HER FRIEND...
...I CAN TELL.

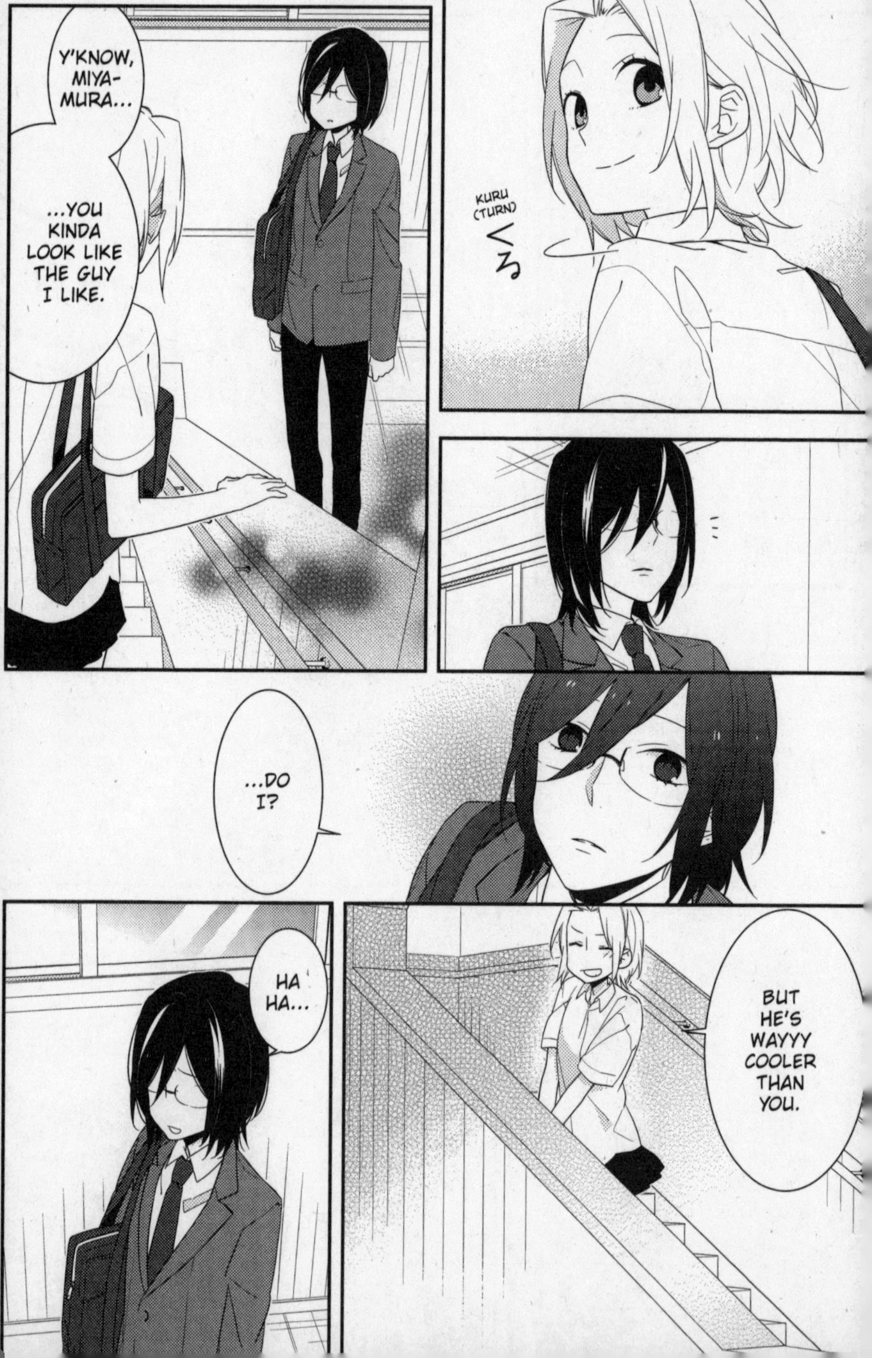
KURU (TURN)
くる
Y'KNOW, MIYA-MURA...
...YOU KINDA LOOK LIKE THE GUY I LIKE.
...DO I?
BUT HE'S WAYYY COOLER THAN YOU.
HA HA...

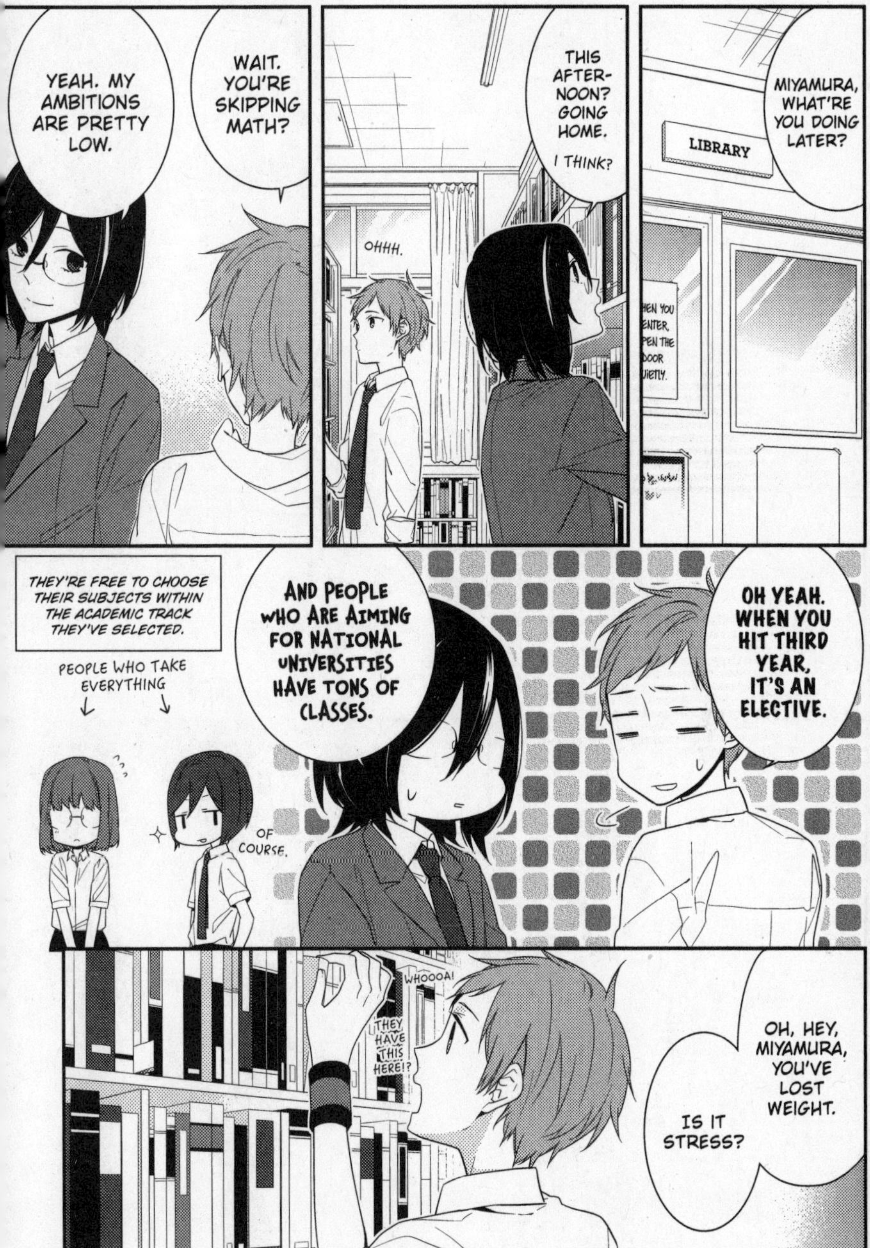
MIYAMURA, WHAT'RE YOU DOING LATER?
LIBRARY
HEN YOU ENTER, PEN THE DOOR UIETLY.
THIS AFTERNOON? GOING HOME.
I THINK?
OHHH.
WAIT. YOU'RE SKIPPING MATH?
YEAH. MY AMBITIONS ARE PRETTY LOW.
OH YEAH. WHEN YOU HIT THIRD YEAR, IT'S AN ELECTIVE.
AND PEOPLE WHO ARE AIMING FOR NATIONAL UNIVERSITIES HAVE TONS OF CLASSES.
THEY'RE FREE TO CHOOSE THEIR SUBJECTS WITHIN THE ACADEMIC TRACK THEY'VE SELECTED.
PEOPLE WHO TAKE EVERYTHING
OF COURSE.
OH, HEY, MIYAMURA, YOU'VE LOST WEIGHT.
IS IT STRESS?
WHOOOA!
THEY HAVE THIS HERE!?

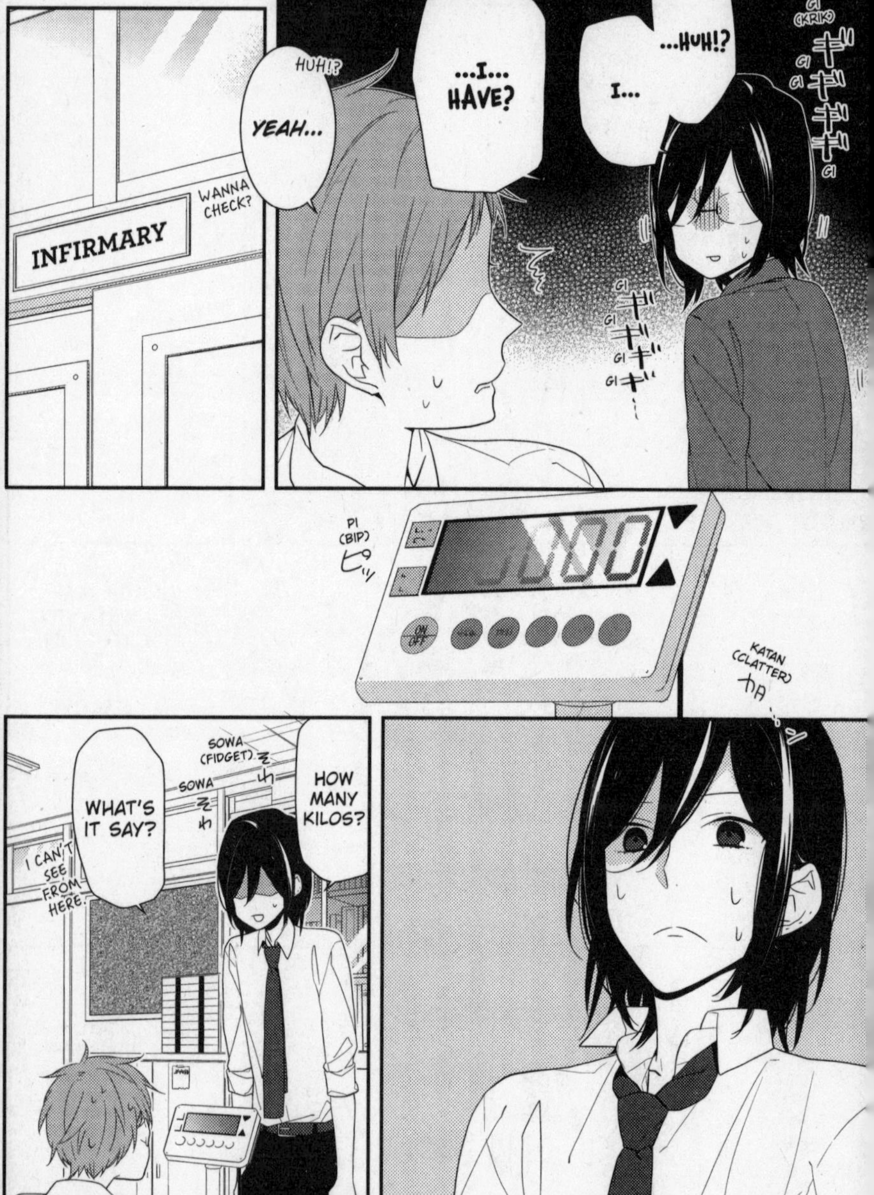
GI (KRIK) GI GI GI GI
...HUH!?
I...
...I... HAVE?
HUH!?
YEAH...
GI GI GI GI
INFIRMARY
WANNA CHECK?
PI (BIP)
KATAN (CLATTER)
HOW MANY KILOS?
SOWA (FIDGET) SOWA
WHAT'S IT SAY?
I CAN'T SEE FROM HERE.

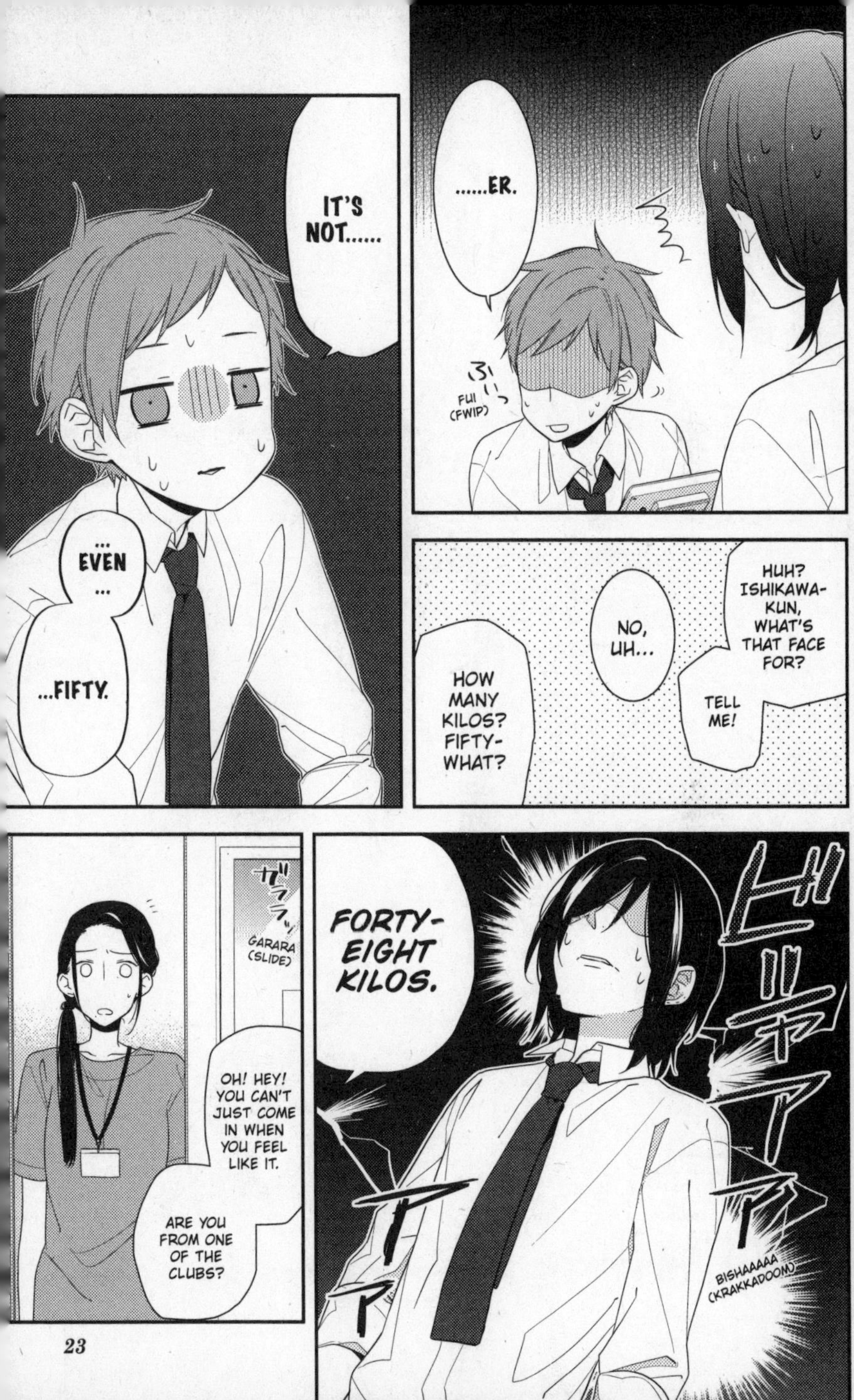

......ER.
ふいっ
FUI (FWIP)
HUH? ISHIKAWA-KUN, WHAT'S THAT FACE FOR?
TELL ME!
NO, UH...
HOW MANY KILOS? FIFTY-WHAT?
IT'S NOT......
...EVEN...
...FIFTY.
FORTY-EIGHT KILOS.
BISHAAAAA (KRAKKADOOM)
GARARA (SLIDE)
OH! HEY! YOU CAN'T JUST COME IN WHEN YOU FEEL LIKE IT.
ARE YOU FROM ONE OF THE CLUBS?

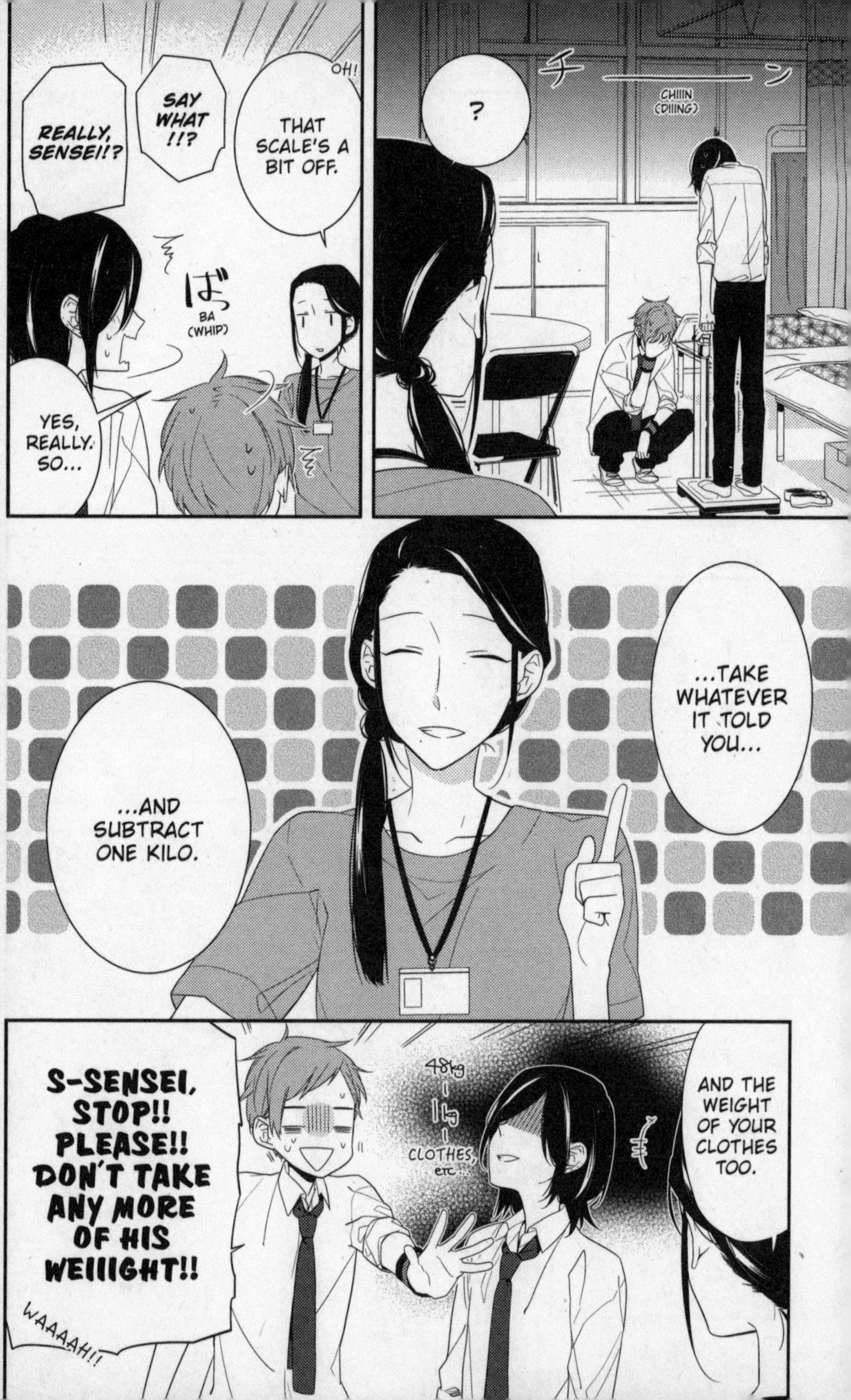
チーン
CHIIIN (DIIING)
?
OH!
THAT SCALE'S A BIT OFF.
SAY WHAT!!?
REALLY, SENSEI!?
ばっ
BA (WHIP)
YES, REALLY. SO...
...TAKE WHATEVER IT TOLD YOU...
...AND SUBTRACT ONE KILO.
AND THE WEIGHT OF YOUR CLOTHES TOO.
48kg - 1kg - CLOTHES, etc...
S-SENSEI, STOP!! PLEASE!! DON'T TAKE ANY MORE OF HIS WEIIIGHT!!
WAAAAAH!!

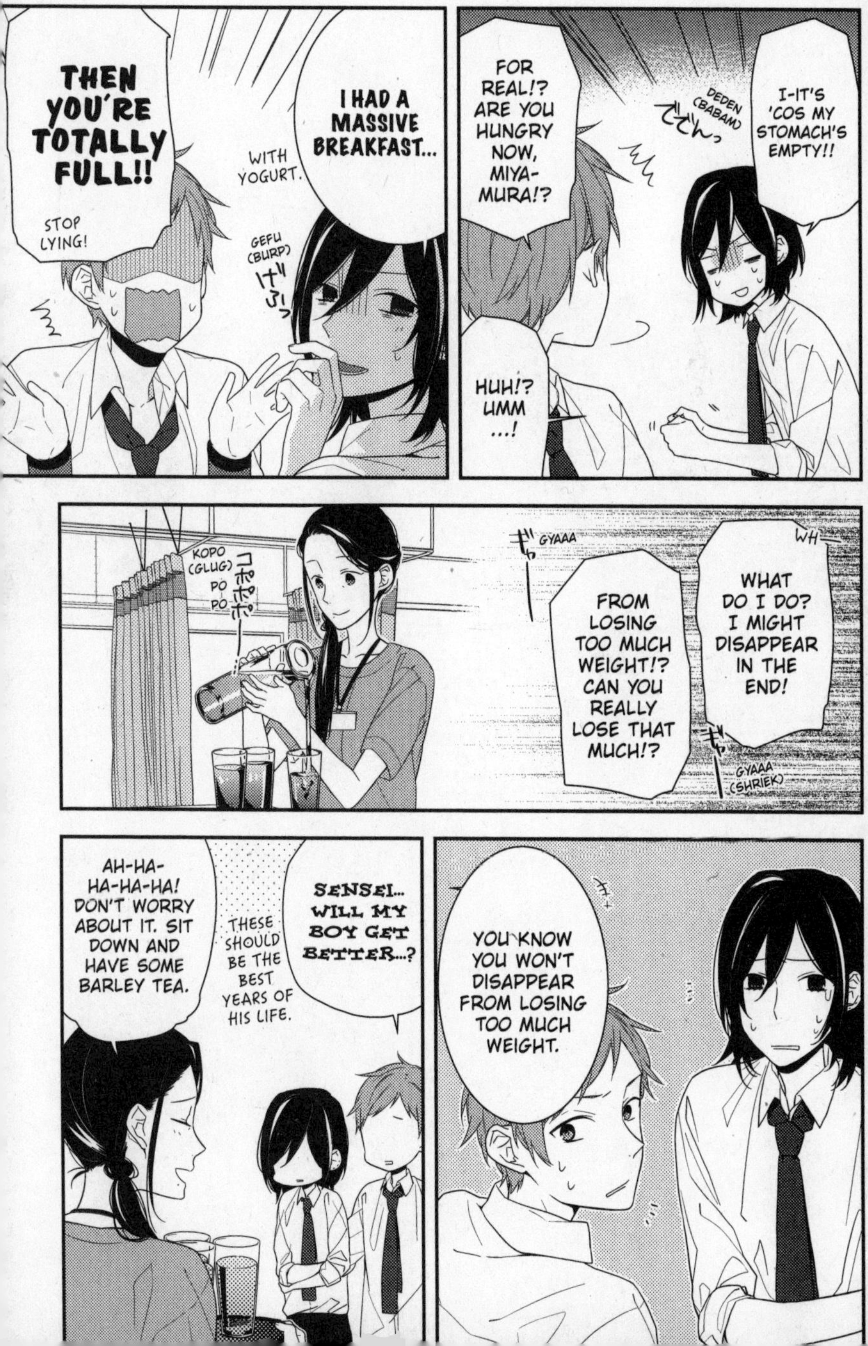
I-IT'S 'COS MY STOMACH'S EMPTY!!
DEDEN (BABAM)
ででんっ
FOR REAL!? ARE YOU HUNGRY NOW, MIYA-MURA!?
HUH!? UMM ...!
I HAD A MASSIVE BREAKFAST...
WITH YOGURT.
GEFU (BURP)
げふっ
THEN YOU'RE TOTALLY FULL!!
STOP LYING!
WH—
WHAT DO I DO? I MIGHT DISAPPEAR IN THE END!
GYAAA (SHRIEK)
FROM LOSING TOO MUCH WEIGHT!? CAN YOU REALLY LOSE THAT MUCH!?
GYAAA
KOPO (GLUG) PO PO
コポポポ
YOU KNOW YOU WON'T DISAPPEAR FROM LOSING TOO MUCH WEIGHT.
SENSEI... WILL MY BOY GET BETTER...?
THESE SHOULD BE THE BEST YEARS OF HIS LIFE.
AH-HA-HA-HA-HA! DON'T WORRY ABOUT IT. SIT DOWN AND HAVE SOME BARLEY TEA.

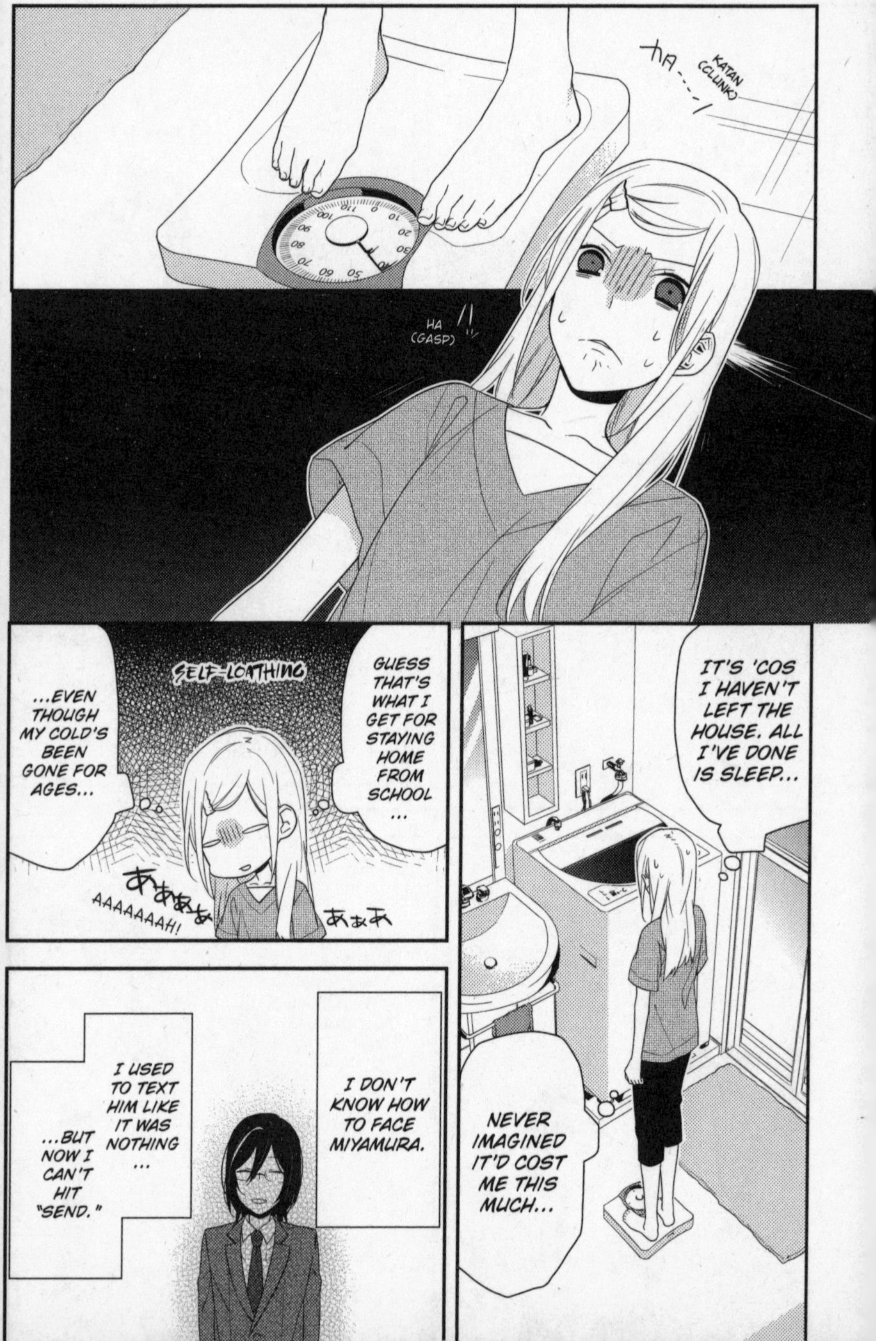
KATAN (CLUNK)
HA (GASP)
IT'S 'COS I HAVEN'T LEFT THE HOUSE. ALL I'VE DONE IS SLEEP...
NEVER IMAGINED IT'D COST ME THIS MUCH...
GUESS THAT'S WHAT I GET FOR STAYING HOME FROM SCHOOL...
...EVEN THOUGH MY COLD'S BEEN GONE FOR AGES...
SELF-LOATHING
AAAAAAAAH!
I DON'T KNOW HOW TO FACE MIYAMURA.
I USED TO TEXT HIM LIKE IT WAS NOTHING...
...BUT NOW I CAN'T HIT "SEND."

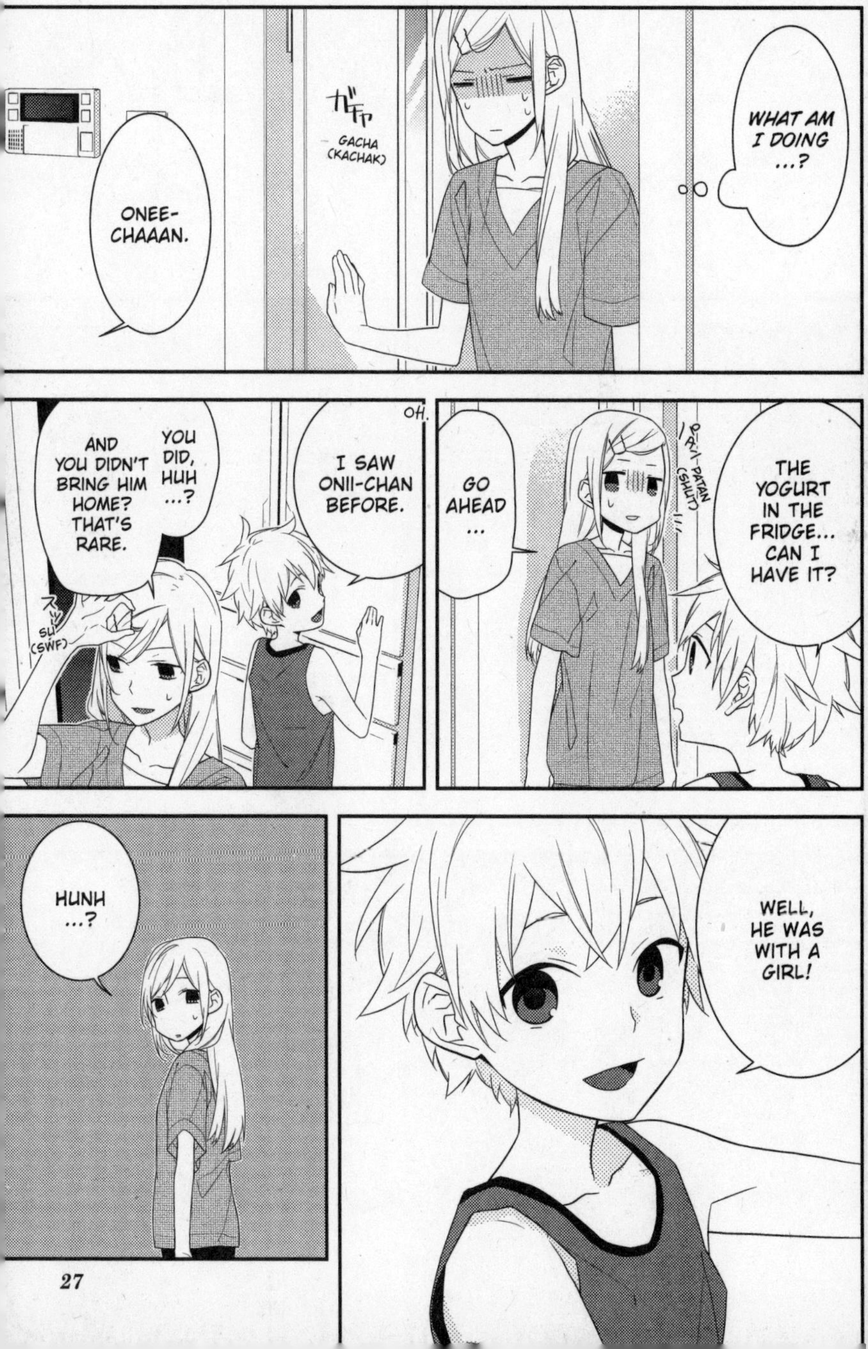
WHAT AM I DOING ...?
ガチャ
GACHA (KACHAK)
ONEE-CHAAAN.
THE YOGURT IN THE FRIDGE... CAN I HAVE IT?
パタン
PATAN (SHUT)
GO AHEAD ...
OH.
I SAW ONII-CHAN BEFORE.
YOU DID, HUH ...?
AND YOU DIDN'T BRING HIM HOME? THAT'S RARE.
スッ
SU (SWF)
WELL, HE WAS WITH A GIRL!
HUNH ...?

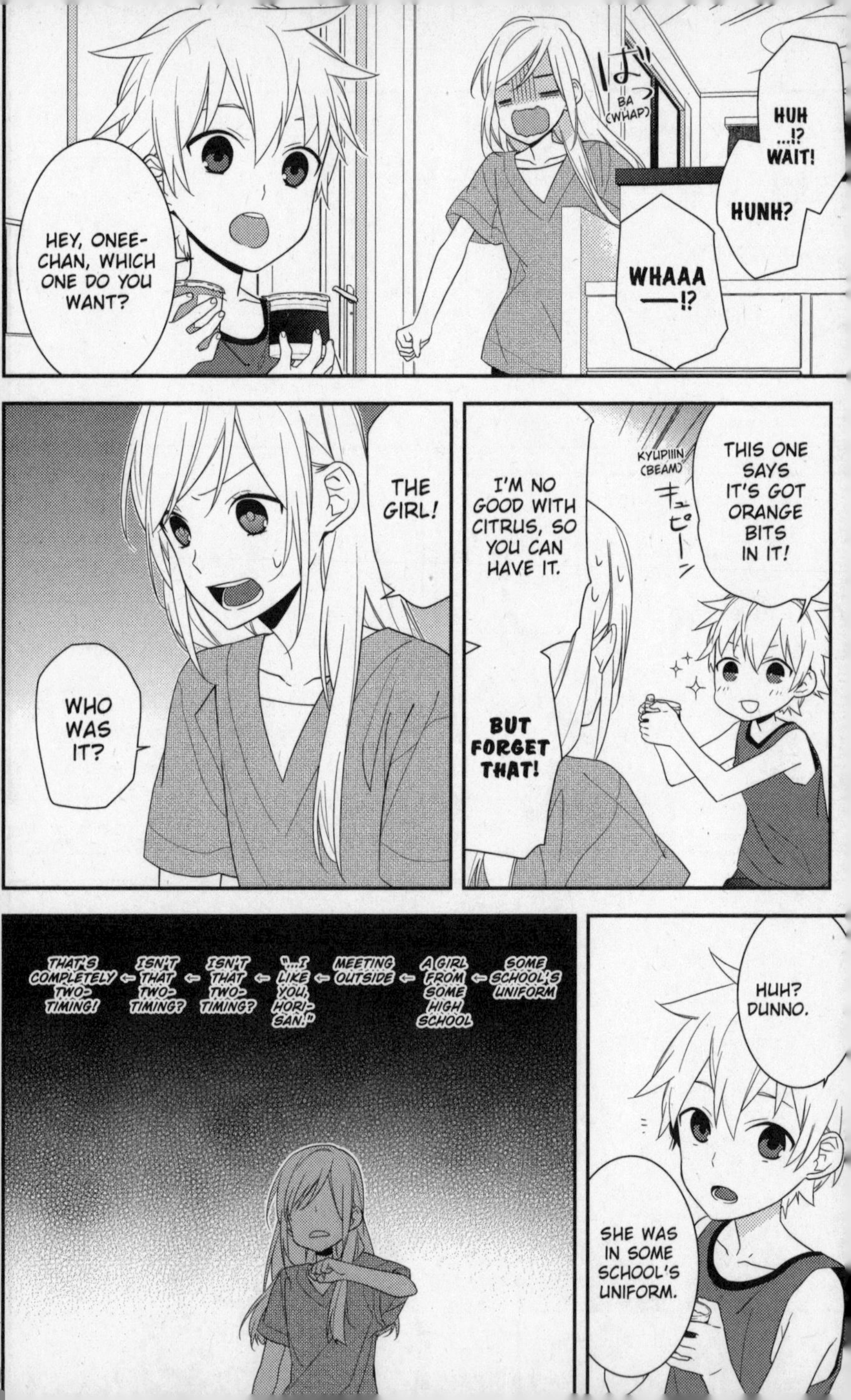
HUH ...!? WAIT!
HUNH?
ばっ
BA (WHAP)
WHAAA—!?
HEY, ONEE-CHAN, WHICH ONE DO YOU WANT?
THIS ONE SAYS IT'S GOT ORANGE BITS IN IT!
キュピーン
KYUPIIIN (BEAM)
I'M NO GOOD WITH CITRUS, SO YOU CAN HAVE IT.
BUT FORGET THAT!
THE GIRL!
WHO WAS IT?
HUH? DUNNO.
SHE WAS IN SOME SCHOOL'S UNIFORM.
SOME SCHOOL'S UNIFORM
A GIRL FROM SOME HIGH SCHOOL
MEETING OUTSIDE
"...I LIKE YOU, HORI-SAN."
ISN'T THAT TWO-TIMING?
ISN'T THAT TWO-TIMING?
THAT'S COMPLETELY TWO-TIMING!

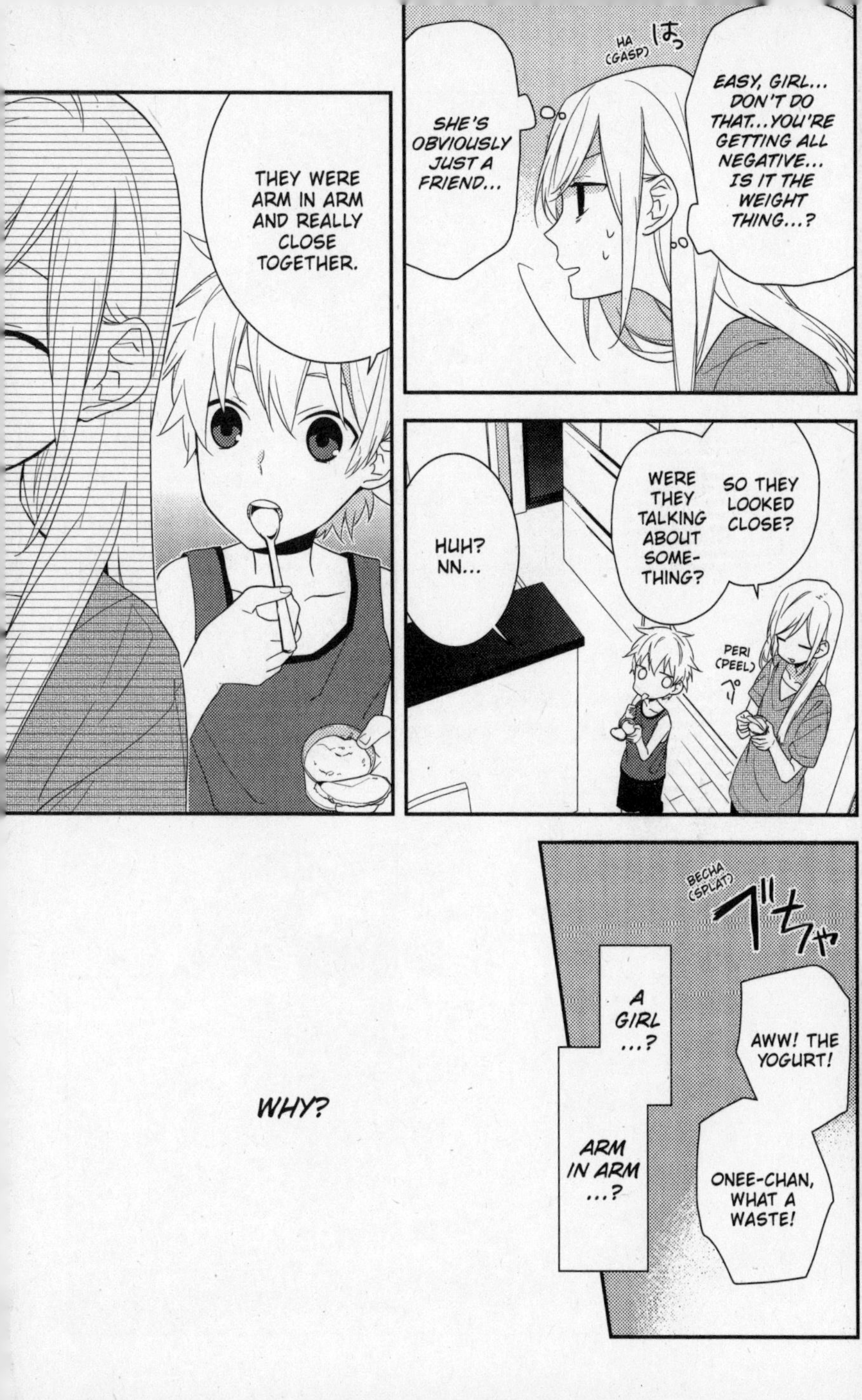
HA (GASP)
はっ
EASY, GIRL... DON'T DO THAT...YOU'RE GETTING ALL NEGATIVE... IS IT THE WEIGHT THING...?
SHE'S OBVIOUSLY JUST A FRIEND...
SO THEY LOOKED CLOSE?
WERE THEY TALKING ABOUT SOME-THING?
HUH? NN...
PERI (PEEL)
ペリ
THEY WERE ARM IN ARM AND REALLY CLOSE TOGETHER.
BECHA (SPLAT)
べちゃ
AWW! THE YOGURT!
ONEE-CHAN, WHAT A WASTE!
A GIRL ...?
ARM IN ARM ...?
WHY?

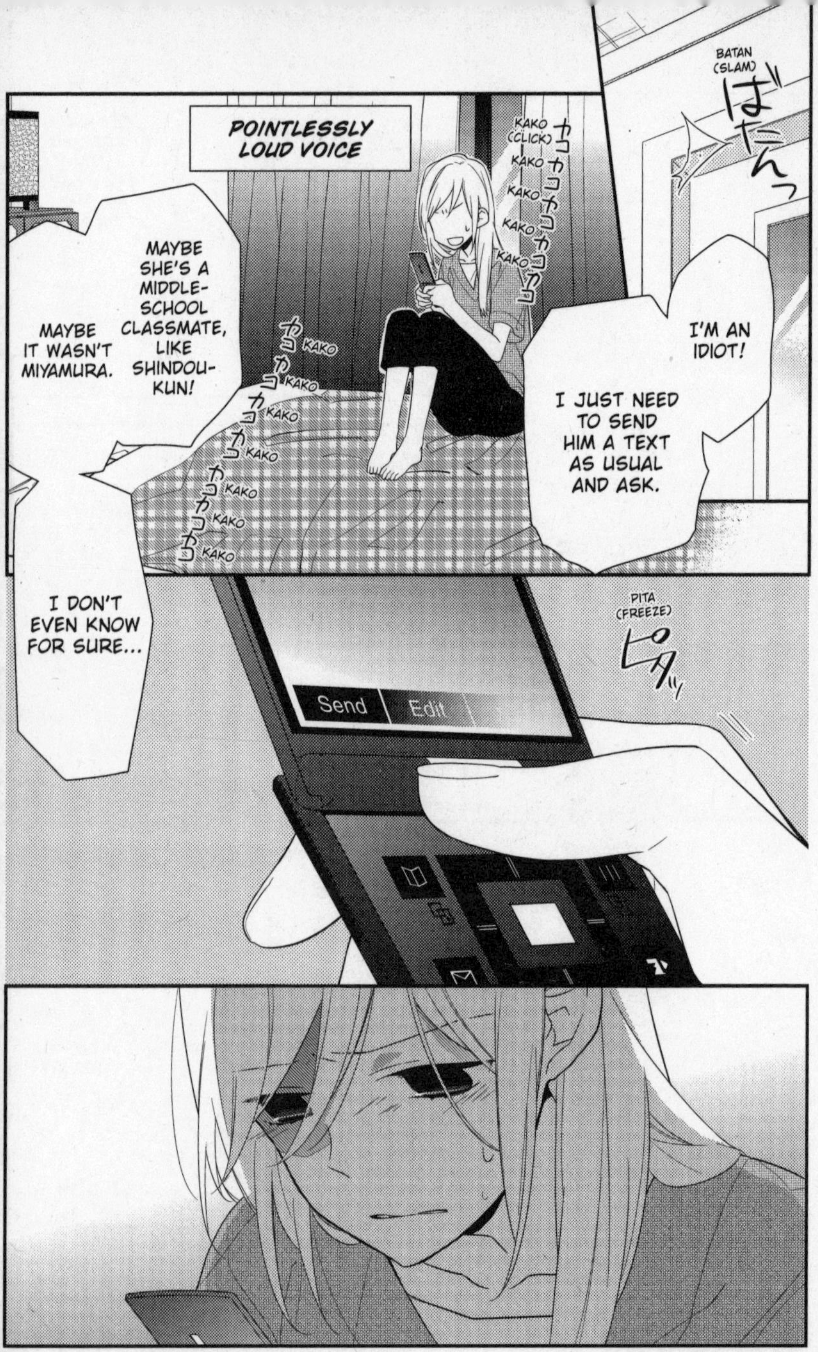

BATAN (SLAM)
ばたんっ
I'M AN IDIOT!
I JUST NEED TO SEND HIM A TEXT AS USUAL AND ASK.
KAKO (CLICK) KAKO KAKO KAKO KAKO
POINTLESSLY LOUD VOICE
MAYBE SHE'S A MIDDLE-SCHOOL CLASSMATE, LIKE SHINDOU-KUN!
MAYBE IT WASN'T MIYAMURA.
KAKO KAKO KAKO KAKO KAKO KAKO KAKO
PITA (FREEZE)
ピタッ
Send
Edit
I DON'T EVEN KNOW FOR SURE...

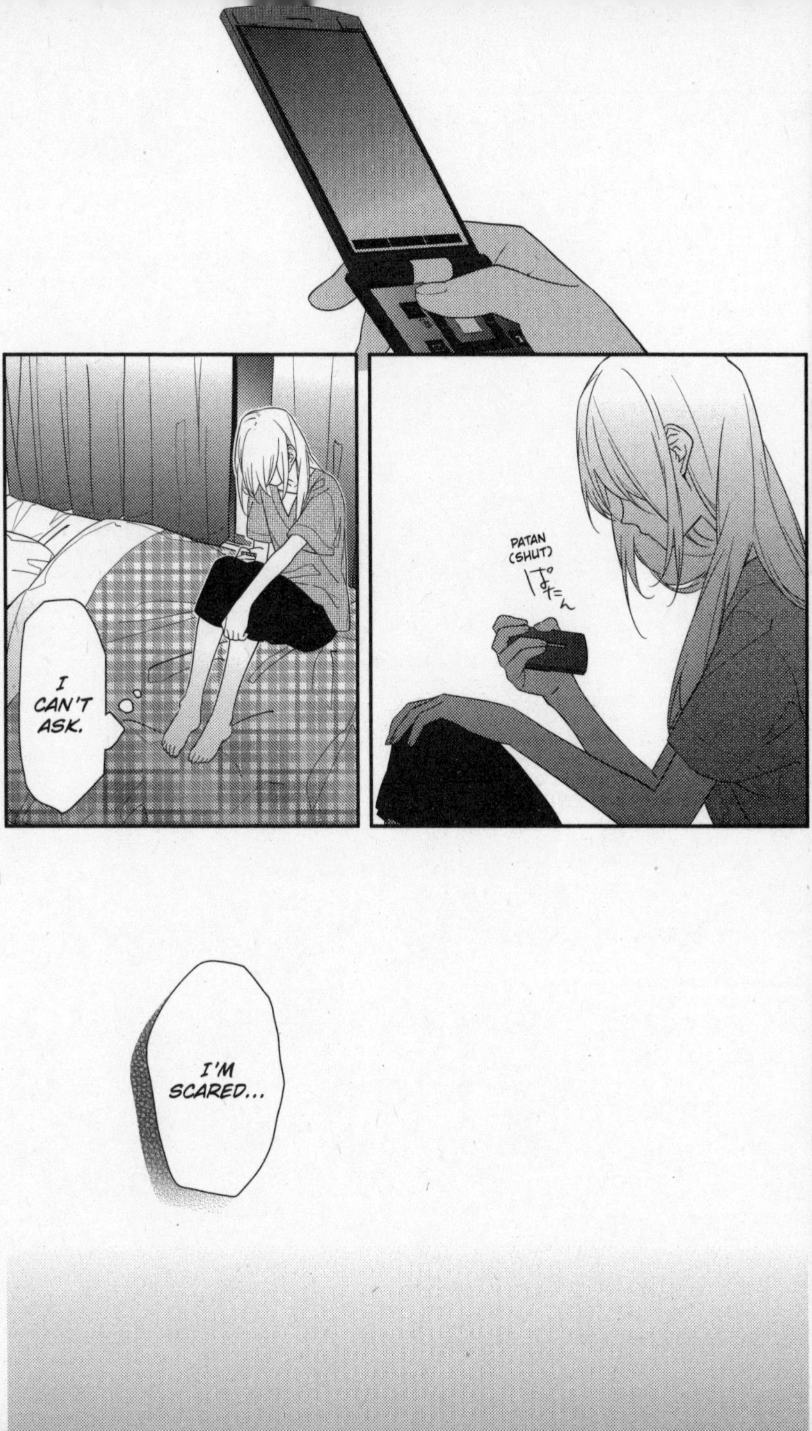
PATAN (SHUT)
ぱたん
I CAN'T ASK.
I'M SCARED...

HORIMIYA

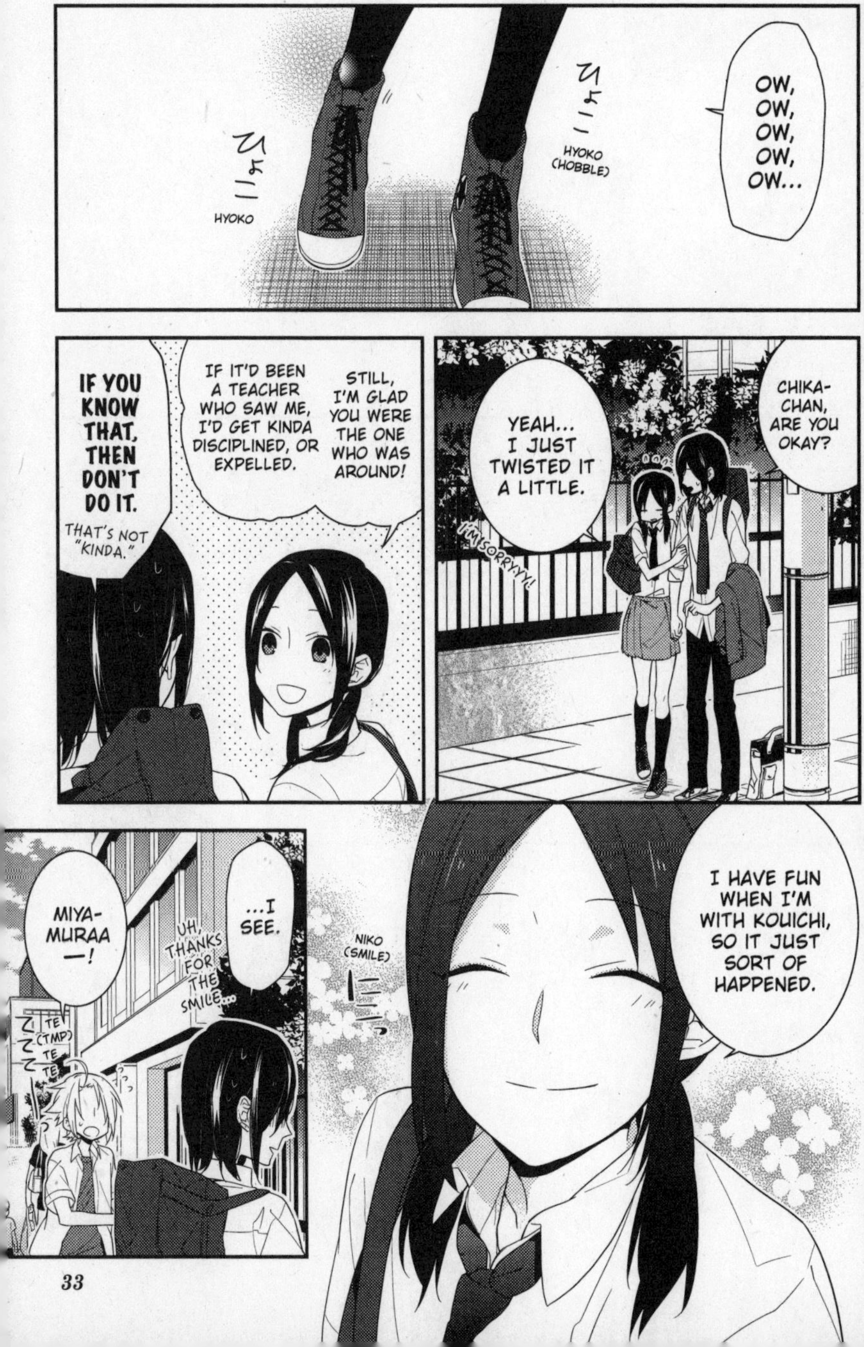
OW, OW, OW, OW, OW...
ひょこ
HYOKO (HOBBLE)
ひょこ
HYOKO
CHIKA-CHAN, ARE YOU OKAY?
YEAH... I JUST TWISTED IT A LITTLE.
I'M SORRYYY!
STILL, I'M GLAD YOU WERE THE ONE WHO WAS AROUND!
IF IT'D BEEN A TEACHER WHO SAW ME, I'D GET KINDA DISCIPLINED, OR EXPELLED.
IF YOU KNOW THAT, THEN DON'T DO IT.
THAT'S NOT "KINDA."
I HAVE FUN WHEN I'M WITH KOUICHI, SO IT JUST SORT OF HAPPENED.
ニコー
NIKO (SMILE)
...I SEE.
UH, THANKS FOR THE SMILE...
MIYA-MURAA—!
TE (TMP) TE TE

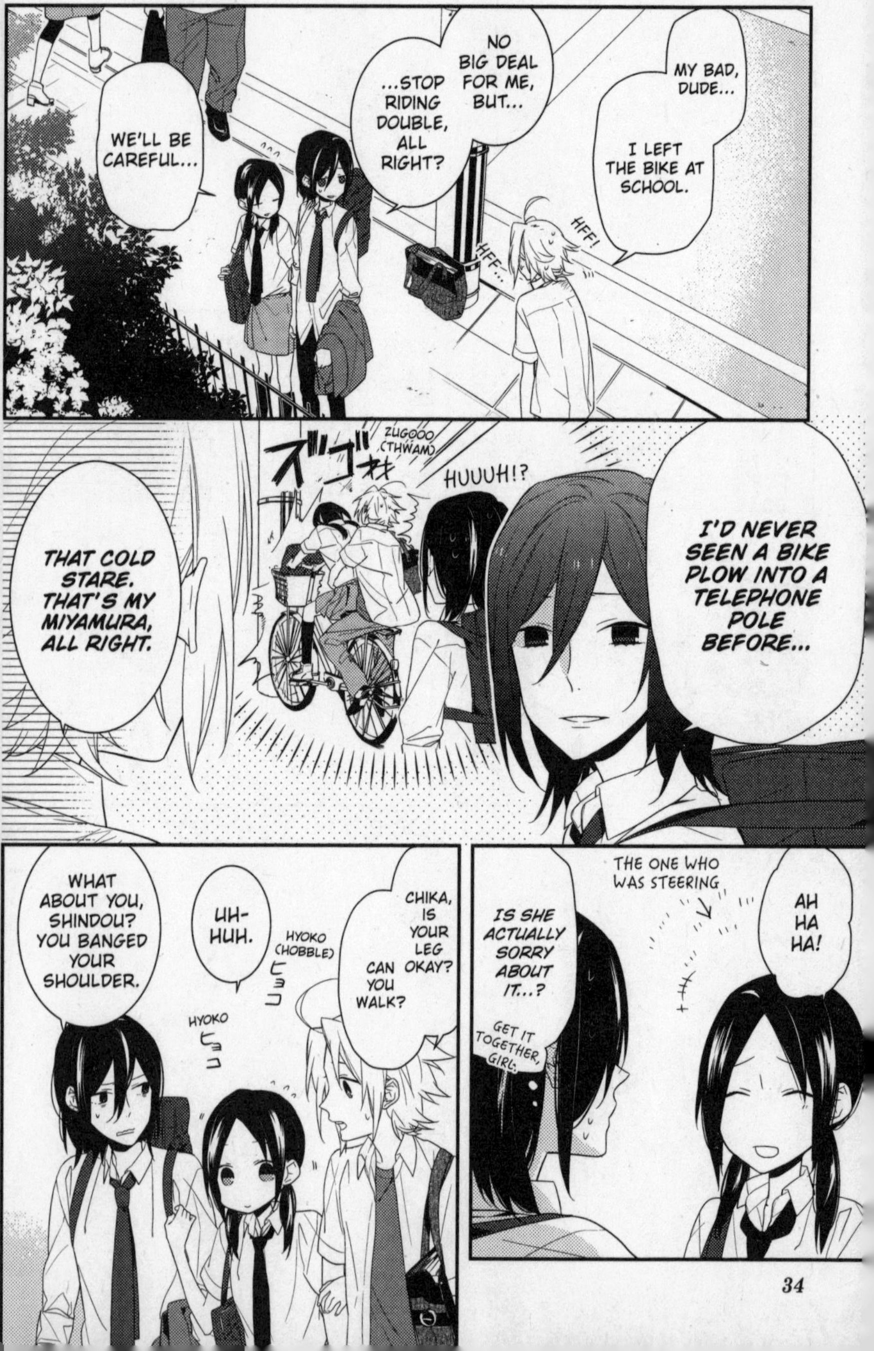

MY BAD, DUDE...
I LEFT THE BIKE AT SCHOOL.
HFF!
HFF...
NO BIG DEAL FOR ME, BUT...
...STOP RIDING DOUBLE, ALL RIGHT?
WE'LL BE CAREFUL...
I'D NEVER SEEN A BIKE PLOW INTO A TELEPHONE POLE BEFORE...
HUUUH!?
ズゴォォ
ZUGOOO (THWAM)
THAT COLD STARE. THAT'S MY MIYAMURA, ALL RIGHT.
AH HA HA!
THE ONE WHO WAS STEERING
IS SHE ACTUALLY SORRY ABOUT IT...?
GET IT TOGETHER, GIRL.
CHIKA, IS YOUR LEG OKAY? CAN YOU WALK?
HYOKO (HOBBLE)
ヒョコ
UH-HUH.
HYOKO
ヒョコ
WHAT ABOUT YOU, SHINDOU? YOU BANGED YOUR SHOULDER.

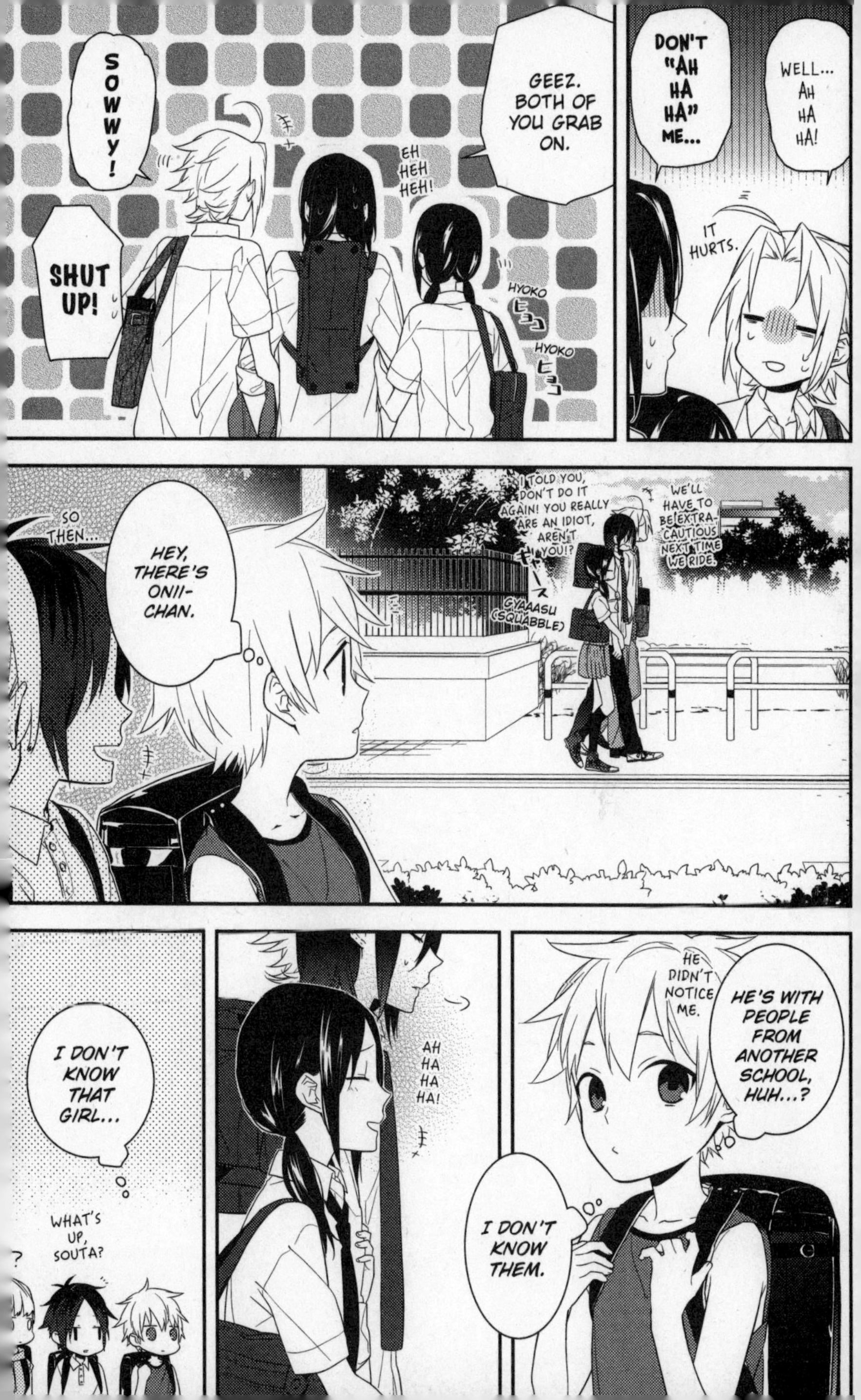
WELL... AH HA HA!
DON'T "AH HA HA" ME...
IT HURTS.
GEEZ. BOTH OF YOU GRAB ON.
EH HEH HEH!
HYOKO ヒョコ
HYOKO ヒョコ
SOWWY!
SHUT UP!
WE'LL HAVE TO BE EXTRA-CAUTIOUS NEXT TIME WE RIDE.
I TOLD YOU, DON'T DO IT AGAIN! YOU REALLY ARE AN IDIOT, AREN'T YOU!?
ギャース GYAAASU (SQUABBLE)
HEY, THERE'S ONII-CHAN.
SO THEN...
HE DIDN'T NOTICE ME.
HE'S WITH PEOPLE FROM ANOTHER SCHOOL, HUH...?
I DON'T KNOW THEM.
AH HA HA HA!
I DON'T KNOW THAT GIRL...
WHAT'S UP, SOUTA?
?

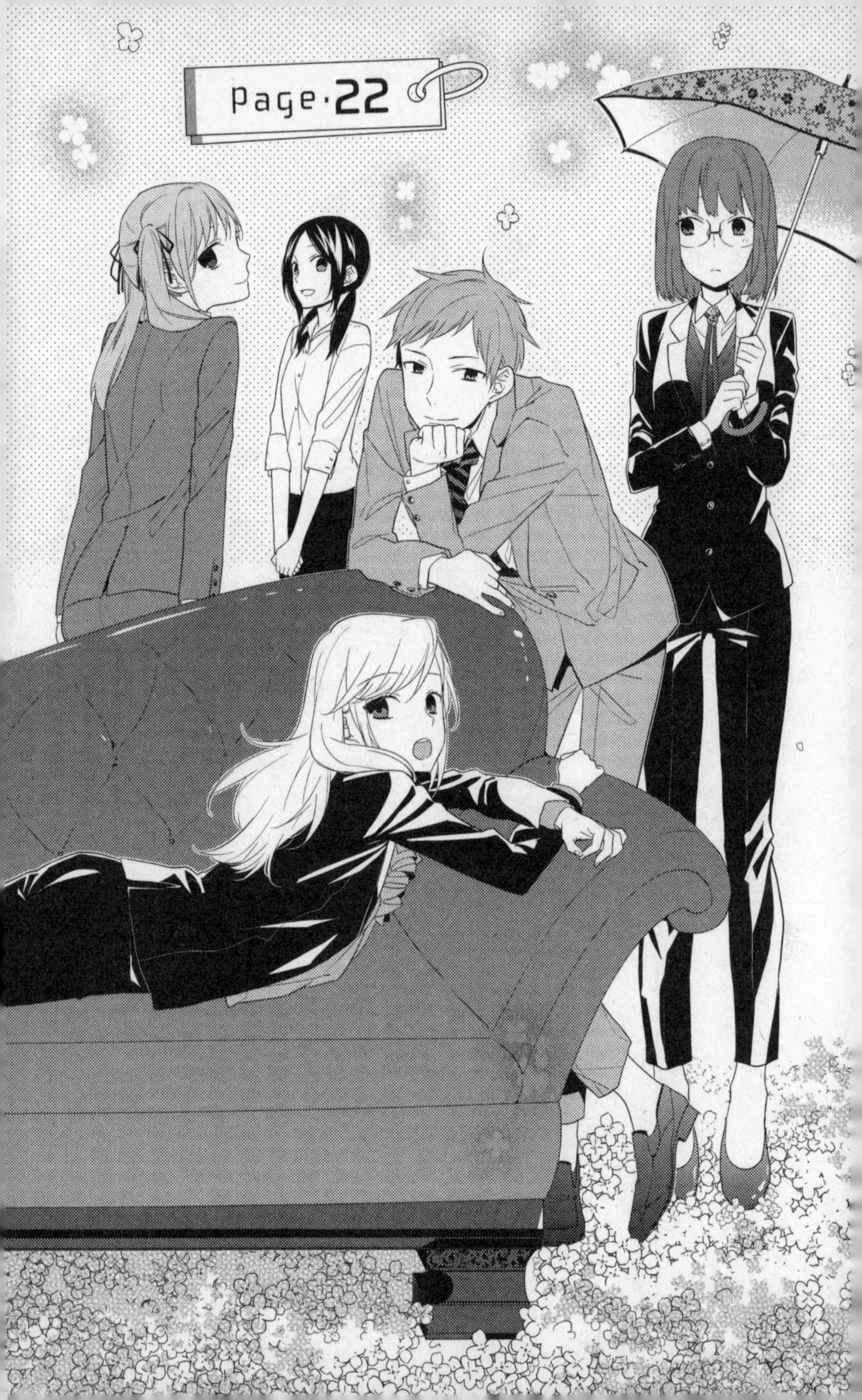
Page·22

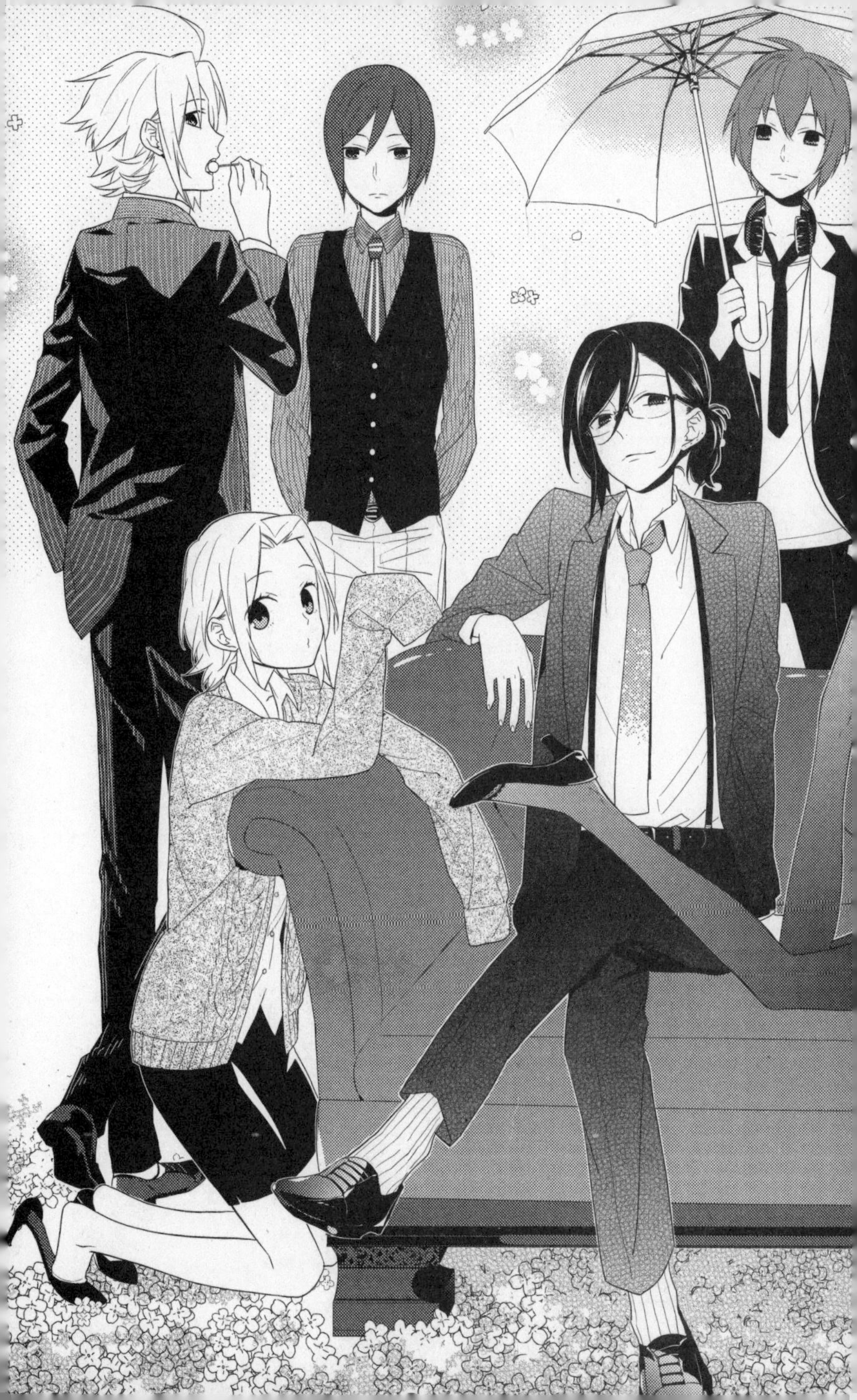

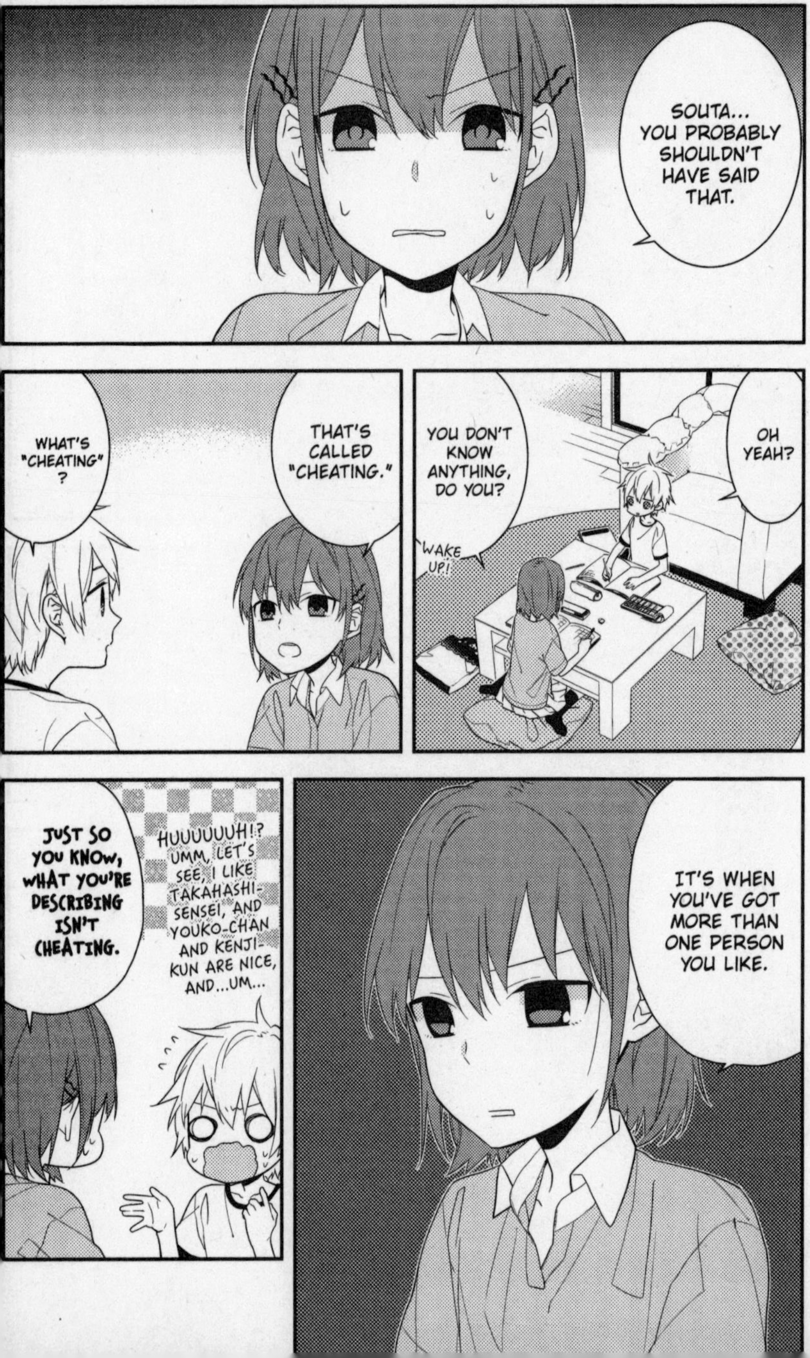
SOUTA... YOU PROBABLY SHOULDN'T HAVE SAID THAT.
OH YEAH?
YOU DON'T KNOW ANYTHING, DO YOU?
WAKE UP!
THAT'S CALLED "CHEATING."
WHAT'S "CHEATING"?
IT'S WHEN YOU'VE GOT MORE THAN ONE PERSON YOU LIKE.
HUUUUUUH!? UMM, LET'S SEE, I LIKE TAKAHASHI-SENSEI, AND YOUKO-CHAN AND KENJI-KUN ARE NICE, AND...UM...
JUST SO YOU KNOW, WHAT YOU'RE DESCRIBING ISN'T CHEATING.

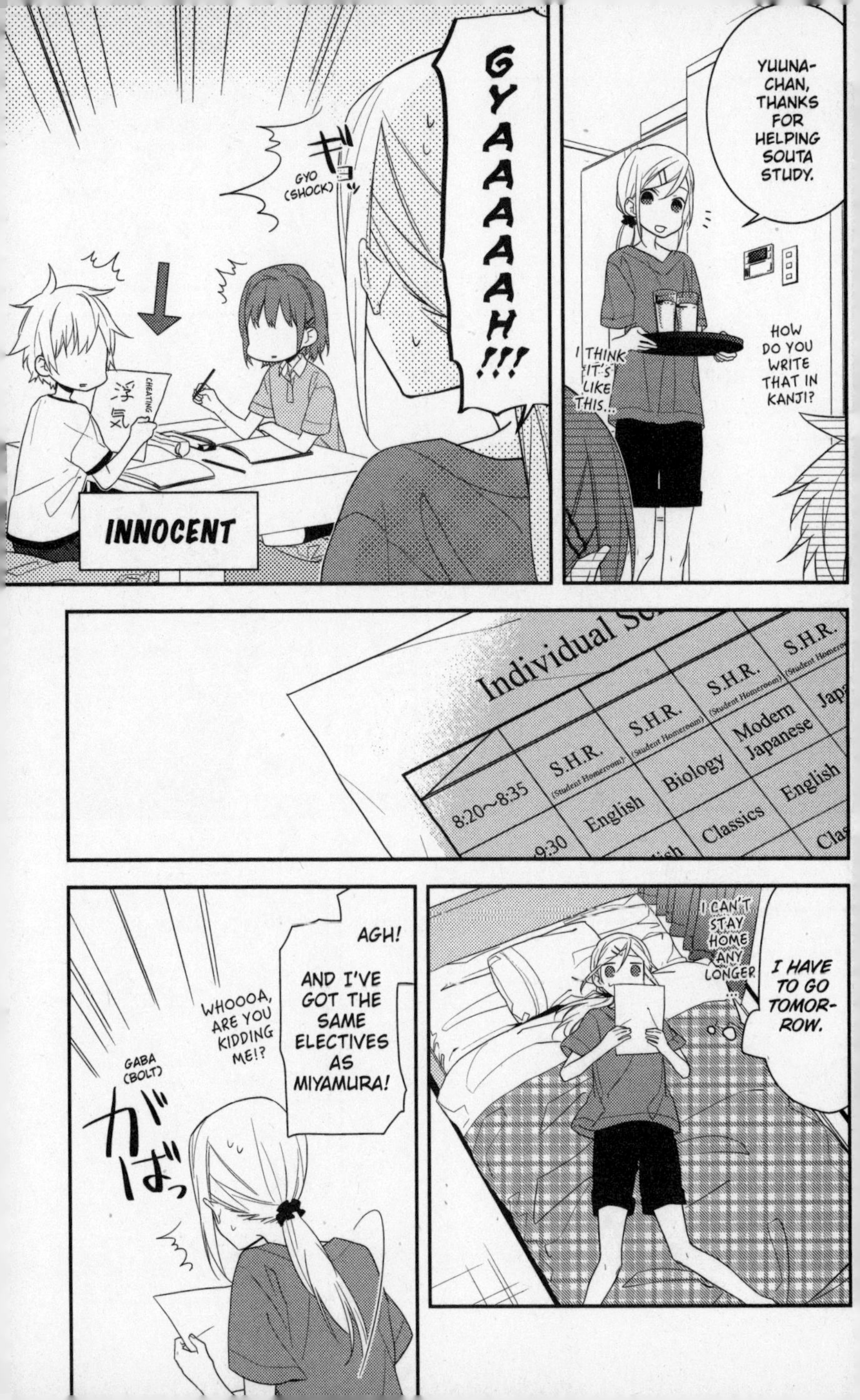
YUUNA-CHAN, THANKS FOR HELPING SOUTA STUDY.
HOW DO YOU WRITE THAT IN KANJI?
I THINK IT'S LIKE THIS...
GYAAAAAH!!!
ギョ
GYO (SHOCK)
浮気
CHEATING
INNOCENT
Individual Sc
8:20~8:35
S.H.R. (Student Homeroom)
English
Biology
Modern Japanese
Classics
English
I CAN'T STAY HOME ANY LONGER...
I HAVE TO GO TOMORROW.
AGH!
AND I'VE GOT THE SAME ELECTIVES AS MIYAMURA!
WHOOOA, ARE YOU KIDDING ME!?
がばっ
GABA (BOLT)

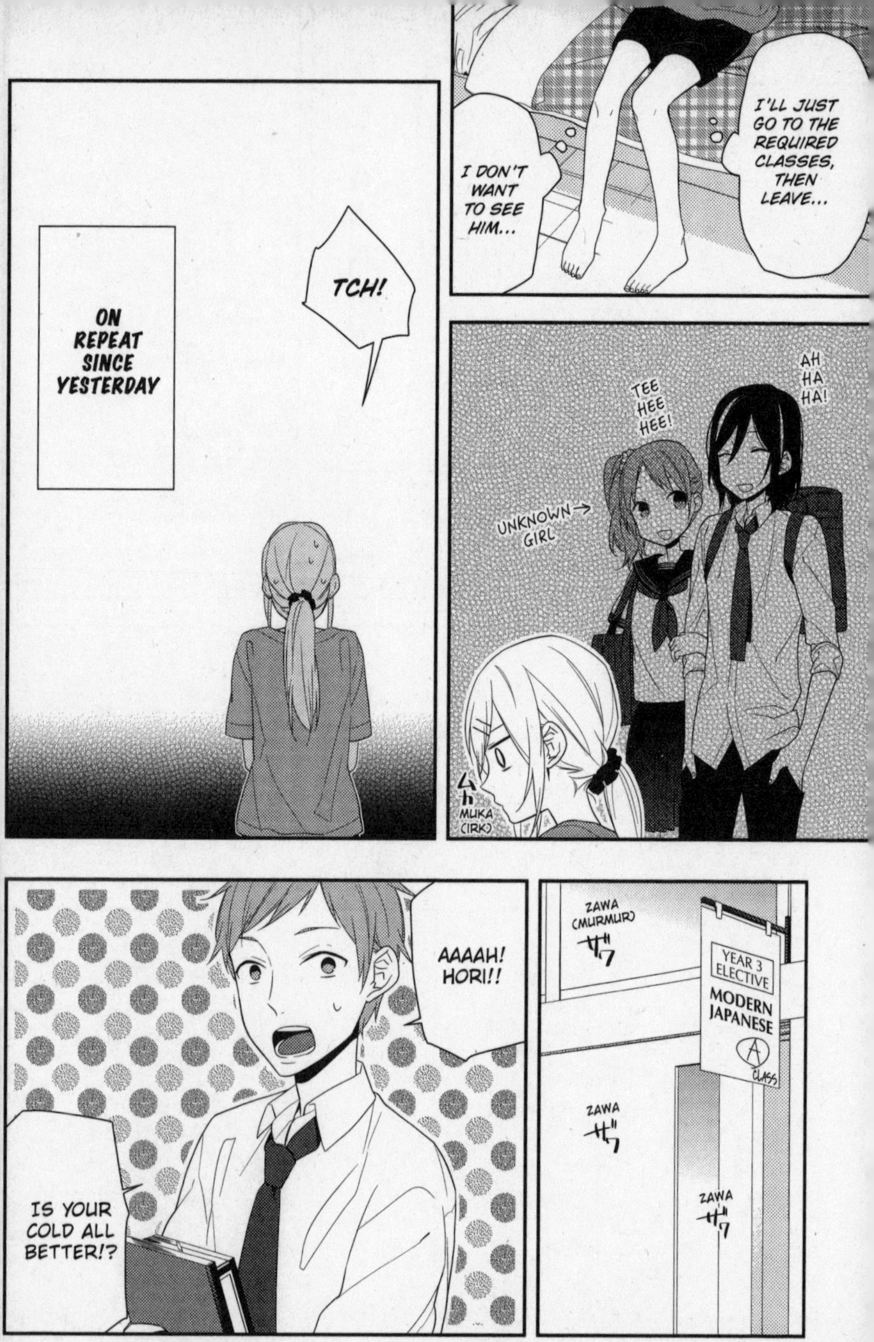
I'LL JUST GO TO THE REQUIRED CLASSES, THEN LEAVE...
I DON'T WANT TO SEE HIM...
AH HA HA!
TEE HEE HEE!
UNKNOWN GIRL
MUKA (IRK)
TCH!
ON REPEAT SINCE YESTERDAY
YEAR 3 ELECTIVE
MODERN JAPANESE
A CLASS
ZAWA (MURMUR)
ZAWA
ZAWA
AAAAH! HORI!!
IS YOUR COLD ALL BETTER!?

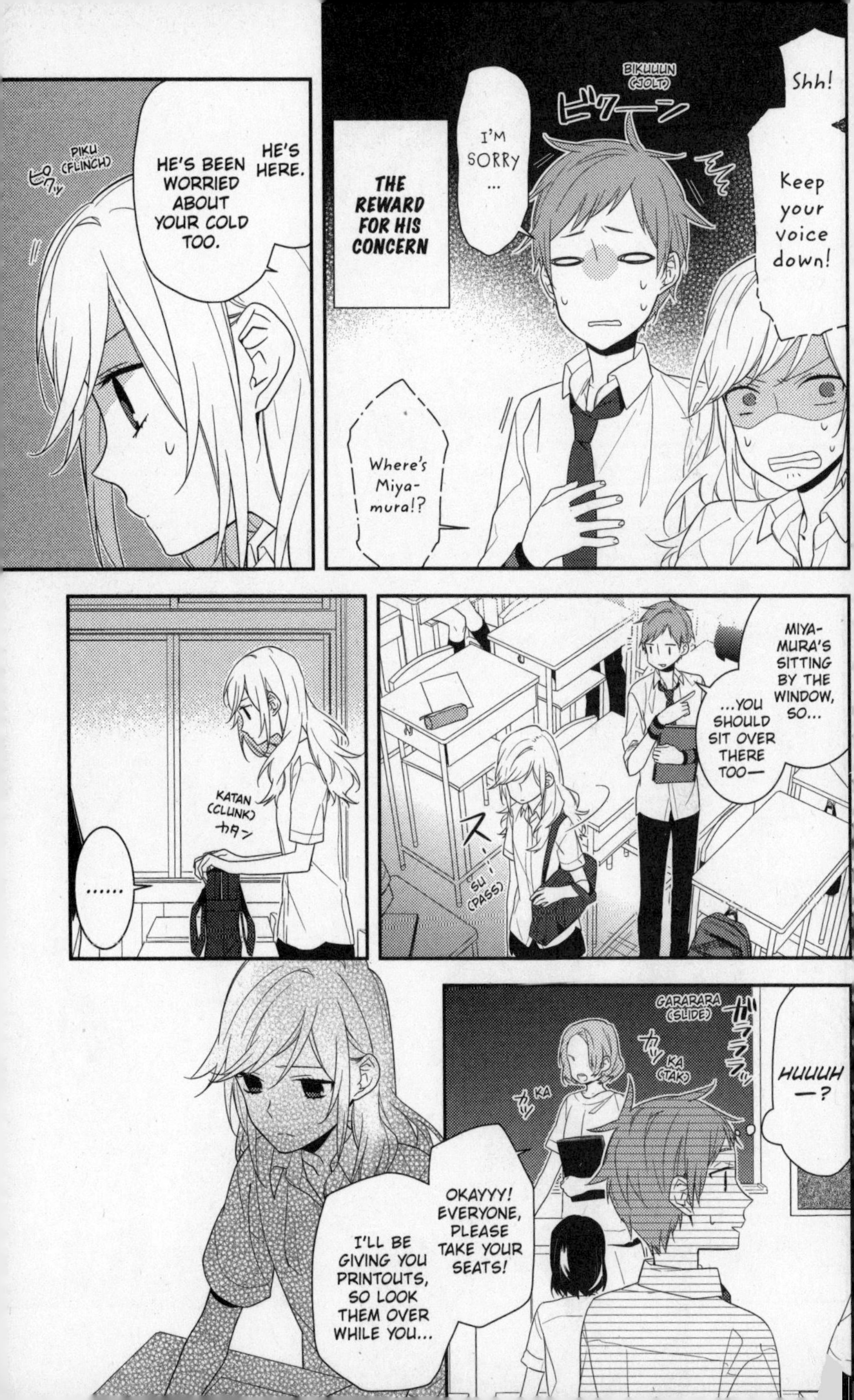
Shh!
Keep your voice down!
BIKUUUN (JOLT)
I'M SORRY ...
THE REWARD FOR HIS CONCERN
Where's Miya-mura!?
HE'S HERE.
HE'S BEEN WORRIED ABOUT YOUR COLD TOO.
PIKU (FLINCH)
MIYA-MURA'S SITTING BY THE WINDOW, SO...
...YOU SHOULD SIT OVER THERE TOO—
SU (PASS)
KATAN (CLUNK)
......
HUUUH—?
GARARARA (SLIDE)
KA (TAK)
KA
OKAYYY! EVERYONE, PLEASE TAKE YOUR SEATS!
I'LL BE GIVING YOU PRINTOUTS, SO LOOK THEM OVER WHILE YOU...

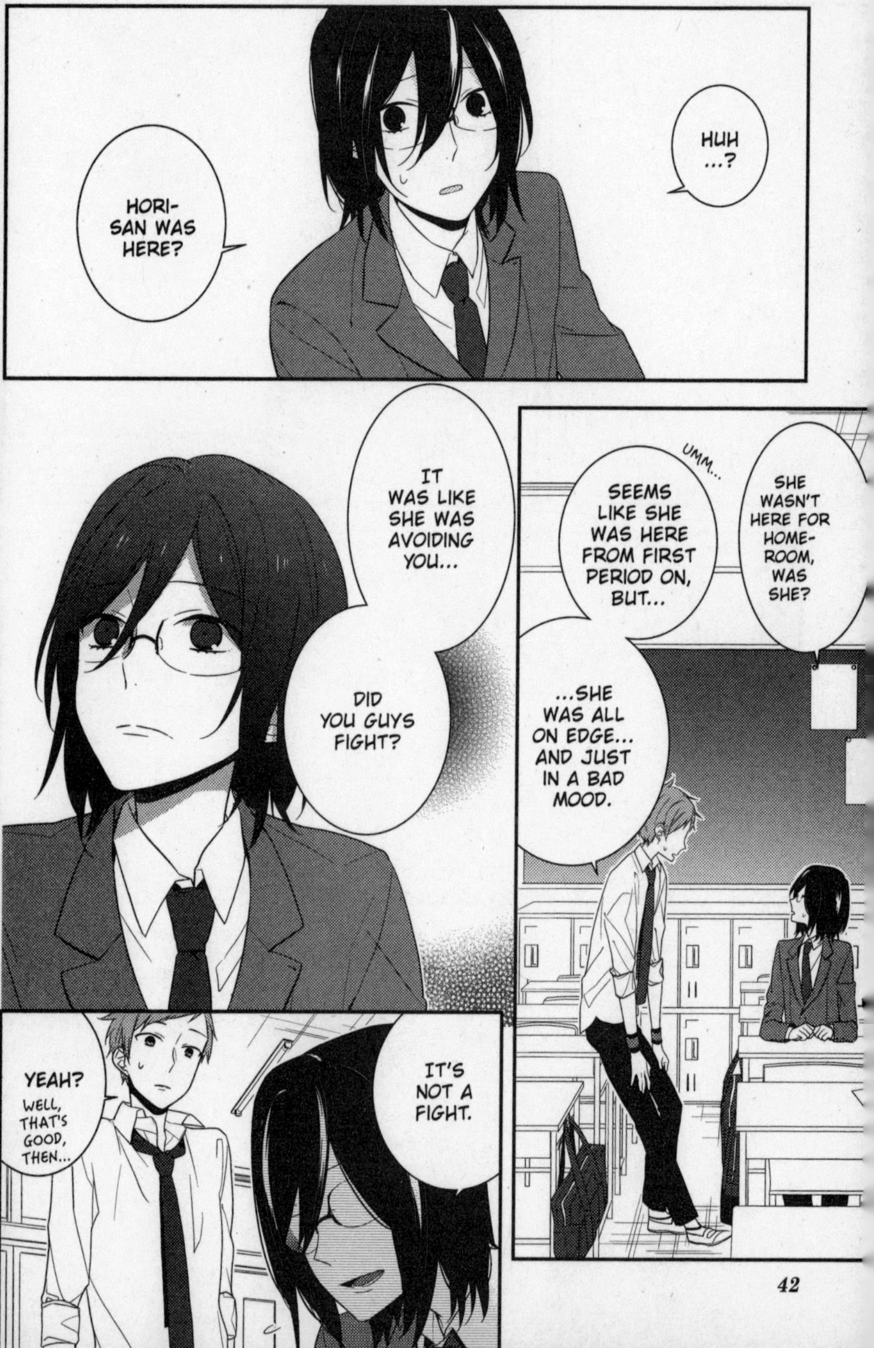
HUH ...?
HORI-SAN WAS HERE?
SHE WASN'T HERE FOR HOME-ROOM, WAS SHE?
UMM...
SEEMS LIKE SHE WAS HERE FROM FIRST PERIOD ON, BUT...
...SHE WAS ALL ON EDGE... AND JUST IN A BAD MOOD.
IT WAS LIKE SHE WAS AVOIDING YOU...
DID YOU GUYS FIGHT?
IT'S NOT A FIGHT.
YEAH? WELL, THAT'S GOOD, THEN...

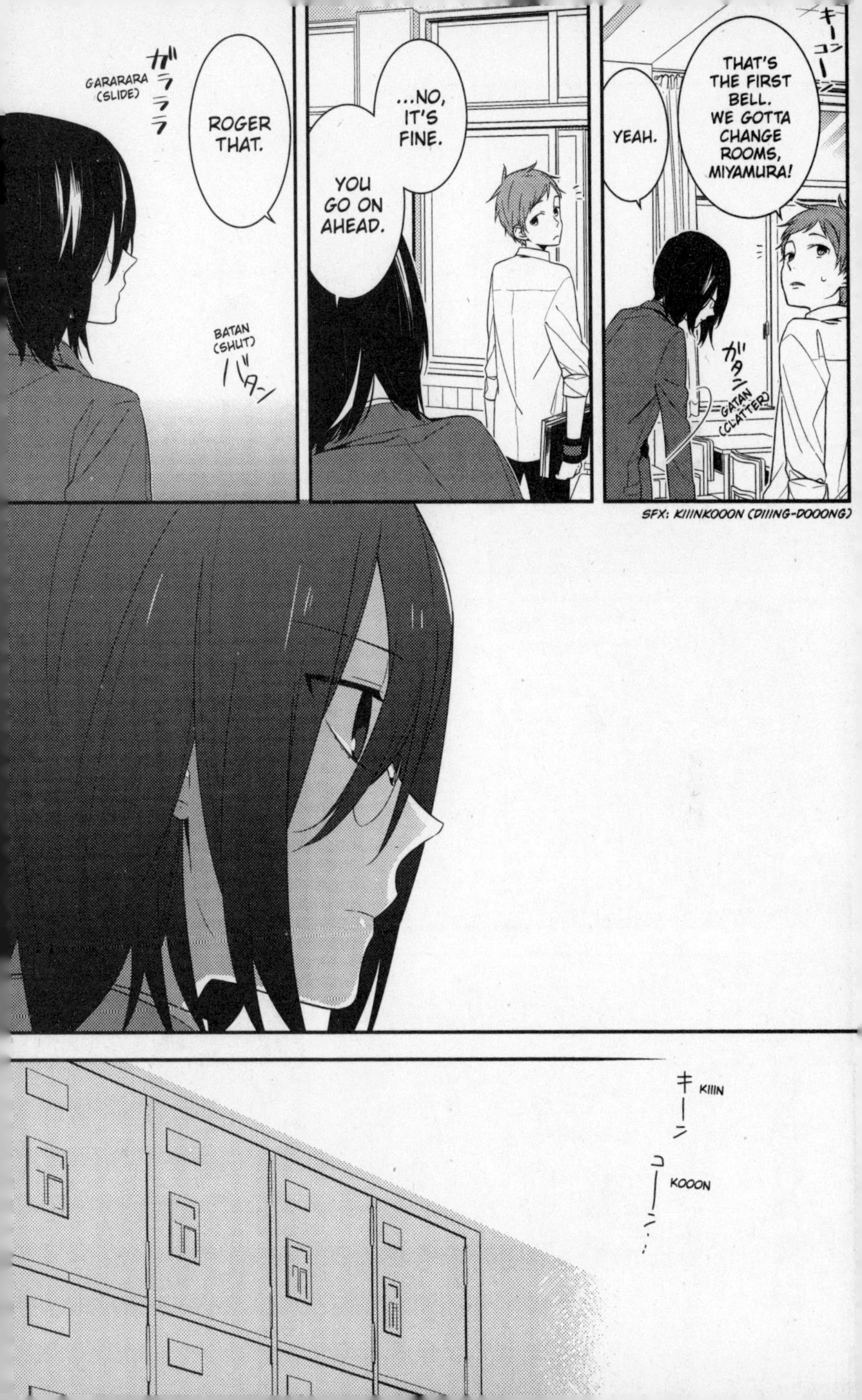
THAT'S THE FIRST BELL. WE GOTTA CHANGE ROOMS, MIYAMURA!
YEAH.
ガタン
GATAN (CLATTER)
...NO, IT'S FINE.
YOU GO ON AHEAD.
ROGER THAT.
ガラララ
GARARARA (SLIDE)
バタン
BATAN (SHUT)
SFX: KIIINKOOON (DIIING-DOOONG)
キーン
KIIIN
コーン
KOOON

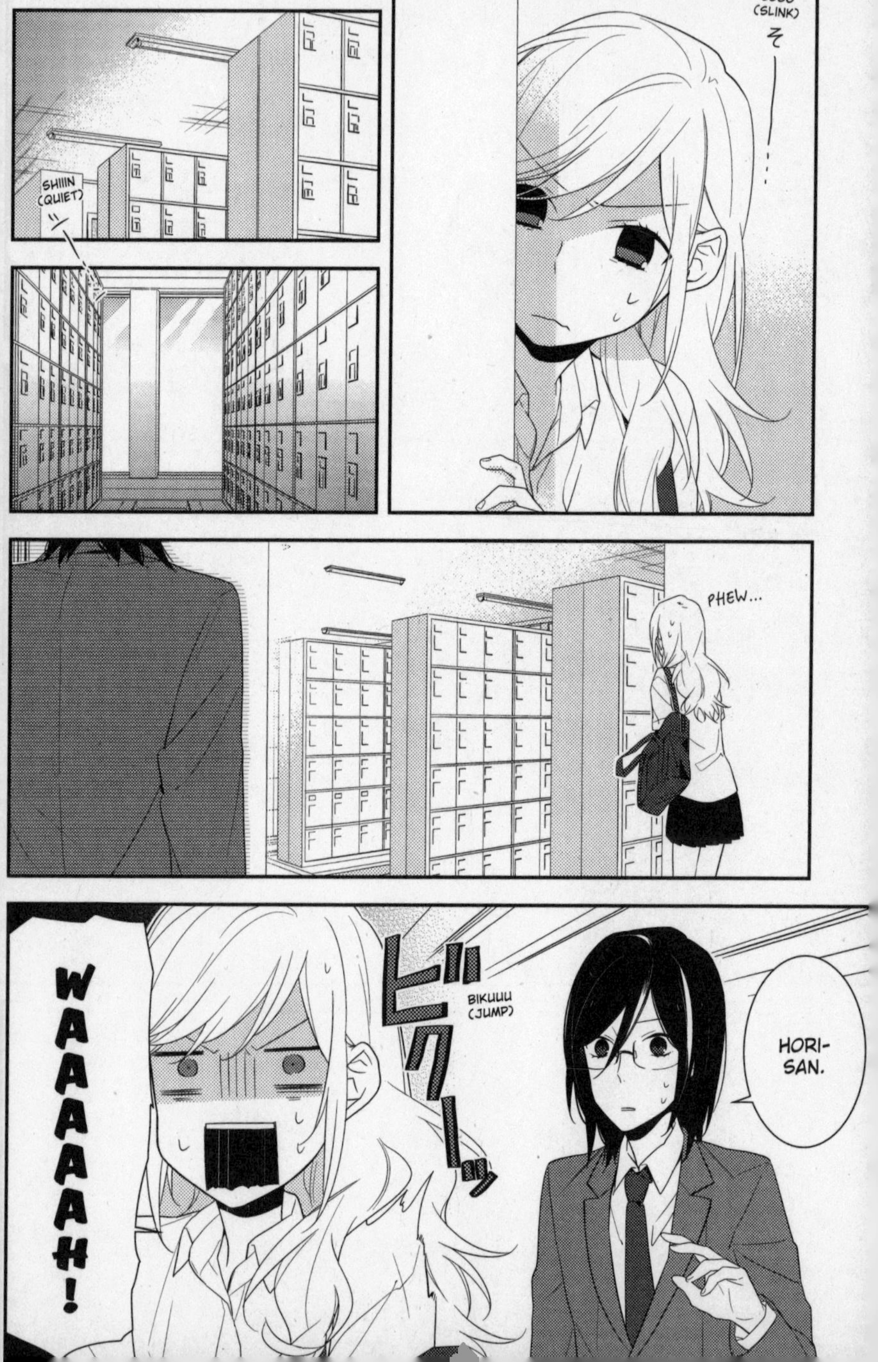
SOOO (SLINK)
そ
SHIIIN (QUIET)
シ
PHEW...
HORI-SAN.
BIKUUU (JUMP)
ビクーッ
WAAAAAAH!

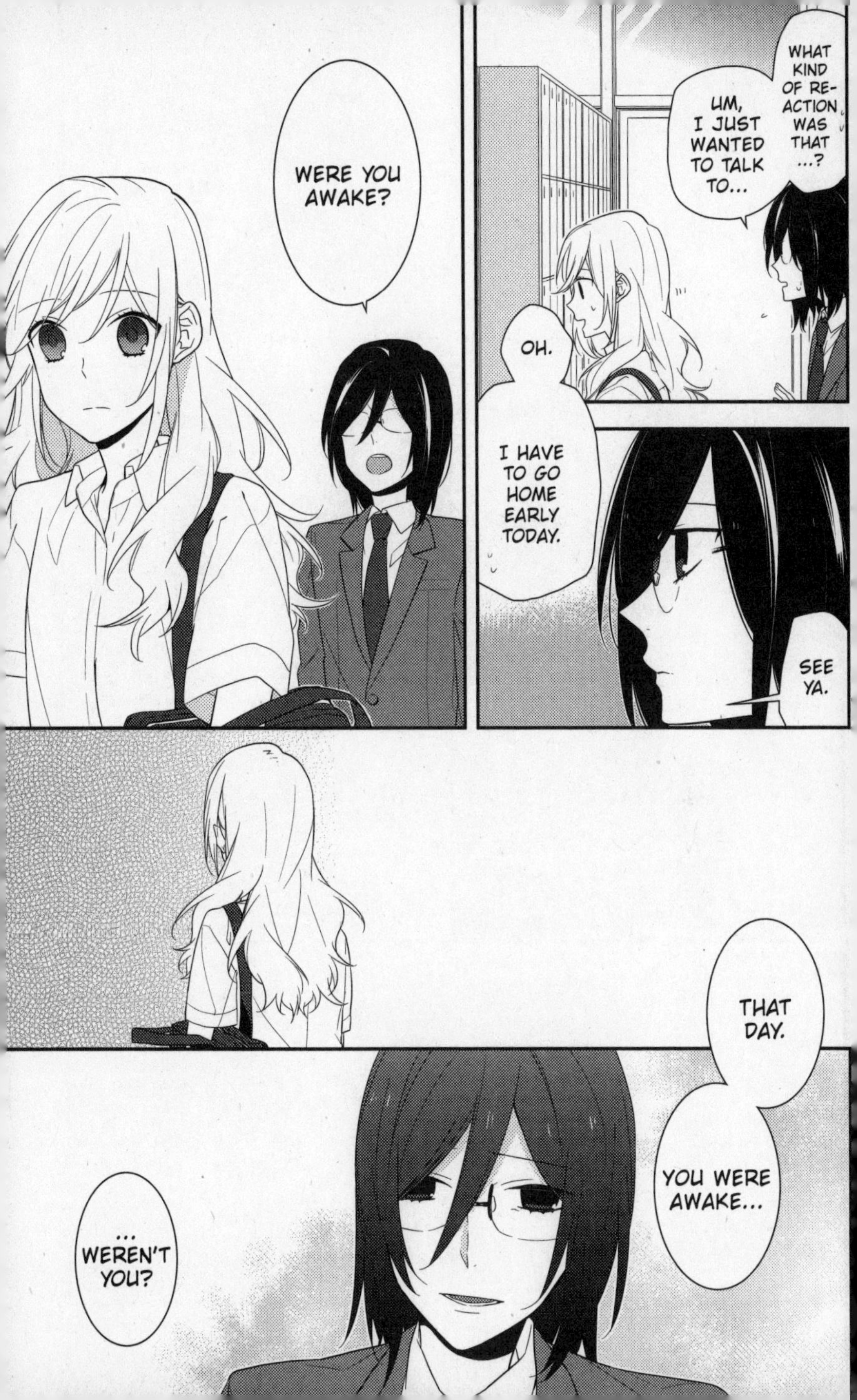
WHAT KIND OF RE-ACTION WAS THAT ...?
UM, I JUST WANTED TO TALK TO...
OH.
I HAVE TO GO HOME EARLY TODAY.
SEE YA.
WERE YOU AWAKE?
THAT DAY.
YOU WERE AWAKE...
...WEREN'T YOU?

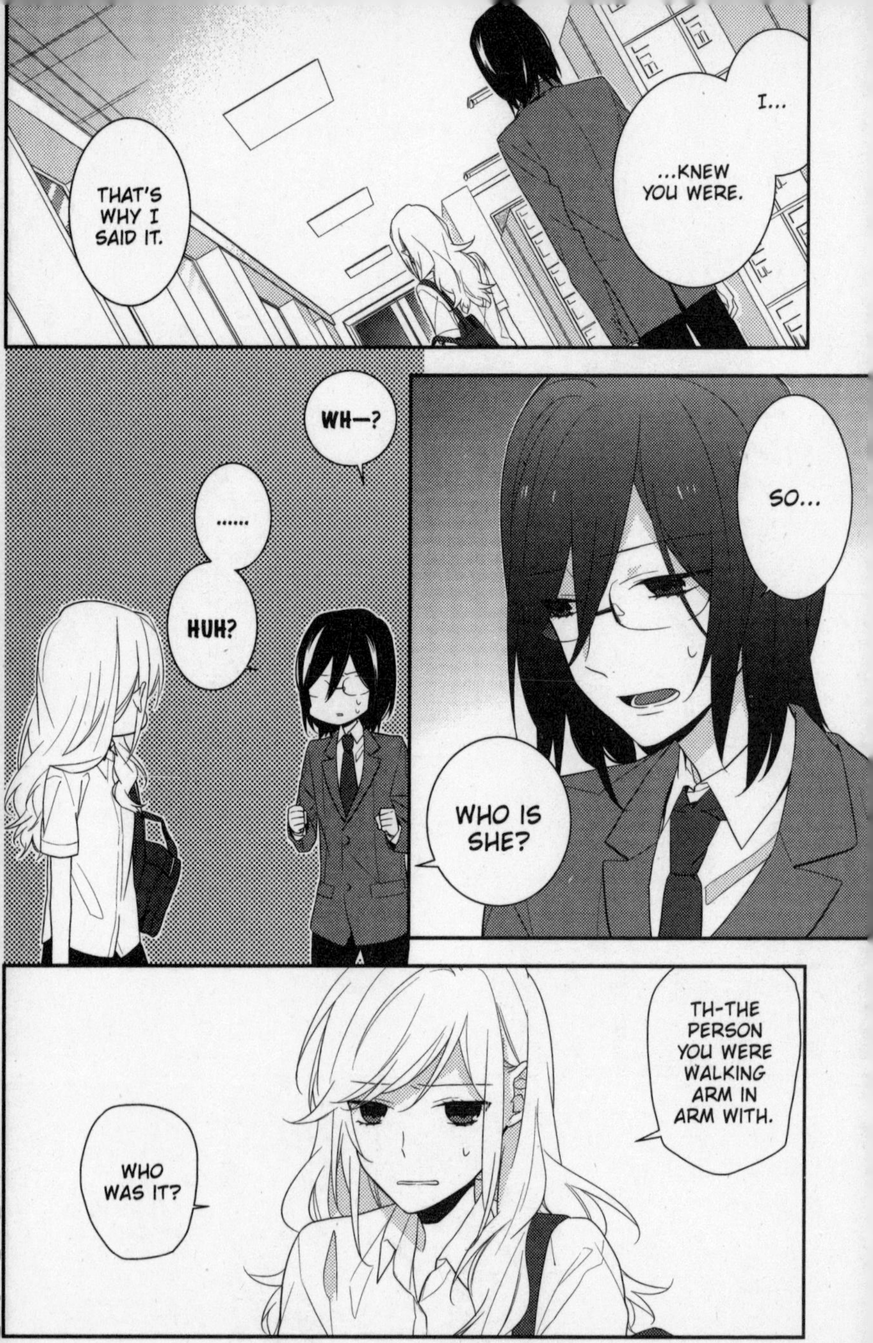
I...
...KNEW YOU WERE.
THAT'S WHY I SAID IT.
SO...
WHO IS SHE?
WH—?
......
HUH?
TH-THE PERSON YOU WERE WALKING ARM IN ARM WITH.
WHO WAS IT?

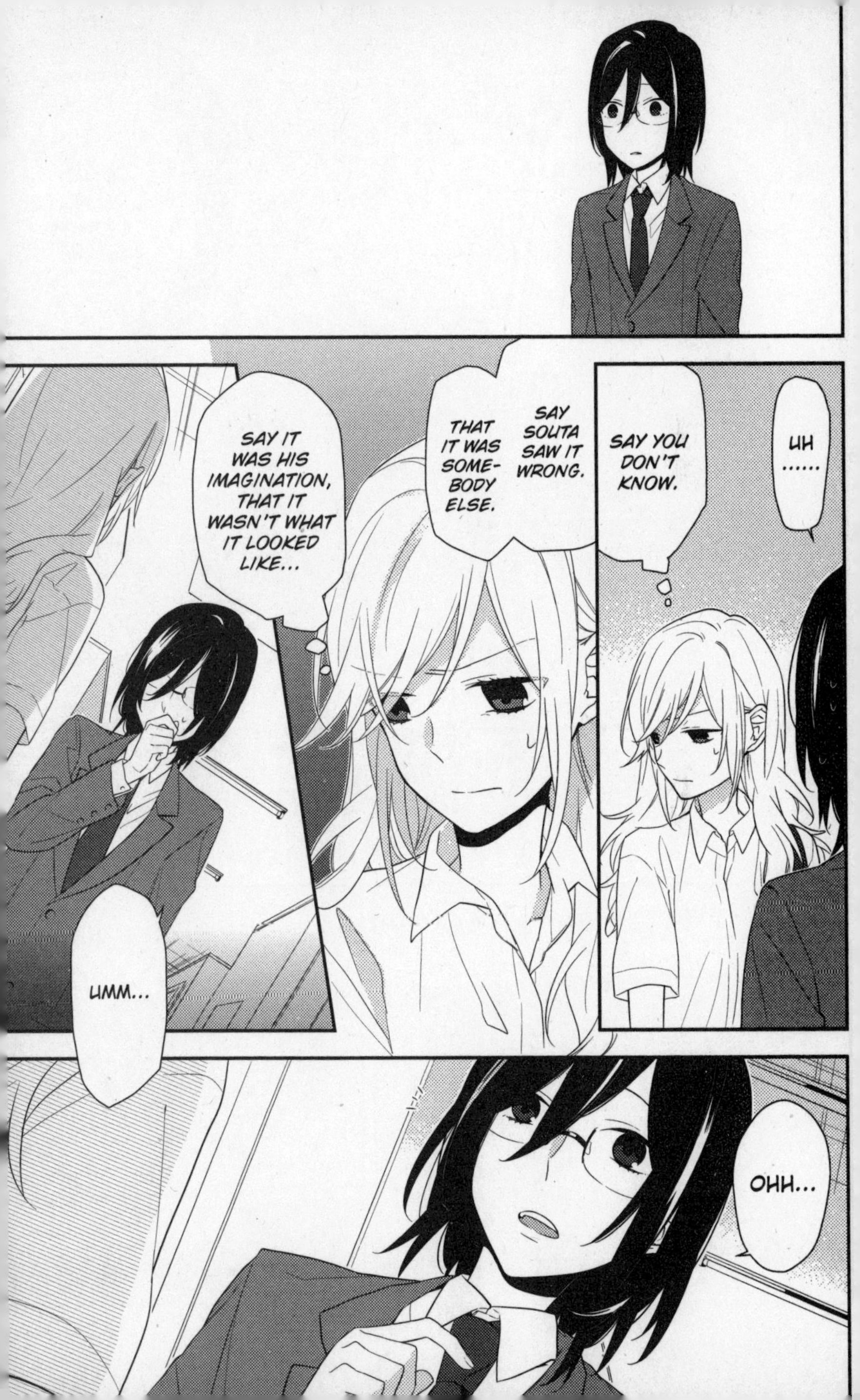
UH ......
SAY YOU DON'T KNOW.
SAY SOUTA SAW IT WRONG.
THAT IT WAS SOMEBODY ELSE.
SAY IT WAS HIS IMAGINATION, THAT IT WASN'T WHAT IT LOOKED LIKE...
UMM...
OHH...

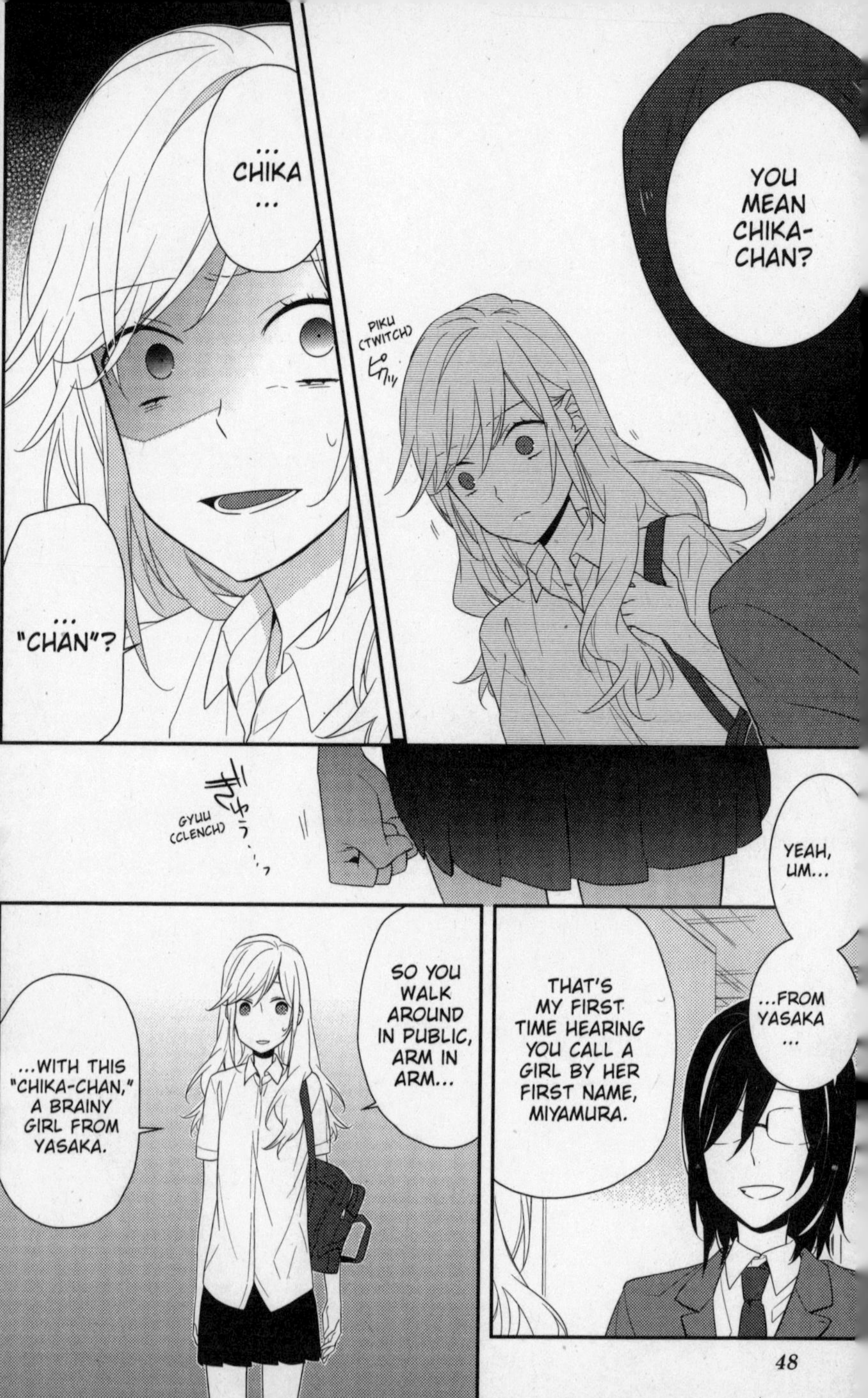
YOU MEAN CHIKA-CHAN?
PIKU (TWITCH)
...CHIKA...
..."CHAN"?
YEAH, UM...
GYUU (CLENCH)
...FROM YASAKA...
THAT'S MY FIRST TIME HEARING YOU CALL A GIRL BY HER FIRST NAME, MIYAMURA.
SO YOU WALK AROUND IN PUBLIC, ARM IN ARM...
...WITH THIS "CHIKA-CHAN," A BRAINY GIRL FROM YASAKA.

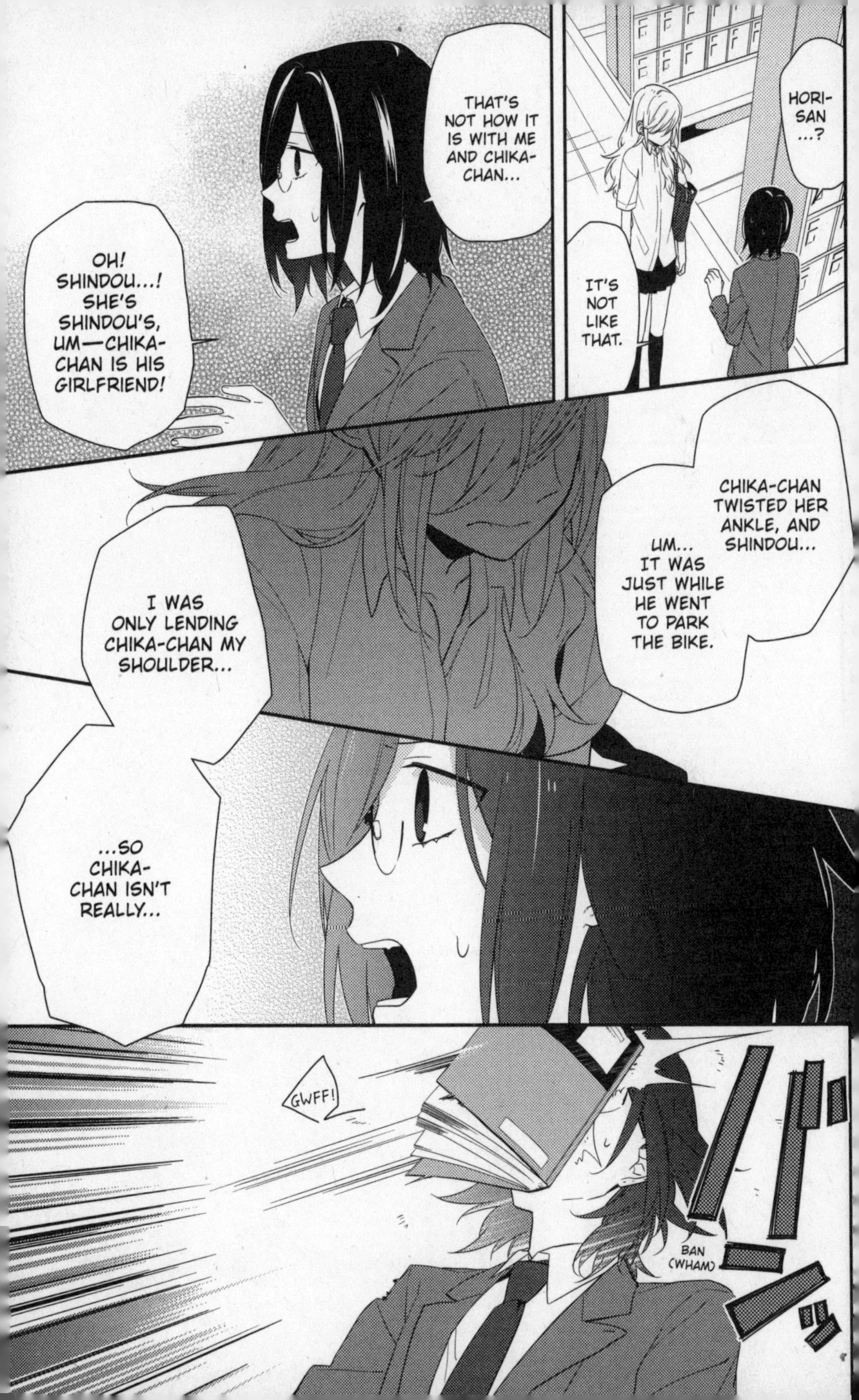
HORI-SAN...?
IT'S NOT LIKE THAT.
THAT'S NOT HOW IT IS WITH ME AND CHIKA-CHAN...
OH! SHINDOU...! SHE'S SHINDOU'S, UM—CHIKA-CHAN IS HIS GIRLFRIEND!
CHIKA-CHAN TWISTED HER ANKLE, AND SHINDOU...
UM... IT WAS JUST WHILE HE WENT TO PARK THE BIKE.
I WAS ONLY LENDING CHIKA-CHAN MY SHOULDER...
...SO CHIKA-CHAN ISN'T REALLY...
GWFF!
BAN (WHAM)

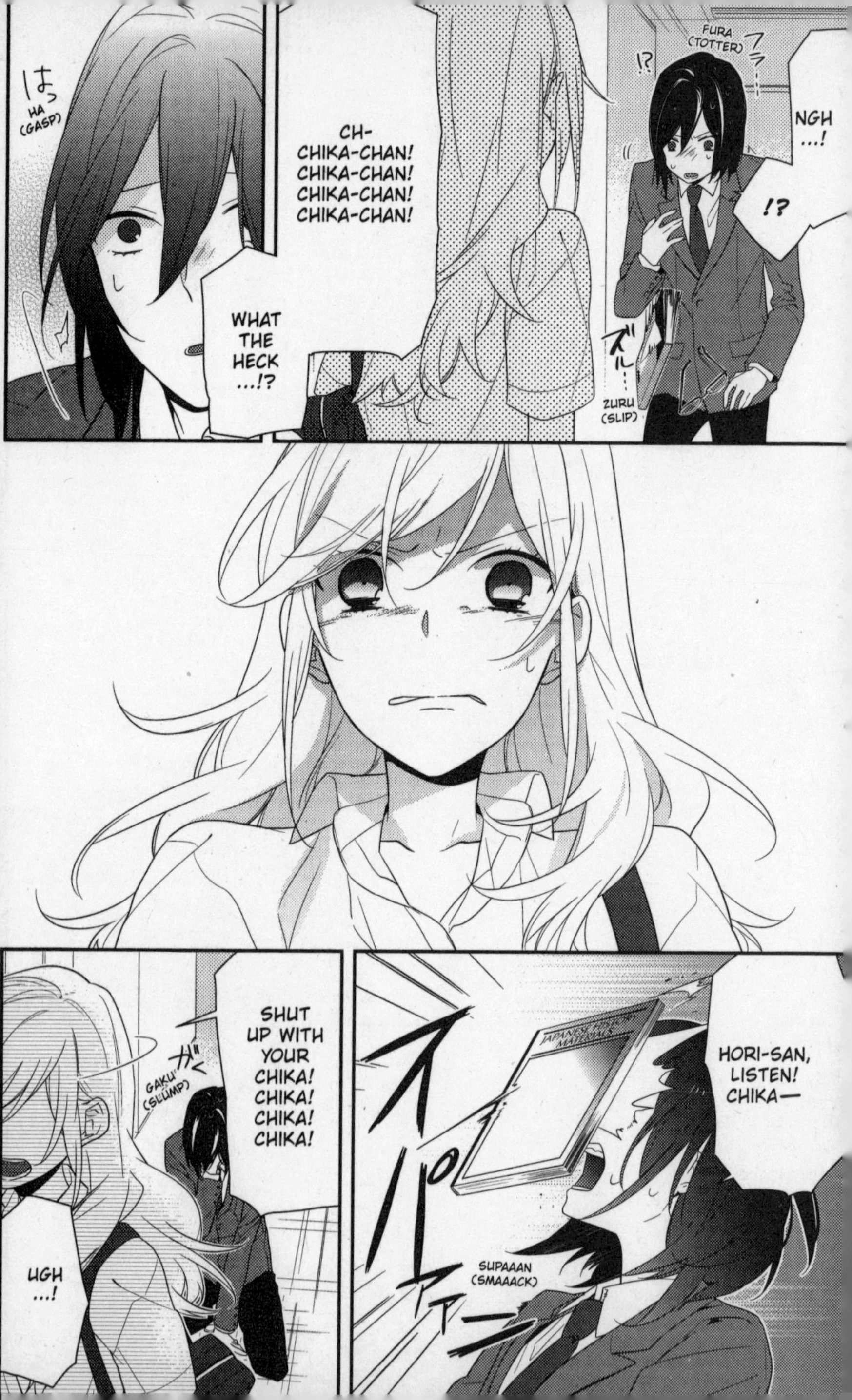
FURA (TOTTER)
フラ…
!?
NGH …!
!?
ズル…
ZURU (SLIP)
CH- CHIKA-CHAN! CHIKA-CHAN! CHIKA-CHAN! CHIKA-CHAN!
はっ
HA (GASP)
WHAT THE HECK …!?
HORI-SAN, LISTEN! CHIKA—
スパーン
SUPAAAN (SMAAACK)
SHUT UP WITH YOUR CHIKA! CHIKA! CHIKA! CHIKA!
がく
GAKU (SLUMP)
UGH …!

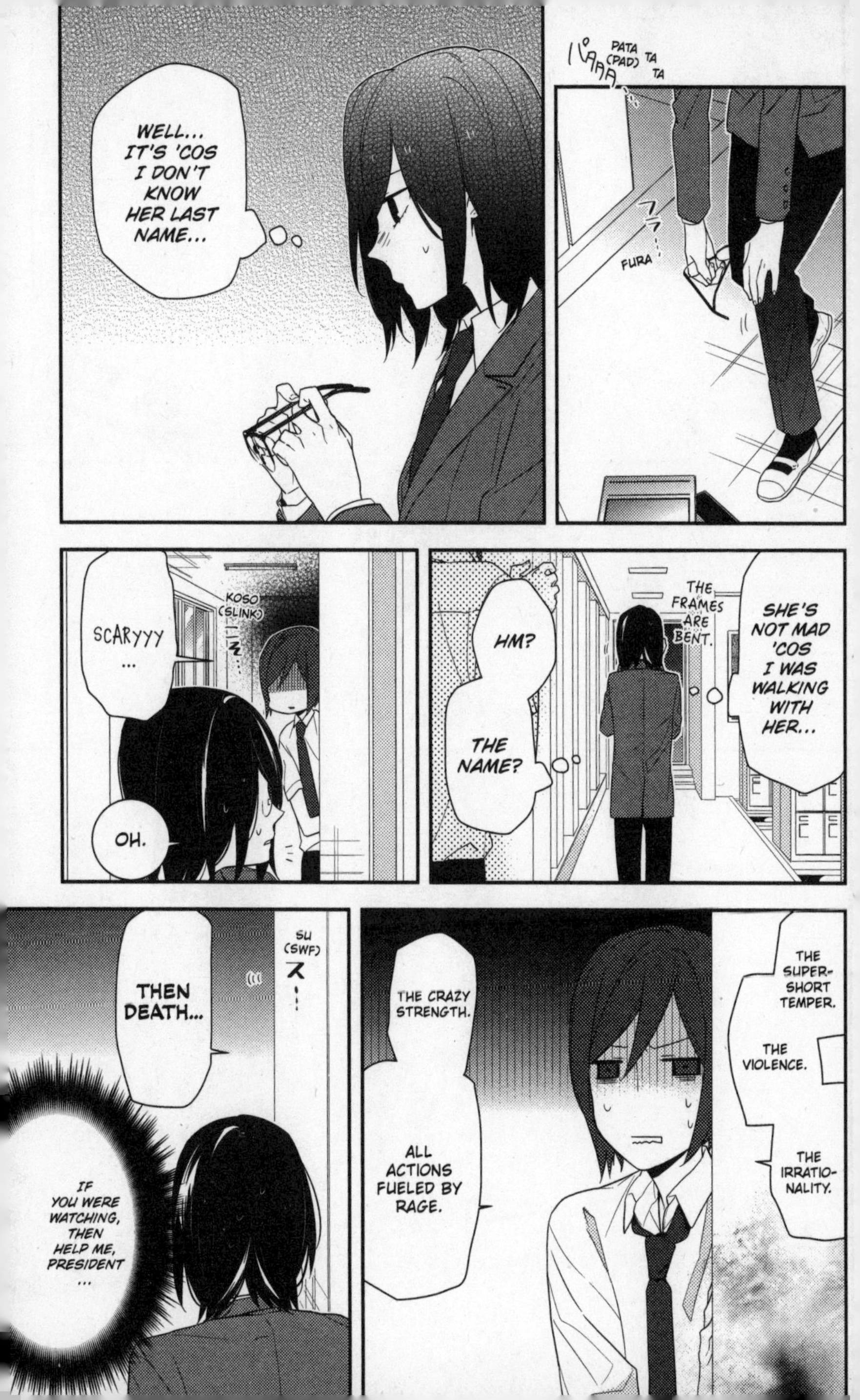
PATA (PAD) TA TA
FURA
WELL... IT'S 'COS I DON'T KNOW HER LAST NAME...
SHE'S NOT MAD 'COS I WAS WALKING WITH HER...
THE FRAMES ARE BENT.
HM?
THE NAME?
KOSO (SLINK)
SCARYYY ...
OH.
THE SUPER-SHORT TEMPER.
THE VIOLENCE.
THE IRRATIONALITY.
THE CRAZY STRENGTH.
ALL ACTIONS FUELED BY RAGE.
SU (SWF)
THEN DEATH...
IF YOU WERE WATCHING, THEN HELP ME, PRESIDENT ...

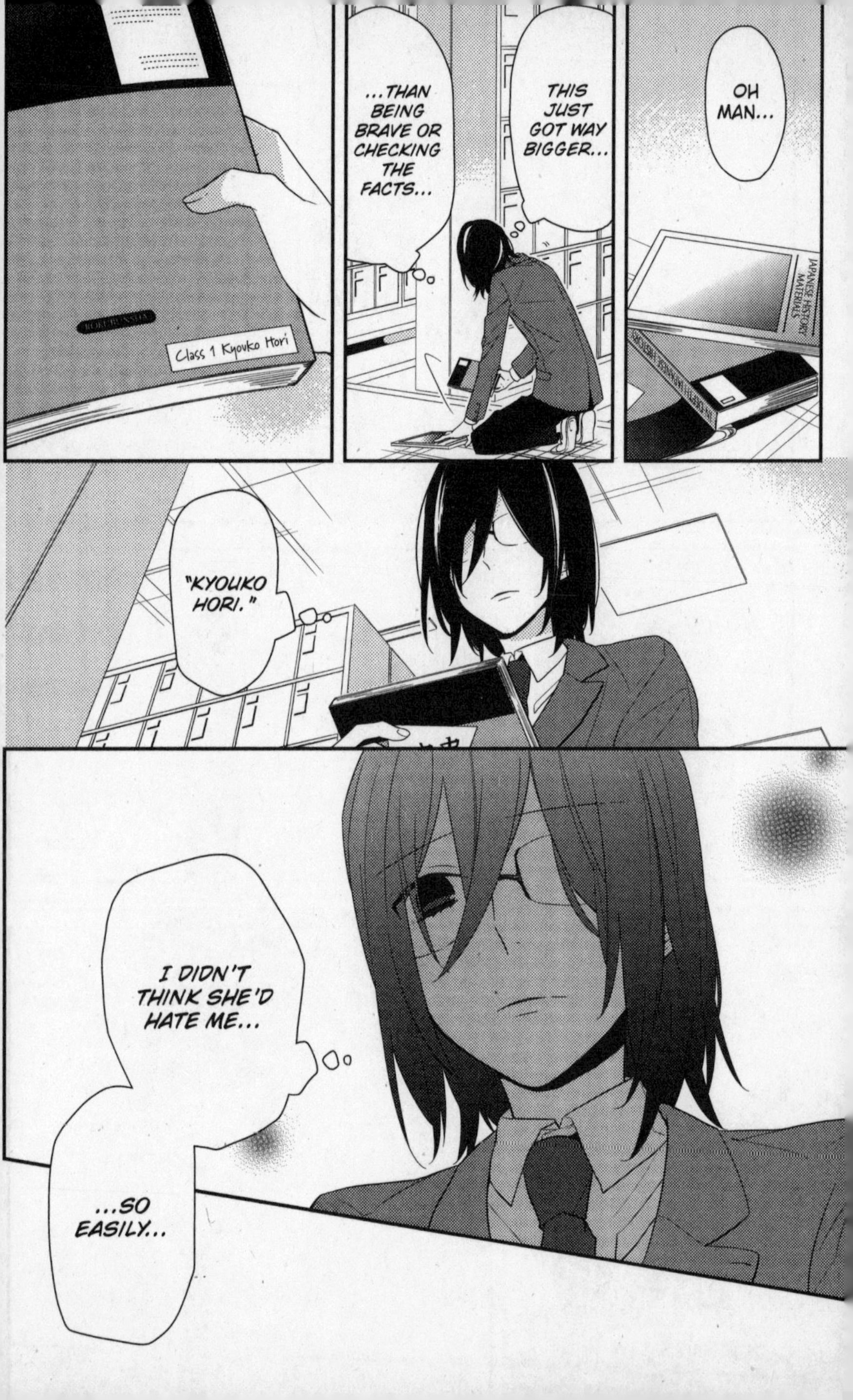
OH MAN...
JAPANESE HISTORY MATERIALS
IN-DEPTH JAPANESE HISTORY
THIS JUST GOT WAY BIGGER...
...THAN BEING BRAVE OR CHECKING THE FACTS...
Class 1 Kyouko Hori
"KYOUKO HORI."
I DIDN'T THINK SHE'D HATE ME...
...SO EASILY...

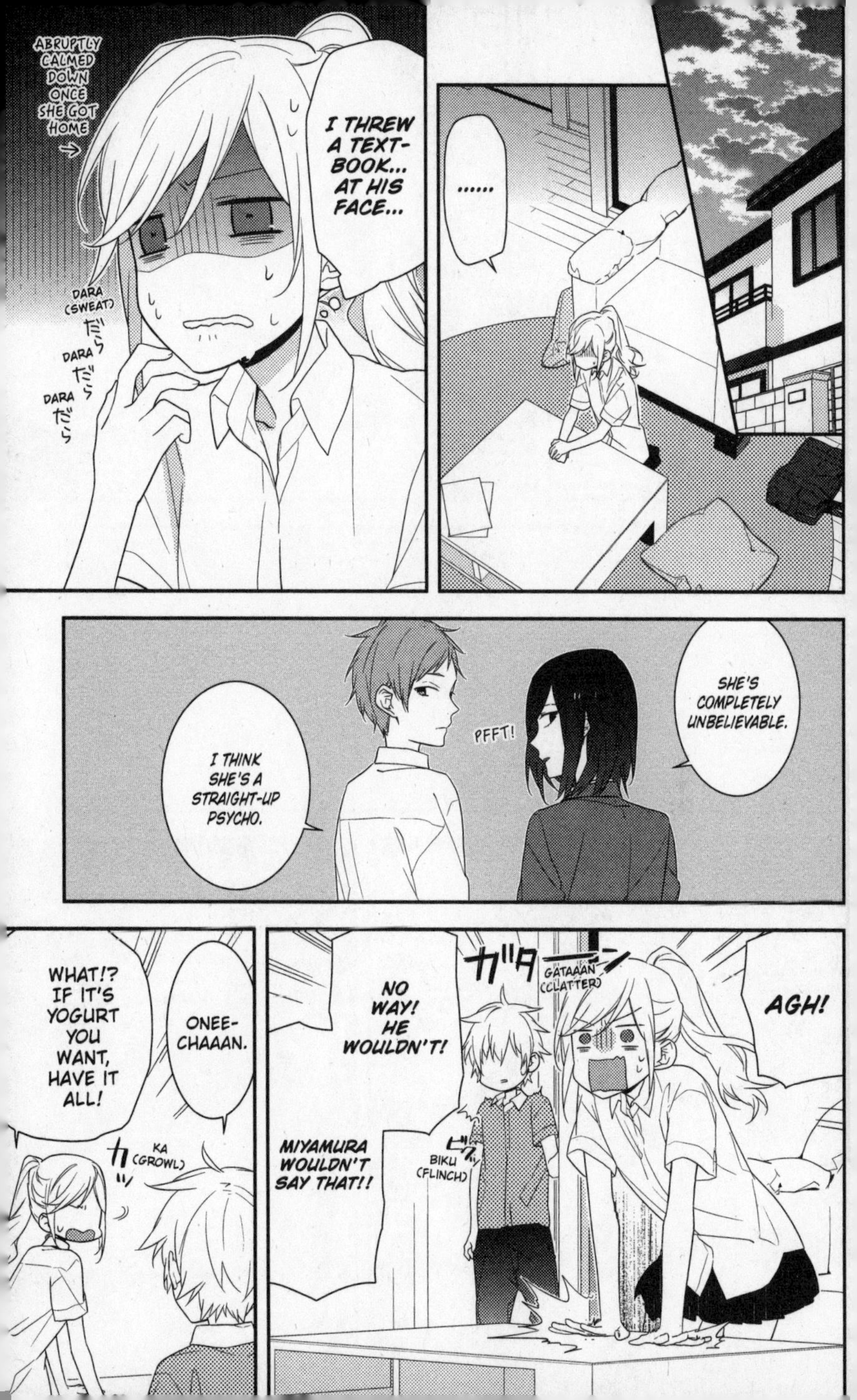
......
I THREW A TEXT-BOOK... AT HIS FACE...
ABRUPTLY CALMED DOWN ONCE SHE GOT HOME →
DARA (SWEAT) だら
DARA だら
DARA だら
SHE'S COMPLETELY UNBELIEVABLE.
PFFT!
I THINK SHE'S A STRAIGHT-UP PSYCHO.
AGH!
ガタ
GATAAAN (CLATTER)
NO WAY! HE WOULDN'T!
MIYAMURA WOULDN'T SAY THAT!!
ビクッ
BIKU (FLINCH)
ONEE-CHAAAN.
WHAT!? IF IT'S YOGURT YOU WANT, HAVE IT ALL!
カッ
KA (GROWL)

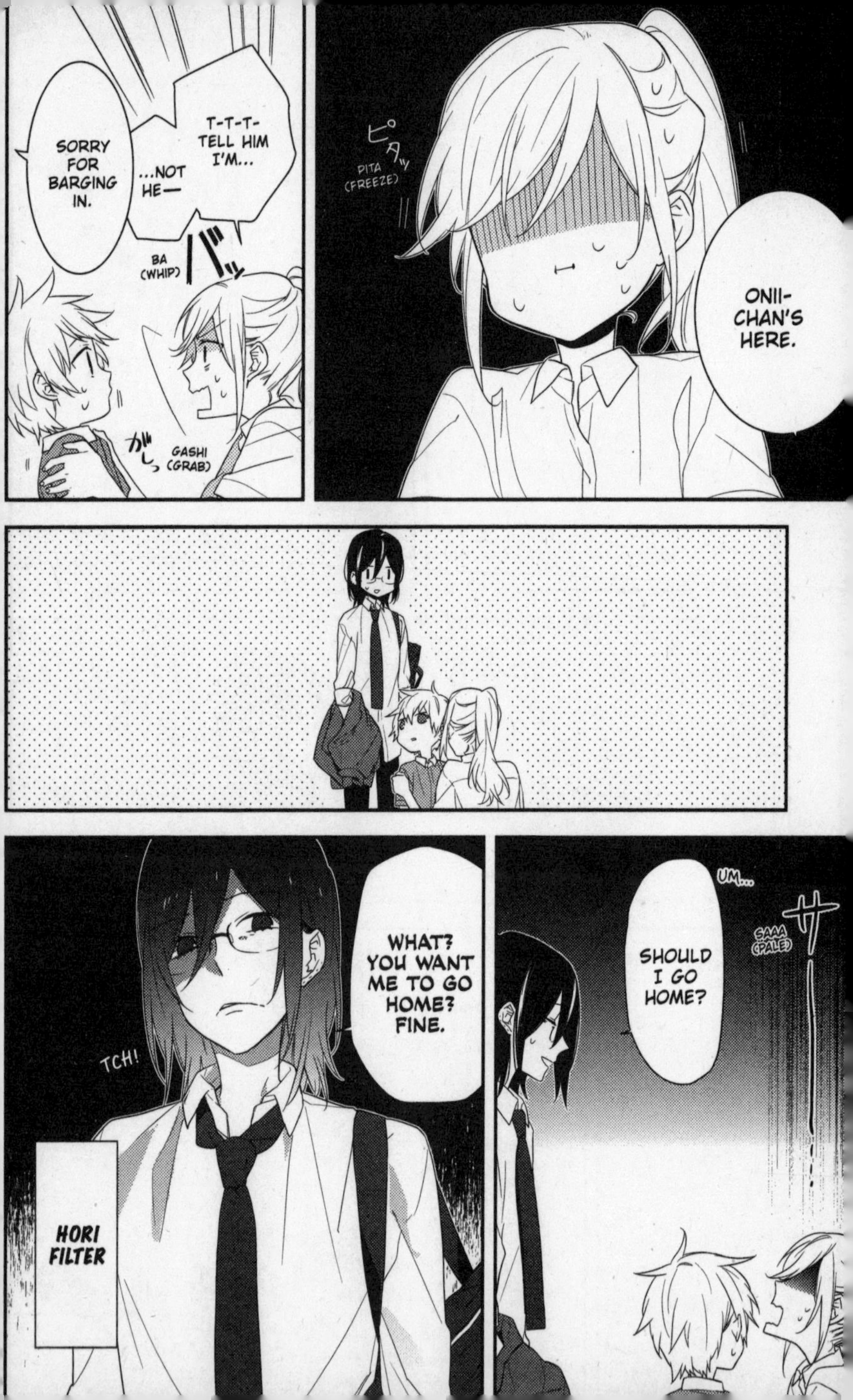
ONII-CHAN'S HERE.
ピタッ
PITA (FREEZE)
T-T-T-TELL HIM I'M...
...NOT HE—
SORRY FOR BARGING IN.
バッ
BA (WHIP)
がしっ
GASHI (GRAB)
UM...
SHOULD I GO HOME?
サー
SAAA (PALE)
WHAT? YOU WANT ME TO GO HOME? FINE.
TCH!
HORI FILTER

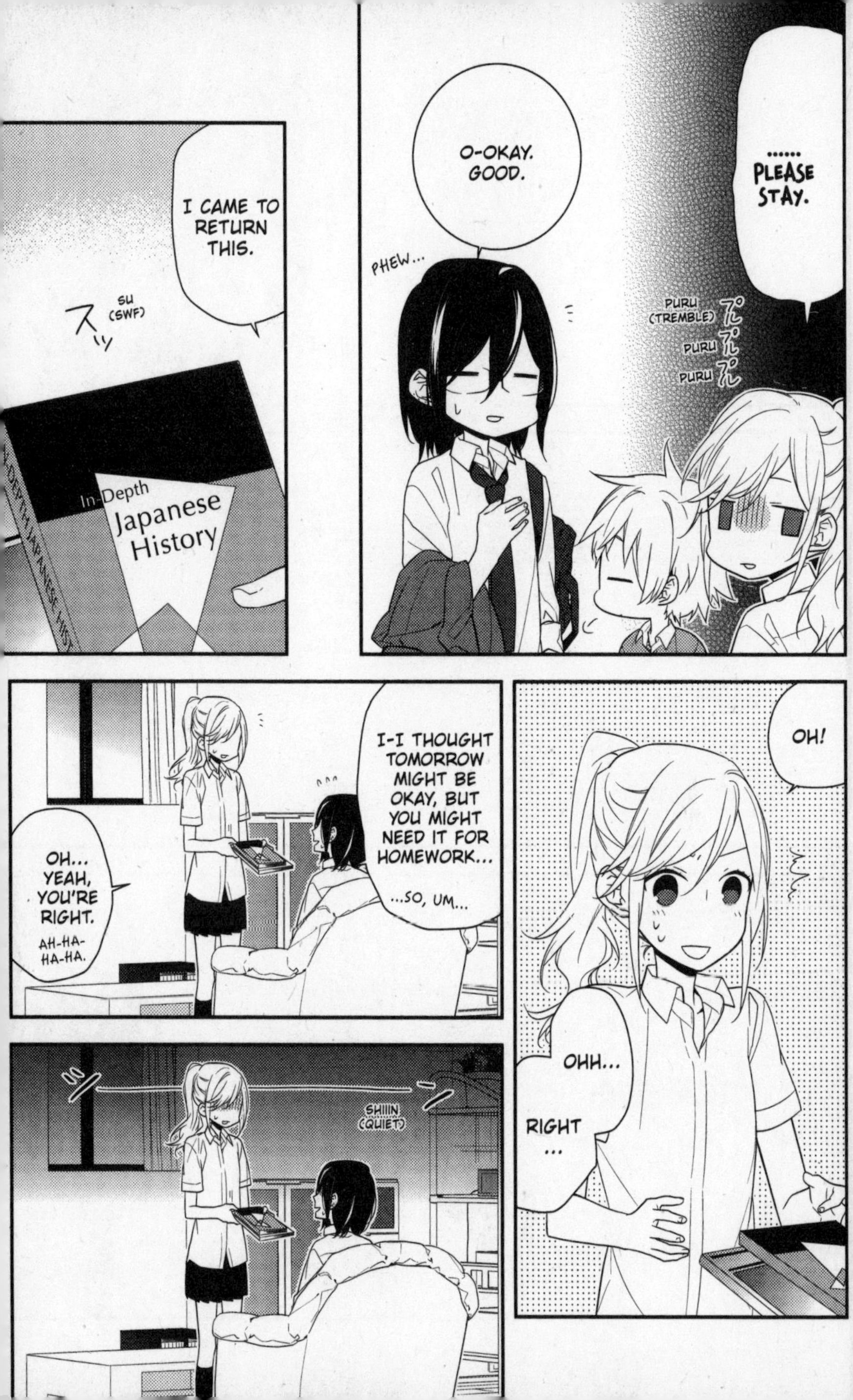

...... PLEASE STAY.
PURU (TREMBLE) PURU PURU
O-OKAY. GOOD.
PHEW...
I CAME TO RETURN THIS.
SU (SWF)
In-Depth Japanese History
OH!
OHH... RIGHT...
I-I THOUGHT TOMORROW MIGHT BE OKAY, BUT YOU MIGHT NEED IT FOR HOMEWORK...
...SO, UM...
OH... YEAH, YOU'RE RIGHT.
AH-HA-HA-HA.
SHIIN (QUIET)

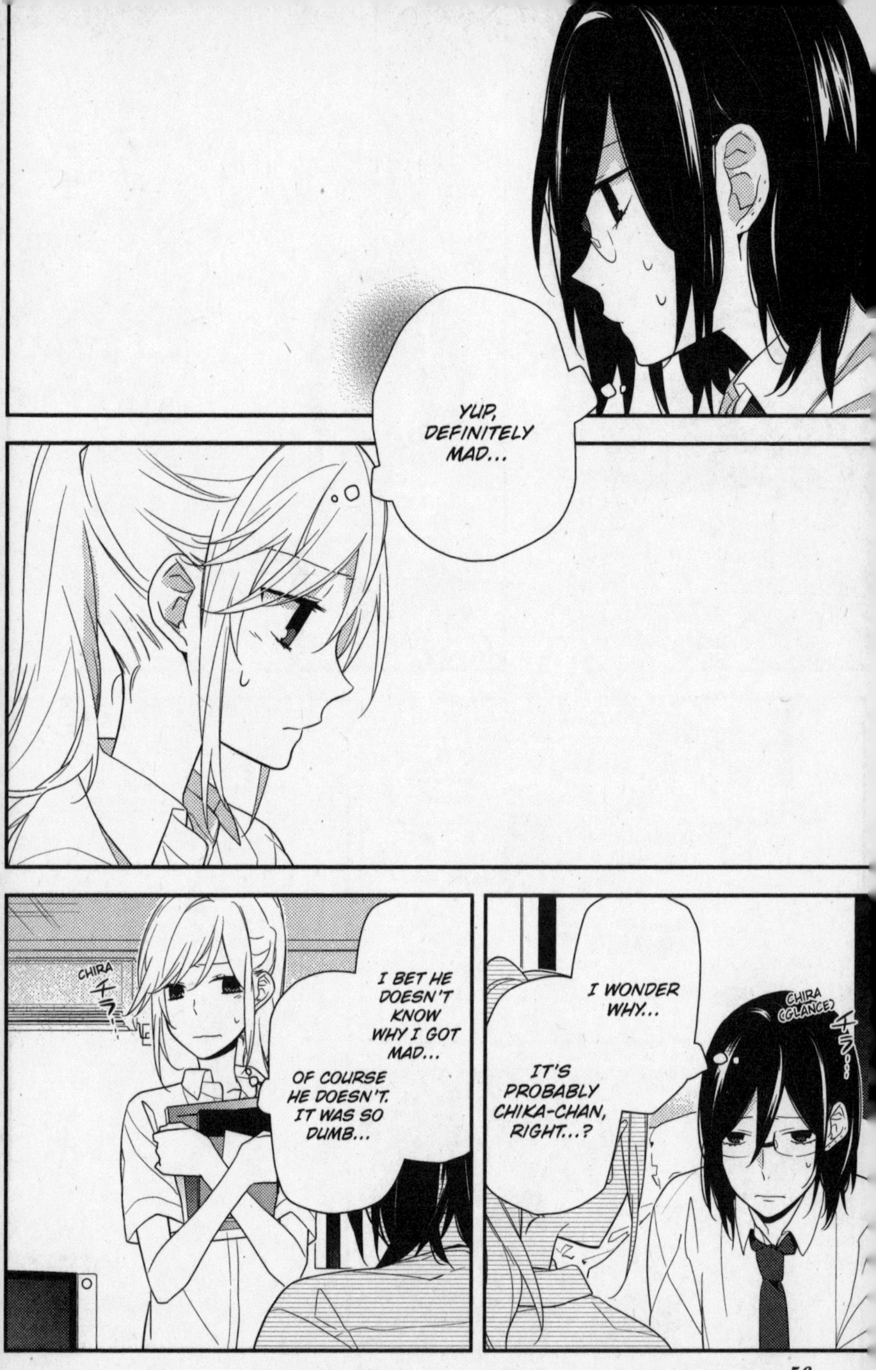
YUP, DEFINITELY MAD...
I WONDER WHY...
CHIRA (GLANCE)
IT'S PROBABLY CHIKA-CHAN, RIGHT...?
I BET HE DOESN'T KNOW WHY I GOT MAD...
OF COURSE HE DOESN'T. IT WAS SO DUMB...
CHIRA

I—

PACHIRI
(SNAP)

I'M SORRY!

I'M SOR—

FOR SMACK-ING YOU WITH IT...

...TWICE...

FOR, UM...

...THIS.

HUH?

NO, IT'S TOTALLY OKAY... IT WAS MY FAULT TO BEGIN WITH, GOING ON ABOUT CHI......

...I MEAN... UMMM...

OHH...

...ABOUT SHINDOU'S GIRLFRIEND. I'M SORRY FOR MAKING YOU FEEL BAD.

PFFT!

WHAT THE HECK?

I DON'T KNOW...

...ACTUALLY...

AH HA!

UH...

UM... WHAT'S CHIKA-CHAN'S LAST NAME...?

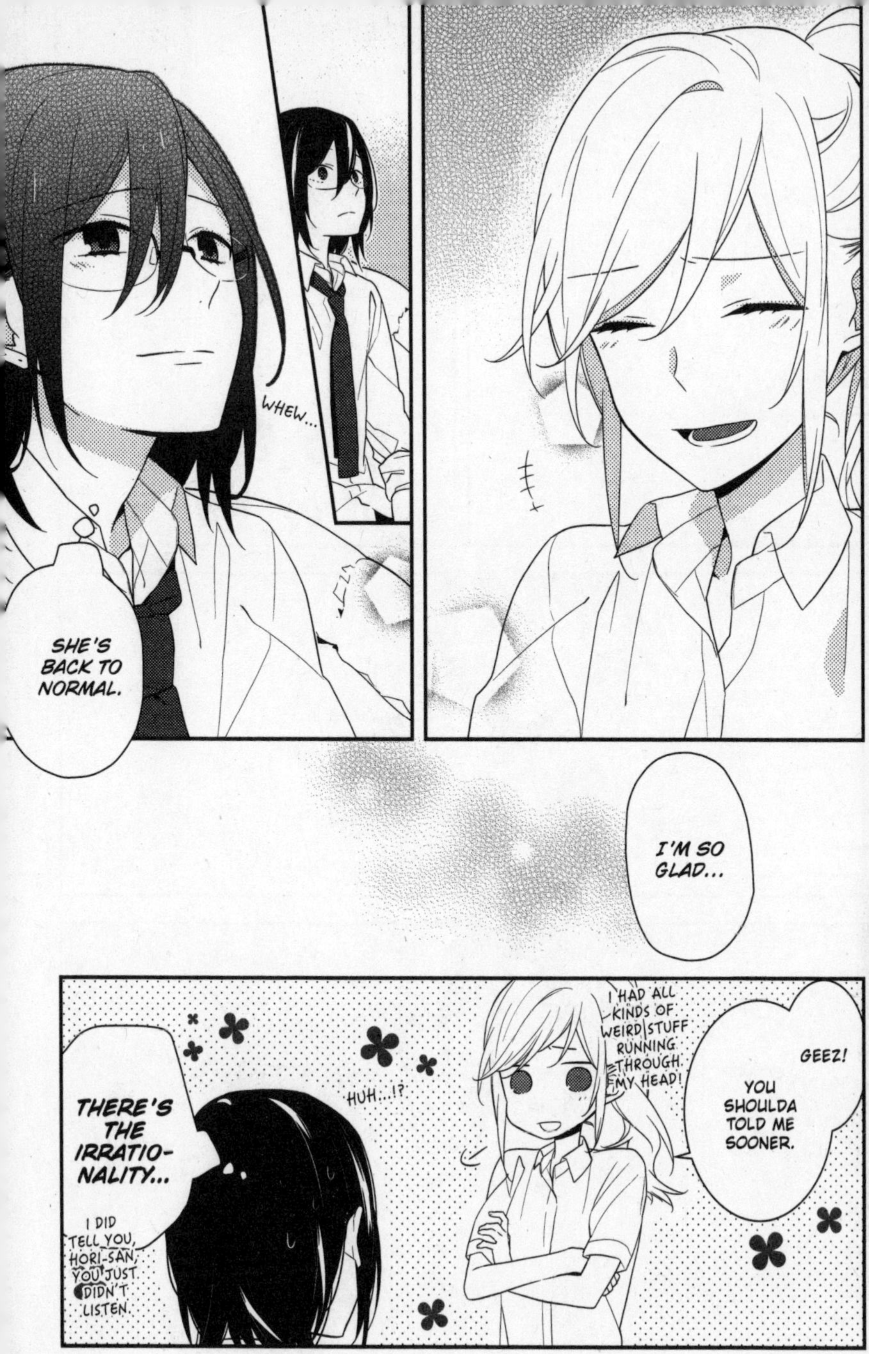
WHEW...
SHE'S BACK TO NORMAL.
I'M SO GLAD...
GEEZ!
YOU SHOULDA TOLD ME SOONER.
I HAD ALL KINDS OF WEIRD STUFF RUNNING THROUGH MY HEAD!
HUH...!?
THERE'S THE IRRATIONALITY...
I DID TELL YOU, HORI-SAN, YOU JUST DIDN'T LISTEN.

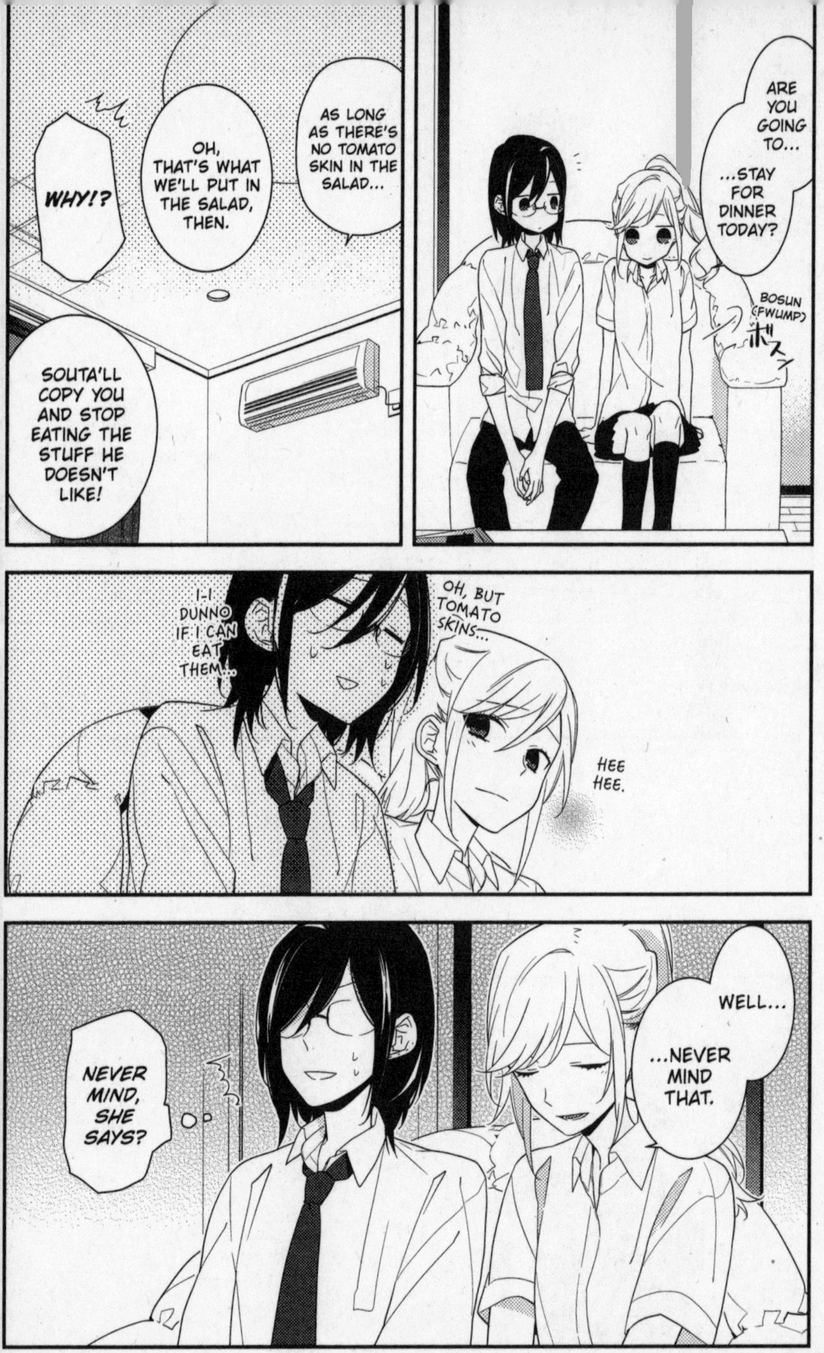
ARE YOU GOING TO...
...STAY FOR DINNER TODAY?
BOSUN (FWUMP)
ボスン
AS LONG AS THERE'S NO TOMATO SKIN IN THE SALAD...
OH, THAT'S WHAT WE'LL PUT IN THE SALAD, THEN.
WHY!?
SOUTA'LL COPY YOU AND STOP EATING THE STUFF HE DOESN'T LIKE!
OH, BUT TOMATO SKINS...
I-I DUNNO IF I CAN EAT THEM...
HEE HEE.
WELL...
...NEVER MIND THAT.
NEVER MIND, SHE SAYS?

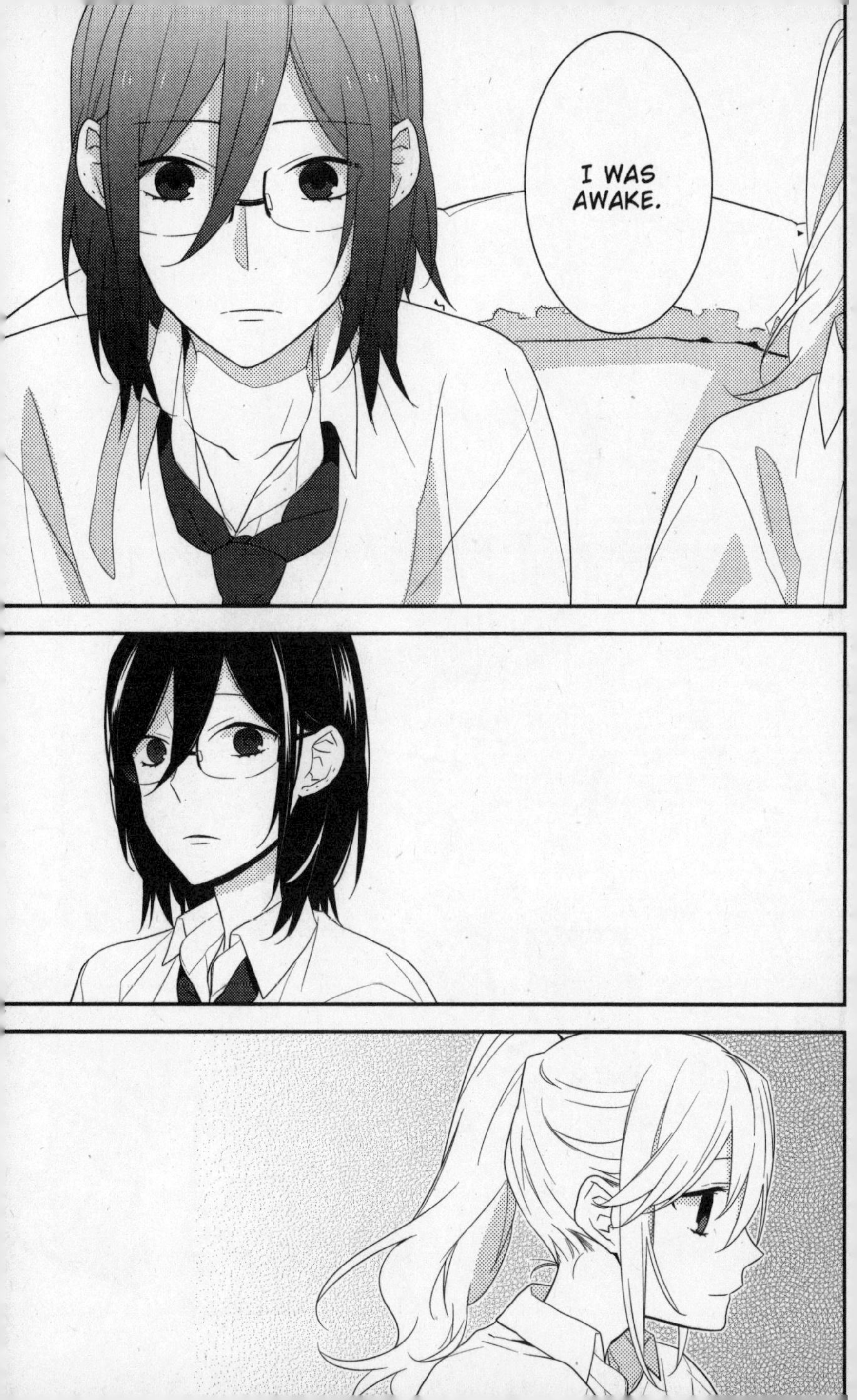
I WAS AWAKE.

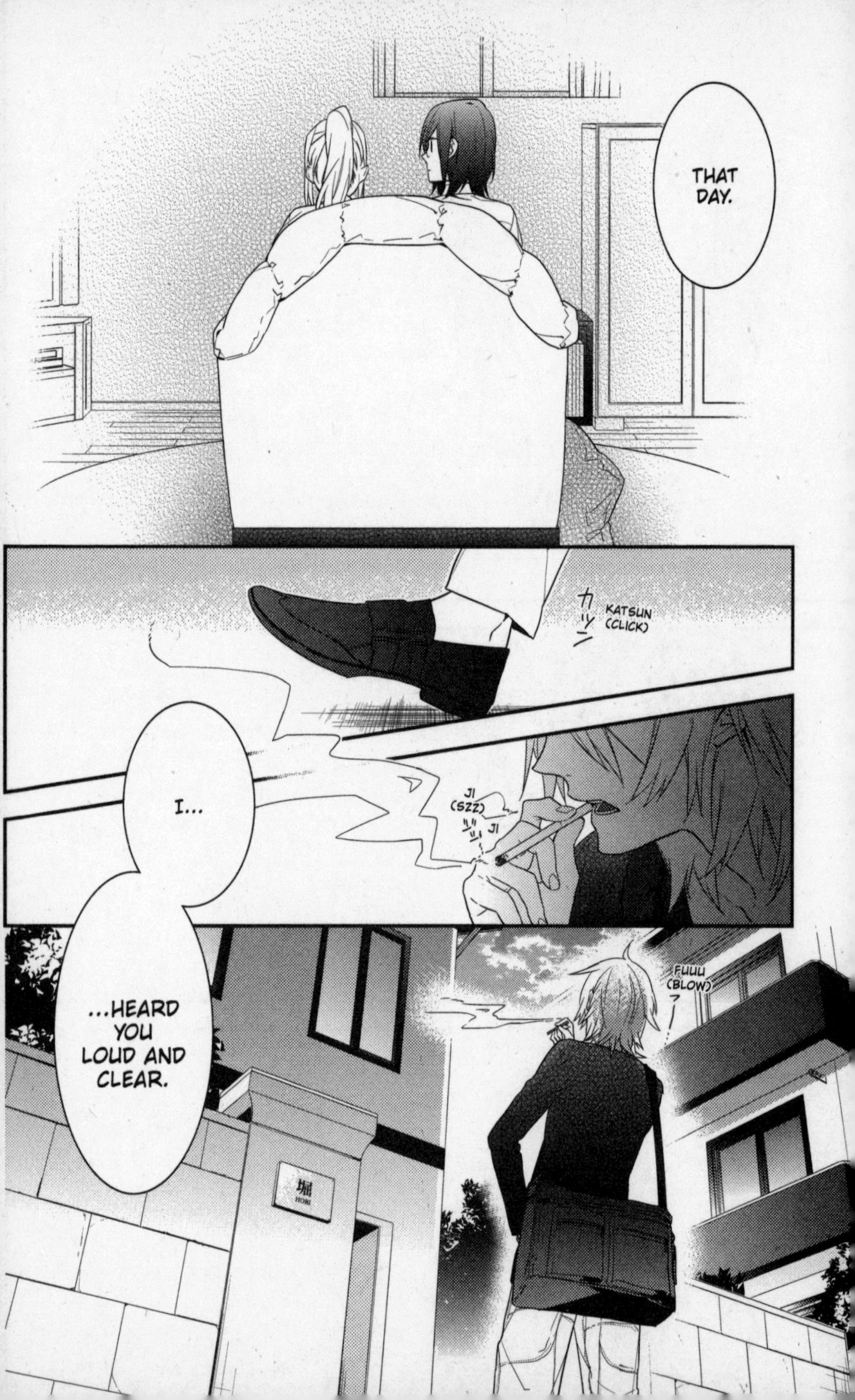
THAT DAY.
KATSUN (CLICK)
I...
JI (SZZ)
JI
...HEARD YOU LOUD AND CLEAR.
FUUU (BLOW)
堀
HORI

HORIMIYA

HORIMIYA

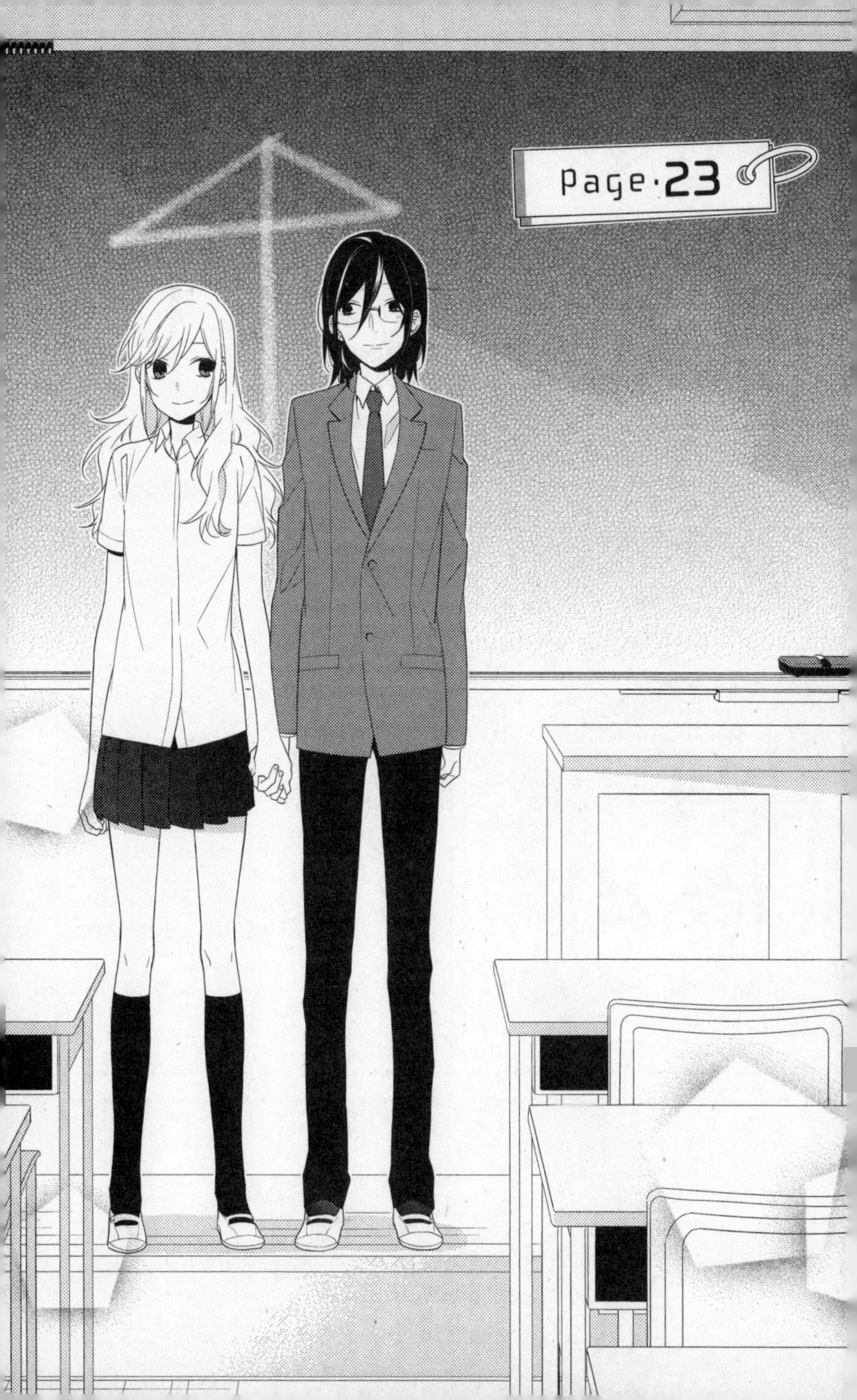
Page·23

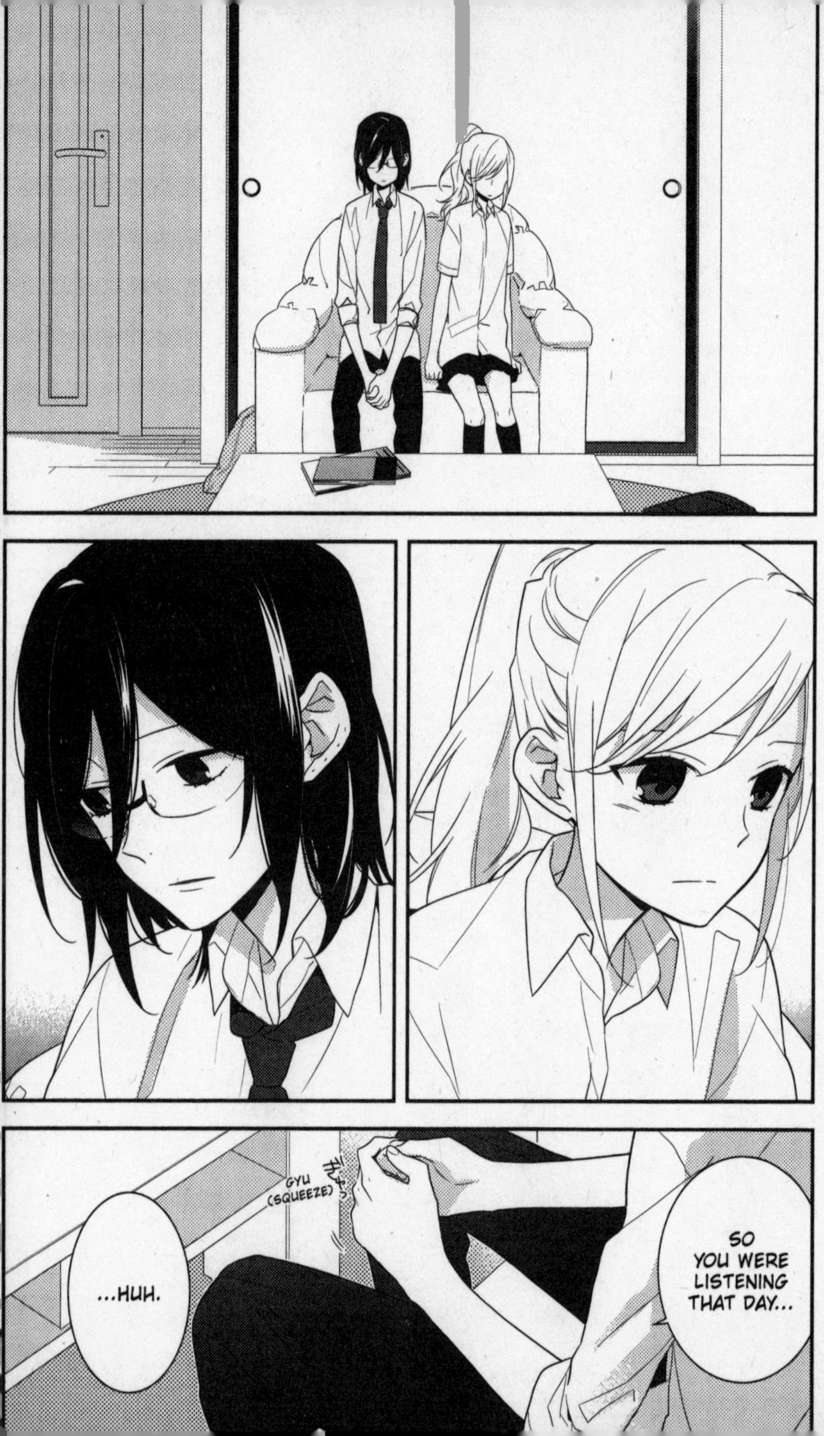
SO YOU WERE LISTENING THAT DAY...
GYU (SQUEEZE)
...HUH.

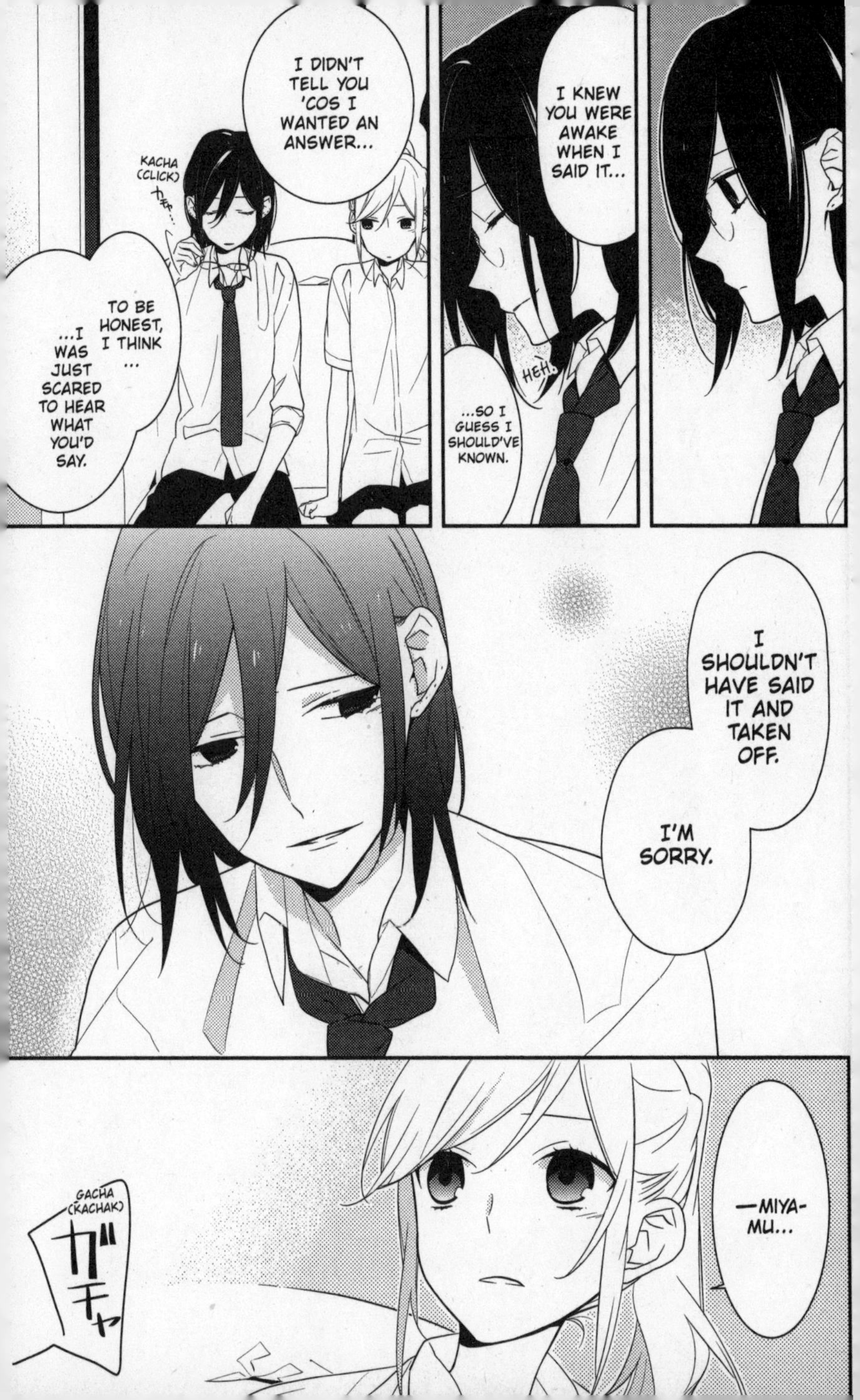
I KNEW YOU WERE AWAKE WHEN I SAID IT...
HEH.
...SO I GUESS I SHOULD'VE KNOWN.
I DIDN'T TELL YOU 'COS I WANTED AN ANSWER...
KACHA (CLICK)
TO BE HONEST, I THINK...
...I WAS JUST SCARED TO HEAR WHAT YOU'D SAY.
I SHOULDN'T HAVE SAID IT AND TAKEN OFF.
I'M SORRY.
—MIYA-MU...
GACHA (KACHAK)
ガチャ

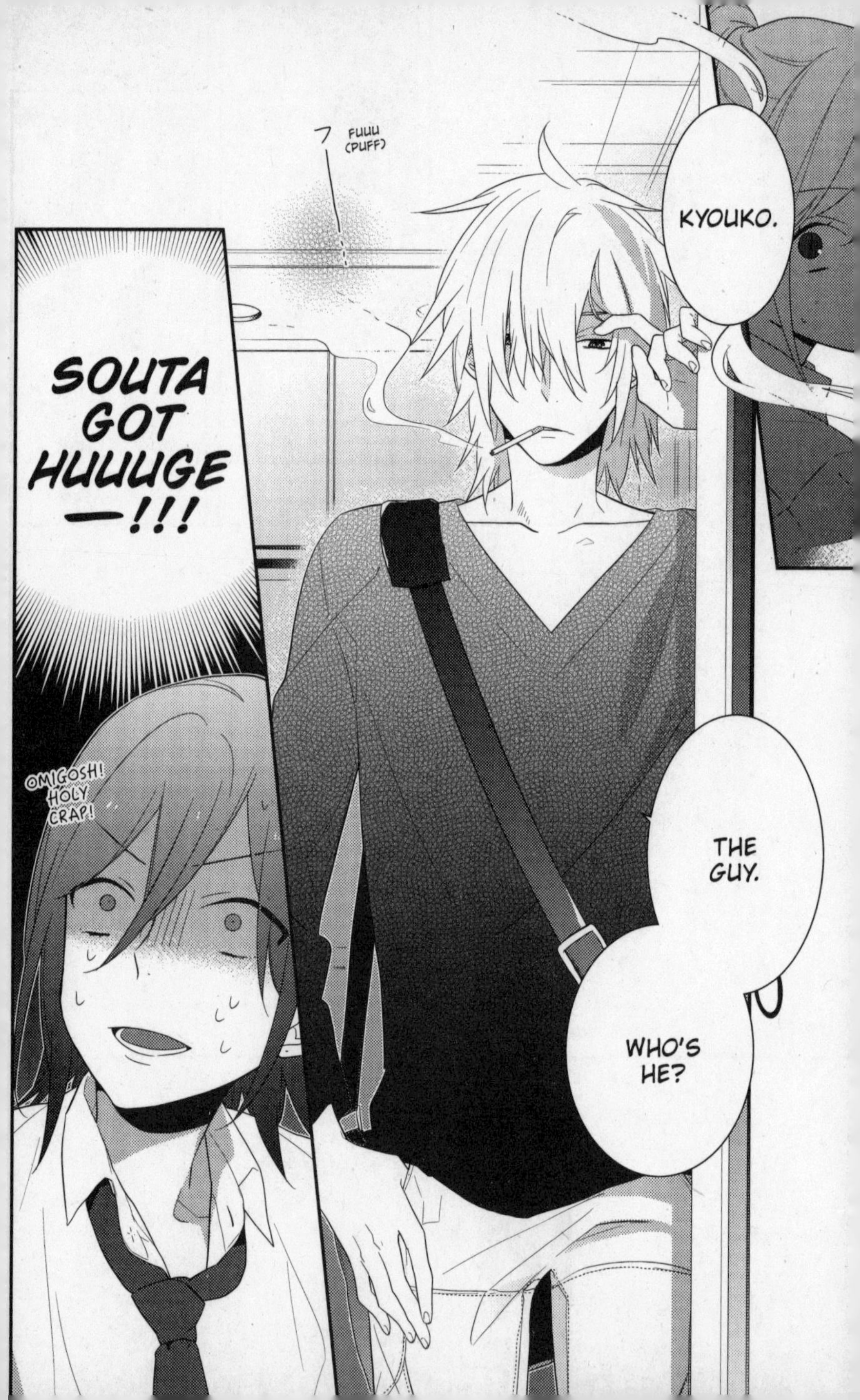
KYOUKO.
FUUU (PUFF)
THE GUY.
WHO'S HE?
SOUTA GOT HUUUGE—!!!
OMIGOSH! HOLY CRAP!

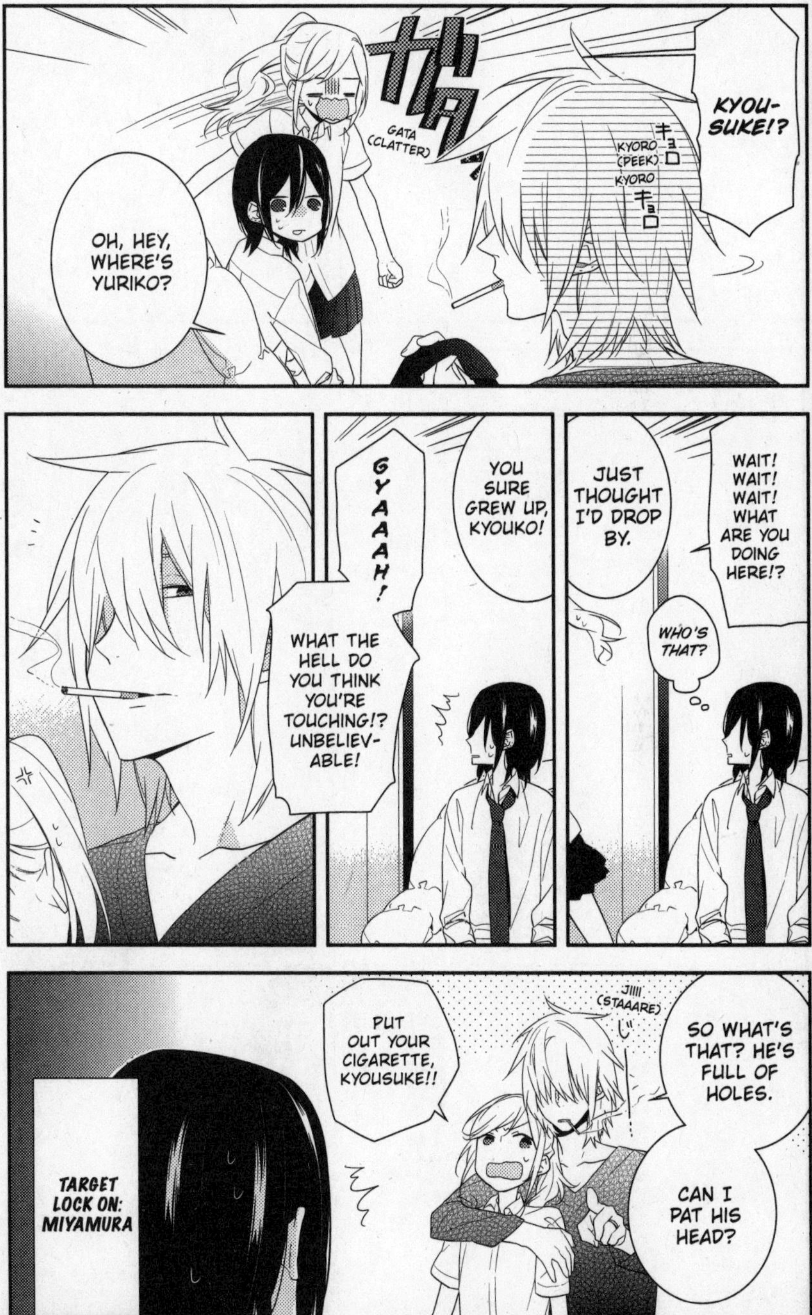
KYOU-SUKE!?
キョロ
KYORO (PEEK)
KYORO
キョロ
ガタ
GATA (CLATTER)
OH, HEY, WHERE'S YURIKO?
WAIT! WAIT! WAIT! WHAT ARE YOU DOING HERE!?
JUST THOUGHT I'D DROP BY.
WHO'S THAT?
YOU SURE GREW UP, KYOUKO!
GYAAAAH!
WHAT THE HELL DO YOU THINK YOU'RE TOUCHING!? UNBELIEVABLE!
SO WHAT'S THAT? HE'S FULL OF HOLES.
JIIII (STAAARE)
CAN I PAT HIS HEAD?
PUT OUT YOUR CIGARETTE, KYOUSUKE!!
TARGET LOCK ON: MIYAMURA

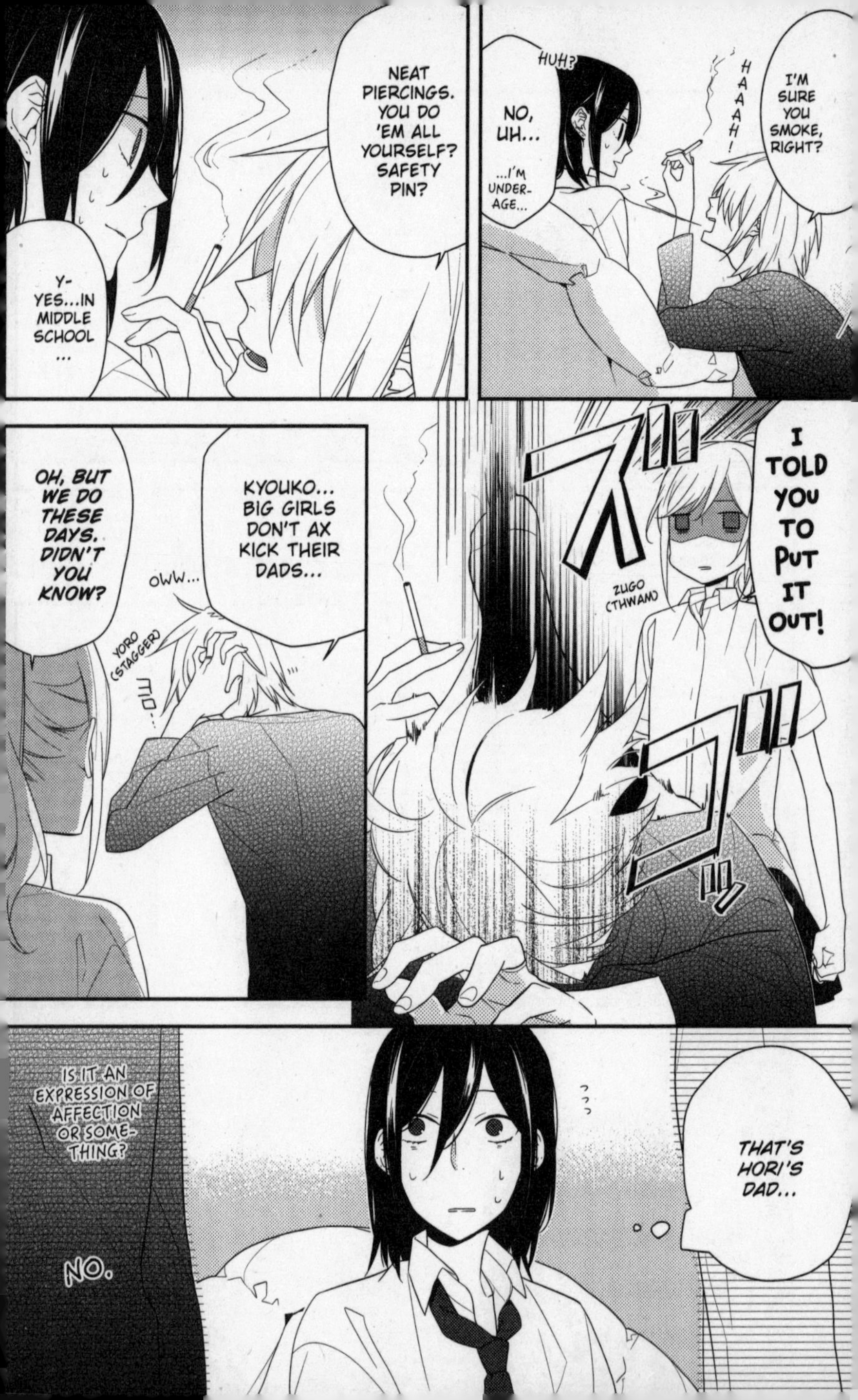
I'M SURE YOU SMOKE, RIGHT?
HAAAAH!
HUH?
NO, UH...
...I'M UNDER-AGE...
NEAT PIERCINGS. YOU DO 'EM ALL YOURSELF? SAFETY PIN?
Y-YES...IN MIDDLE SCHOOL...
I TOLD YOU TO PUT IT OUT!
ZUGO (THWAM)
KYOUKO... BIG GIRLS DON'T AX KICK THEIR DADS...
OWW...
YORO (STAGGER)
OH, BUT WE DO THESE DAYS. DIDN'T YOU KNOW?
THAT'S HORI'S DAD...
IS IT AN EXPRESSION OF AFFECTION OR SOME-THING?
NO.

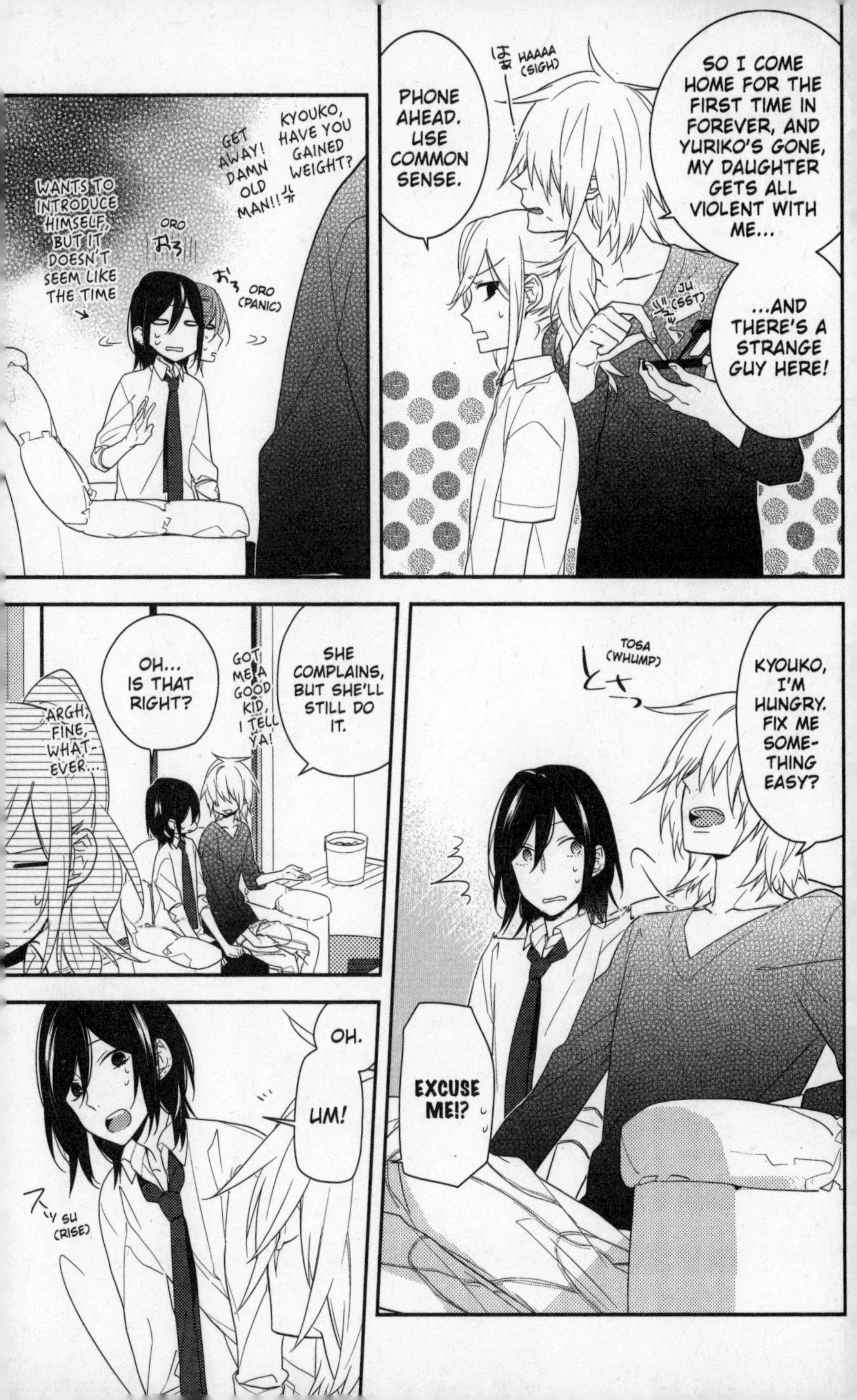

SO I COME HOME FOR THE FIRST TIME IN FOREVER, AND YURIKO'S GONE, MY DAUGHTER GETS ALL VIOLENT WITH ME...
...AND THERE'S A STRANGE GUY HERE!
JU (SST)
HAAAA (SIGH)
PHONE AHEAD. USE COMMON SENSE.
KYOUKO, HAVE YOU GAINED WEIGHT?
GET AWAY! DAMN OLD MAN!!
ORO
ORO (PANIC)
WANTS TO INTRODUCE HIMSELF, BUT IT DOESN'T SEEM LIKE THE TIME
KYOUKO, I'M HUNGRY. FIX ME SOME-THING EASY?
TOSA (WHUMP)
EXCUSE ME!?
SHE COMPLAINS, BUT SHE'LL STILL DO IT.
GOT ME A GOOD KID, I TELL YA!
OH... IS THAT RIGHT?
ARGH, FINE, WHAT-EVER...
OH.
UM!
SU (RISE)

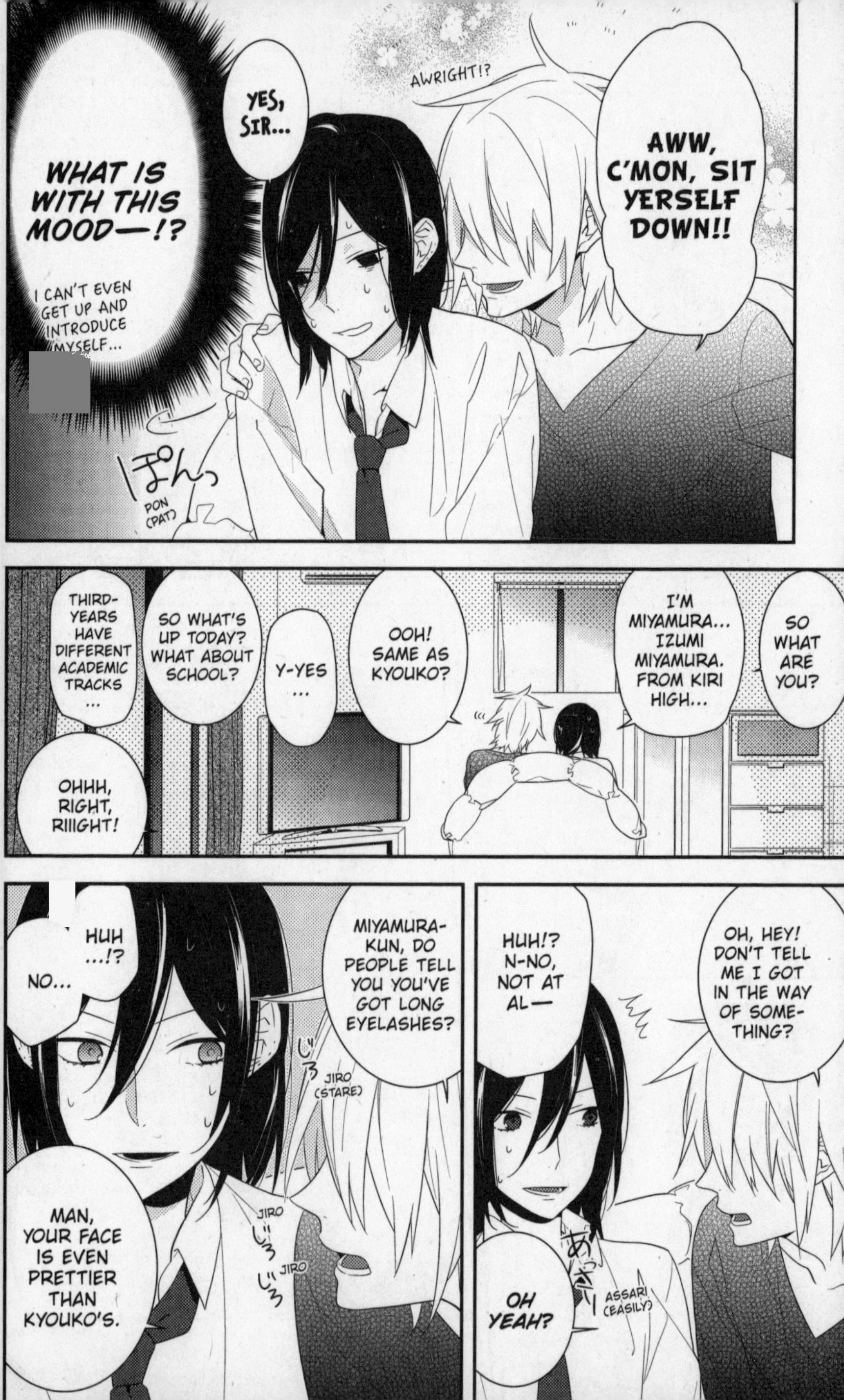
AWW, C'MON, SIT YERSELF DOWN!!
AWRIGHT!?
YES, SIR...
WHAT IS WITH THIS MOOD—!?
I CAN'T EVEN GET UP AND INTRODUCE MYSELF...
ぽんっ
PON (PAT)
SO WHAT ARE YOU?
I'M MIYAMURA... IZUMI MIYAMURA. FROM KIRI HIGH...
OOH! SAME AS KYOUKO?
Y-YES ...
SO WHAT'S UP TODAY? WHAT ABOUT SCHOOL?
THIRD-YEARS HAVE DIFFERENT ACADEMIC TRACKS ...
OHHH, RIGHT, RIIIGHT!
OH, HEY! DON'T TELL ME I GOT IN THE WAY OF SOME-THING?
HUH!? N-NO, NOT AT AL—
ASSARI (EASILY)
OH YEAH?
MIYAMURA-KUN, DO PEOPLE TELL YOU YOU'VE GOT LONG EYELASHES?
HUH ...!?
NO...
じろ
JIRO (STARE)
JIRO じろ
JIRO じろ
MAN, YOUR FACE IS EVEN PRETTIER THAN KYOUKO'S.

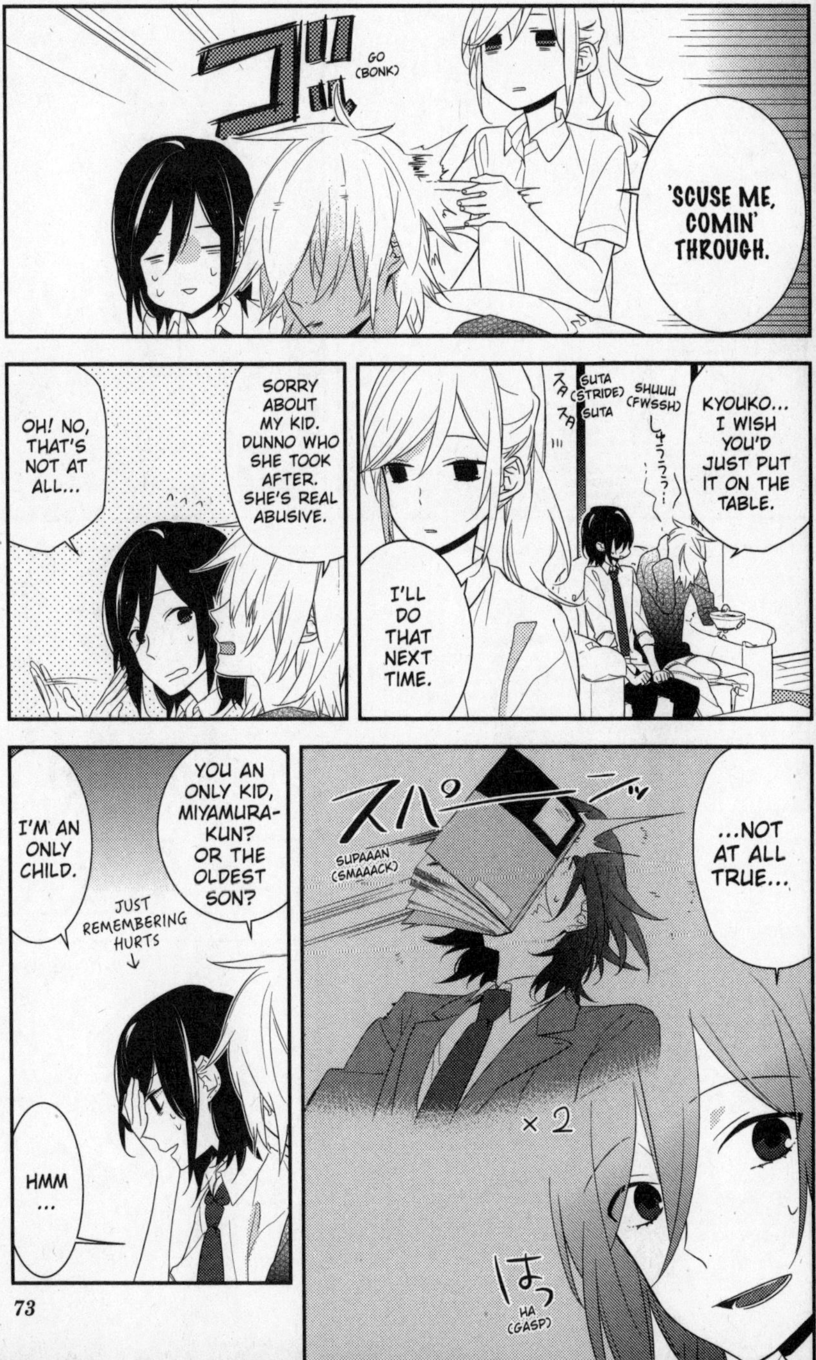

GO (BONK)
'SCUSE ME, COMIN' THROUGH.
KYOUKO... I WISH YOU'D JUST PUT IT ON THE TABLE.
SUTA (STRIDE) SUTA
SHUUU (FWSSH)
I'LL DO THAT NEXT TIME.
SORRY ABOUT MY KID. DUNNO WHO SHE TOOK AFTER. SHE'S REAL ABUSIVE.
OH! NO, THAT'S NOT AT ALL...
...NOT AT ALL TRUE...
SUPAAAN (SMAAACK)
× 2
HA (GASP)
YOU AN ONLY KID, MIYAMURA-KUN? OR THE OLDEST SON?
I'M AN ONLY CHILD.
JUST REMEMBERING HURTS
HMM ...

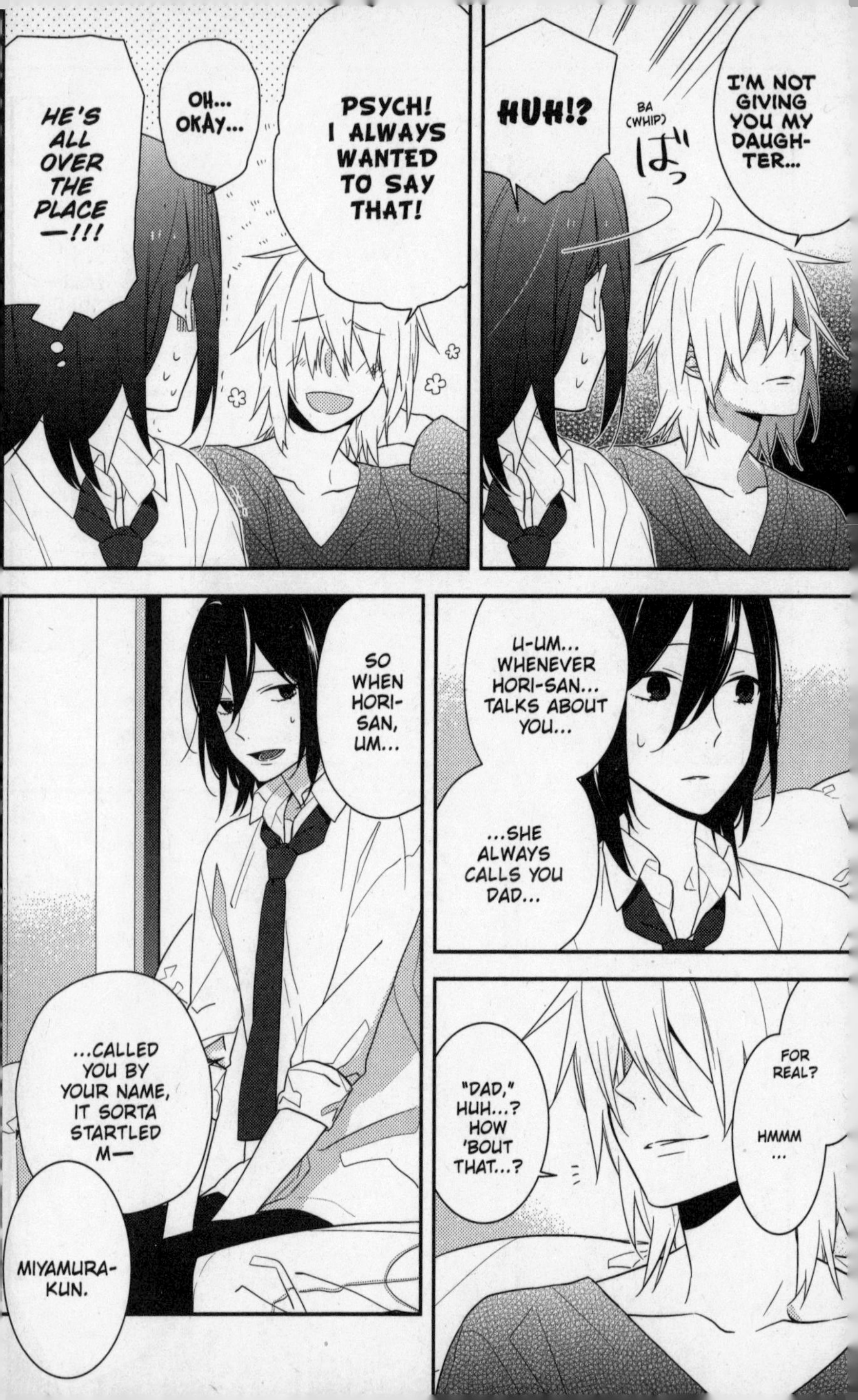
I'M NOT GIVING YOU MY DAUGHTER...
BA (WHIP)
ばっ
HUH!?
PSYCH! I ALWAYS WANTED TO SAY THAT!
OH... OKAY...
HE'S ALL OVER THE PLACE—!!!
U-UM... WHENEVER HORI-SAN... TALKS ABOUT YOU...
...SHE ALWAYS CALLS YOU DAD...
FOR REAL?
HMMM...
"DAD," HUH...? HOW 'BOUT THAT...?
SO WHEN HORI-SAN, UM...
...CALLED YOU BY YOUR NAME, IT SORTA STARTLED M—
MIYAMURA-KUN.

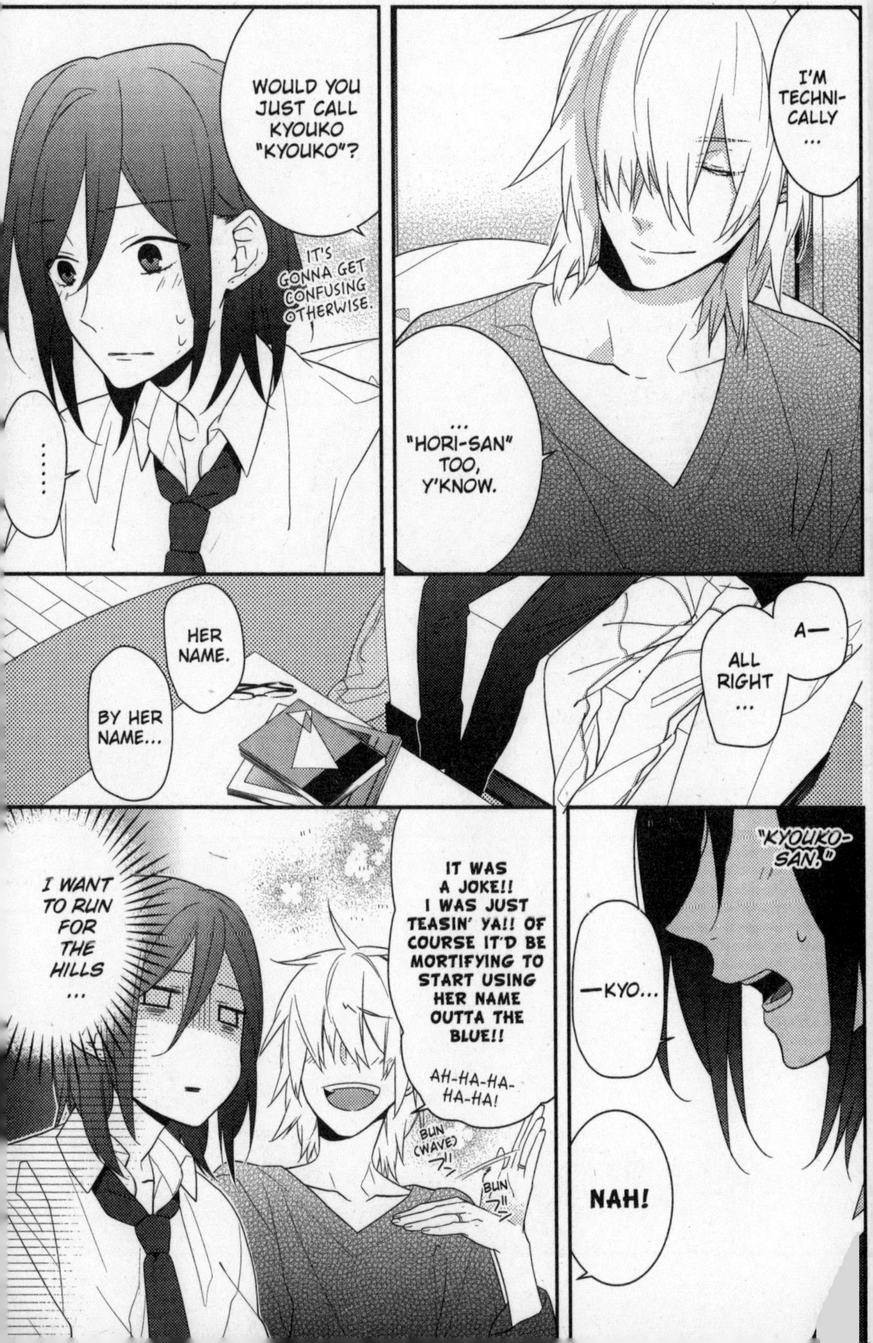
I'M TECHNICALLY ...
... "HORI-SAN" TOO, Y'KNOW.
WOULD YOU JUST CALL KYOUKO "KYOUKO"?
IT'S GONNA GET CONFUSING OTHERWISE.
......
A— ALL RIGHT ...
HER NAME.
BY HER NAME...
"KYOUKO-SAN."
—KYO...
NAH!
IT WAS A JOKE!! I WAS JUST TEASIN' YA!! OF COURSE IT'D BE MORTIFYING TO START USING HER NAME OUTTA THE BLUE!!
AH-HA-HA-HA-HA!
BUN (WAVE)
BUN
I WANT TO RUN FOR THE HILLS ...

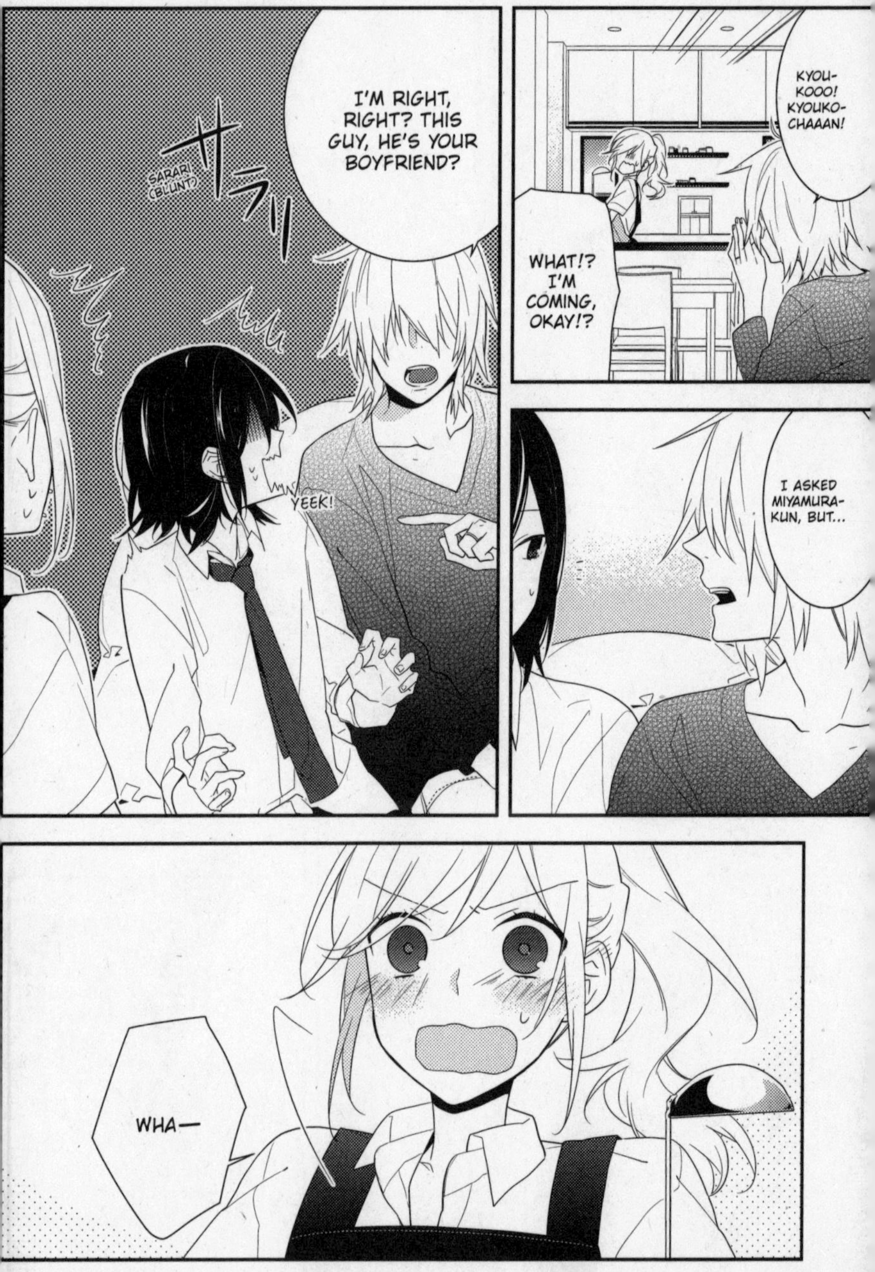
KYOU-KOOO! KYOUKO-CHAAAN!
WHAT!? I'M COMING, OKAY!?
I ASKED MIYAMURA-KUN, BUT...
I'M RIGHT, RIGHT? THIS GUY, HE'S YOUR BOYFRIEND?
SARARI (BLUNT)
YEEK!
WHA—

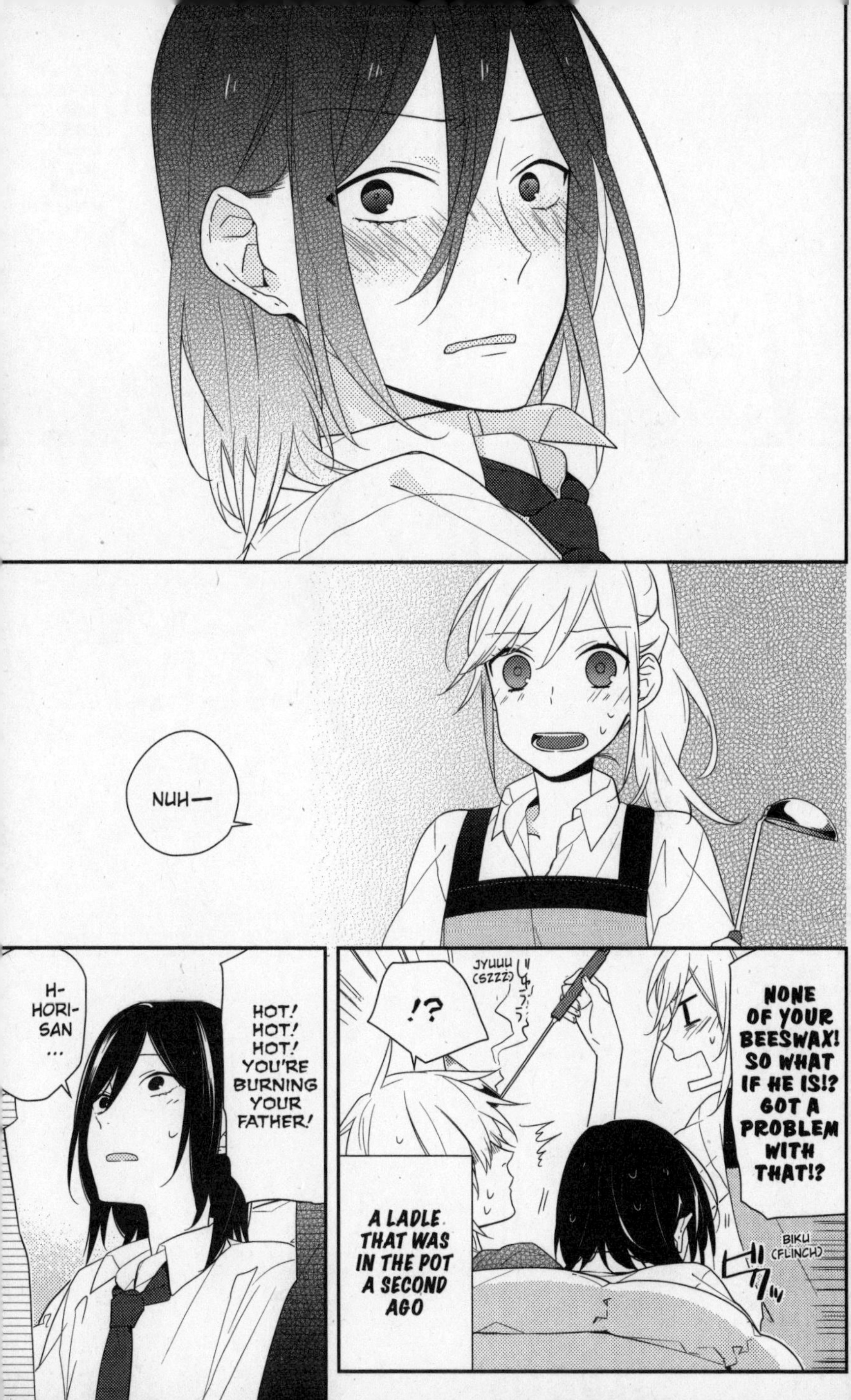
NUH—
NONE OF YOUR BEESWAX! SO WHAT IF HE IS!? GOT A PROBLEM WITH THAT!?
JYUUU (SZZZ)
!?
BIKU (FLINCH)
A LADLE THAT WAS IN THE POT A SECOND AGO
HOT! HOT! HOT! YOU'RE BURNING YOUR FATHER!
H-HORI-SAN ...

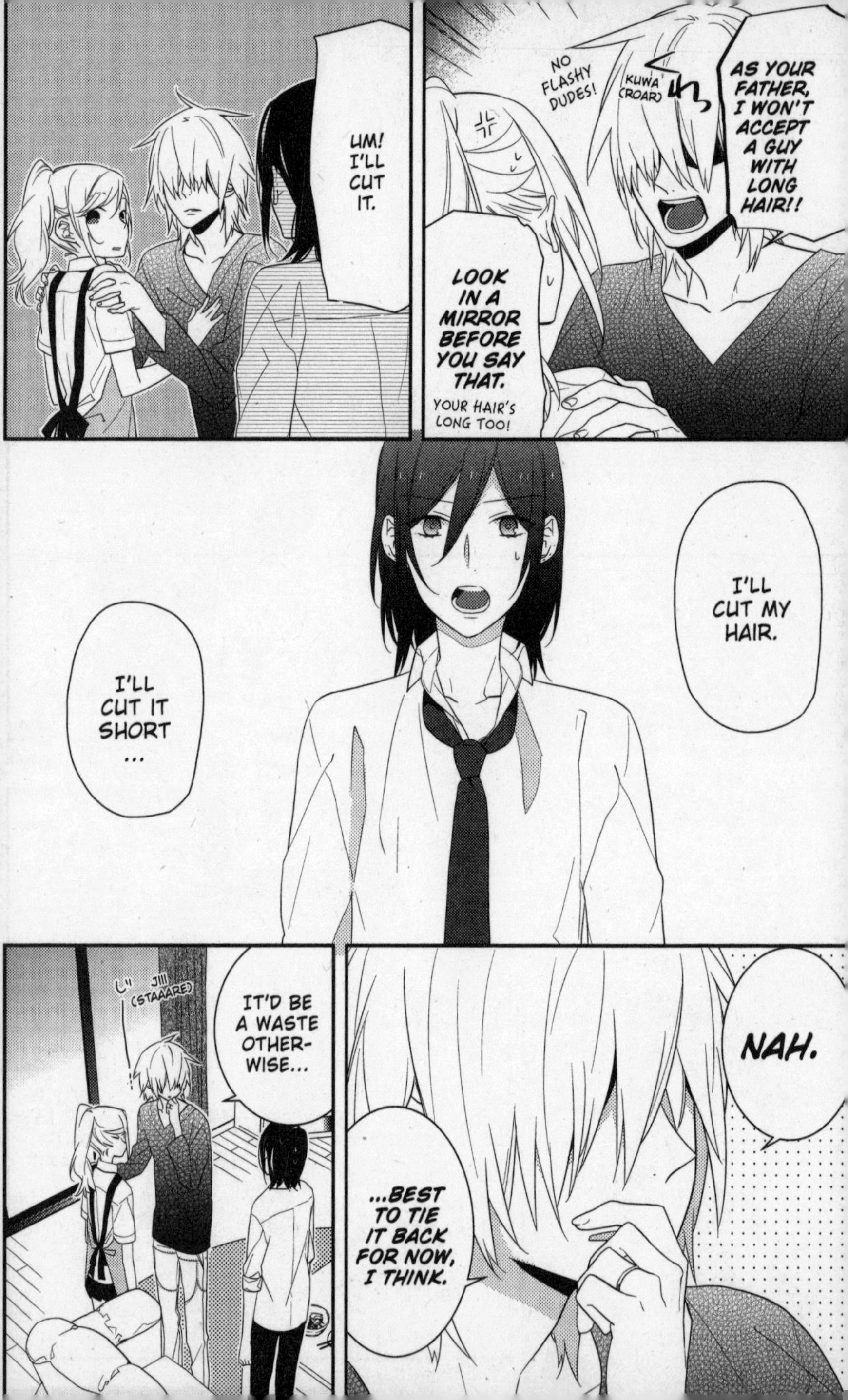

AS YOUR FATHER, I WON'T ACCEPT A GUY WITH LONG HAIR!!
KUWA (ROAR)
NO FLASHY DUDES!
LOOK IN A MIRROR BEFORE YOU SAY THAT.
YOUR HAIR'S LONG TOO!
UM! I'LL CUT IT.
I'LL CUT MY HAIR.
I'LL CUT IT SHORT...
NAH.
...BEST TO TIE IT BACK FOR NOW, I THINK.
IT'D BE A WASTE OTHERWISE...
JIII (STAAARE)

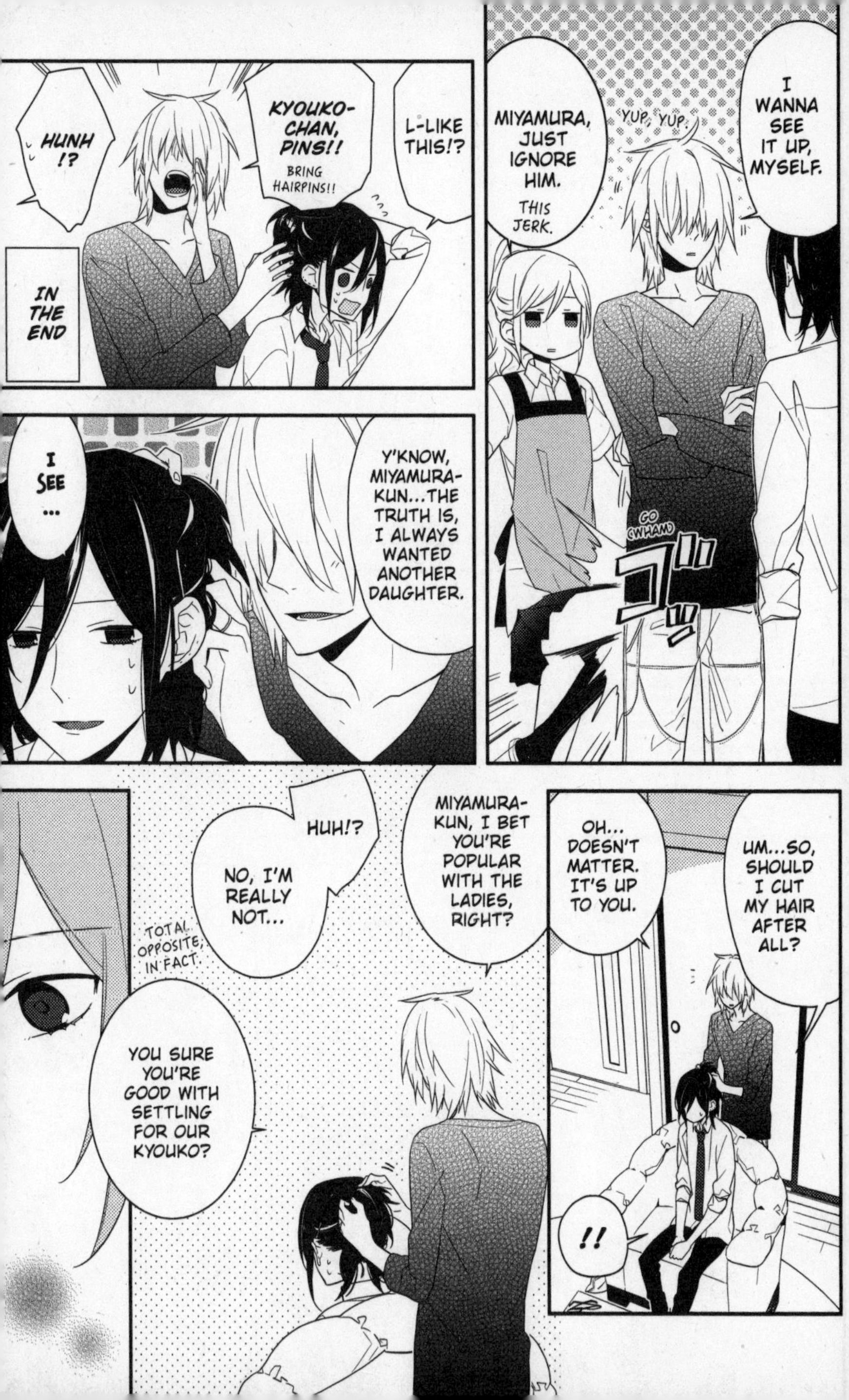
I WANNA SEE IT UP, MYSELF.
YUP, YUP.
MIYAMURA, JUST IGNORE HIM.
THIS JERK.
GO (WHAM)
L-LIKE THIS!?
KYOUKO-CHAN, PINS!!
BRING HAIRPINS!!
HUNH!?
IN THE END
Y'KNOW, MIYAMURA-KUN...THE TRUTH IS, I ALWAYS WANTED ANOTHER DAUGHTER.
I SEE...
UM...SO, SHOULD I CUT MY HAIR AFTER ALL?
OH... DOESN'T MATTER. IT'S UP TO YOU.
!!
MIYAMURA-KUN, I BET YOU'RE POPULAR WITH THE LADIES, RIGHT?
HUH!?
NO, I'M REALLY NOT...
TOTAL OPPOSITE, IN FACT.
YOU SURE YOU'RE GOOD WITH SETTLING FOR OUR KYOUKO?

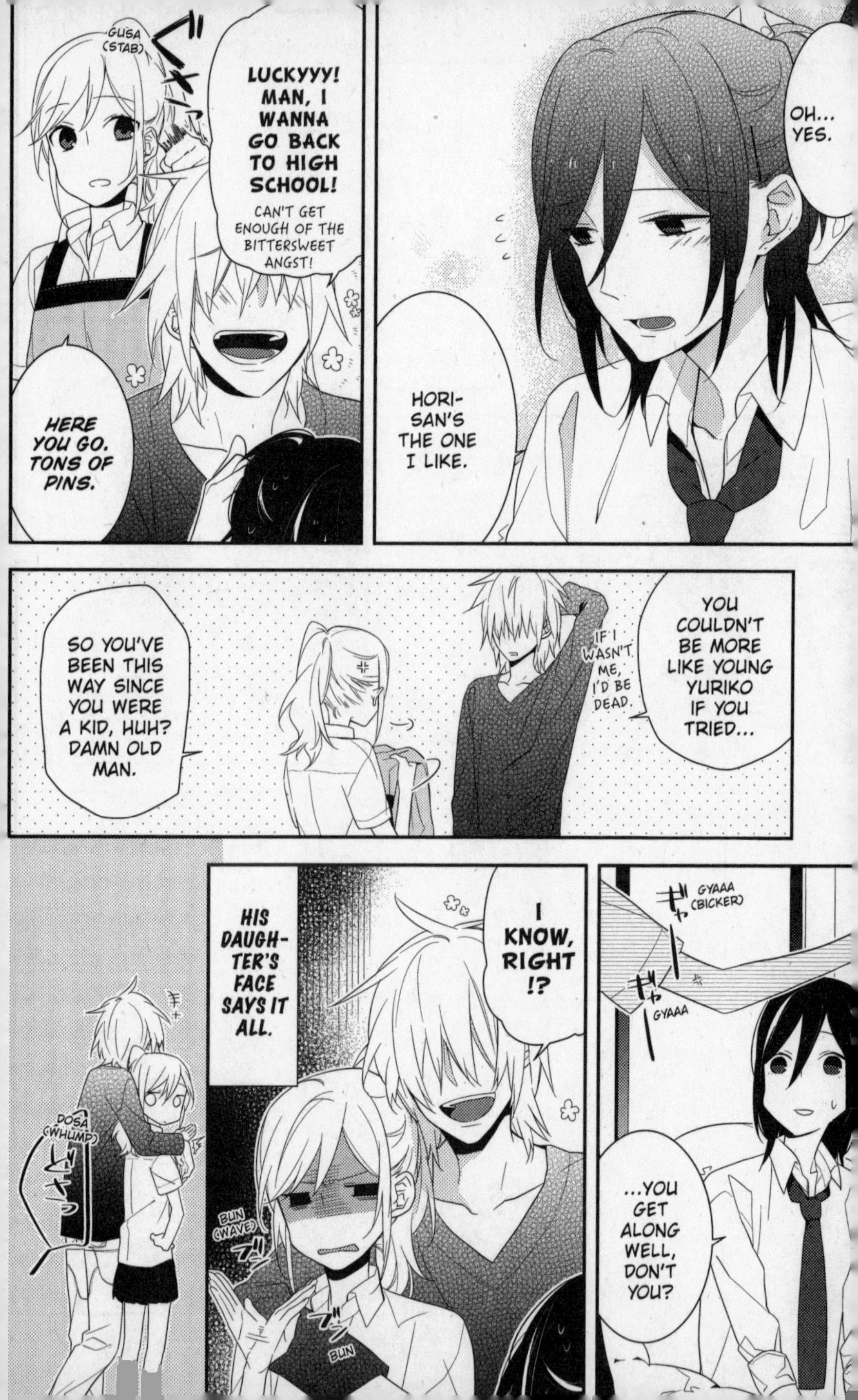
OH... YES.
HORI-SAN'S THE ONE I LIKE.
GUSA (STAB)
LUCKYYY! MAN, I WANNA GO BACK TO HIGH SCHOOL!
CAN'T GET ENOUGH OF THE BITTERSWEET ANGST!
HERE YOU GO. TONS OF PINS.
YOU COULDN'T BE MORE LIKE YOUNG YURIKO IF YOU TRIED...
IF I WASN'T ME, I'D BE DEAD.
SO YOU'VE BEEN THIS WAY SINCE YOU WERE A KID, HUH? DAMN OLD MAN.
GYAAA (BICKER)
GYAAA
...YOU GET ALONG WELL, DON'T YOU?
I KNOW, RIGHT!?
HIS DAUGHTER'S FACE SAYS IT ALL.
BUN (WAVE)
BUN
DOSA (WHUMP)

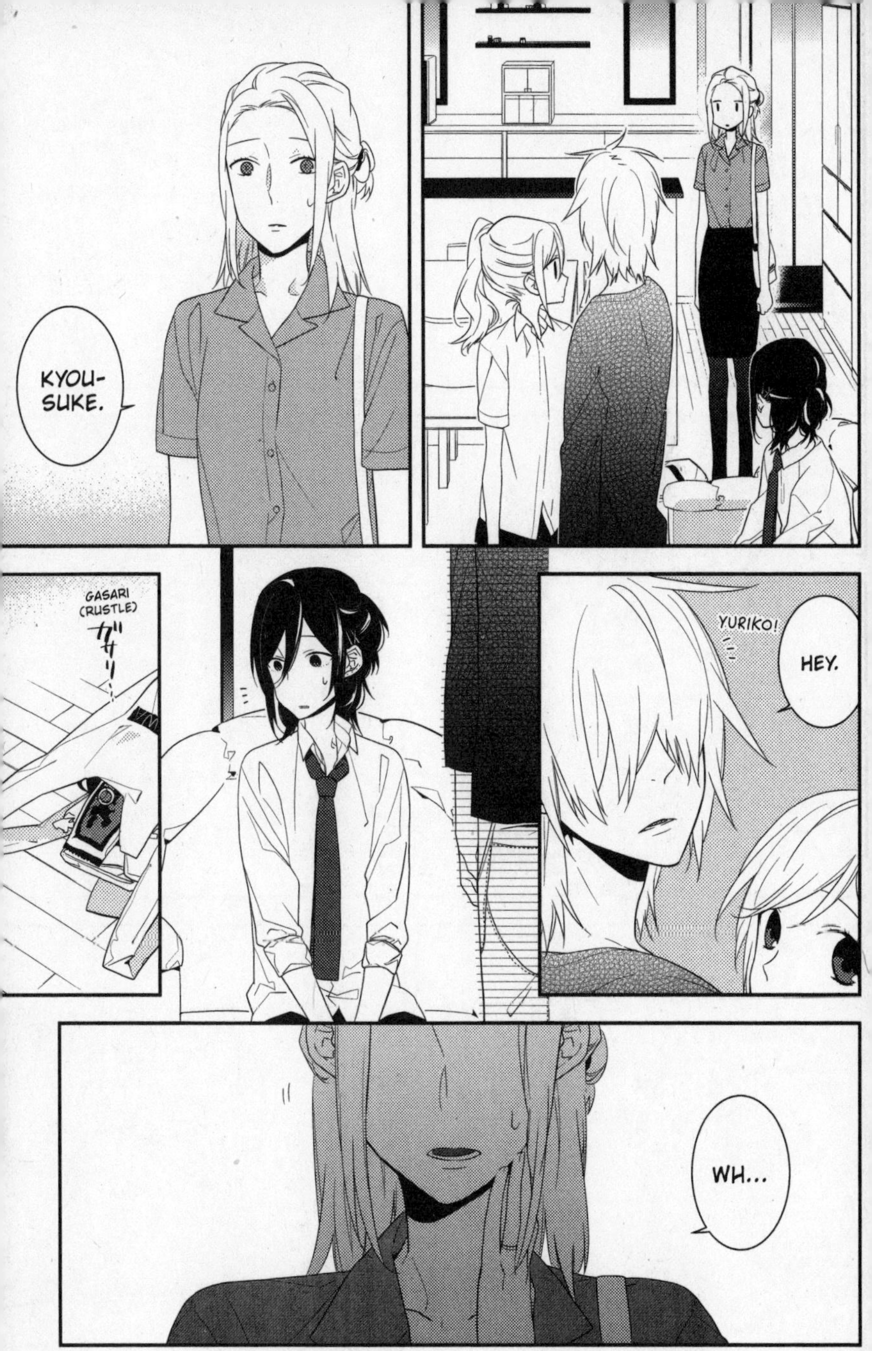
KYOU-SUKE.
HEY.
YURIKO!
GASARI (RUSTLE)
ガサリ
WH...

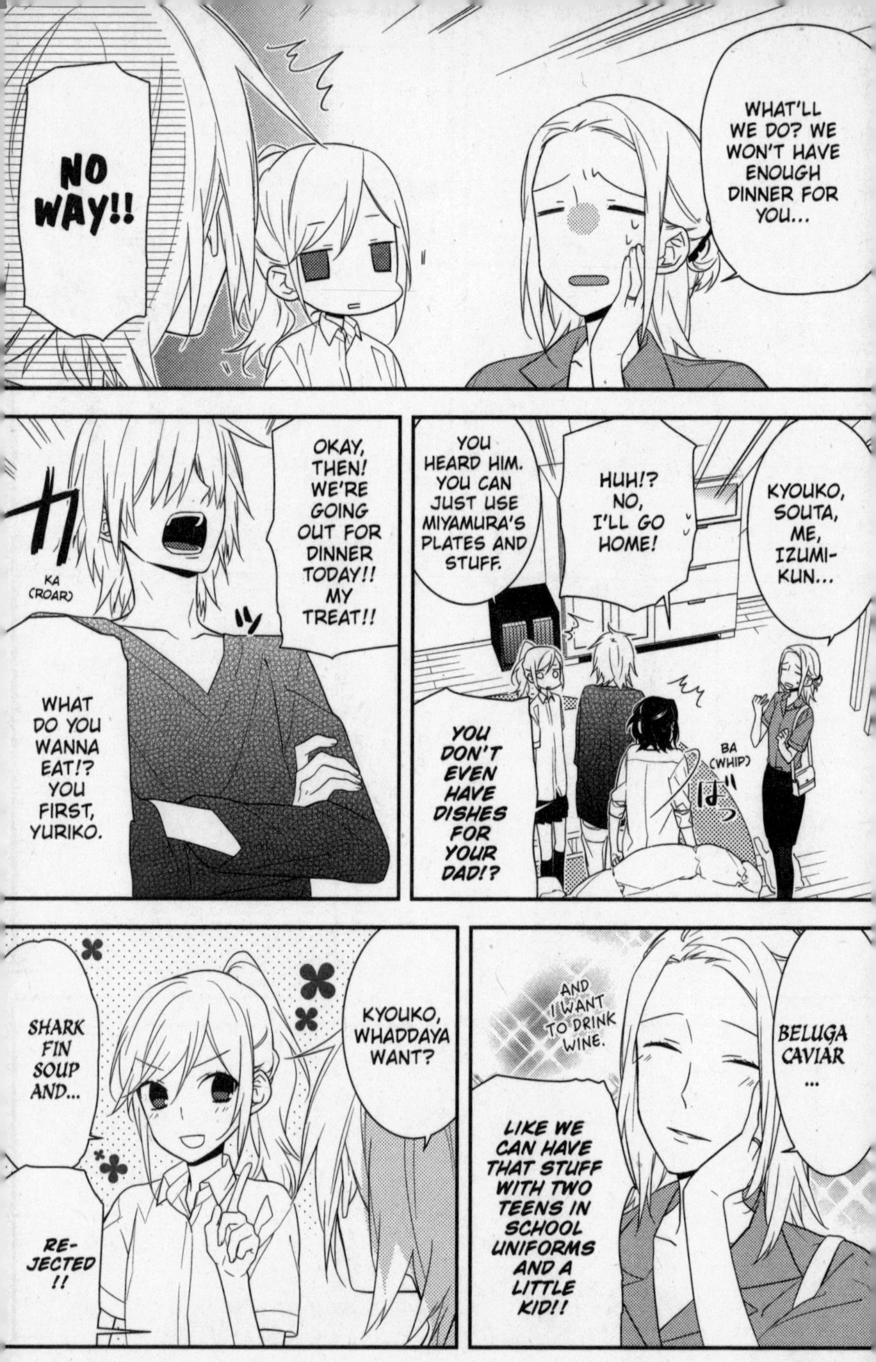
WHAT'LL WE DO? WE WON'T HAVE ENOUGH DINNER FOR YOU...
NO WAY!!
KYOUKO, SOUTA, ME, IZUMI-KUN...
HUH!? NO, I'LL GO HOME!
YOU HEARD HIM. YOU CAN JUST USE MIYAMURA'S PLATES AND STUFF.
BA (WHIP)
YOU DON'T EVEN HAVE DISHES FOR YOUR DAD!?
OKAY, THEN! WE'RE GOING OUT FOR DINNER TODAY!! MY TREAT!!
KA (ROAR)
WHAT DO YOU WANNA EAT!? YOU FIRST, YURIKO.
BELUGA CAVIAR...
AND I WANT TO DRINK WINE.
LIKE WE CAN HAVE THAT STUFF WITH TWO TEENS IN SCHOOL UNIFORMS AND A LITTLE KID!!
KYOUKO, WHADDAYA WANT?
SHARK FIN SOUP AND...
RE-JECTED!!

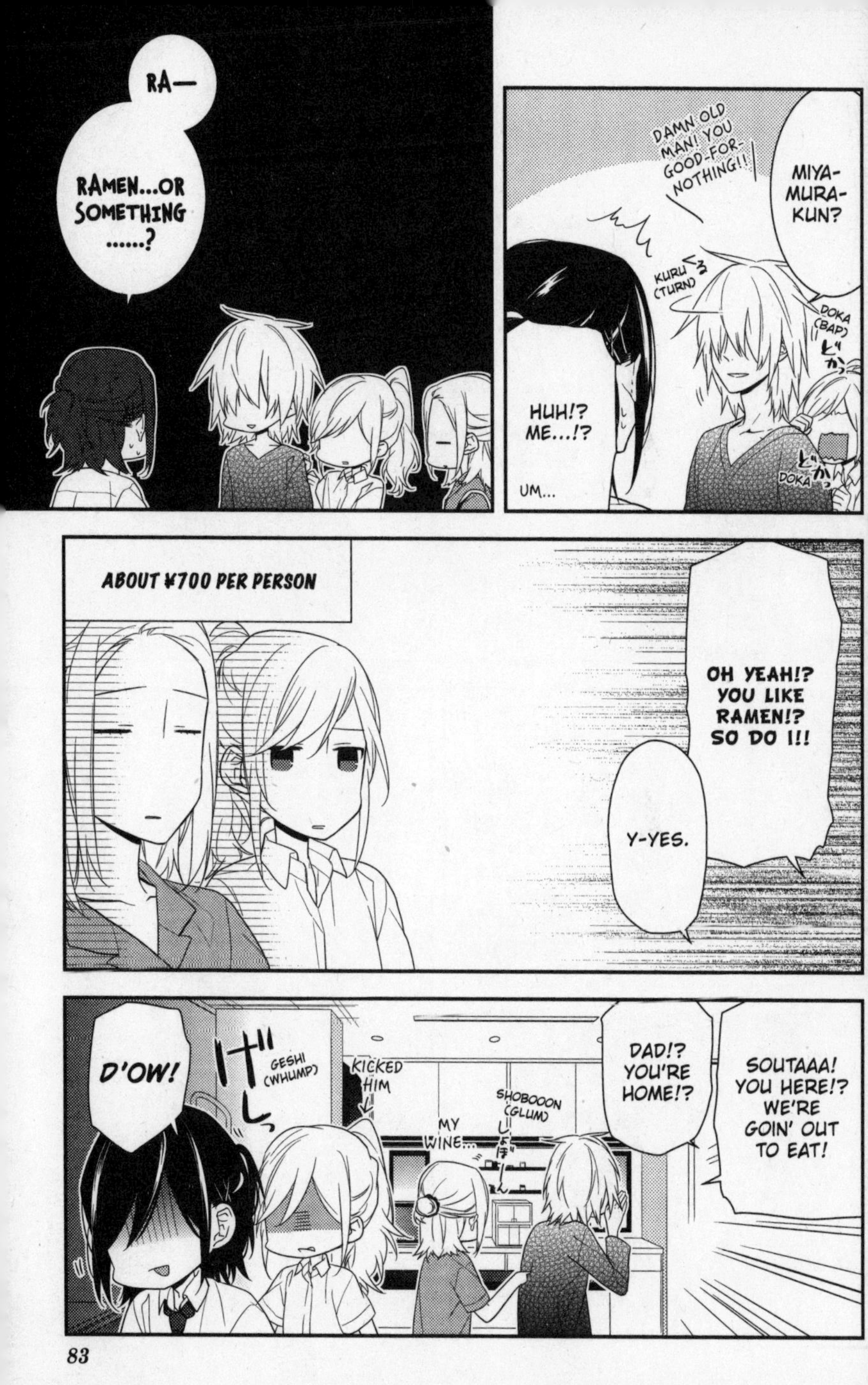
MIYA-MURA-KUN?
DAMN OLD MAN! YOU GOOD-FOR-NOTHING!!
KURU (TURN)
DOKA (BAP)
HUH!? ME...!?
DOKA
UM...
RA—
RAMEN...OR SOMETHING ......?
OH YEAH!? YOU LIKE RAMEN!? SO DO I!!
Y-YES.
ABOUT ¥700 PER PERSON
SOUTAAA! YOU HERE!? WE'RE GOIN' OUT TO EAT!
DAD!? YOU'RE HOME!?
SHOBOOON (GLUM)
MY WINE...
KICKED HIM
GESHI (WHUMP)
D'OW!

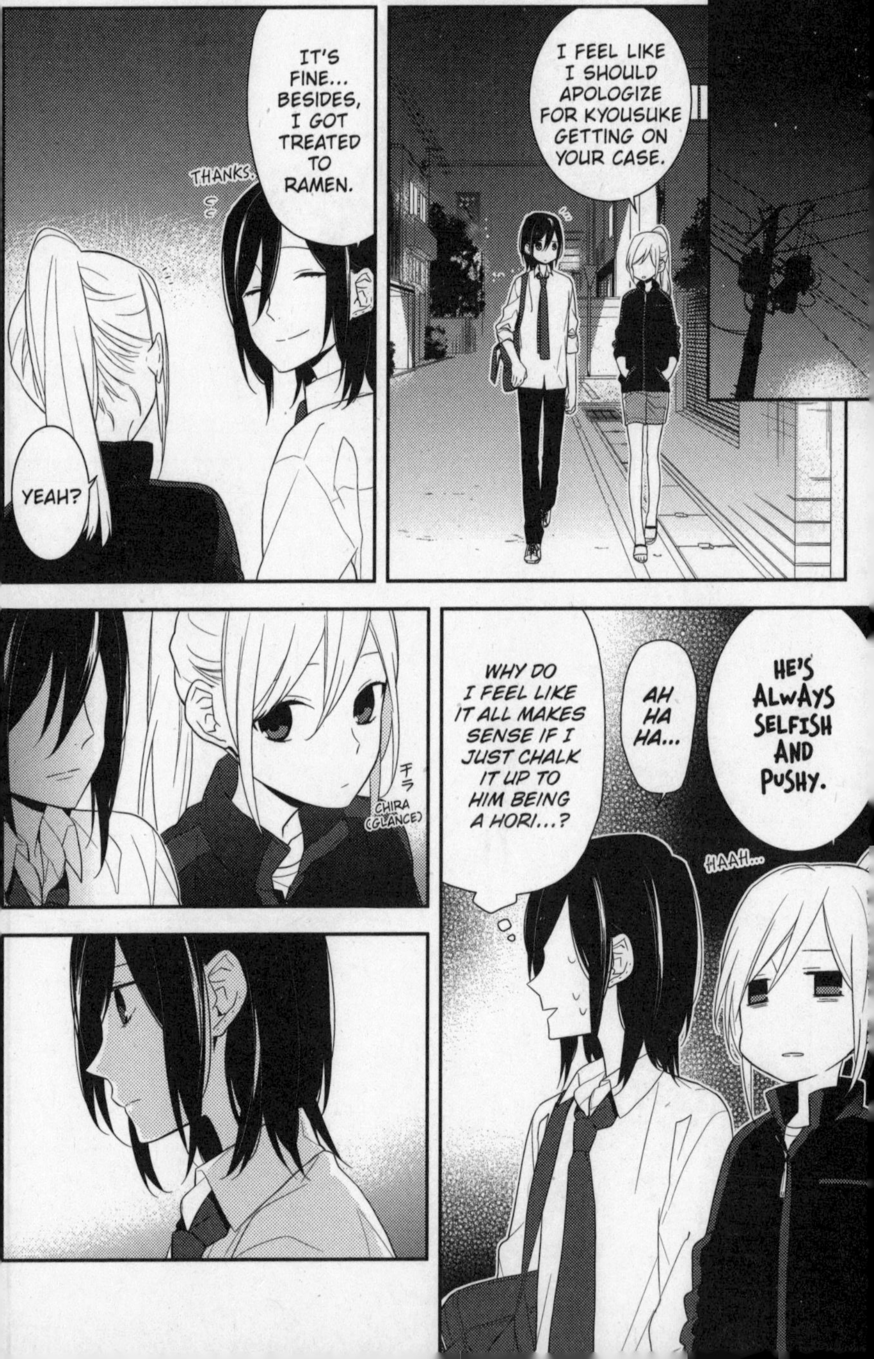
I FEEL LIKE I SHOULD APOLOGIZE FOR KYOUSUKE GETTING ON YOUR CASE.
IT'S FINE... BESIDES, I GOT TREATED TO RAMEN.
THANKS.
YEAH?
HE'S ALWAYS SELFISH AND PUSHY.
AH HA HA...
WHY DO I FEEL LIKE IT ALL MAKES SENSE IF I JUST CHALK IT UP TO HIM BEING A HORI...?
HAAH...
チラ
CHIRA (GLANCE)

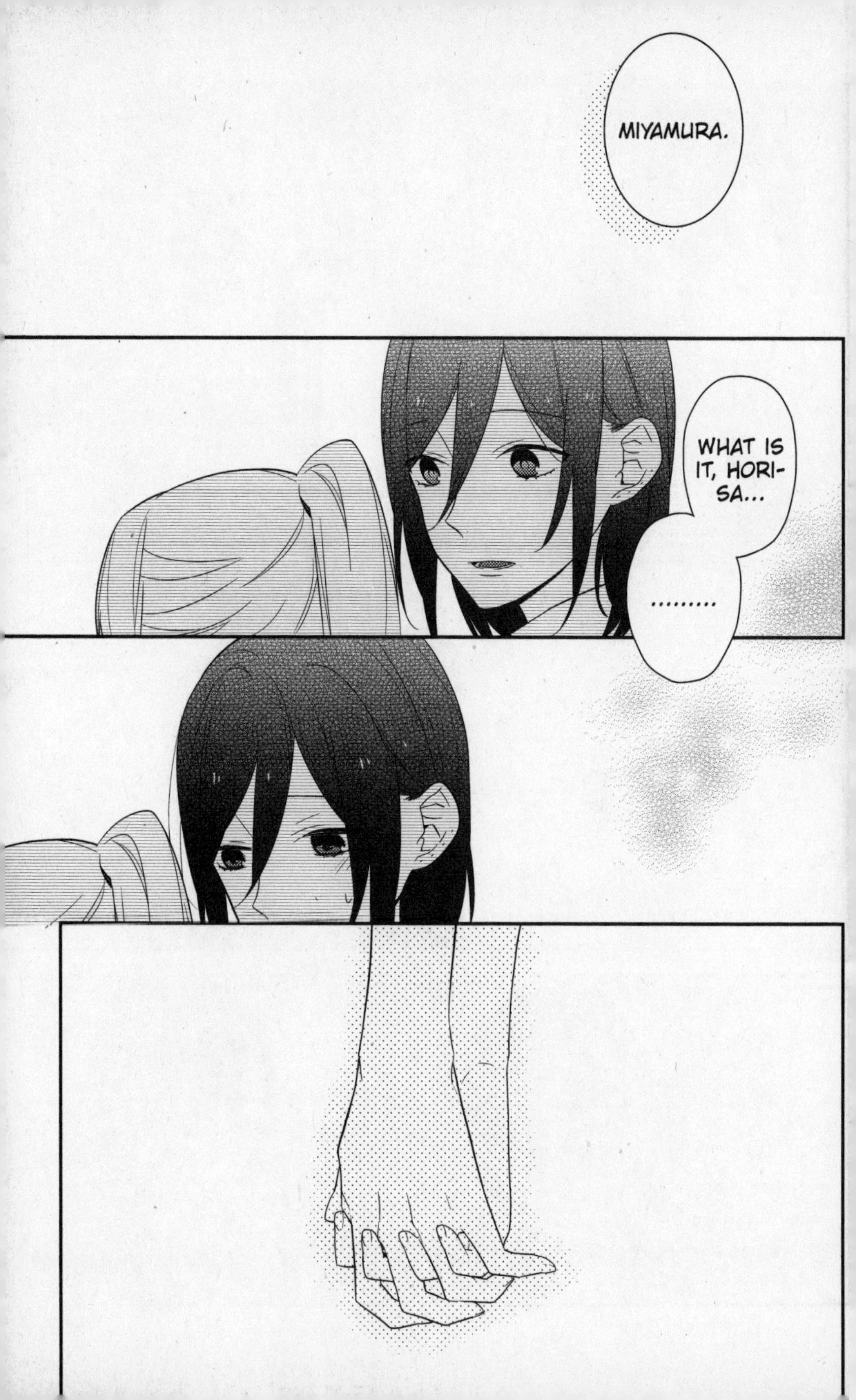
MIYAMURA.
WHAT IS IT, HORI-SA...
....

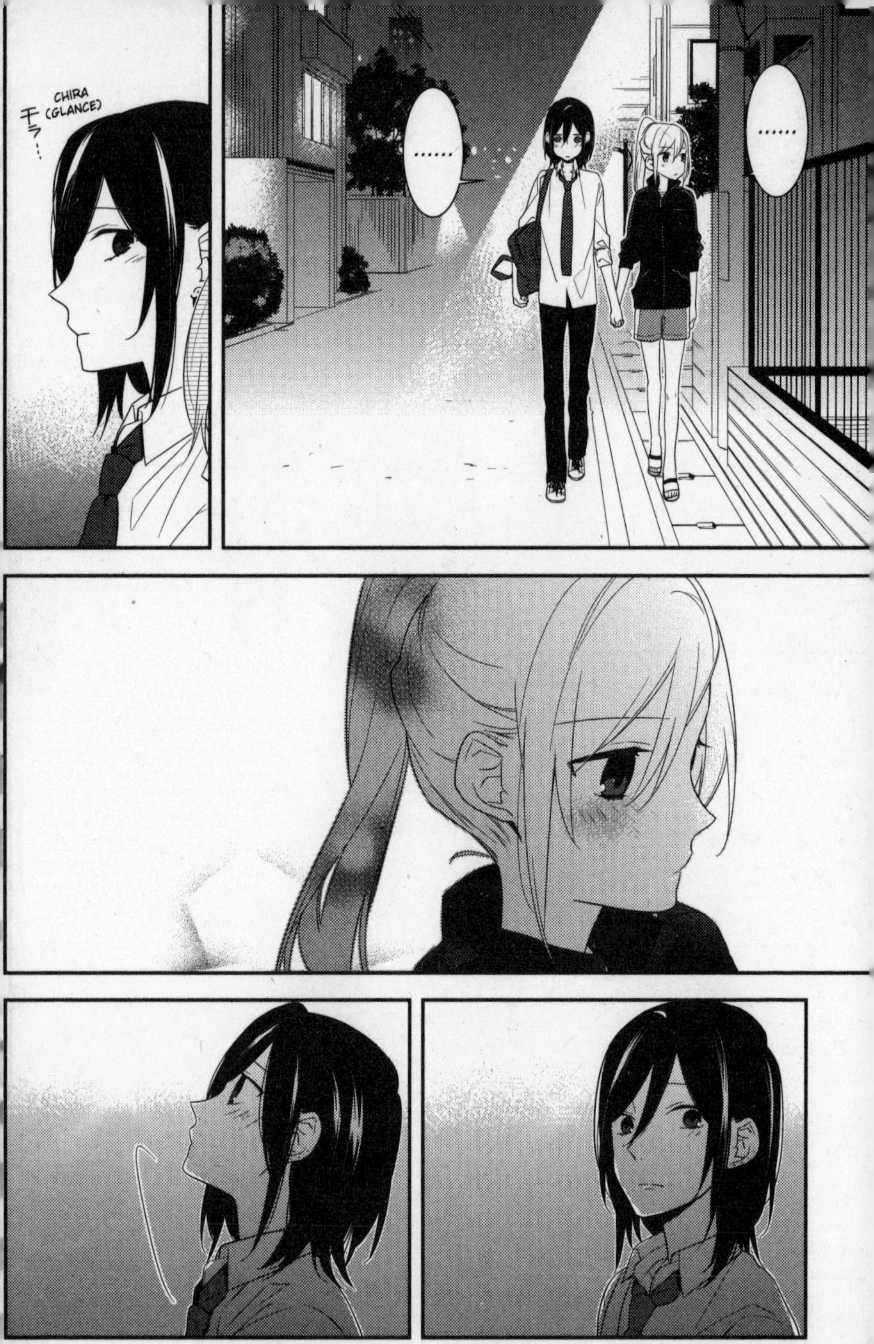
......
......
チラ…
CHIRA (GLANCE)

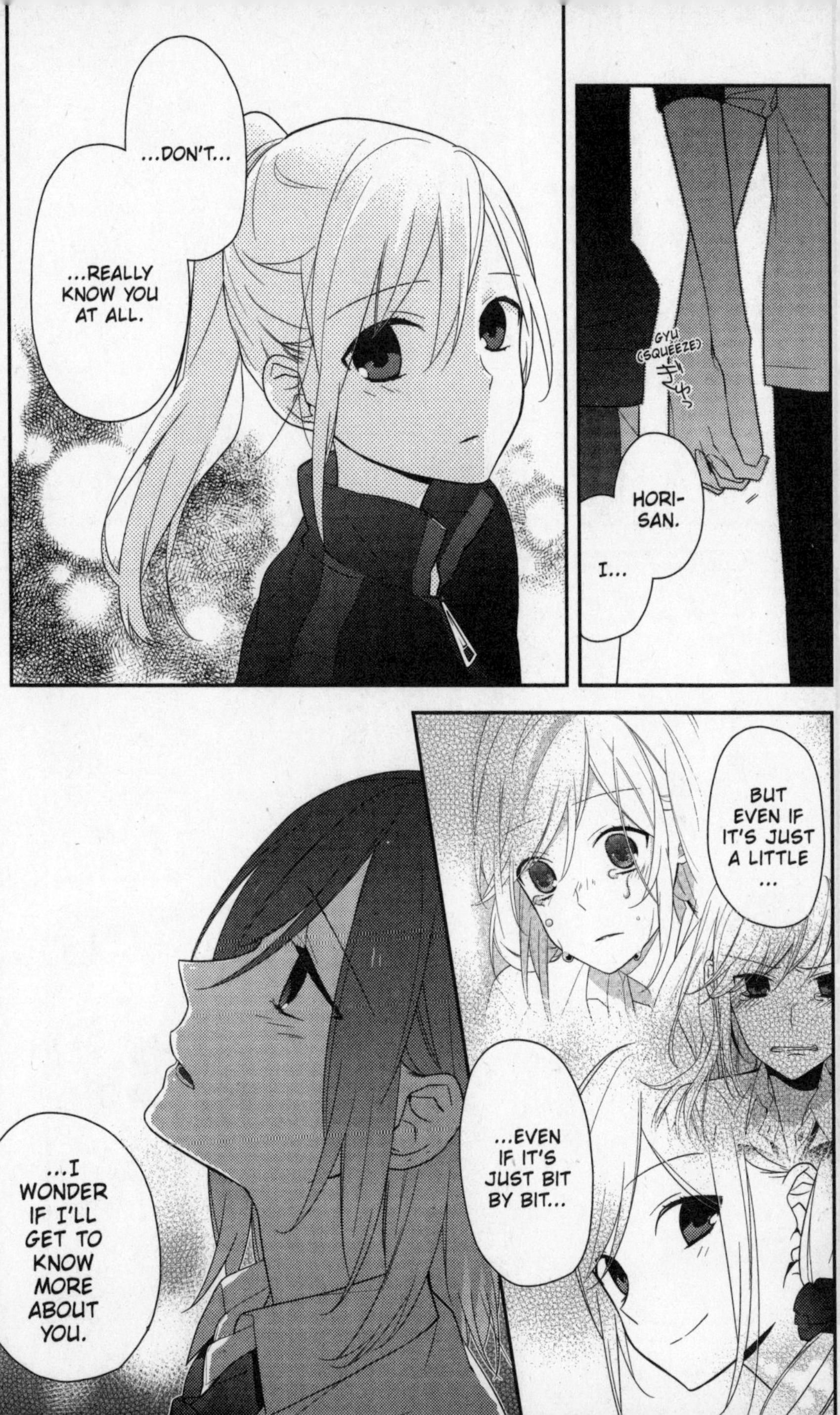
GYU (SQUEEZE)
HORI-SAN.
I...
...DON'T...
...REALLY KNOW YOU AT ALL.
BUT EVEN IF IT'S JUST A LITTLE ...
...EVEN IF IT'S JUST BIT BY BIT...
...I WONDER IF I'LL GET TO KNOW MORE ABOUT YOU.

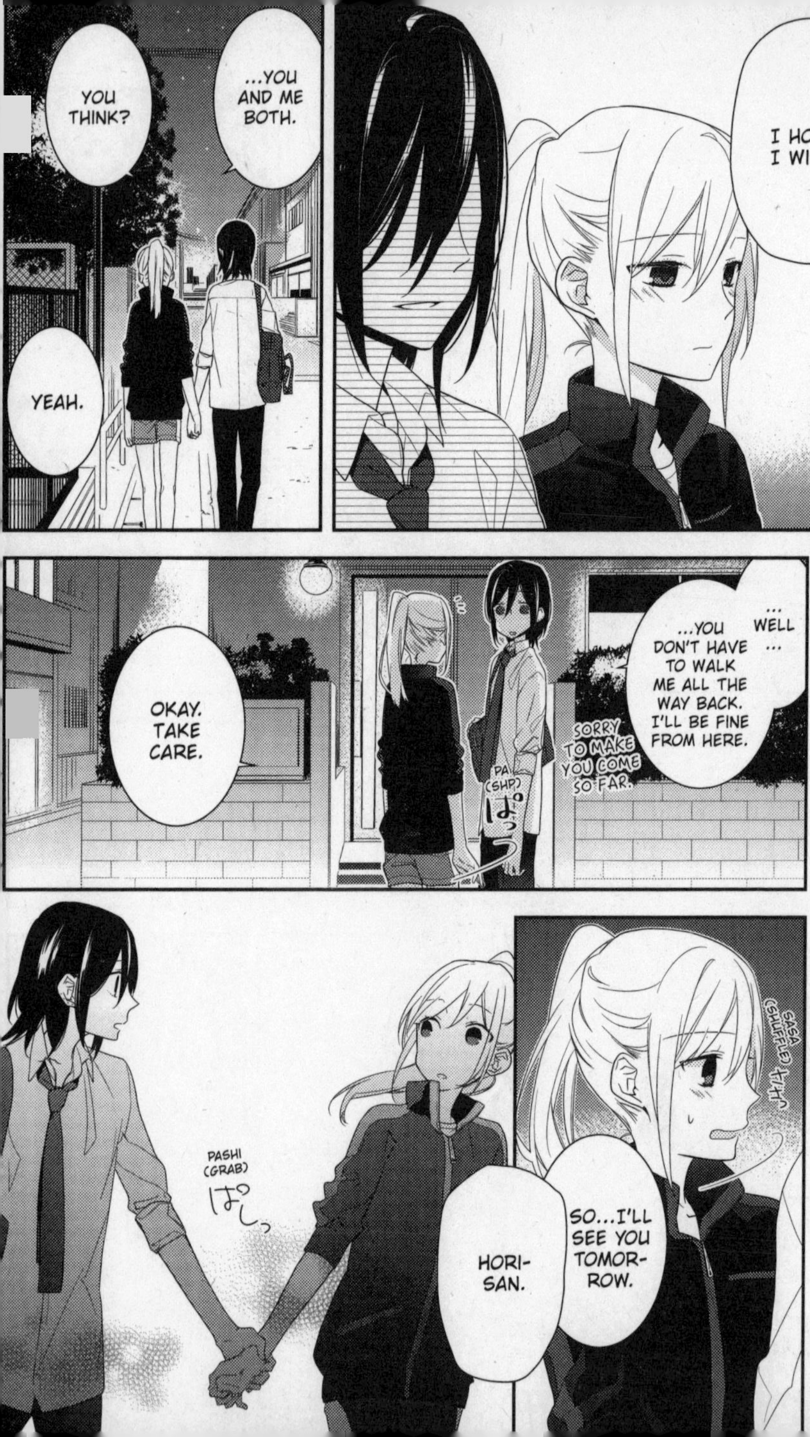
I HOPE I WILL.
...YOU AND ME BOTH.
YOU THINK?
YEAH.
... WELL ...
...YOU DON'T HAVE TO WALK ME ALL THE WAY BACK. I'LL BE FINE FROM HERE.
SORRY TO MAKE YOU COME SO FAR.
PA (SHP) ぱっ
OKAY. TAKE CARE.
SASA (SHUFFLE)
SO...I'LL SEE YOU TOMOR-ROW.
HORI-SAN.
PASHI (GRAB) ぱしっ

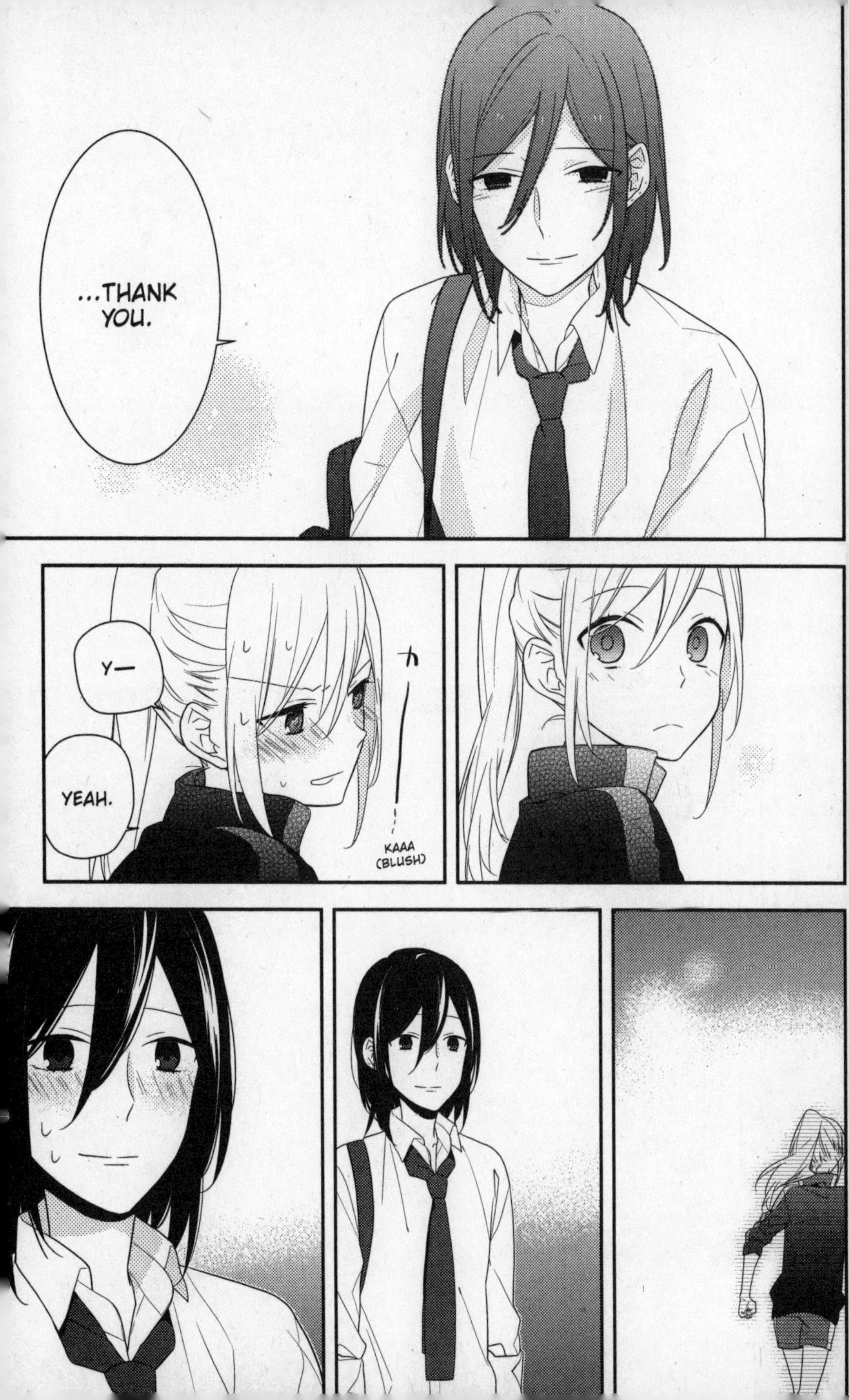
...THANK YOU.
カ
Y—
KAAA (BLUSH)
YEAH.

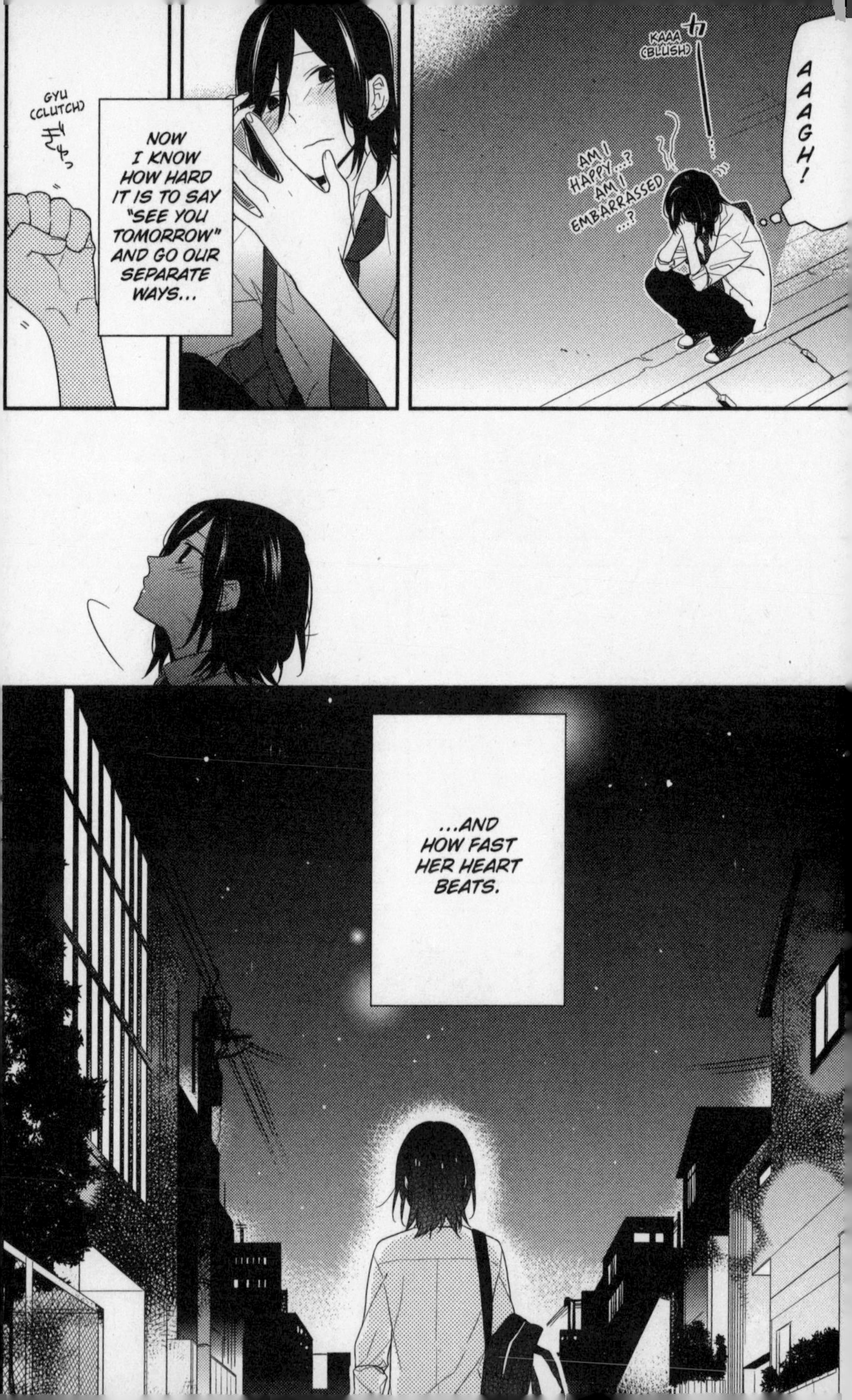

AAAAGH!
KAAA (BLUSH)
カ
AM I HAPPY...? AM I EMBARRASSED...?
NOW I KNOW HOW HARD IT IS TO SAY "SEE YOU TOMORROW" AND GO OUR SEPARATE WAYS...
GYU (CLUTCH)
ぎゅっ
...AND HOW FAST HER HEART BEATS.

HORIMIYA

HORIMIYA

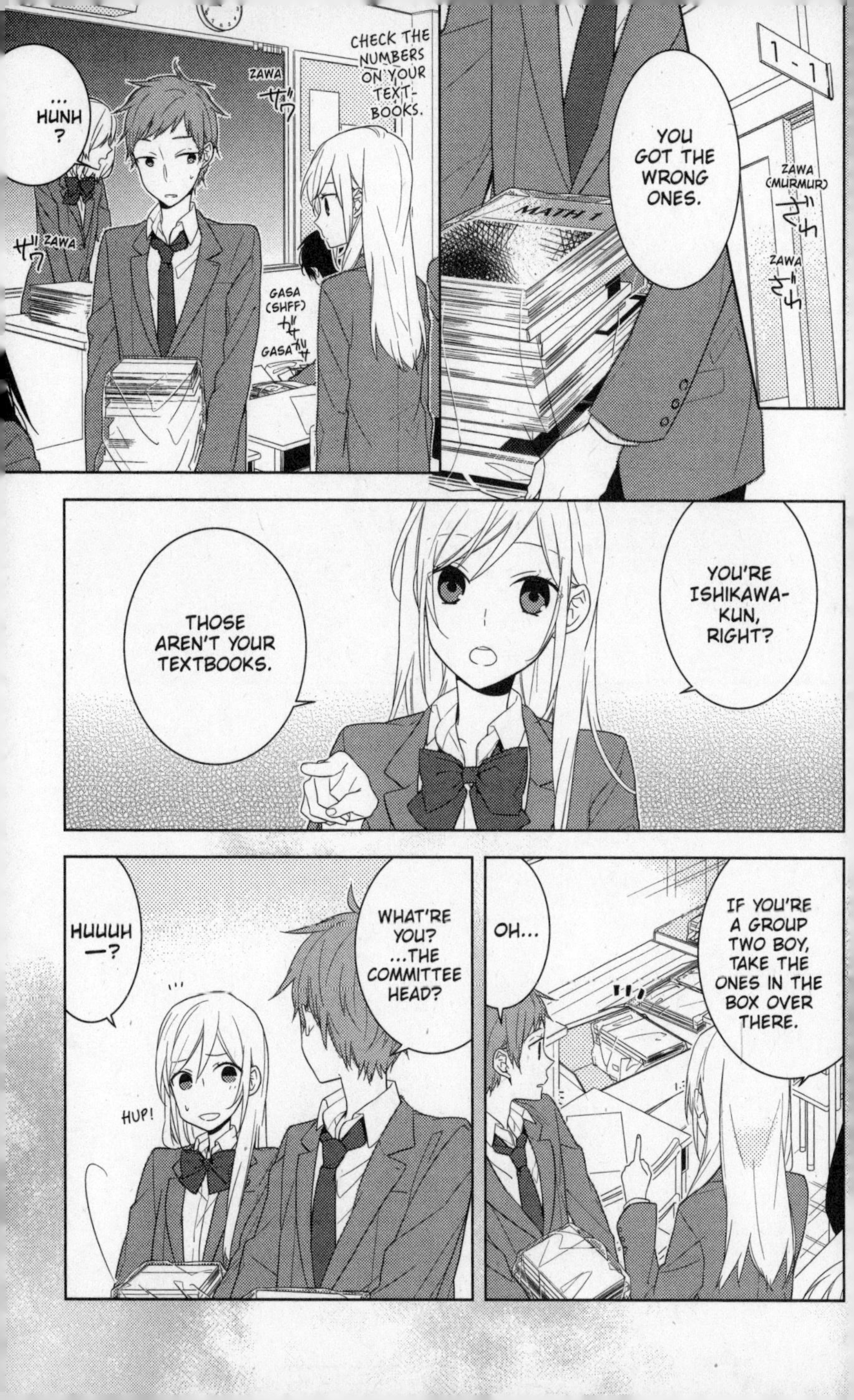
YOU GOT THE WRONG ONES.
ZAWA (MURMUR)
ZAWA
CHECK THE NUMBERS ON YOUR TEXTBOOKS.
ZAWA
... HUNH ?
ZAWA
GASA (SHFF)
GASA
YOU'RE ISHIKAWA-KUN, RIGHT?
THOSE AREN'T YOUR TEXTBOOKS.
IF YOU'RE A GROUP TWO BOY, TAKE THE ONES IN THE BOX OVER THERE.
OH...
WHAT'RE YOU? ...THE COMMITTEE HEAD?
HUUUH—?
HUP!

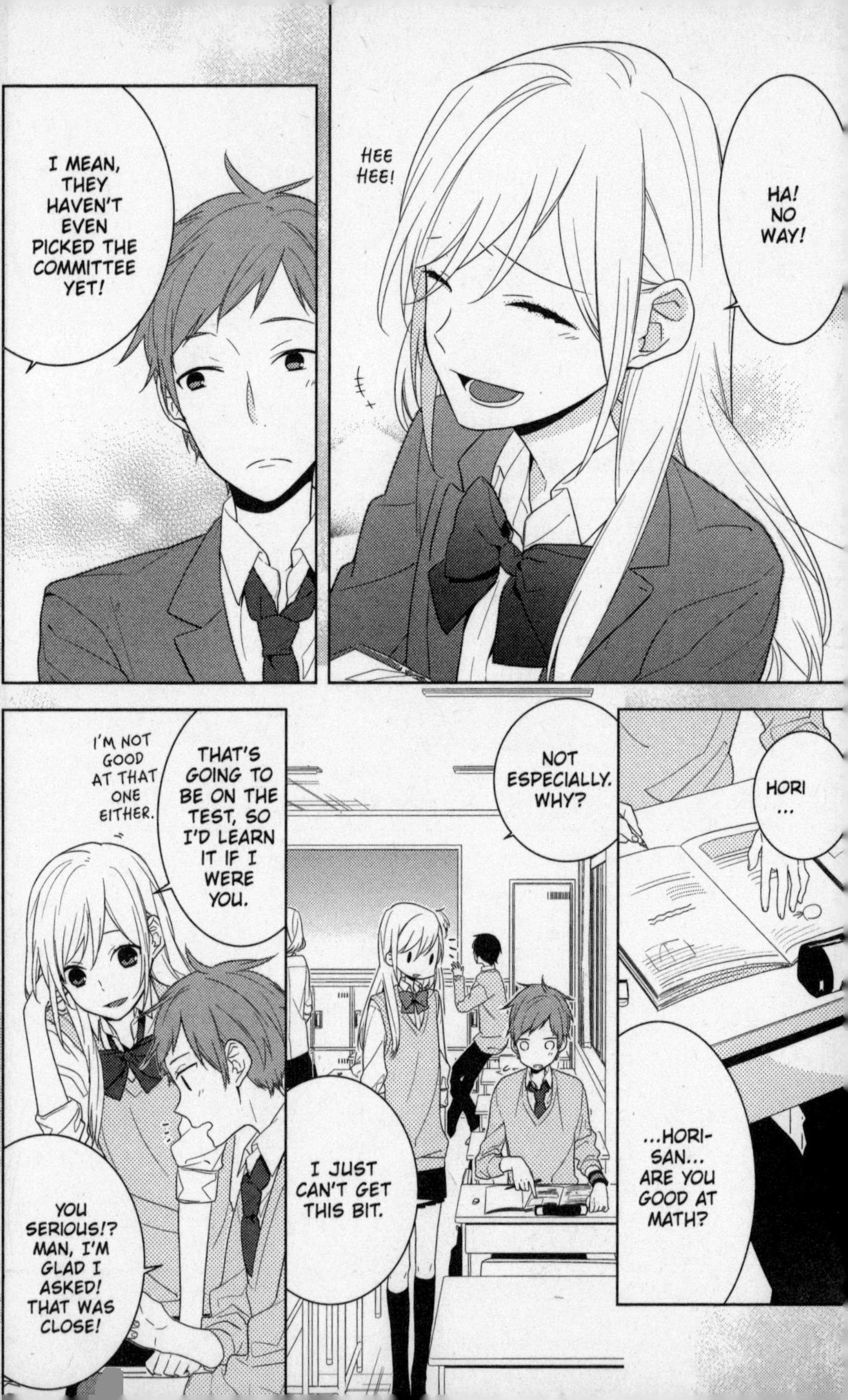
HA! NO WAY!
HEE HEE!
I MEAN, THEY HAVEN'T EVEN PICKED THE COMMITTEE YET!
HORI...
...HORI-SAN... ARE YOU GOOD AT MATH?
NOT ESPECIALLY. WHY?
I JUST CAN'T GET THIS BIT.
THAT'S GOING TO BE ON THE TEST, SO I'D LEARN IT IF I WERE YOU.
I'M NOT GOOD AT THAT ONE EITHER.
YOU SERIOUS!? MAN, I'M GLAD I ASKED! THAT WAS CLOSE!

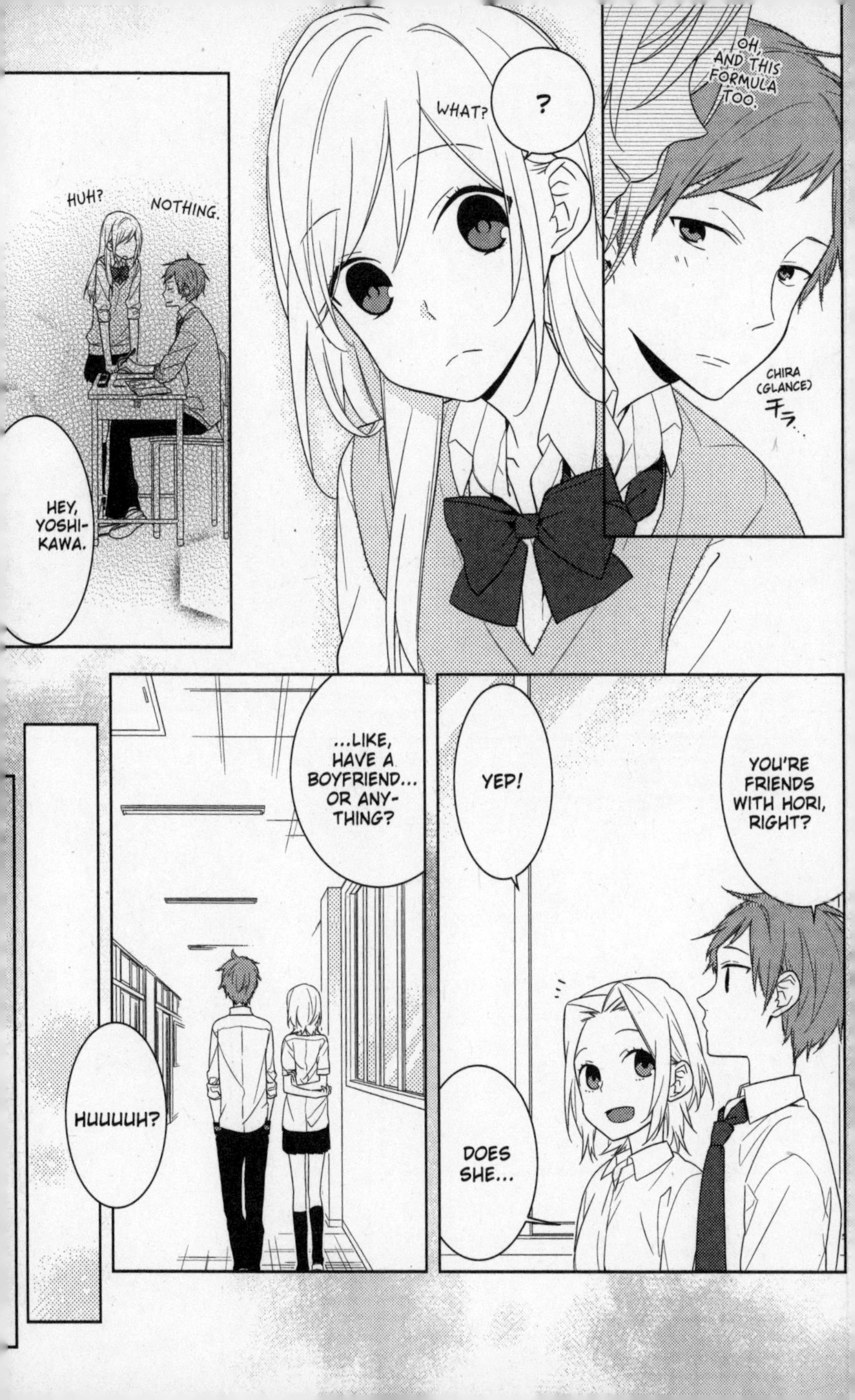
OH, AND THIS FORMULA TOO.
CHIRA (GLANCE)
チラ…
?
WHAT?
NOTHING.
HUH?
HEY, YOSHIKAWA.
YOU'RE FRIENDS WITH HORI, RIGHT?
YEP!
DOES SHE...
...LIKE, HAVE A BOYFRIEND... OR ANYTHING?
HUUUUH?

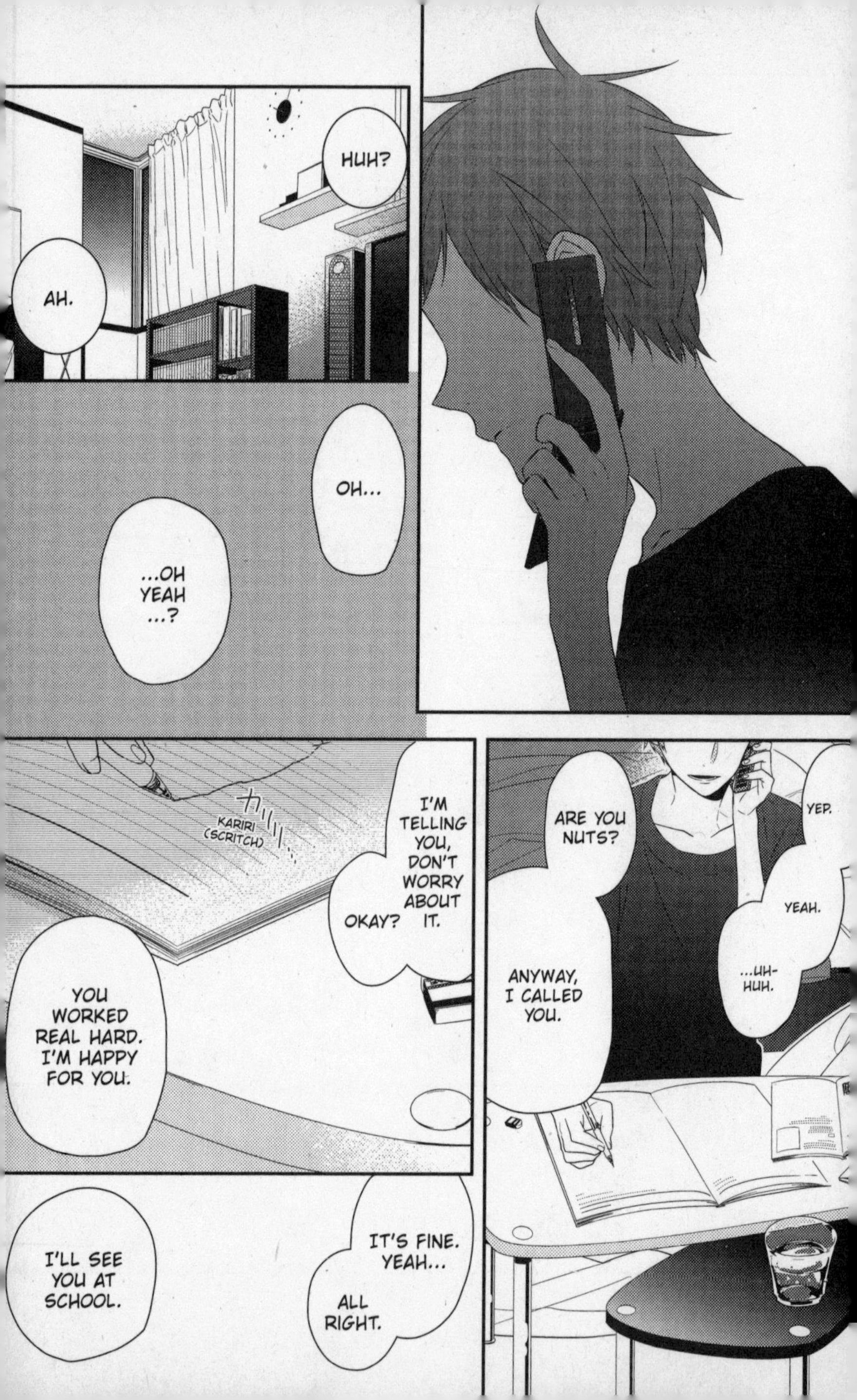
HUH?
AH.
OH...
...OH YEAH ...?
YEP.
ARE YOU NUTS?
YEAH.
...UH-HUH.
ANYWAY, I CALLED YOU.
I'M TELLING YOU, DON'T WORRY ABOUT IT.
OKAY?
KARIRI (SCRITCH)
YOU WORKED REAL HARD. I'M HAPPY FOR YOU.
IT'S FINE. YEAH...
ALL RIGHT.
I'LL SEE YOU AT SCHOOL.

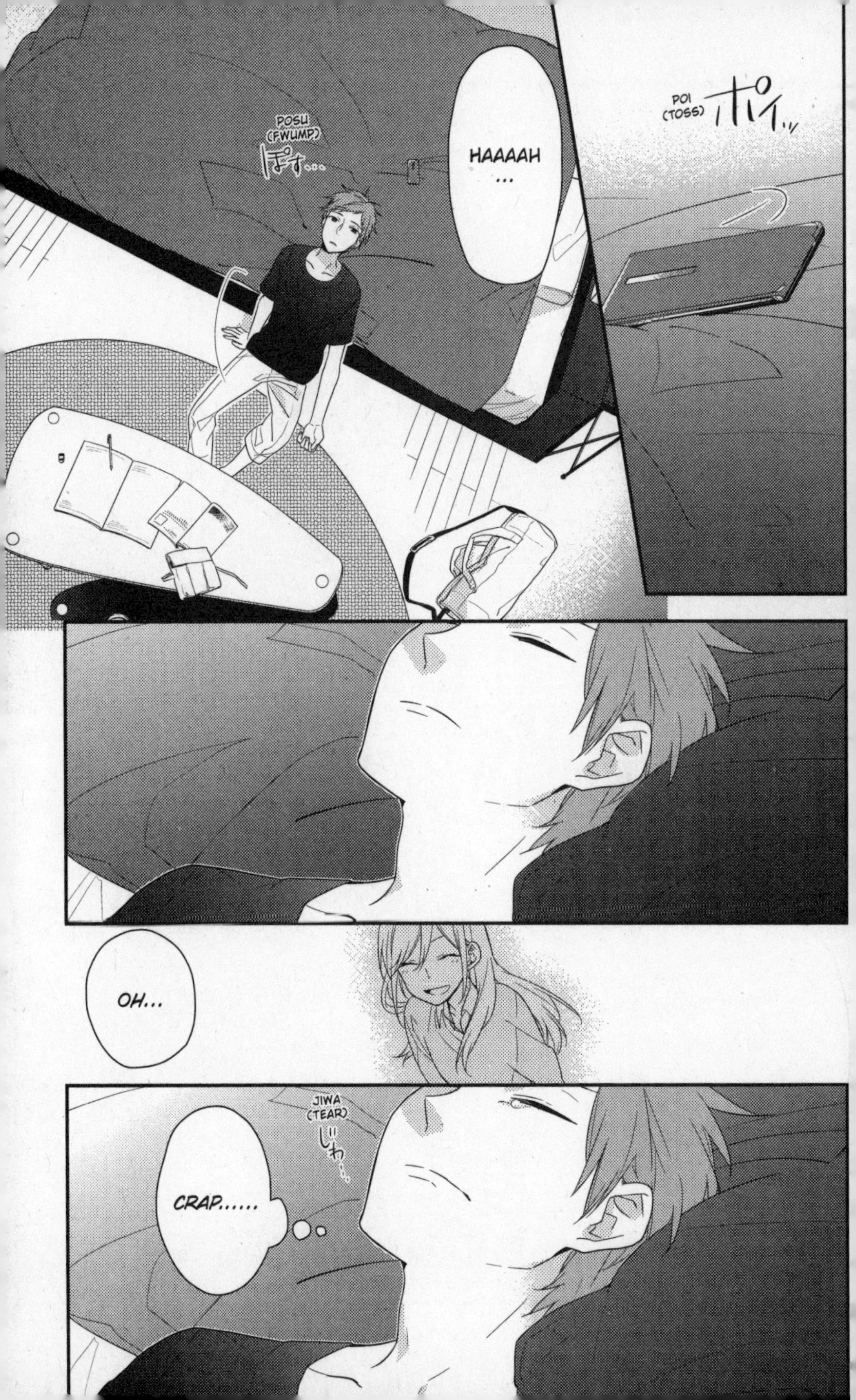
POI (TOSS) ポイッ
HAAAAH ...
POSU (FWUMP) ぽす...
OH...
JIWA (TEAR) じわ...
CRAP......

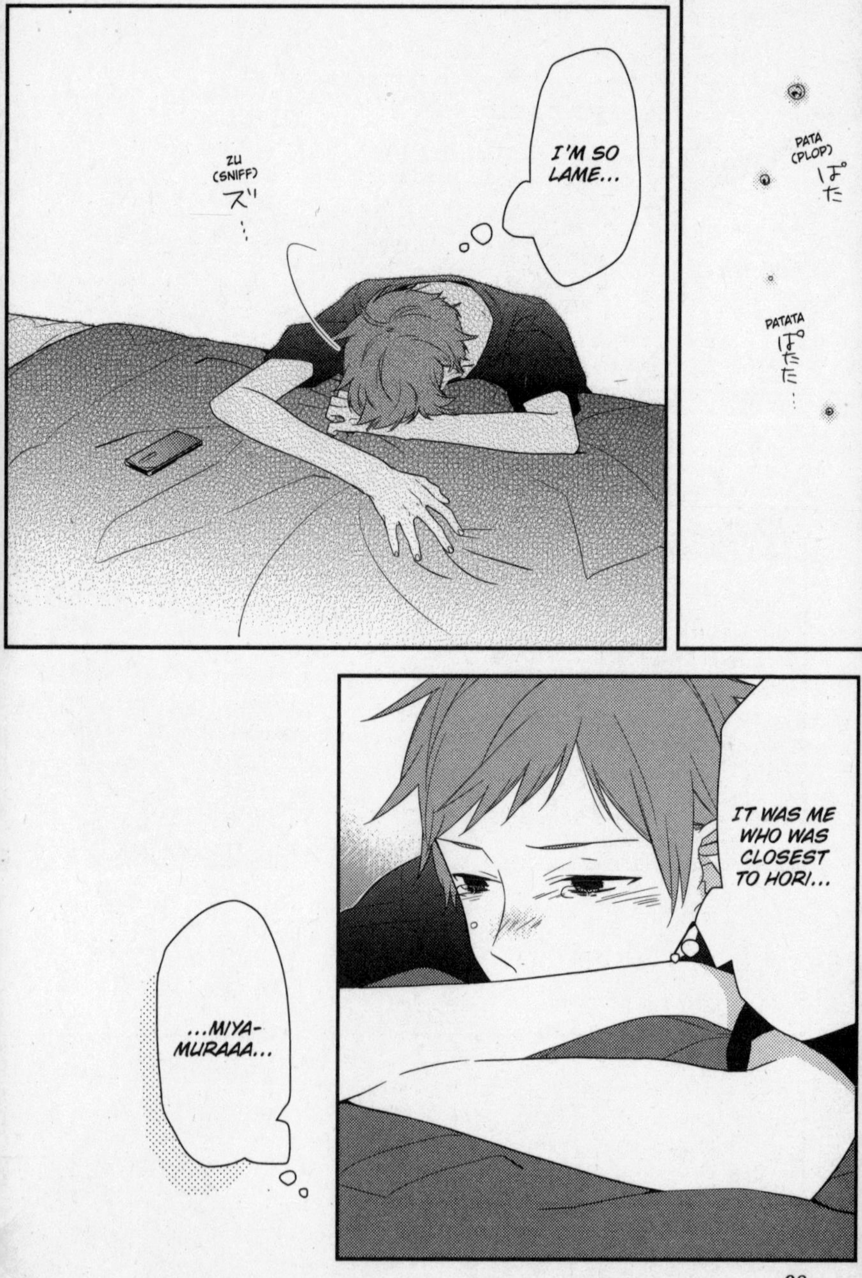
PATA (PLOP) ぱた
PATATA ぱたた…
I'M SO LAME...
ZU (SNIFF) ズ…
IT WAS ME WHO WAS CLOSEST TO HORI...
...MIYA-MURAAA...

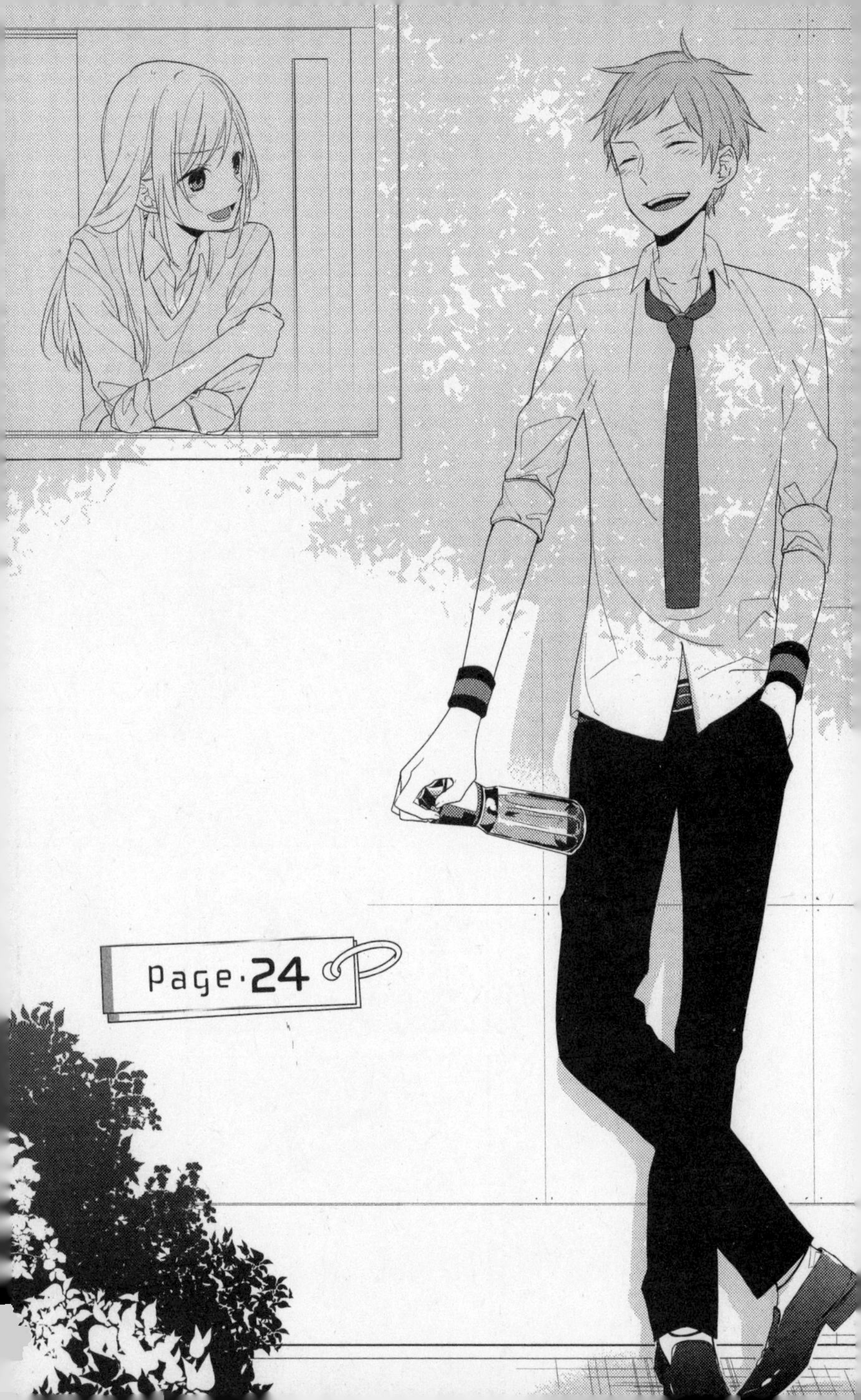
page·24

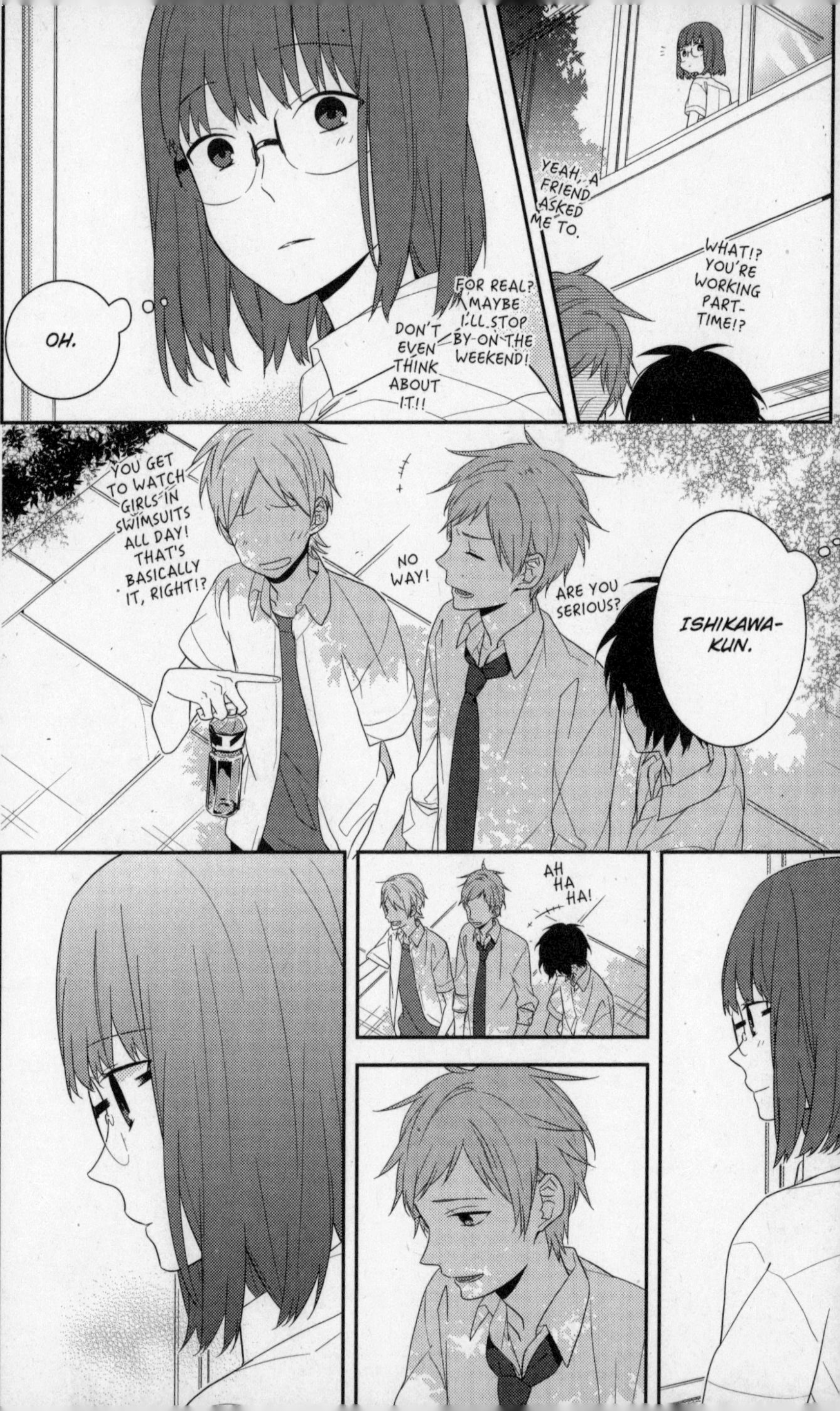
WHAT!? YOU'RE WORKING PART-TIME!?
YEAH, A FRIEND ASKED ME TO.
FOR REAL? MAYBE I'LL STOP BY ON THE WEEKEND!
DON'T EVEN THINK ABOUT IT!!
OH.
ISHIKAWA-KUN.
ARE YOU SERIOUS?
NO WAY!
YOU GET TO WATCH GIRLS IN SWIMSUITS ALL DAY! THAT'S BASICALLY IT, RIGHT!?
AH HA HA!

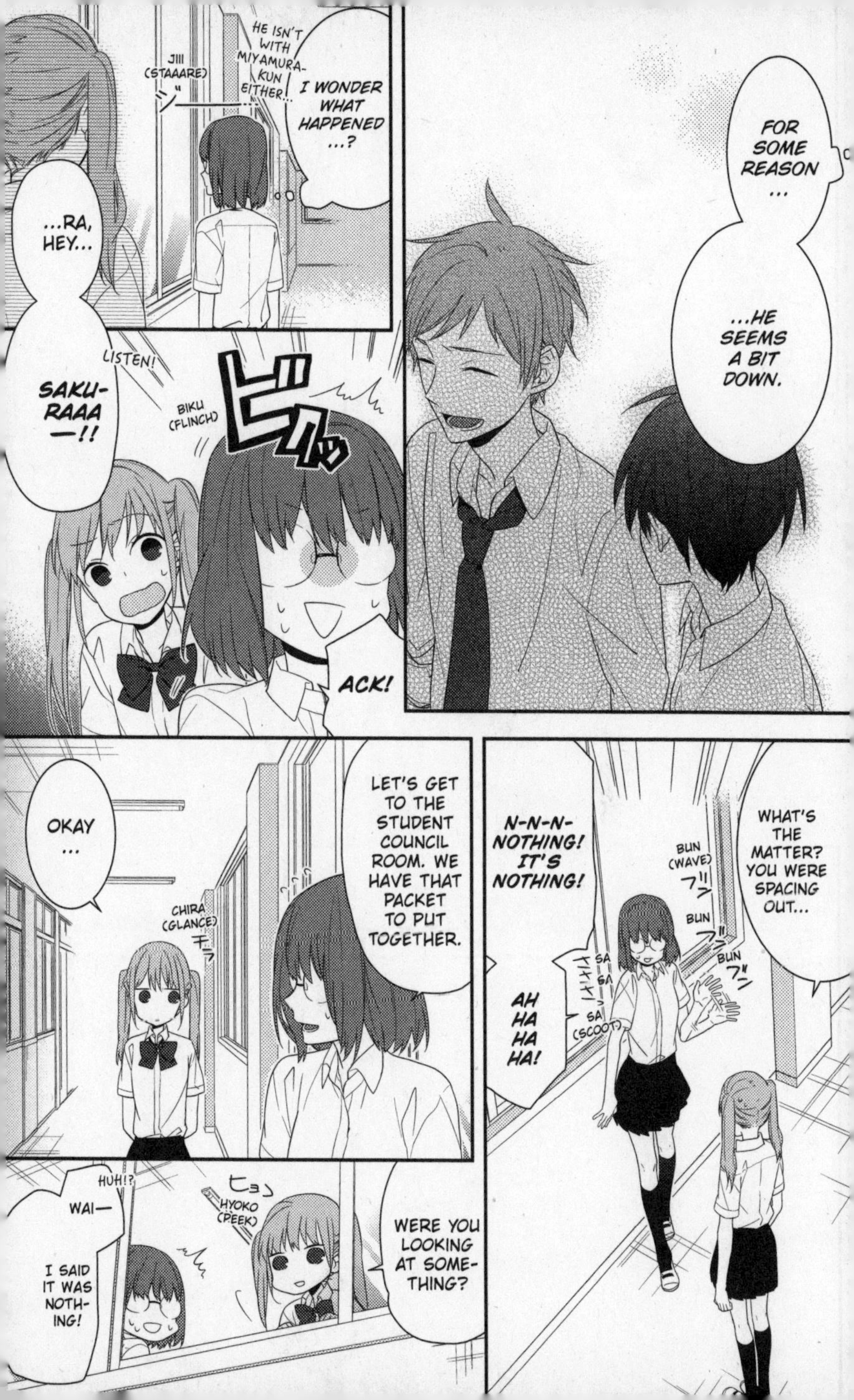
FOR SOME REASON...
...HE SEEMS A BIT DOWN.
HE ISN'T WITH MIYAMURA-KUN EITHER...
I WONDER WHAT HAPPENED...?
JIII (STAAARE)
...RA, HEY...
SAKU-RAAA—!!
LISTEN!
BIKU (FLINCH)
ACK!
WHAT'S THE MATTER? YOU WERE SPACING OUT...
BUN (WAVE)
BUN
BUN
N-N-N-NOTHING! IT'S NOTHING!
AH HA HA HA!
SA
SA
SA (SCOOT)
LET'S GET TO THE STUDENT COUNCIL ROOM. WE HAVE THAT PACKET TO PUT TOGETHER.
OKAY...
CHIRA (GLANCE)
WERE YOU LOOKING AT SOME-THING?
HYOKO (PEEK)
HUH!?
WAI—
I SAID IT WAS NOTHING!

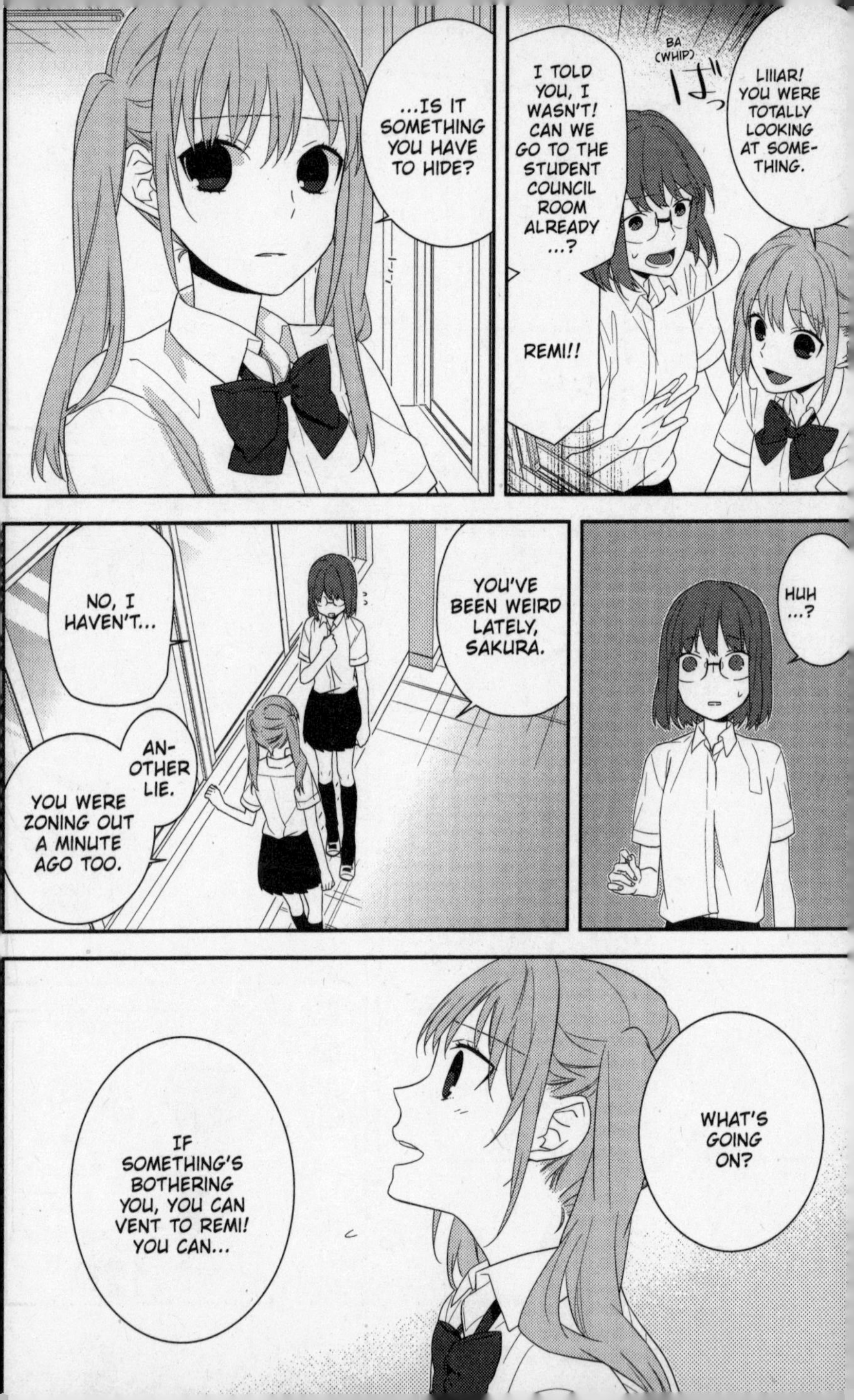
LIIIAR! YOU WERE TOTALLY LOOKING AT SOMETHING.
BA (WHIP)
ばっ
I TOLD YOU, I WASN'T! CAN WE GO TO THE STUDENT COUNCIL ROOM ALREADY ...?
REMI!!
...IS IT SOMETHING YOU HAVE TO HIDE?
HUH ...?
YOU'VE BEEN WEIRD LATELY, SAKURA.
NO, I HAVEN'T...
AN-OTHER LIE.
YOU WERE ZONING OUT A MINUTE AGO TOO.
WHAT'S GOING ON?
IF SOMETHING'S BOTHERING YOU, YOU CAN VENT TO REMI! YOU CAN...

...SHARE ANYTHING...

BIG EYES.

A SMALL, SLIM BODY.

HORI-SAN, THE GIRL ISHIKAWA-KUN LIKES...

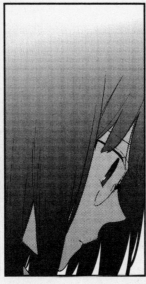

....IS PRETTY AND CUTE TOO.

YOU...

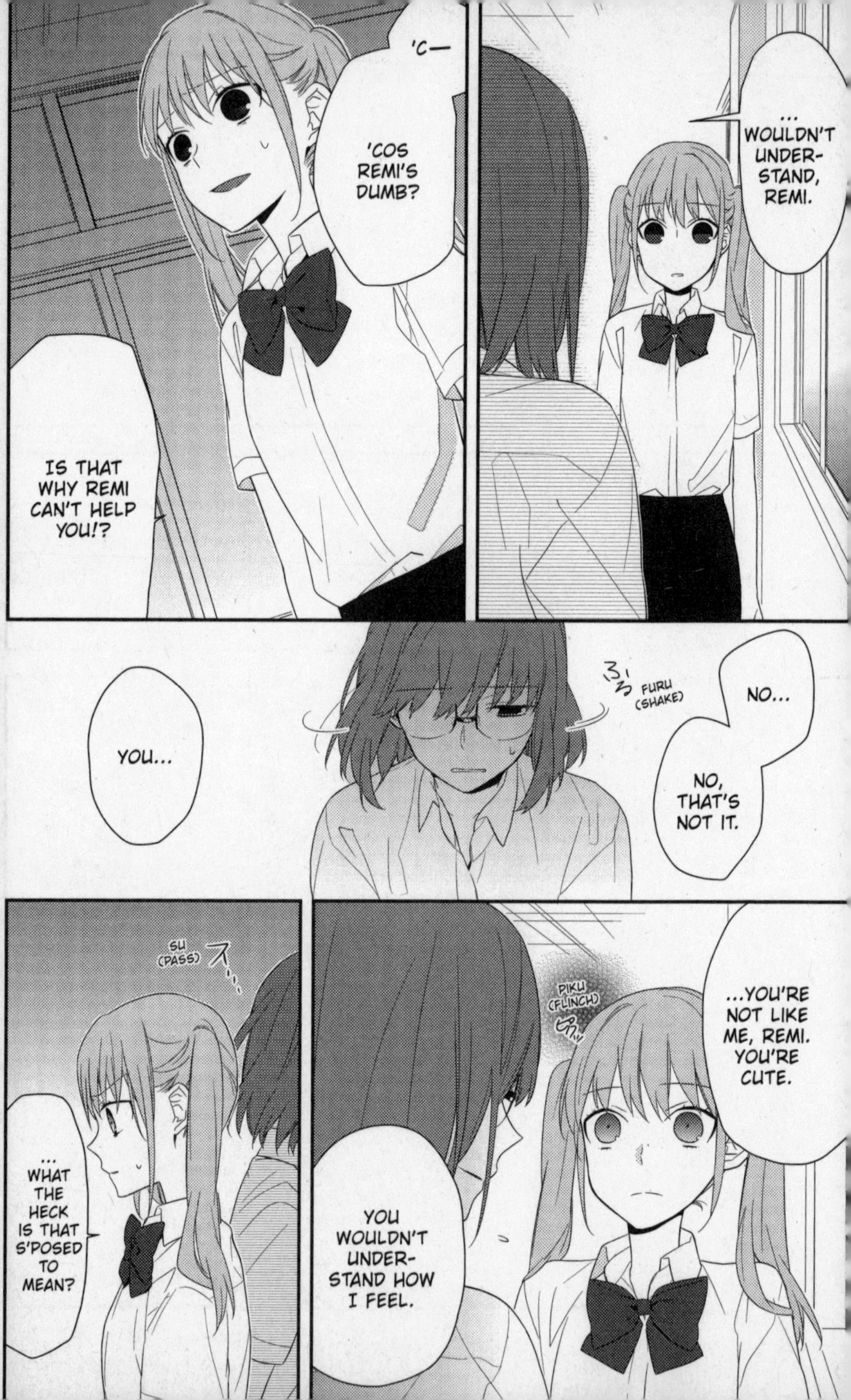
... WOULDN'T UNDER-STAND, REMI.
'C—
'COS REMI'S DUMB?
IS THAT WHY REMI CAN'T HELP YOU!?
FURU (SHAKE)
NO...
NO, THAT'S NOT IT.
YOU...
PIKU (FLINCH)
...YOU'RE NOT LIKE ME, REMI. YOU'RE CUTE.
YOU WOULDN'T UNDER-STAND HOW I FEEL.
SU (PASS)
... WHAT THE HECK IS THAT S'POSED TO MEAN?

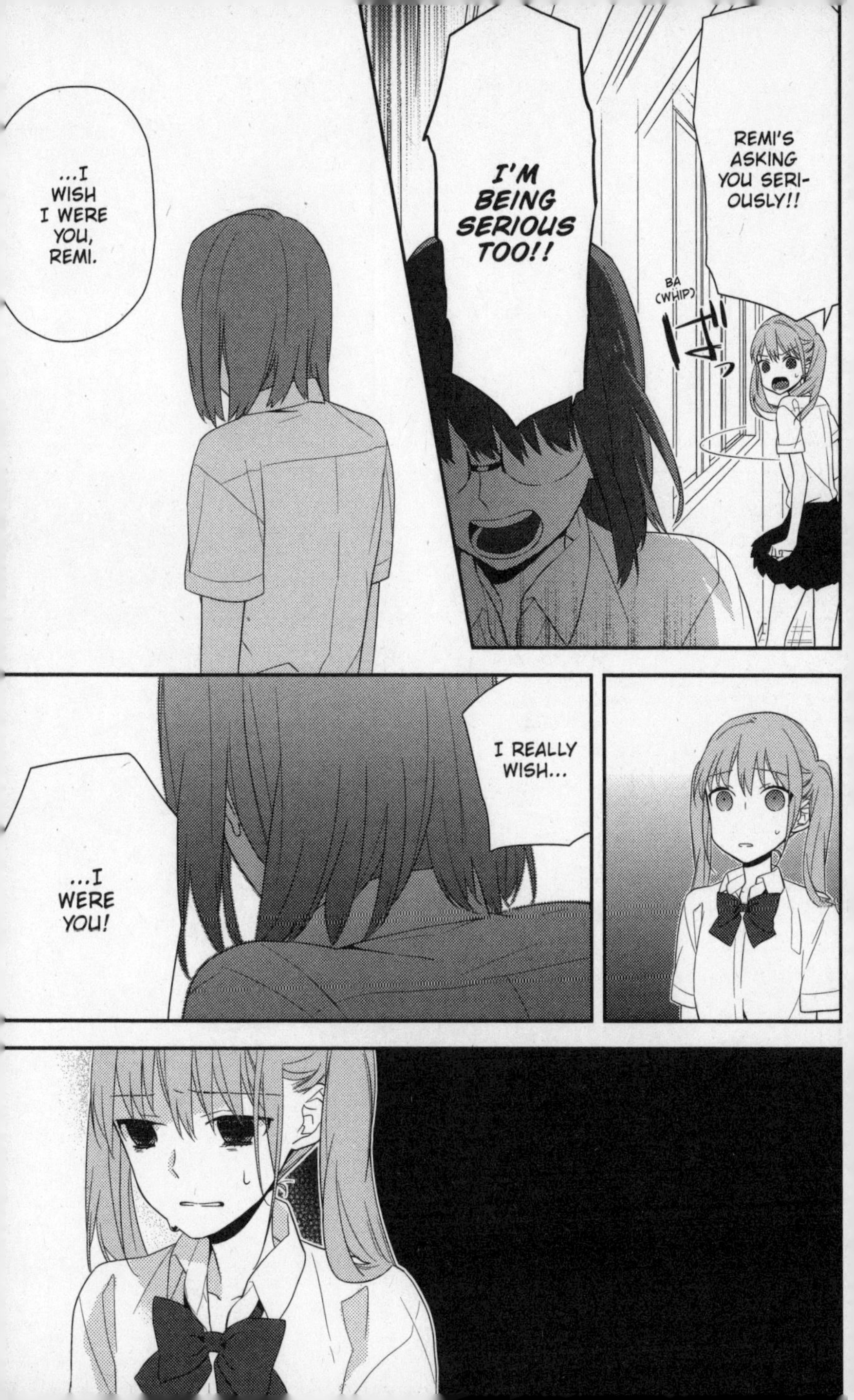
REMI'S ASKING YOU SERI-OUSLY!!
BA (WHIP)
I'M BEING SERIOUS TOO!!
...I WISH I WERE YOU, REMI.
I REALLY WISH...
...I WERE YOU!

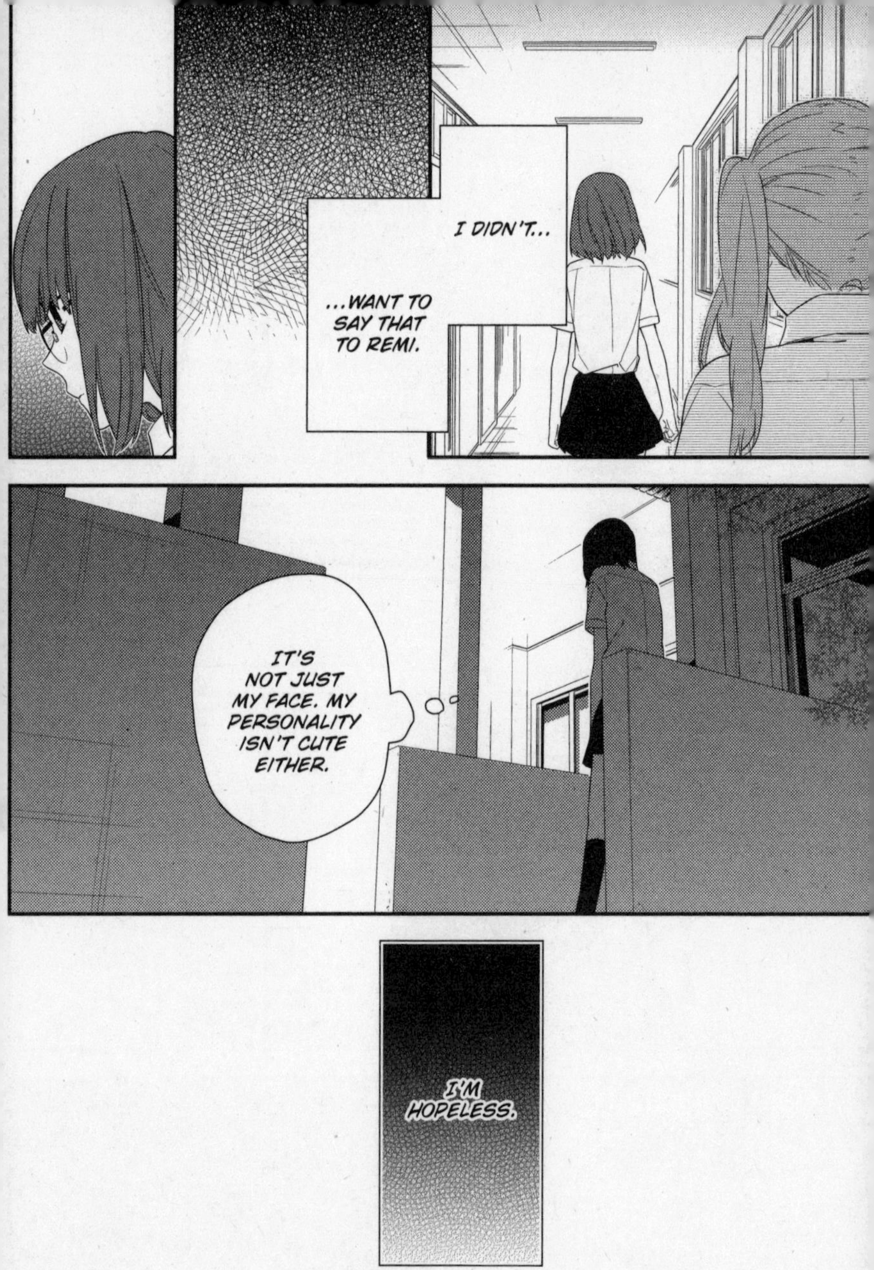
I DIDN'T...
...WANT TO SAY THAT TO REMI.
IT'S NOT JUST MY FACE. MY PERSONALITY ISN'T CUTE EITHER.
I'M HOPELESS.

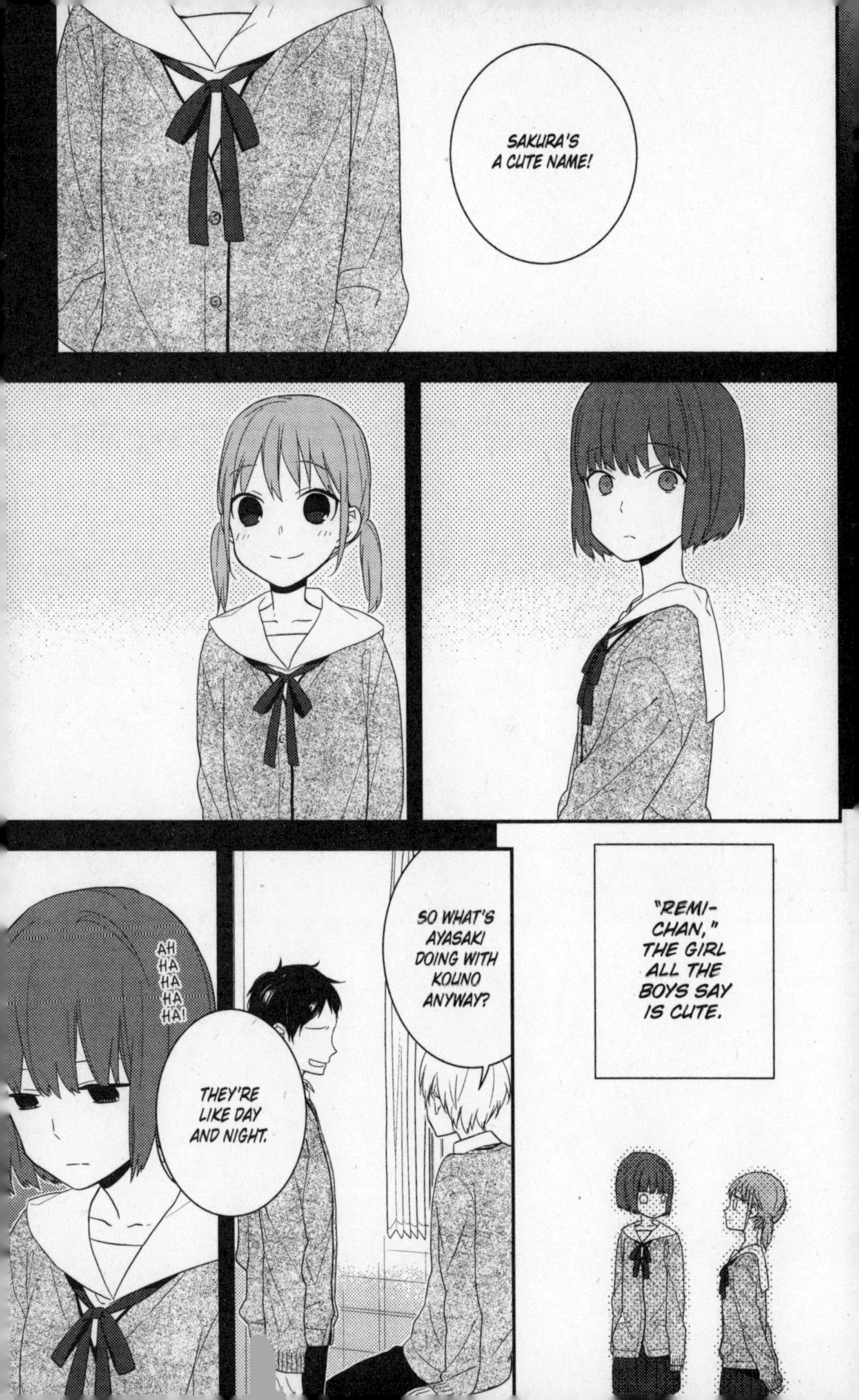
SAKURA'S A CUTE NAME!
"REMI-CHAN," THE GIRL ALL THE BOYS SAY IS CUTE.
SO WHAT'S AYASAKI DOING WITH KOUNO ANYWAY?
AH HA HA HA HA!
THEY'RE LIKE DAY AND NIGHT.

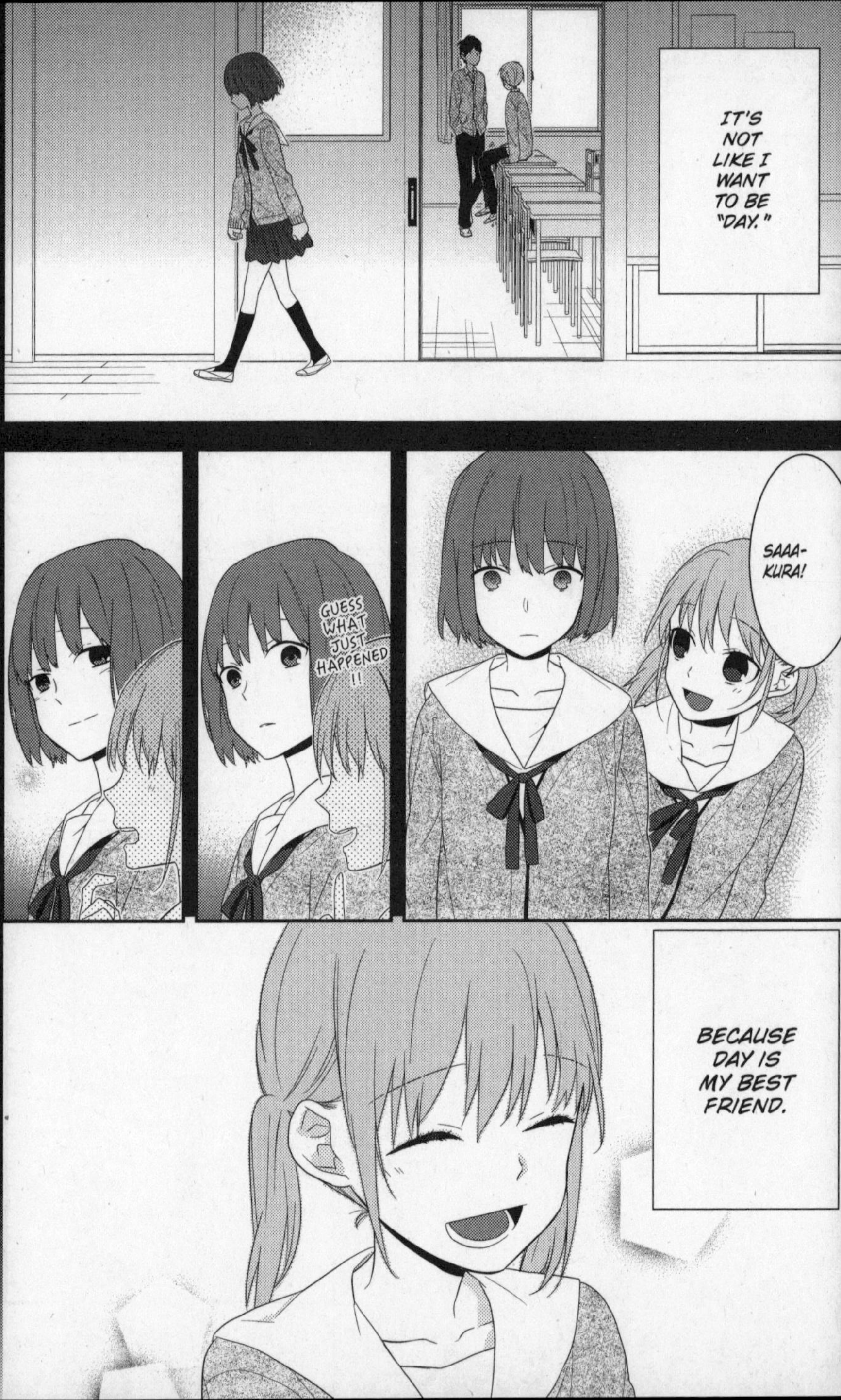
IT'S NOT LIKE I WANT TO BE "DAY."
SAAA-KURA!
GUESS WHAT JUST HAPPENED !!
BECAUSE DAY IS MY BEST FRIEND.

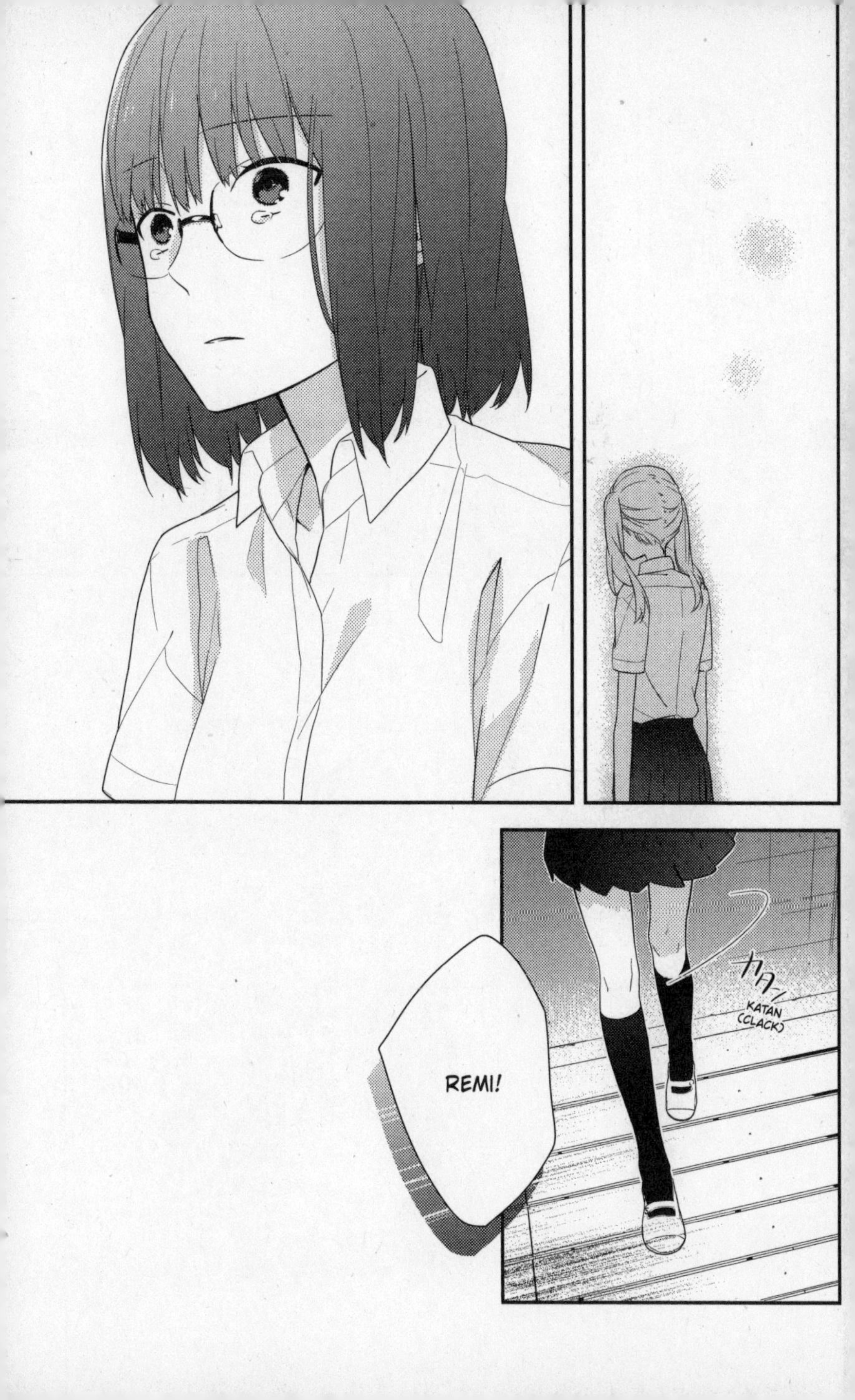
カタン
KATAN (CLACK)
REMI!

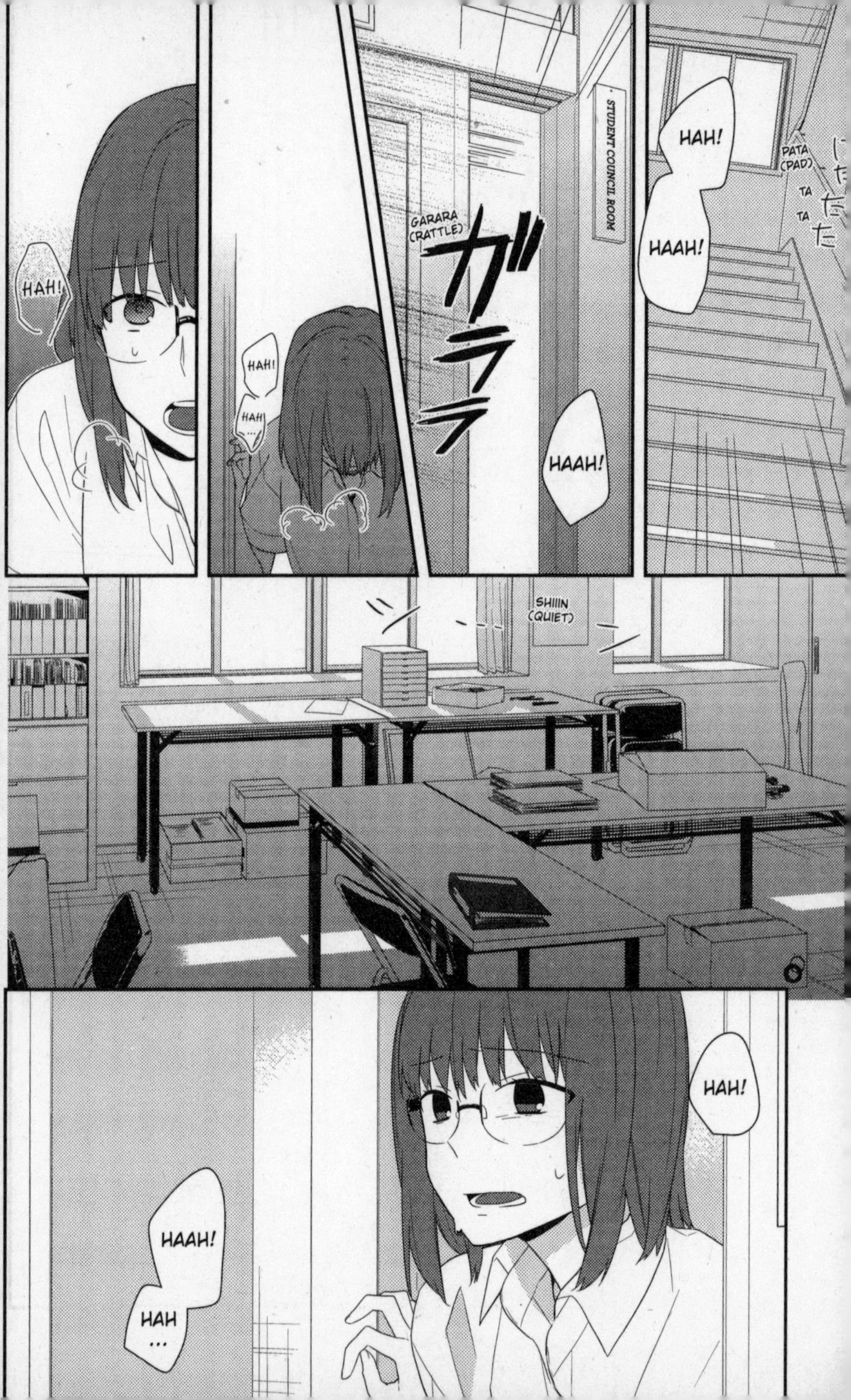
HAH!
PATA (PAD)
TA
TA
HAAH!
STUDENT COUNCIL ROOM
GARARA (RATTLE)
HAAH!
HAH!
HAH! ...
HAH!
SHIIN (QUIET)
HAH!
HAAH!
HAH ...

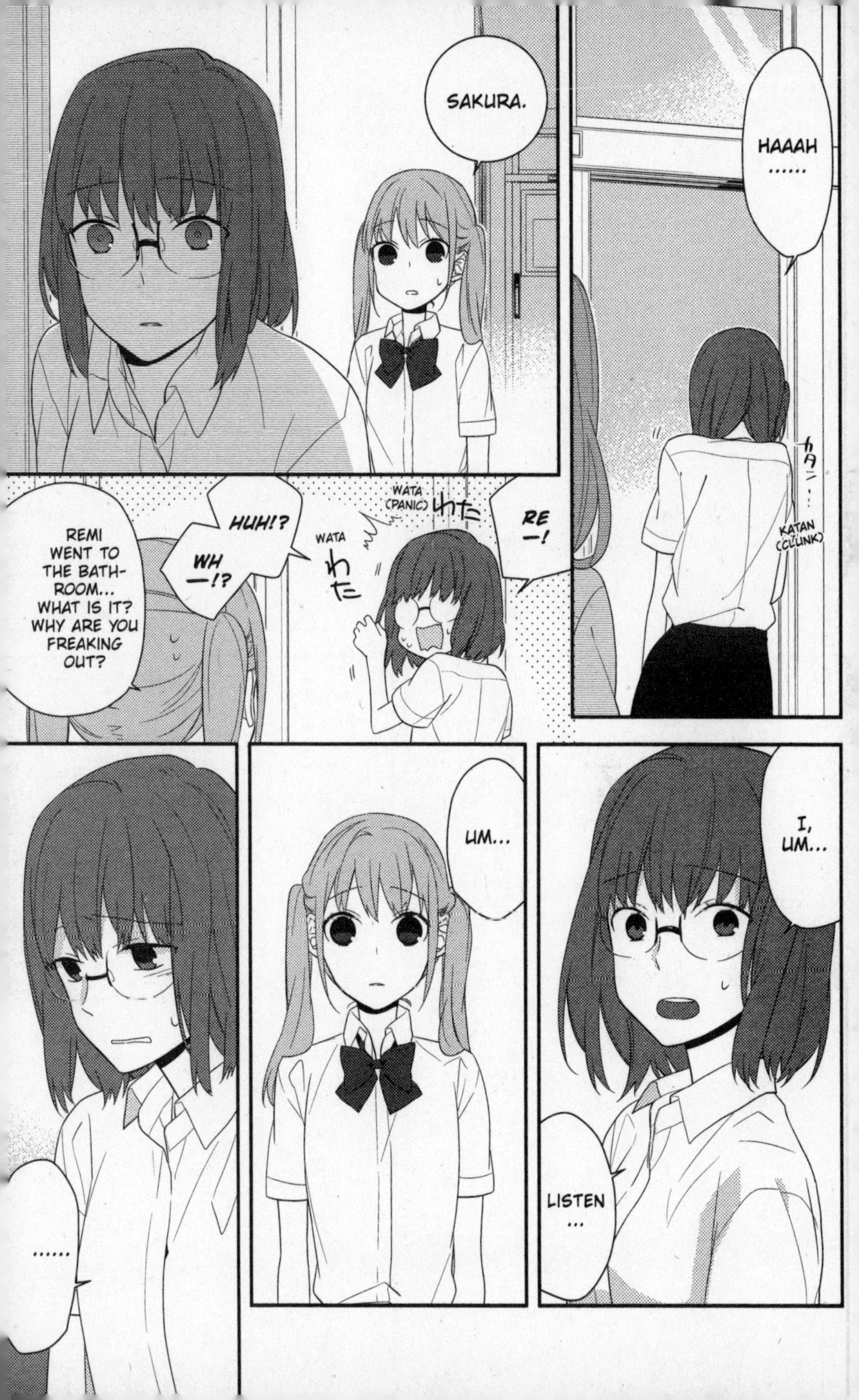
HAAAH ......
カタ…
KATAN (CLUNK)
SAKURA.
RE—!
WATA (PANIC) わた
WATA わた
HUH!?
WH—!?
REMI WENT TO THE BATH-ROOM... WHAT IS IT? WHY ARE YOU FREAKING OUT?
I, UM...
LISTEN ...
UM...
......

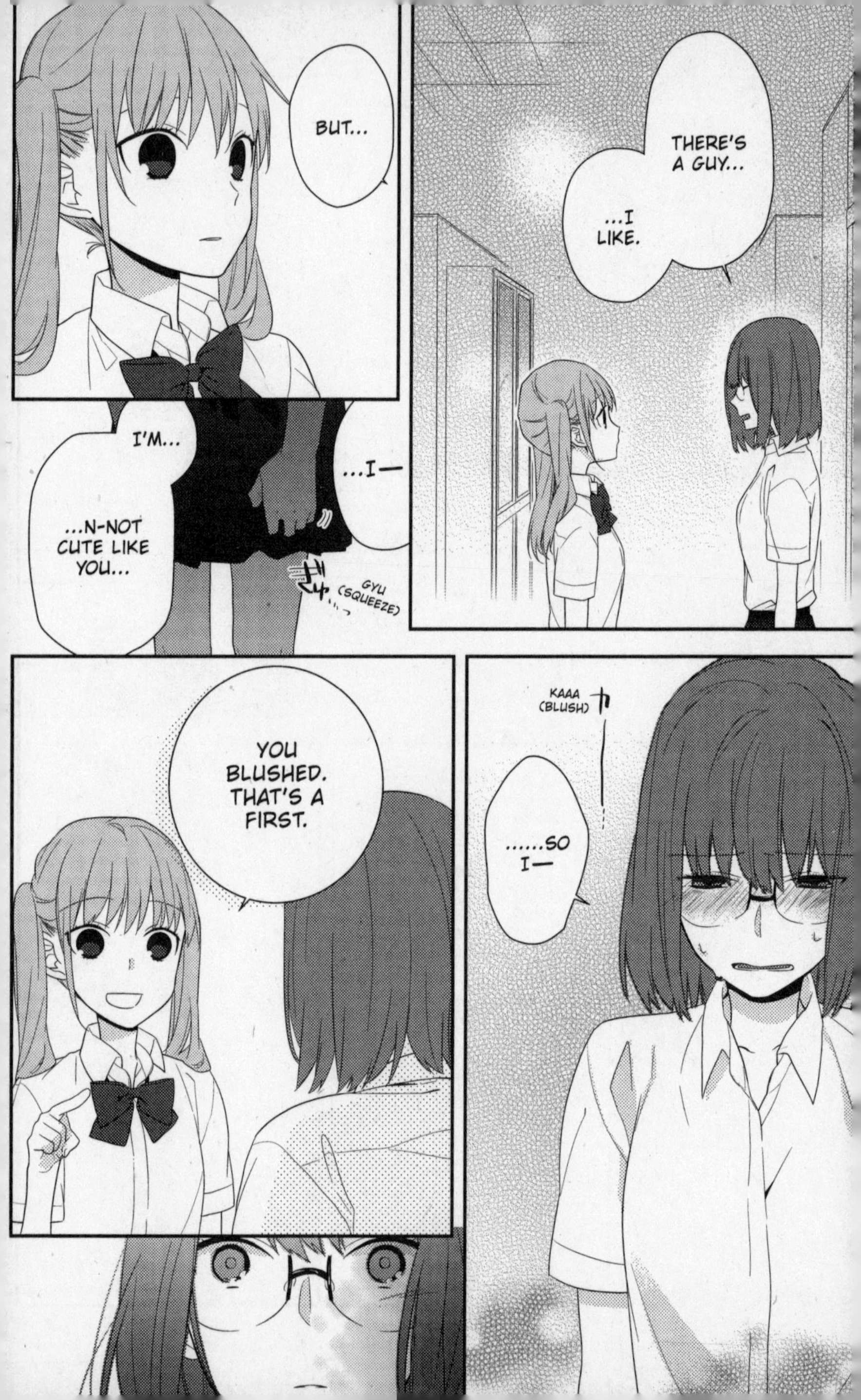
THERE'S A GUY...
...I LIKE.
BUT...
I'M...
...N-NOT CUTE LIKE YOU...
...I—
GYU (SQUEEZE)
KAAA (BLUSH)
......SO I—
YOU BLUSHED. THAT'S A FIRST.

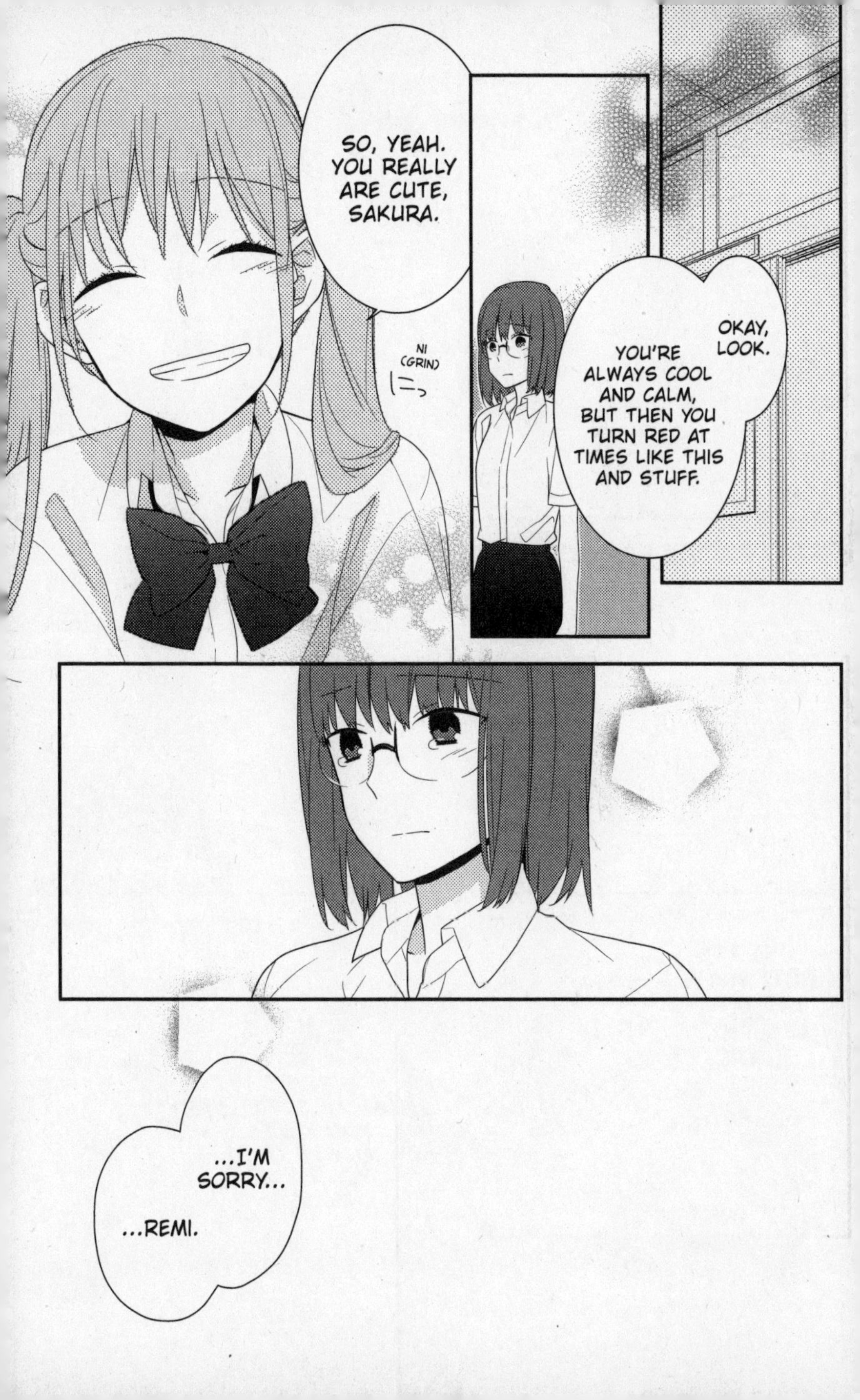
OKAY, LOOK. YOU'RE ALWAYS COOL AND CALM, BUT THEN YOU TURN RED AT TIMES LIKE THIS AND STUFF.
SO, YEAH. YOU REALLY ARE CUTE, SAKURA.
NI (GRIN)
...I'M SORRY...
...REMI.

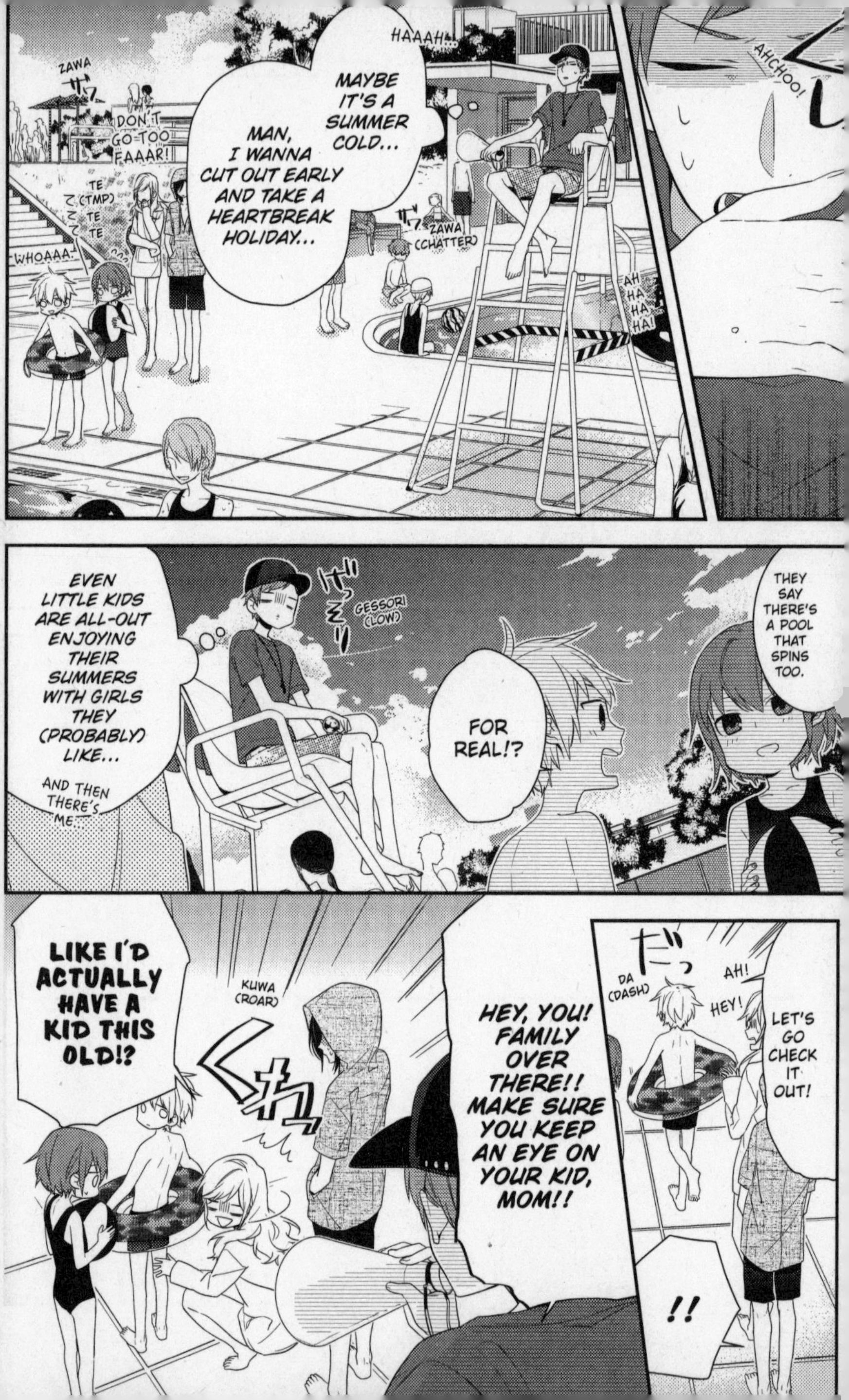
AHCHOO!
HAAAH...
MAYBE IT'S A SUMMER COLD...
MAN, I WANNA CUT OUT EARLY AND TAKE A HEARTBREAK HOLIDAY...
ZAWA
DON'T GO TOO FAAAR!
TE (TMP) TE TE
WHOAAA.
ZAWA (CHATTER)
AH HA HA HA!
THEY SAY THERE'S A POOL THAT SPINS TOO.
FOR REAL!?
GESSORI (LOW)
EVEN LITTLE KIDS ARE ALL-OUT ENJOYING THEIR SUMMERS WITH GIRLS THEY (PROBABLY) LIKE...
AND THEN THERE'S ME...
DA (DASH)
AH!
HEY!
LET'S GO CHECK IT OUT!
!!
HEY, YOU! FAMILY OVER THERE!! MAKE SURE YOU KEEP AN EYE ON YOUR KID, MOM!!
KUWA (ROAR)
LIKE I'D ACTUALLY HAVE A KID THIS OLD!?

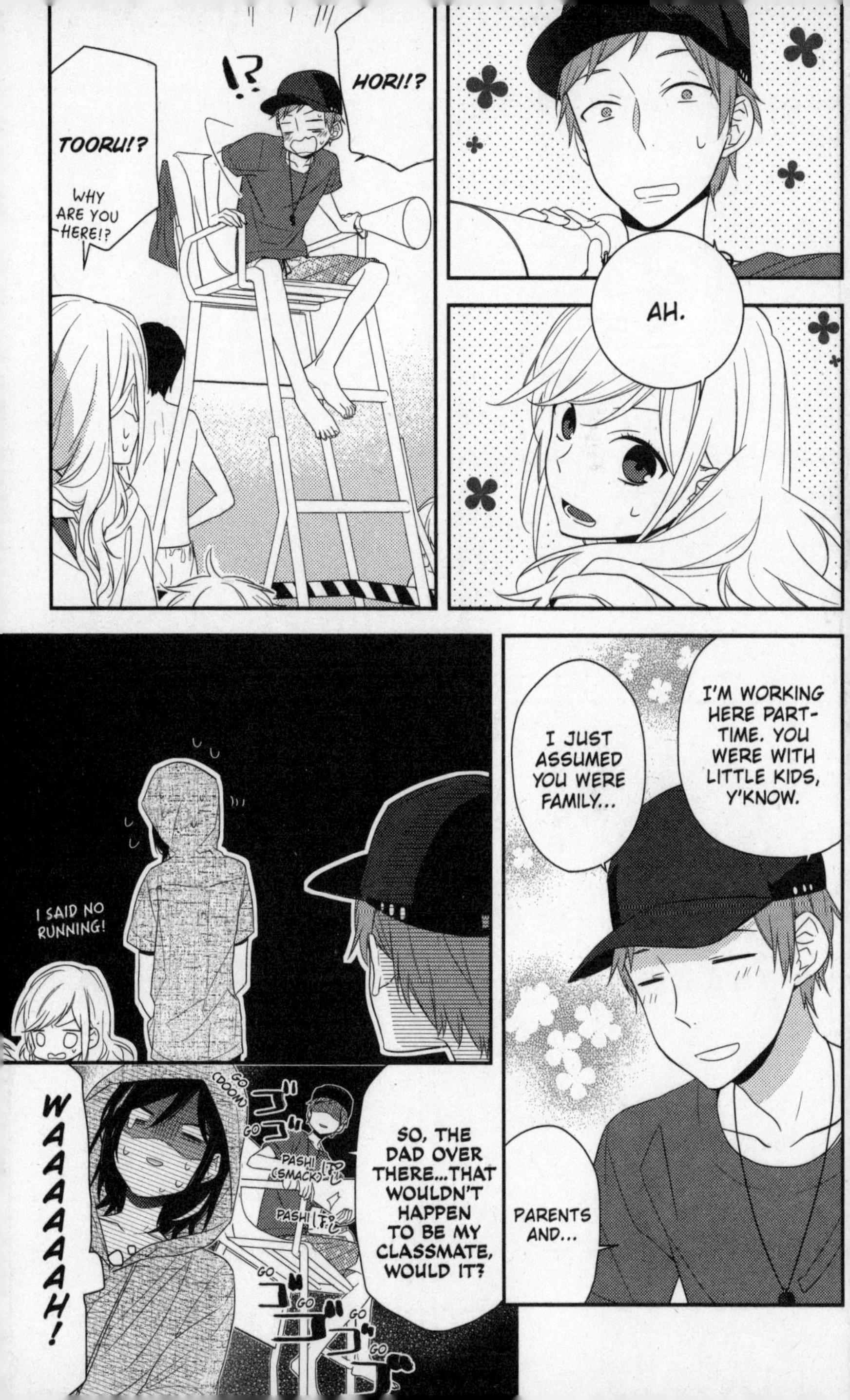
AH.
!?
HORI!?
TOORU!?
WHY ARE YOU HERE!?
I'M WORKING HERE PART-TIME. YOU WERE WITH LITTLE KIDS, Y'KNOW.
I JUST ASSUMED YOU WERE FAMILY...
PARENTS AND...
I SAID NO RUNNING!
SO, THE DAD OVER THERE...THAT WOULDN'T HAPPEN TO BE MY CLASSMATE, WOULD IT?
GO (DOOM)
GO
PASH! (SMACK)
PASH!
GO GO GO GO
WAAAAAAAAH!

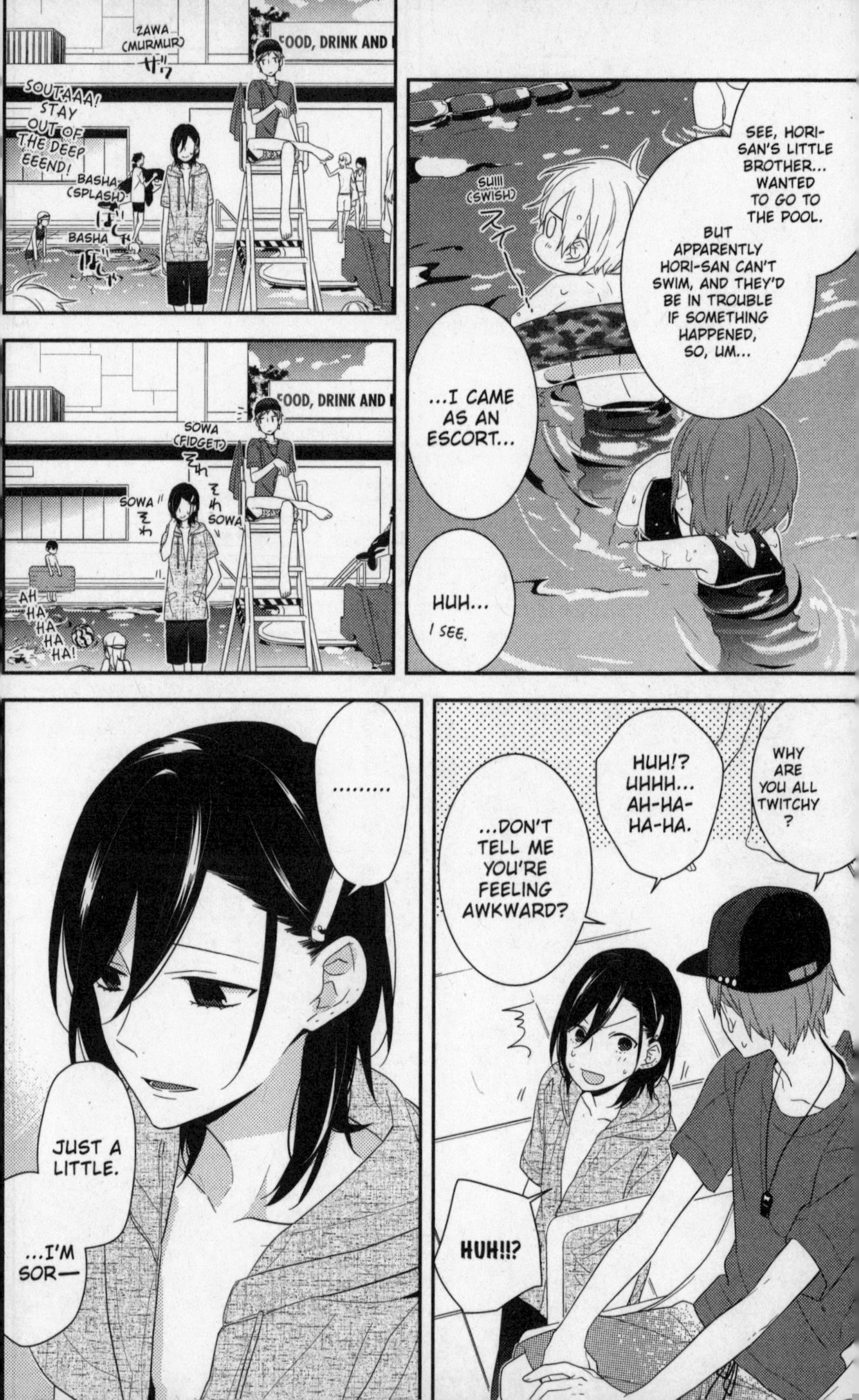
SEE, HORI-SAN'S LITTLE BROTHER... WANTED TO GO TO THE POOL.
BUT APPARENTLY HORI-SAN CAN'T SWIM, AND THEY'D BE IN TROUBLE IF SOMETHING HAPPENED, SO, UM...
SUIII (SWISH)
...I CAME AS AN ESCORT...
HUH... I SEE.
FOOD, DRINK AND
ZAWA (MURMUR)
SOUTAAA! STAY OUT OF THE DEEP EEEND!
BASHA (SPLASH)
BASHA
FOOD, DRINK AND
SOWA (FIDGET)
SOWA
SOWA
AH HA HA HA HA!
WHY ARE YOU ALL TWITCHY?
HUH!? UHHH... AH-HA-HA-HA.
...DON'T TELL ME YOU'RE FEELING AWKWARD?
HUH!!?
....
JUST A LITTLE.
...I'M SOR—

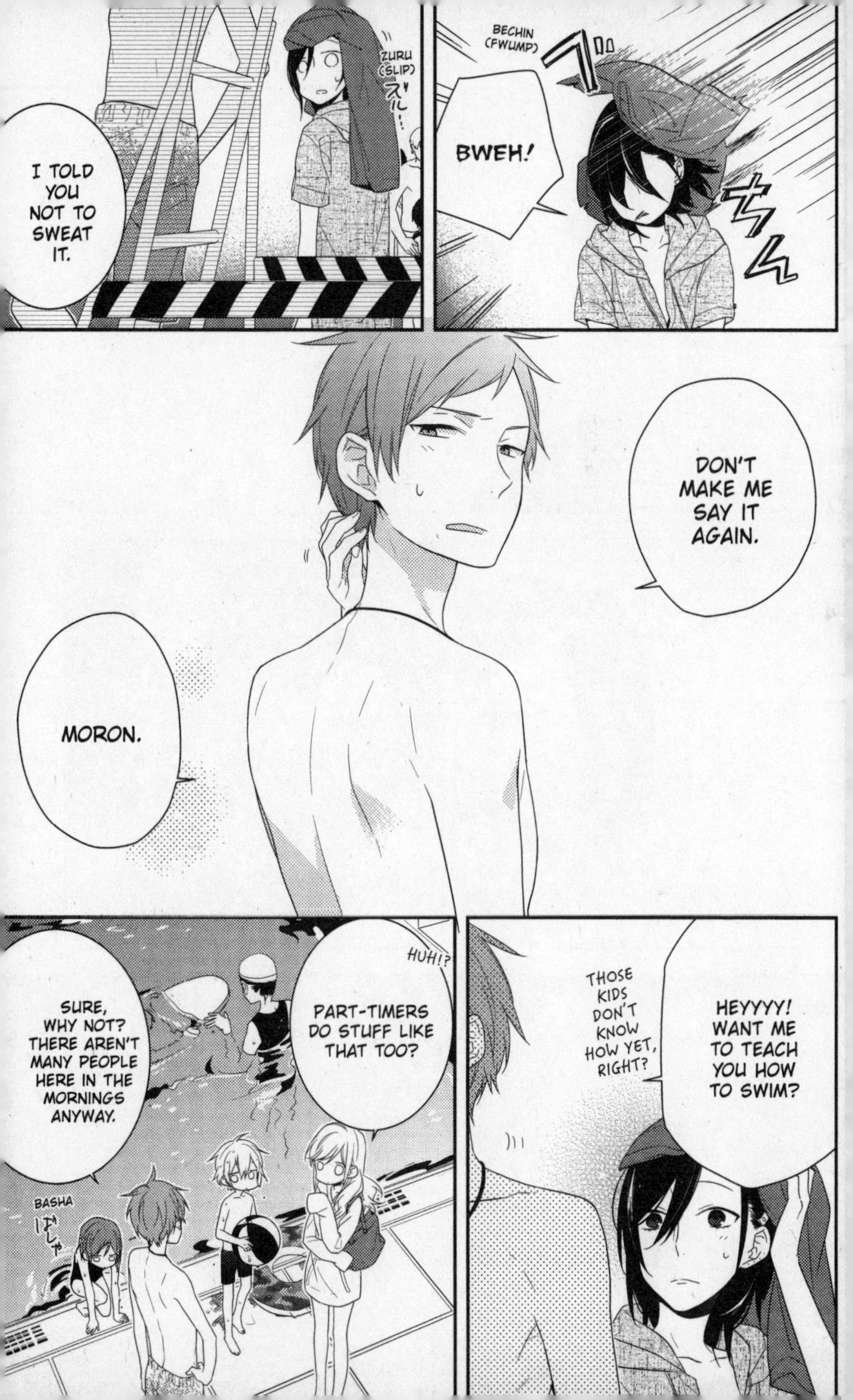
BECHIN (FWUMP)
BWEH!
ZURU (SLIP)
I TOLD YOU NOT TO SWEAT IT.
DON'T MAKE ME SAY IT AGAIN.
MORON.
HEYYYY! WANT ME TO TEACH YOU HOW TO SWIM?
THOSE KIDS DON'T KNOW HOW YET, RIGHT?
HUH!?
PART-TIMERS DO STUFF LIKE THAT TOO?
SURE, WHY NOT? THERE AREN'T MANY PEOPLE HERE IN THE MORNINGS ANYWAY.
BASHA

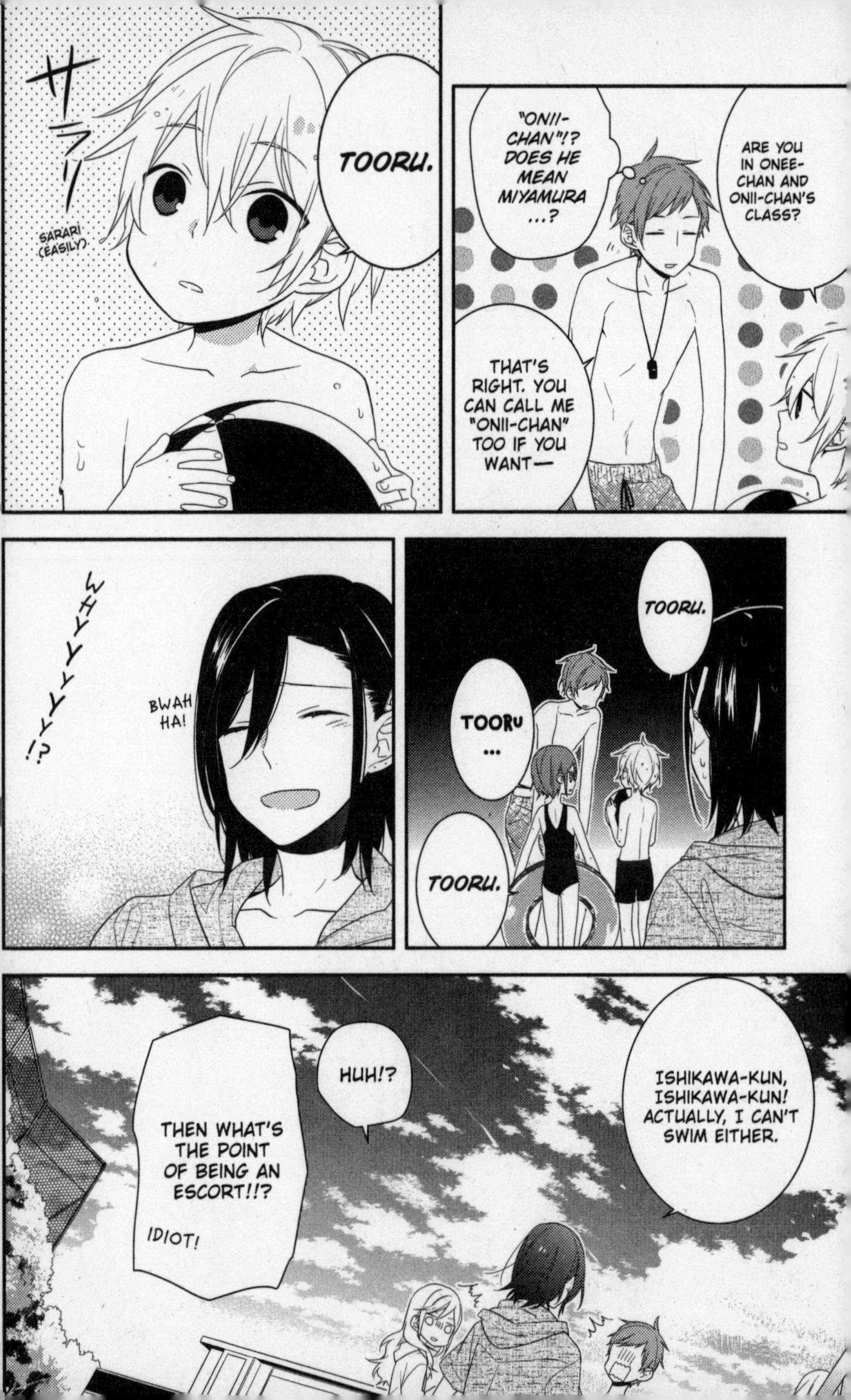
ARE YOU IN ONEE-CHAN AND ONII-CHAN'S CLASS?
"ONII-CHAN"!? DOES HE MEAN MIYAMURA ...?
THAT'S RIGHT. YOU CAN CALL ME "ONII-CHAN" TOO IF YOU WANT—
TOORU.
SARARI (EASILY)
TOORU.
TOORU ...
TOORU.
WHYYYYYYY!?
BWAH HA!
ISHIKAWA-KUN, ISHIKAWA-KUN! ACTUALLY, I CAN'T SWIM EITHER.
HUH!?
THEN WHAT'S THE POINT OF BEING AN ESCORT!!?
IDIOT!

HORIMIYA

HORIMIYA

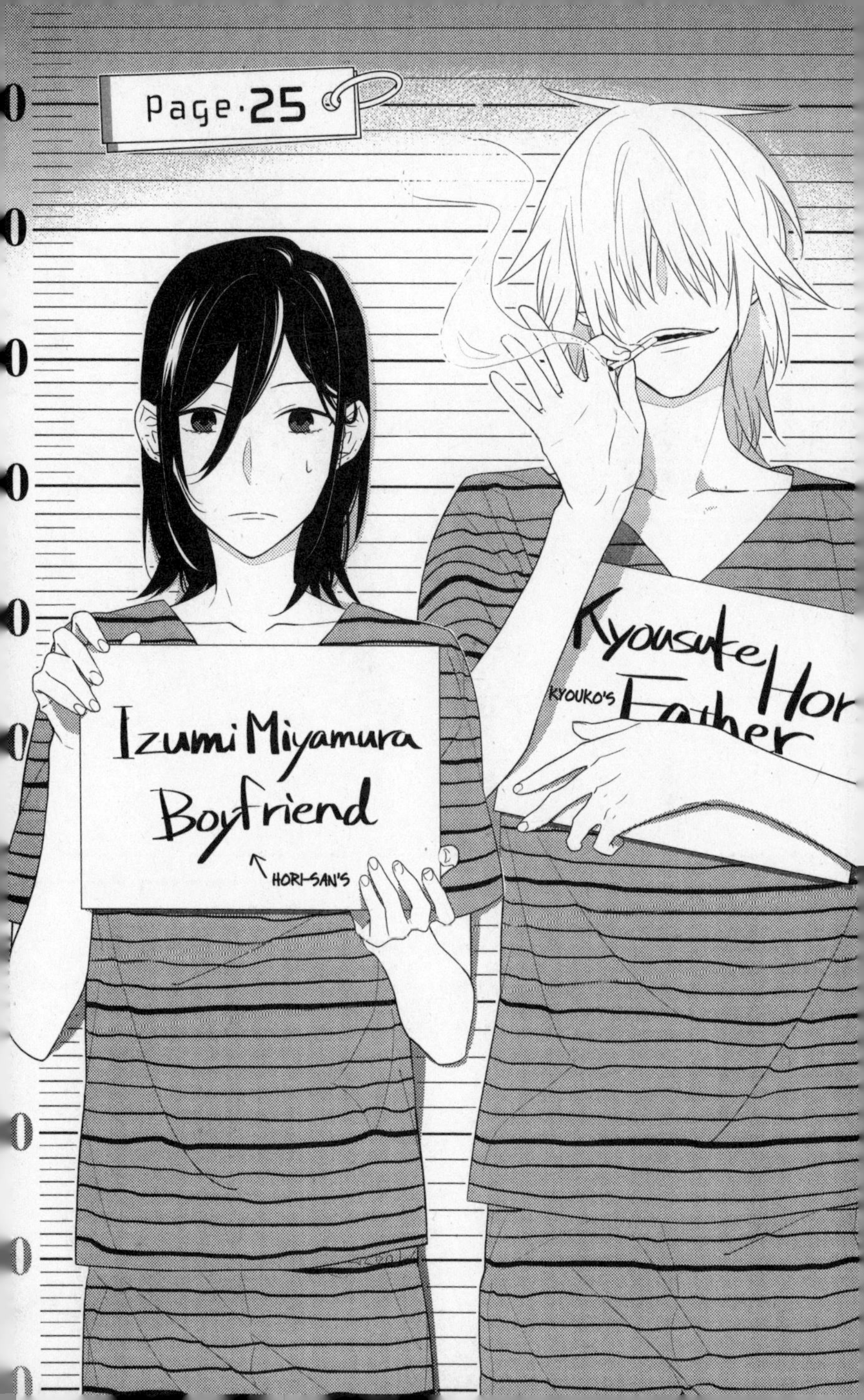
page·25
Kyousuke Hori
Kyouko's Father
Izumi Miyamura
Boyfriend
↑ Hori-san's

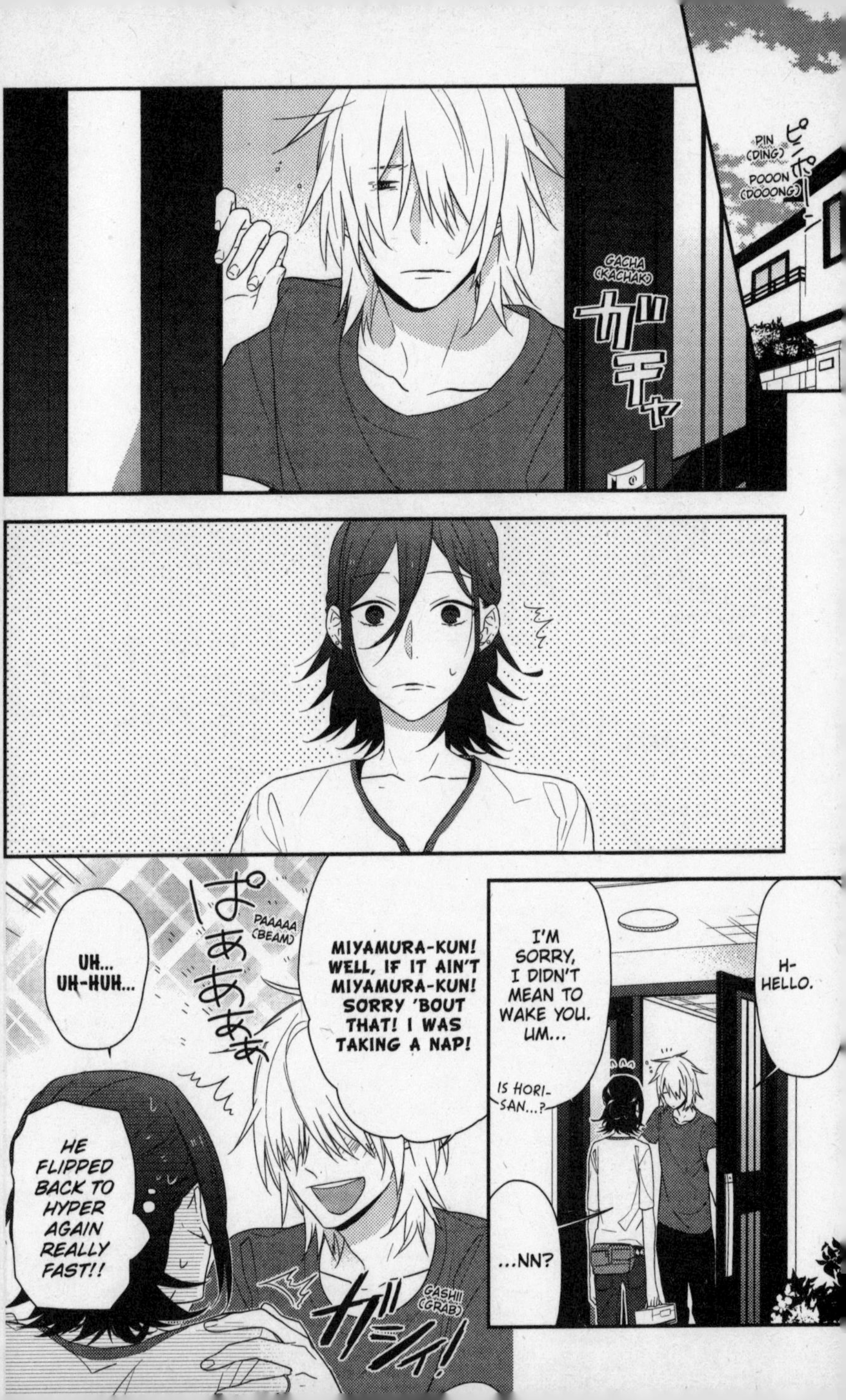
PIN (DING)
POOON (DOOONG)
GACHA (KACHAK)
H-HELLO.
I'M SORRY, I DIDN'T MEAN TO WAKE YOU. UM...
IS HORI-SAN...?
...NN?
MIYAMURA-KUN! WELL, IF IT AIN'T MIYAMURA-KUN! SORRY 'BOUT THAT! I WAS TAKING A NAP!
PAAAAA (BEAM)
UH... UH-HUH...
HE FLIPPED BACK TO HYPER AGAIN REALLY FAST!!
GASHI! (GRAB)

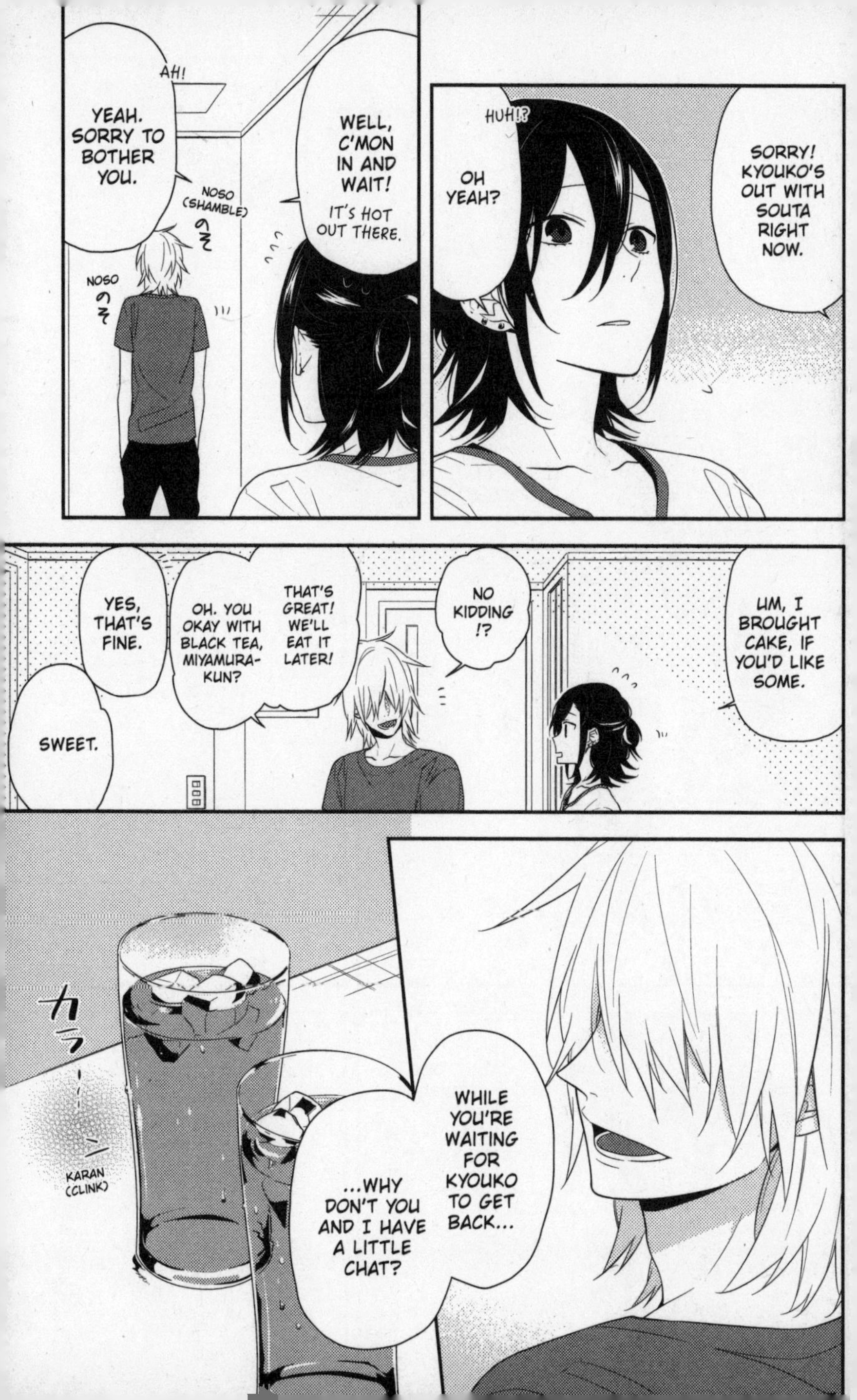
SORRY! KYOUKO'S OUT WITH SOUTA RIGHT NOW.
HUH!?
OH YEAH?
WELL, C'MON IN AND WAIT!
IT'S HOT OUT THERE.
AH!
YEAH. SORRY TO BOTHER YOU.
NOSO (SHAMBLE)
NOSO
UM, I BROUGHT CAKE, IF YOU'D LIKE SOME.
NO KIDDING !?
THAT'S GREAT! WE'LL EAT IT LATER!
OH. YOU OKAY WITH BLACK TEA, MIYAMURA-KUN?
YES, THAT'S FINE.
SWEET.
WHILE YOU'RE WAITING FOR KYOUKO TO GET BACK...
...WHY DON'T YOU AND I HAVE A LITTLE CHAT?
KARAN (CLINK)

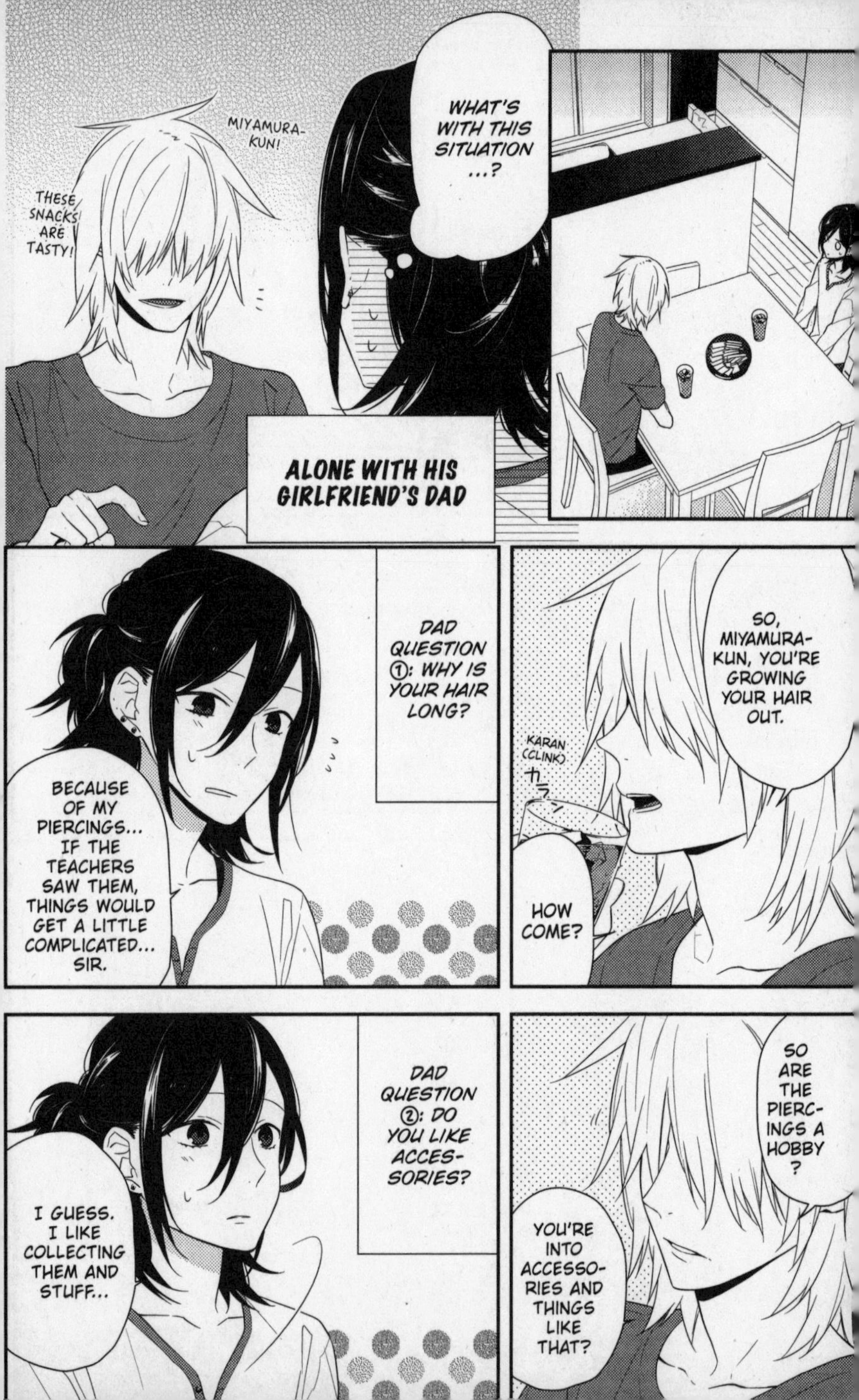
WHAT'S WITH THIS SITUATION ...?
MIYAMURA-KUN!
THESE SNACKS ARE TASTY!
ALONE WITH HIS GIRLFRIEND'S DAD
SO, MIYAMURA-KUN, YOU'RE GROWING YOUR HAIR OUT.
KARAN (CLINK)
カラン
HOW COME?
DAD QUESTION ①: WHY IS YOUR HAIR LONG?
BECAUSE OF MY PIERCINGS... IF THE TEACHERS SAW THEM, THINGS WOULD GET A LITTLE COMPLICATED... SIR.
SO ARE THE PIERCINGS A HOBBY?
YOU'RE INTO ACCESSORIES AND THINGS LIKE THAT?
DAD QUESTION ②: DO YOU LIKE ACCESSORIES?
I GUESS. I LIKE COLLECTING THEM AND STUFF...

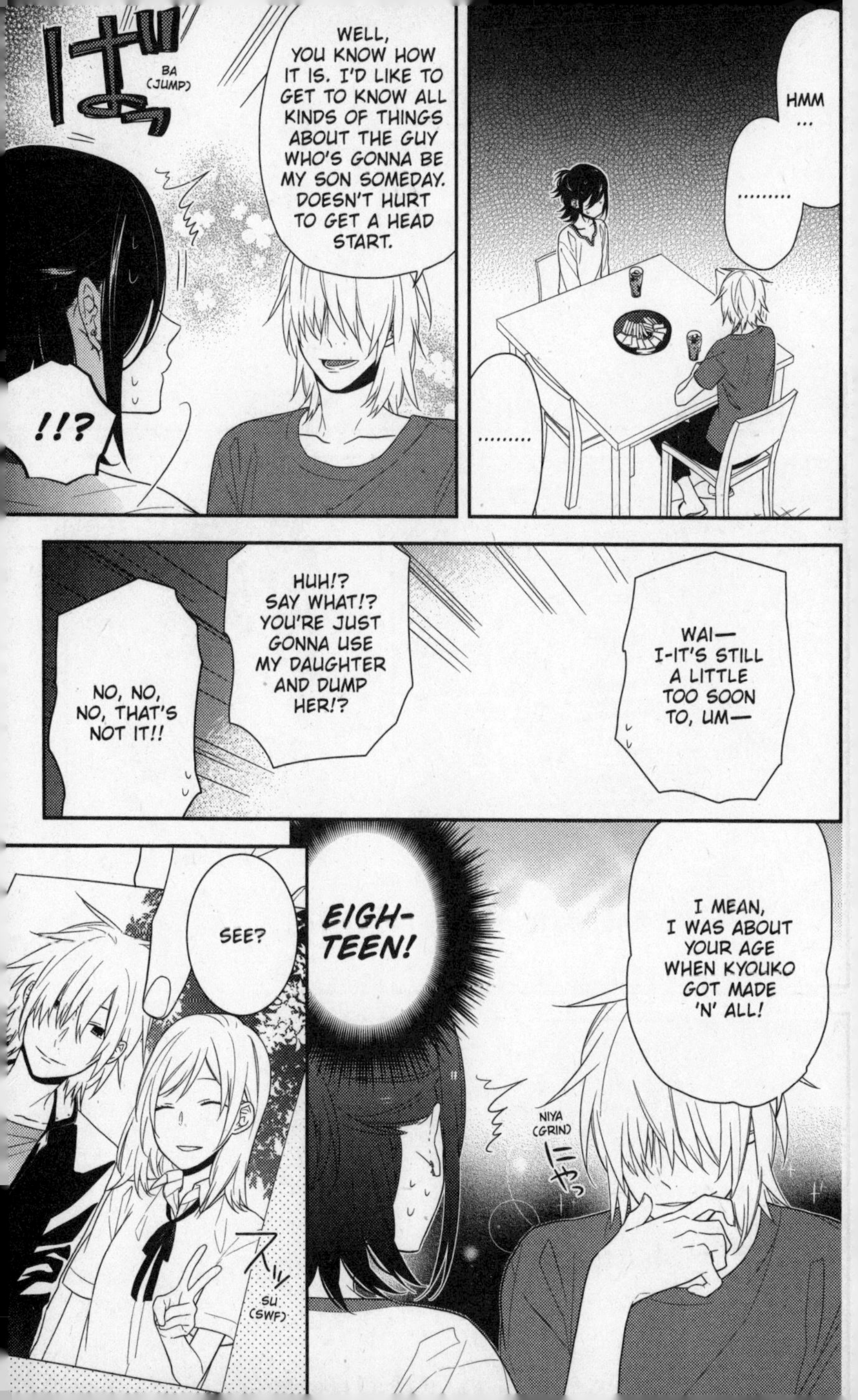
HMM ...
....
....
WELL, YOU KNOW HOW IT IS. I'D LIKE TO GET TO KNOW ALL KINDS OF THINGS ABOUT THE GUY WHO'S GONNA BE MY SON SOMEDAY. DOESN'T HURT TO GET A HEAD START.
ばっ
BA (JUMP)
!!?
WAI— I-IT'S STILL A LITTLE TOO SOON TO, UM—
HUH!? SAY WHAT!? YOU'RE JUST GONNA USE MY DAUGHTER AND DUMP HER!?
NO, NO, NO, THAT'S NOT IT!!
I MEAN, I WAS ABOUT YOUR AGE WHEN KYOUKO GOT MADE 'N' ALL!
NIYA (GRIN)
にやっ
EIGH-TEEN!
SEE?
スッ
SU (SWF)

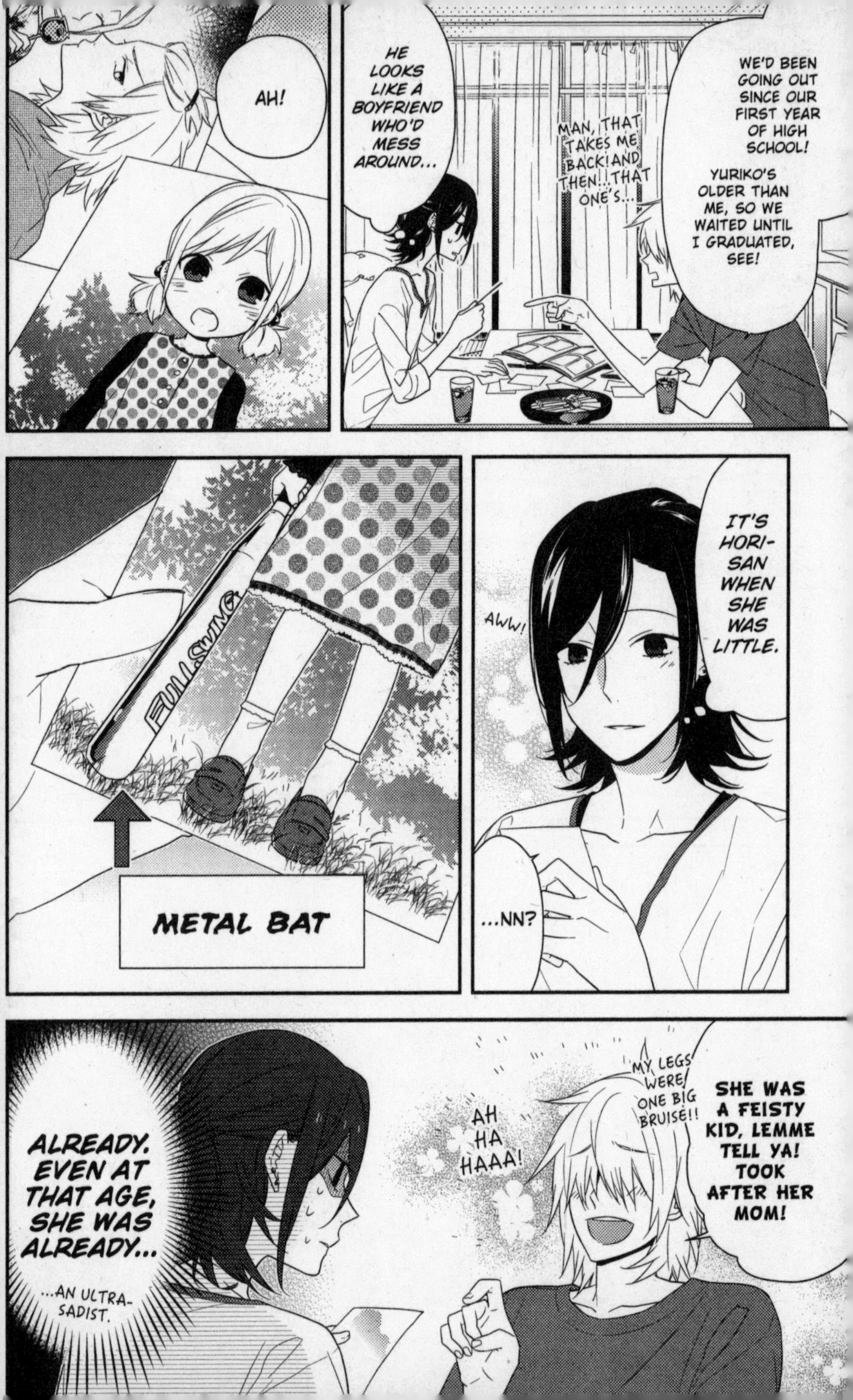
WE'D BEEN GOING OUT SINCE OUR FIRST YEAR OF HIGH SCHOOL!
YURIKO'S OLDER THAN ME, SO WE WAITED UNTIL I GRADUATED, SEE!
MAN, THAT TAKES ME BACK! AND THEN... THAT ONE'S...
HE LOOKS LIKE A BOYFRIEND WHO'D MESS AROUND...
AH!
IT'S HORI-SAN WHEN SHE WAS LITTLE.
AWW!
...NN?
FULLSWING
METAL BAT
SHE WAS A FEISTY KID, LEMME TELL YA! TOOK AFTER HER MOM!
MY LEGS WERE ONE BIG BRUISE!!
AH HA HAAA!
ALREADY. EVEN AT THAT AGE, SHE WAS ALREADY...
...AN ULTRA-SADIST.

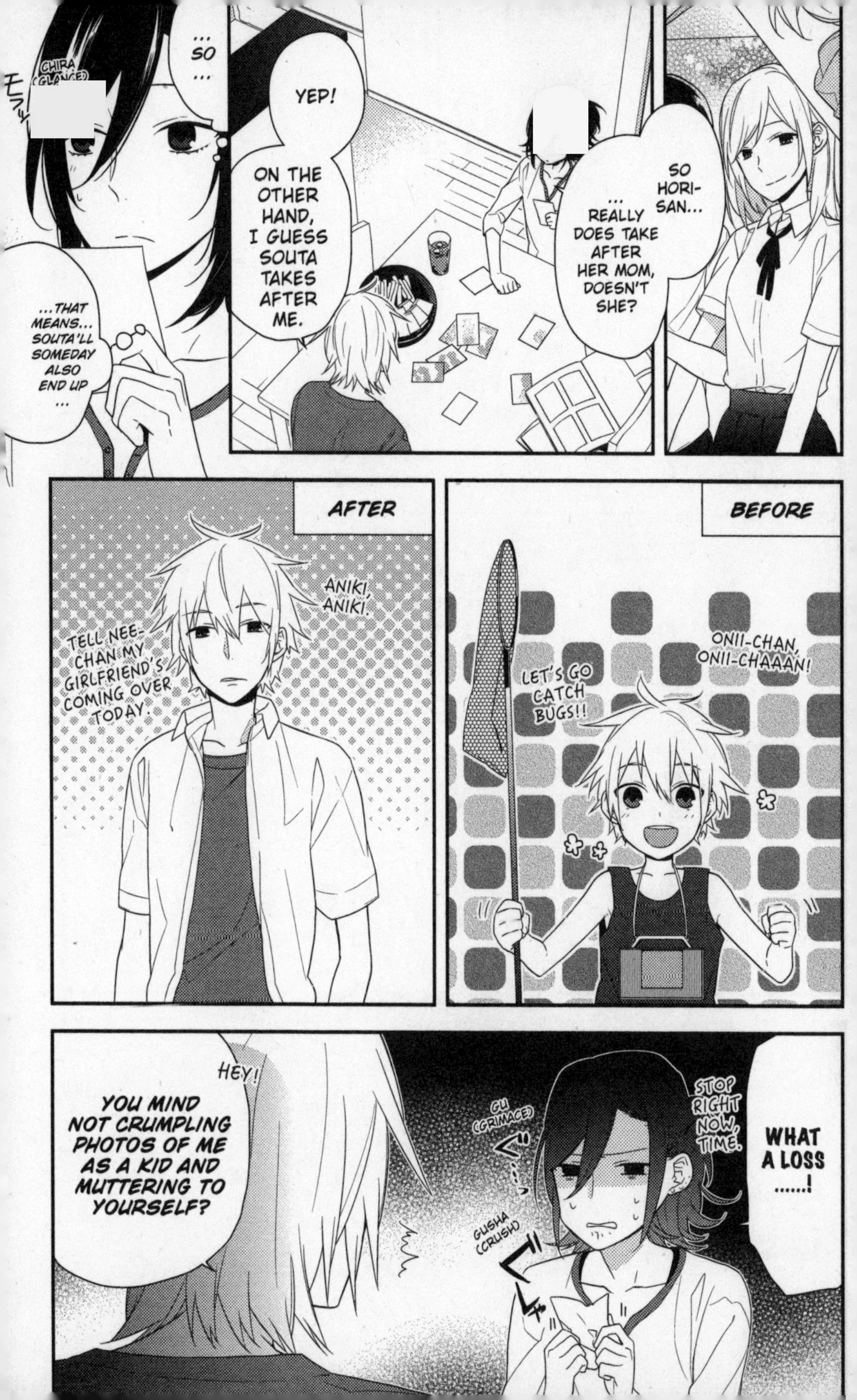
SO HORI-SAN... ...REALLY DOES TAKE AFTER HER MOM, DOESN'T SHE?
YEP!
ON THE OTHER HAND, I GUESS SOUTA TAKES AFTER ME.
...SO...
CHIRA (GLANCE)
...THAT MEANS... SOUTA'LL SOMEDAY ALSO END UP ...
BEFORE
ONII-CHAN, ONII-CHAAAN!
LET'S GO CATCH BUGS!!
AFTER
ANIKI, ANIKI.
TELL NEE-CHAN MY GIRLFRIEND'S COMING OVER TODAY.
WHAT A LOSS ......!
STOP RIGHT NOW, TIME.
GU (GRIMACE)
GUSHA (CRUSH)
HEY!
YOU MIND NOT CRUMPLING PHOTOS OF ME AS A KID AND MUTTERING TO YOURSELF?

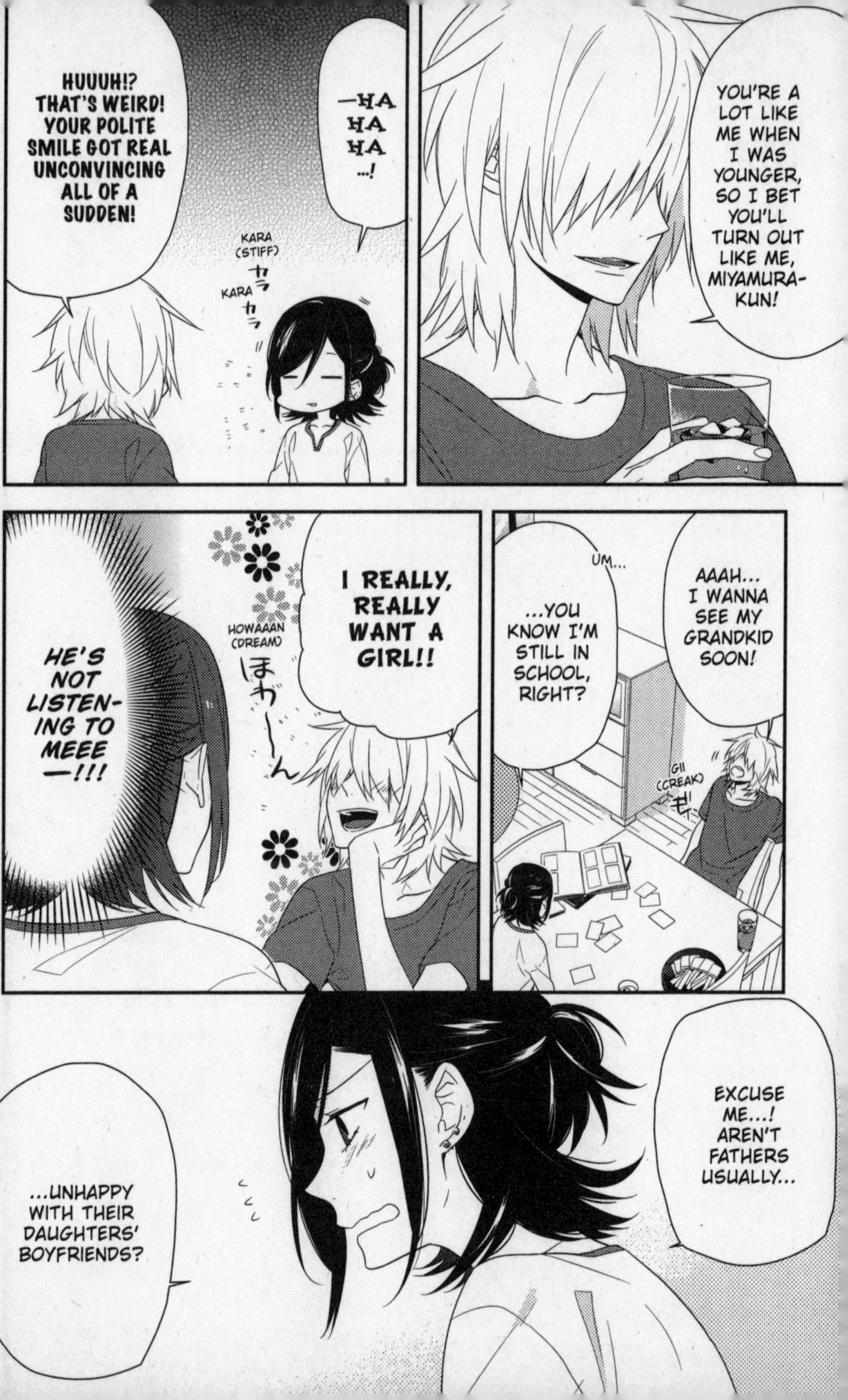
YOU'RE A LOT LIKE ME WHEN I WAS YOUNGER, SO I BET YOU'LL TURN OUT LIKE ME, MIYAMURA-KUN!
—HA HA HA ...!
HUUUH!? THAT'S WEIRD! YOUR POLITE SMILE GOT REAL UNCONVINCING ALL OF A SUDDEN!
KARA (STIFF) カラ
KARA カラ
AAAH... I WANNA SEE MY GRANDKID SOON!
UM...
...YOU KNOW I'M STILL IN SCHOOL, RIGHT?
GII (CREAK)
I REALLY, REALLY WANT A GIRL!!
HOWAAAN (DREAM)
HE'S NOT LISTENING TO MEEE—!!!
EXCUSE ME...! AREN'T FATHERS USUALLY...
...UNHAPPY WITH THEIR DAUGHTERS' BOYFRIENDS?

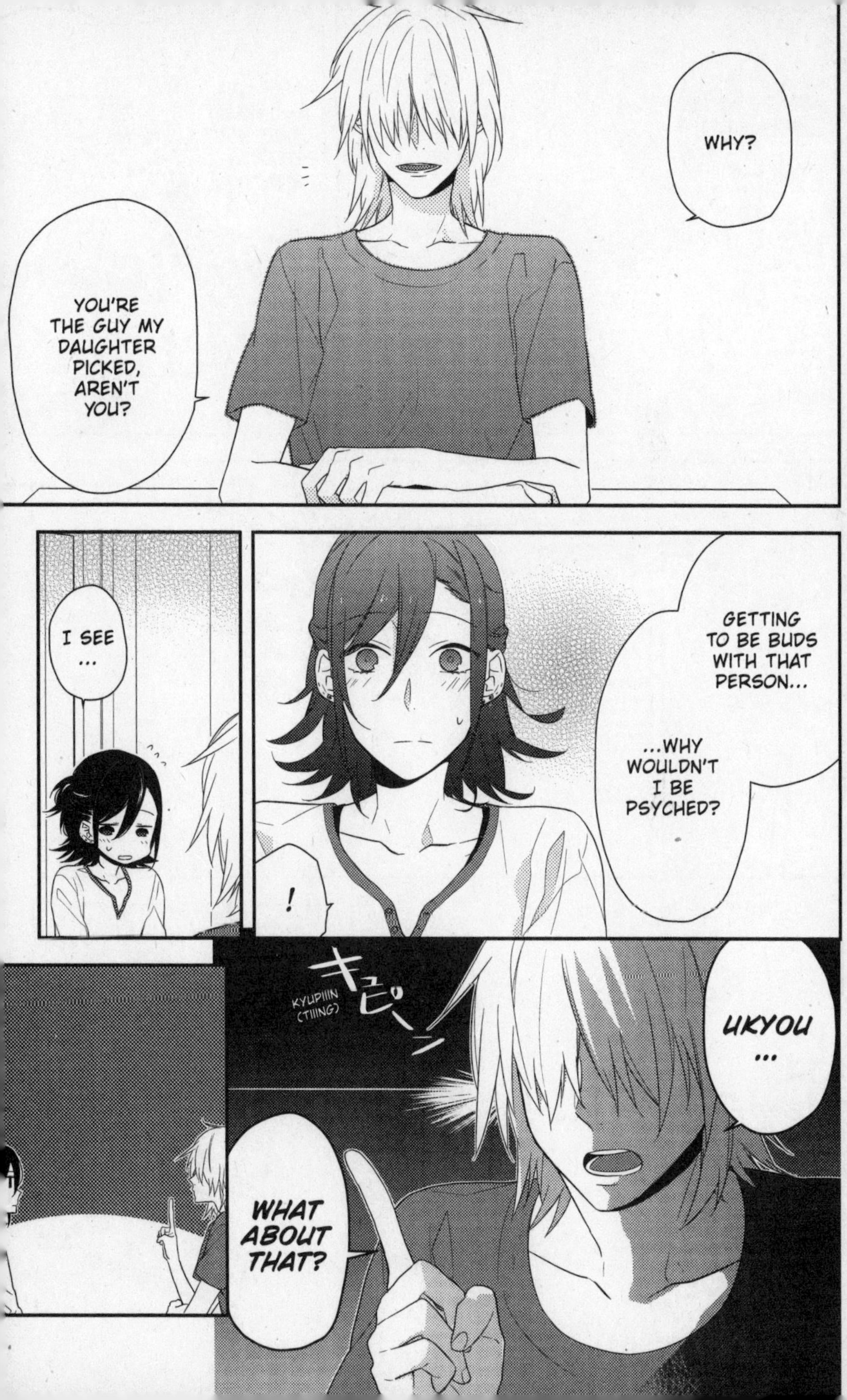
WHY?
YOU'RE THE GUY MY DAUGHTER PICKED, AREN'T YOU?
GETTING TO BE BUDS WITH THAT PERSON...
...WHY WOULDN'T I BE PSYCHED?
!
I SEE ...
UKYOU ...
キュピーン
KYUPIIIN (TIIING)
WHAT ABOUT THAT?

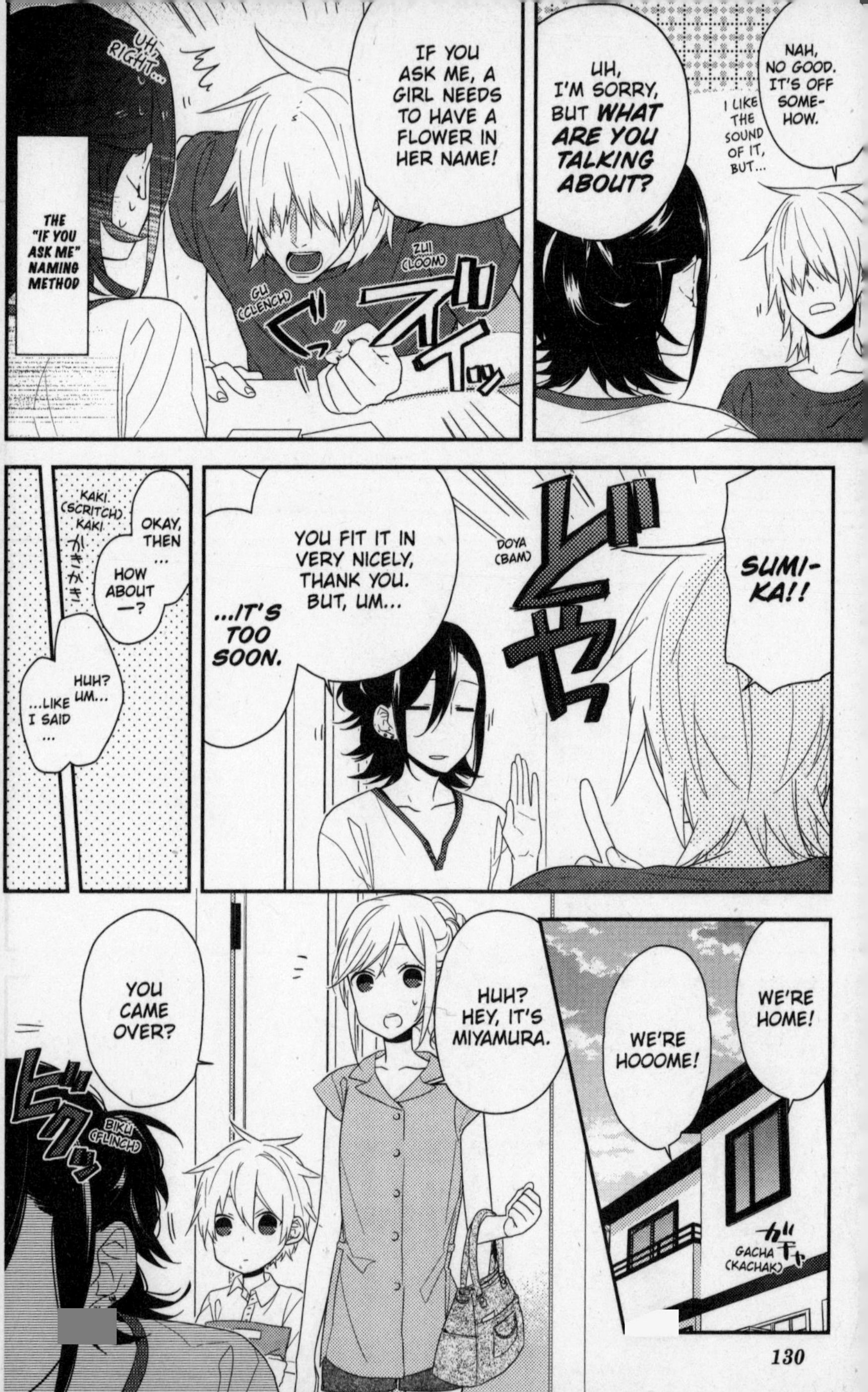
NAH, NO GOOD. IT'S OFF SOME-HOW.
I LIKE THE SOUND OF IT, BUT...
UH, I'M SORRY, BUT WHAT ARE YOU TALKING ABOUT?
IF YOU ASK ME, A GIRL NEEDS TO HAVE A FLOWER IN HER NAME!
UH, RIGHT...
ZUI (LOOM)
GU (CLENCH)
THE "IF YOU ASK ME" NAMING METHOD
SUMI-KA!!
DOYA (BAM)
YOU FIT IT IN VERY NICELY, THANK YOU. BUT, UM...
...IT'S TOO SOON.
KAKI (SCRITCH) KAKI
OKAY, THEN... HOW ABOUT—?
HUH? UM...
...LIKE I SAID...
WE'RE HOME!
WE'RE HOOOME!
GACHA (KACHAK)
HUH? HEY, IT'S MIYAMURA.
YOU CAME OVER?
BIKU (FLINCH)

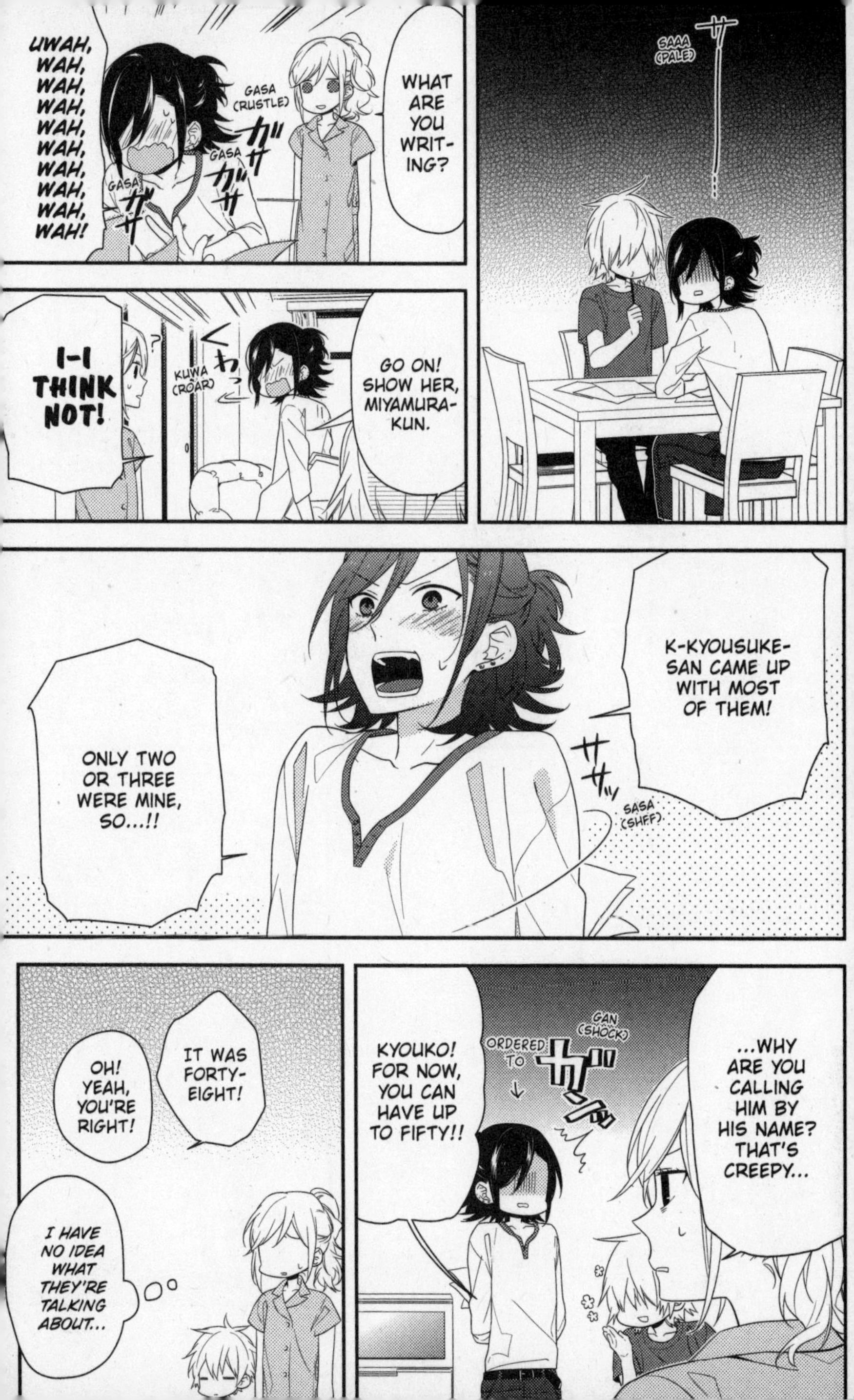

SAAA (PALE)
WHAT ARE YOU WRITING?
GASA (RUSTLE)
GASA
GASA
UWAH, WAH, WAH, WAH, WAH, WAH, WAH, WAH, WAH, WAH!
GO ON! SHOW HER, MIYAMURA-KUN.
KUWA (ROAR)
?
I-I THINK NOT!
K-KYOUSUKE-SAN CAME UP WITH MOST OF THEM!
SASA (SHFF)
ONLY TWO OR THREE WERE MINE, SO...!!
...WHY ARE YOU CALLING HIM BY HIS NAME? THAT'S CREEPY...
GAN (SHOCK)
ORDERED TO
KYOUKO! FOR NOW, YOU CAN HAVE UP TO FIFTY!!
IT WAS FORTY-EIGHT!
OH! YEAH, YOU'RE RIGHT!
I HAVE NO IDEA WHAT THEY'RE TALKING ABOUT...

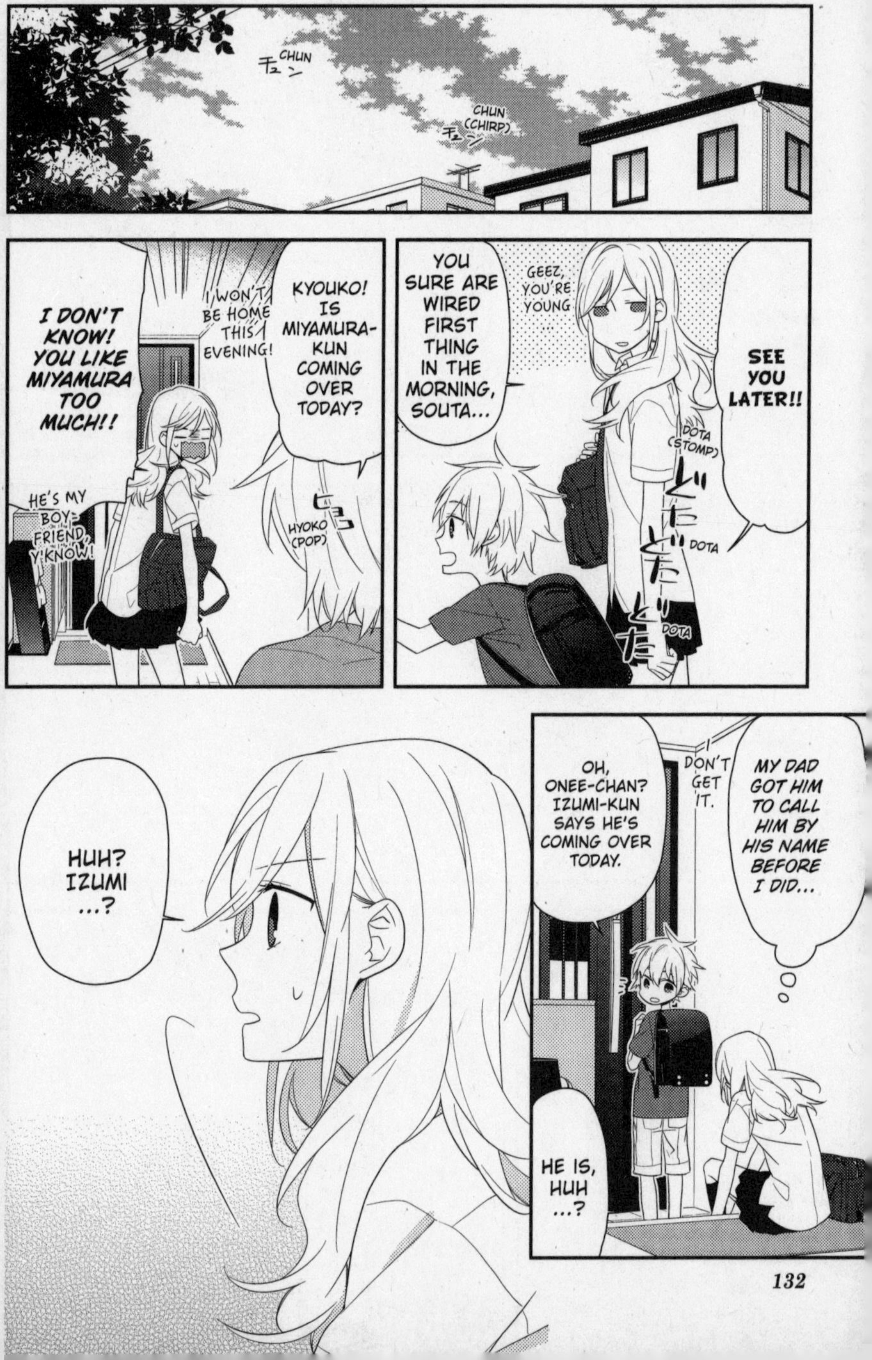
CHUN
チュン
CHUN (CHIRP)
SEE YOU LATER!!
DOTA (STOMP)
DOTA
DOTA
GEEZ, YOU'RE YOUNG...
YOU SURE ARE WIRED FIRST THING IN THE MORNING, SOUTA...
KYOUKO! IS MIYAMURA-KUN COMING OVER TODAY?
I WON'T BE HOME THIS EVENING!
HYOKO (POP)
I DON'T KNOW! YOU LIKE MIYAMURA TOO MUCH!!
HE'S MY BOYFRIEND, Y'KNOW!
MY DAD GOT HIM TO CALL HIM BY HIS NAME BEFORE I DID...
I DON'T GET IT.
OH, ONEE-CHAN? IZUMI-KUN SAYS HE'S COMING OVER TODAY.
HE IS, HUH...?
HUH? IZUMI...?

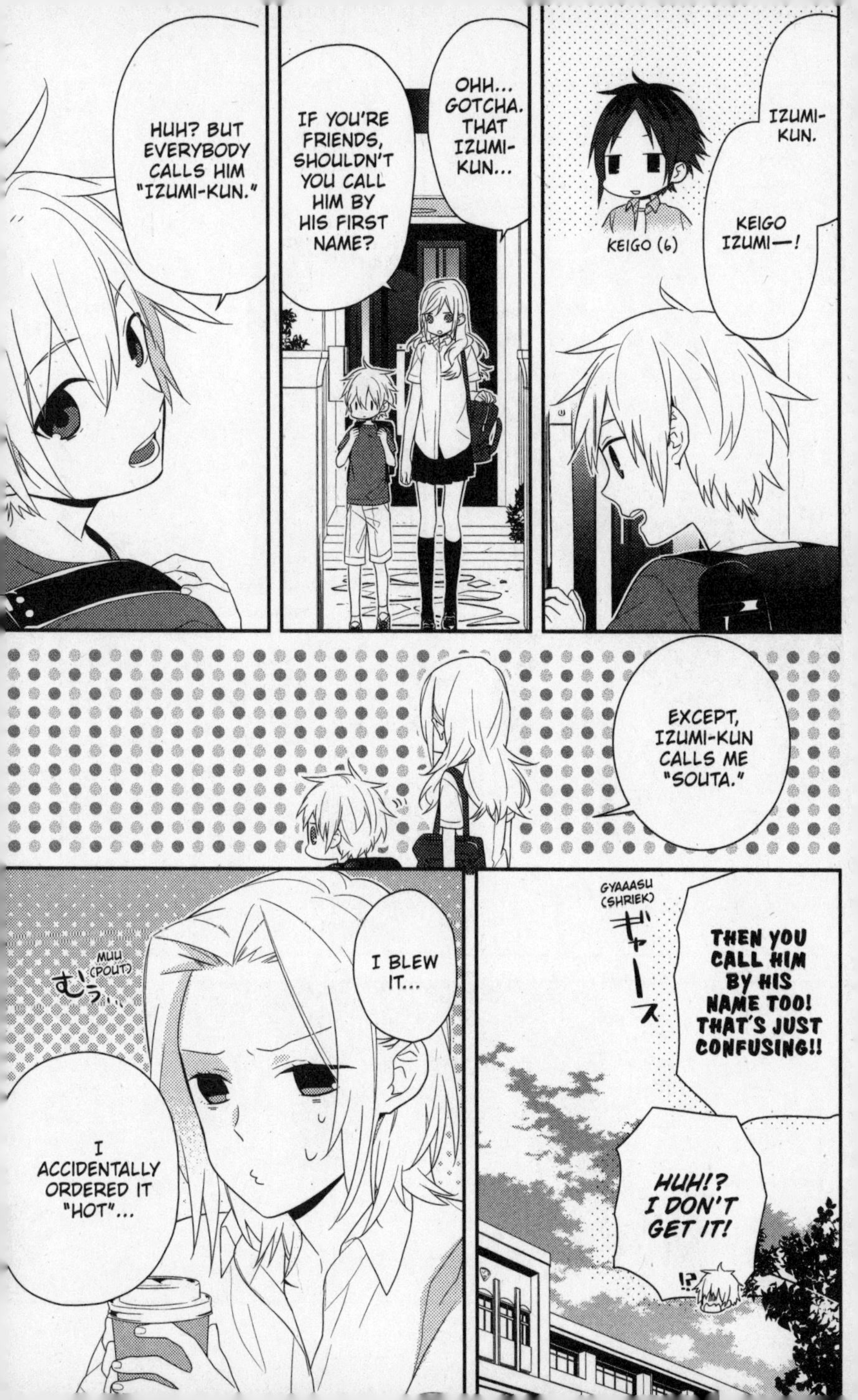
IZUMI-KUN.
KEIGO IZUMI—!
KEIGO (6)
OHH... GOTCHA. THAT IZUMI-KUN...
IF YOU'RE FRIENDS, SHOULDN'T YOU CALL HIM BY HIS FIRST NAME?
HUH? BUT EVERYBODY CALLS HIM "IZUMI-KUN."
EXCEPT, IZUMI-KUN CALLS ME "SOUTA."
GYAAASU (SHRIEK)
ギャース
THEN YOU CALL HIM BY HIS NAME TOO! THAT'S JUST CONFUSING!!
HUH!? I DON'T GET IT!
!?
I BLEW IT...
MUU (POUT)
むぅ...
I ACCIDENTALLY ORDERED IT "HOT"...

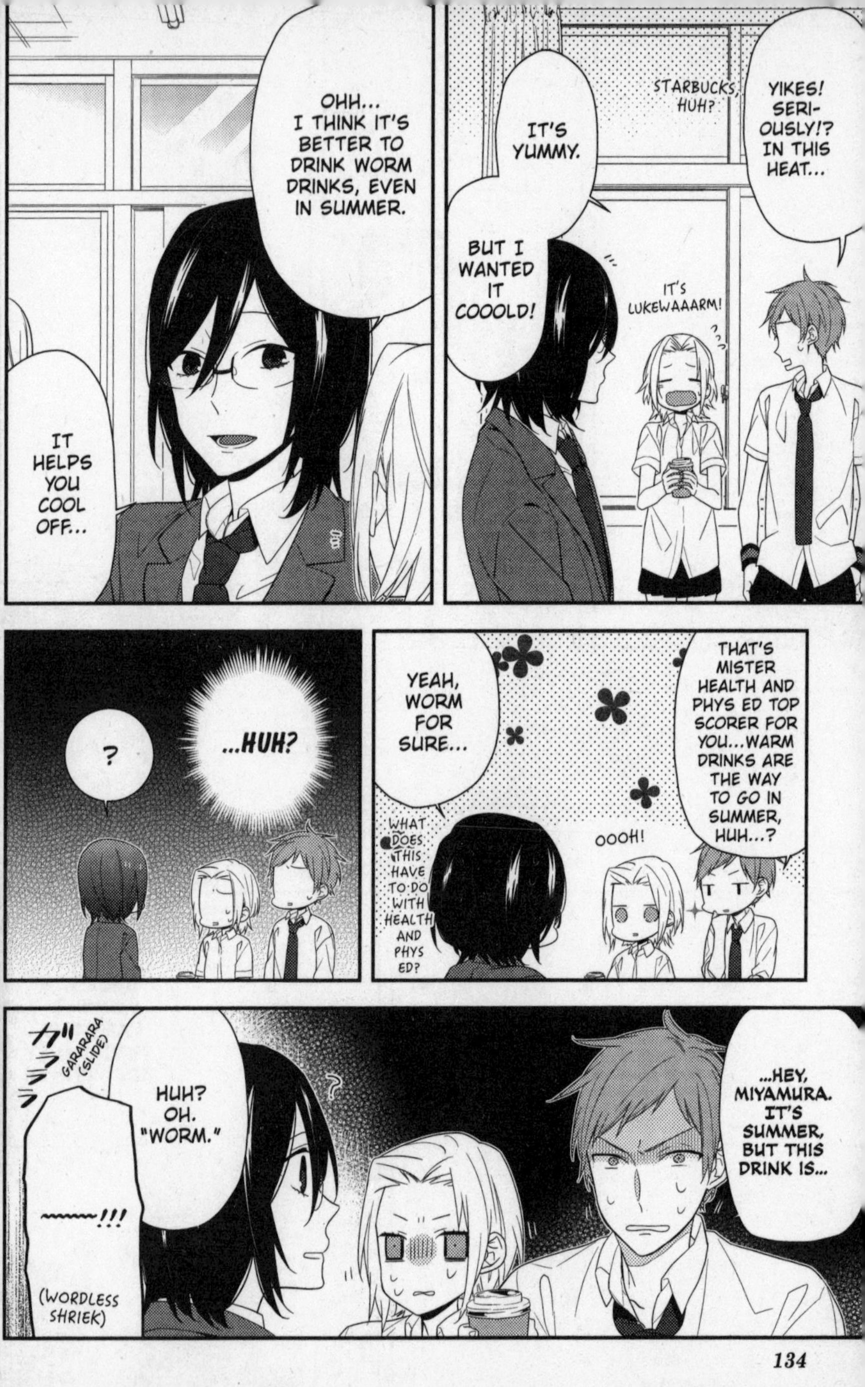

YIKES! SERIOUSLY!? IN THIS HEAT...
STARBUCKS, HUH?
IT'S YUMMY.
IT'S LUKEWAAARM!
BUT I WANTED IT COOOLD!
OHH... I THINK IT'S BETTER TO DRINK WORM DRINKS, EVEN IN SUMMER.
IT HELPS YOU COOL OFF...
THAT'S MISTER HEALTH AND PHYS ED TOP SCORER FOR YOU...WARM DRINKS ARE THE WAY TO GO IN SUMMER, HUH...?
OOOH!
YEAH, WORM FOR SURE...
WHAT DOES THIS HAVE TO DO WITH HEALTH AND PHYS ED?
...HUH?
?
...HEY, MIYAMURA. IT'S SUMMER, BUT THIS DRINK IS...
HUH? OH. "WORM."
?
~~~~!!!
(WORDLESS SHRIEK)
ガラララ
GARARARA (SLIDE)
~~~~

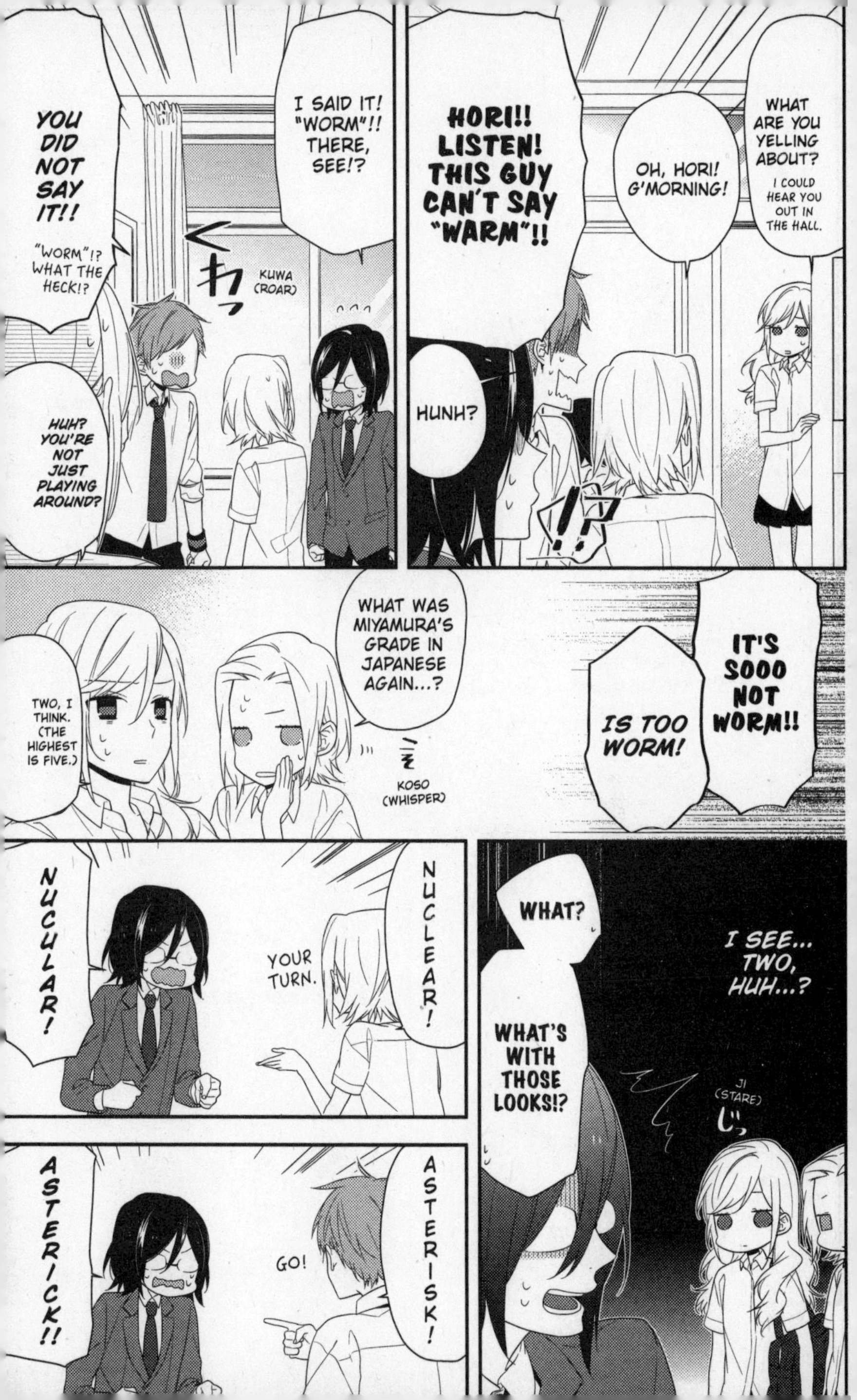
WHAT ARE YOU YELLING ABOUT?
I COULD HEAR YOU OUT IN THE HALL.
OH, HORI! G'MORNING!
HORI!! LISTEN! THIS GUY CAN'T SAY "WARM"!!
HUNH?
I SAID IT! "WORM"!! THERE, SEE!?
KUWA (ROAR)
YOU DID NOT SAY IT!!
"WORM"!? WHAT THE HECK!?
HUH? YOU'RE NOT JUST PLAYING AROUND?
IT'S SOOO NOT WORM!!
IS TOO WORM!
WHAT WAS MIYAMURA'S GRADE IN JAPANESE AGAIN...?
KOSO (WHISPER)
TWO, I THINK. (THE HIGHEST IS FIVE.)
I SEE... TWO, HUH...?
WHAT?
WHAT'S WITH THOSE LOOKS!?
JI (STARE)
NUCLEAR!
YOUR TURN.
NUCULAR!
ASTERISK!
GO!
ASTERICK!!

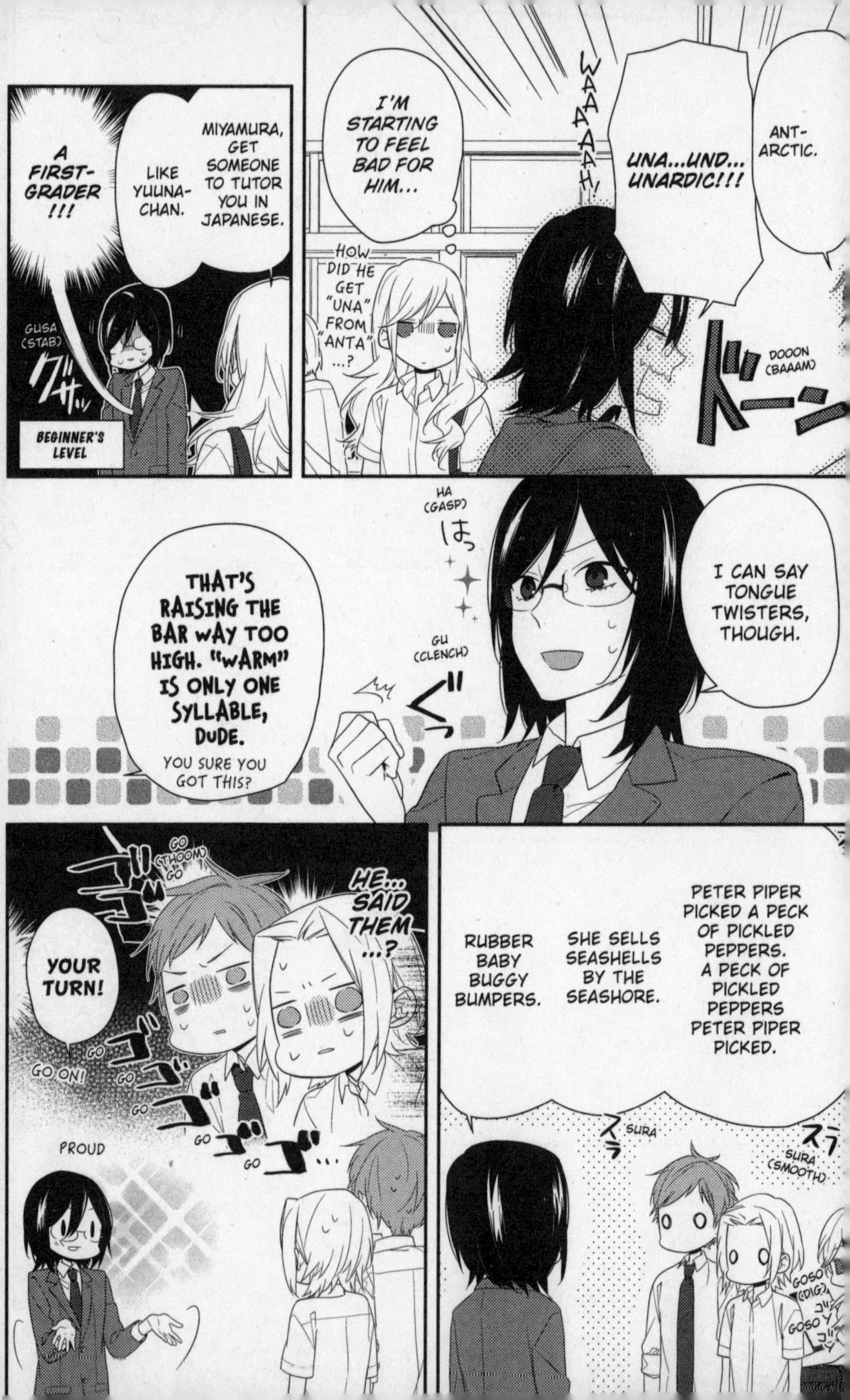

ANT-ARCTIC.
UNA...UND... UNARDIC!!!
WAAAAAH!
DOOON (BAAAM)
I'M STARTING TO FEEL BAD FOR HIM...
HOW DID HE GET "UNA" FROM "ANTA" ...?
MIYAMURA, GET SOMEONE TO TUTOR YOU IN JAPANESE.
LIKE YUUNA-CHAN.
A FIRST-GRADER!!!
GUSA (STAB)
BEGINNER'S LEVEL
I CAN SAY TONGUE TWISTERS, THOUGH.
HA (GASP)
GU (CLENCH)
THAT'S RAISING THE BAR WAY TOO HIGH. "WARM" IS ONLY ONE SYLLABLE, DUDE.
YOU SURE YOU GOT THIS?
PETER PIPER PICKED A PECK OF PICKLED PEPPERS. A PECK OF PICKLED PEPPERS PETER PIPER PICKED.
SHE SELLS SEASHELLS BY THE SEASHORE.
RUBBER BABY BUGGY BUMPERS.
SURA
SURA (SMOOTH)
GOSO (DIG)
GOSO
HE... SAID THEM ...?
GO (THOOM) GO
YOUR TURN!
GO ON!
GO
GO
GO
GO
GO
PROUD

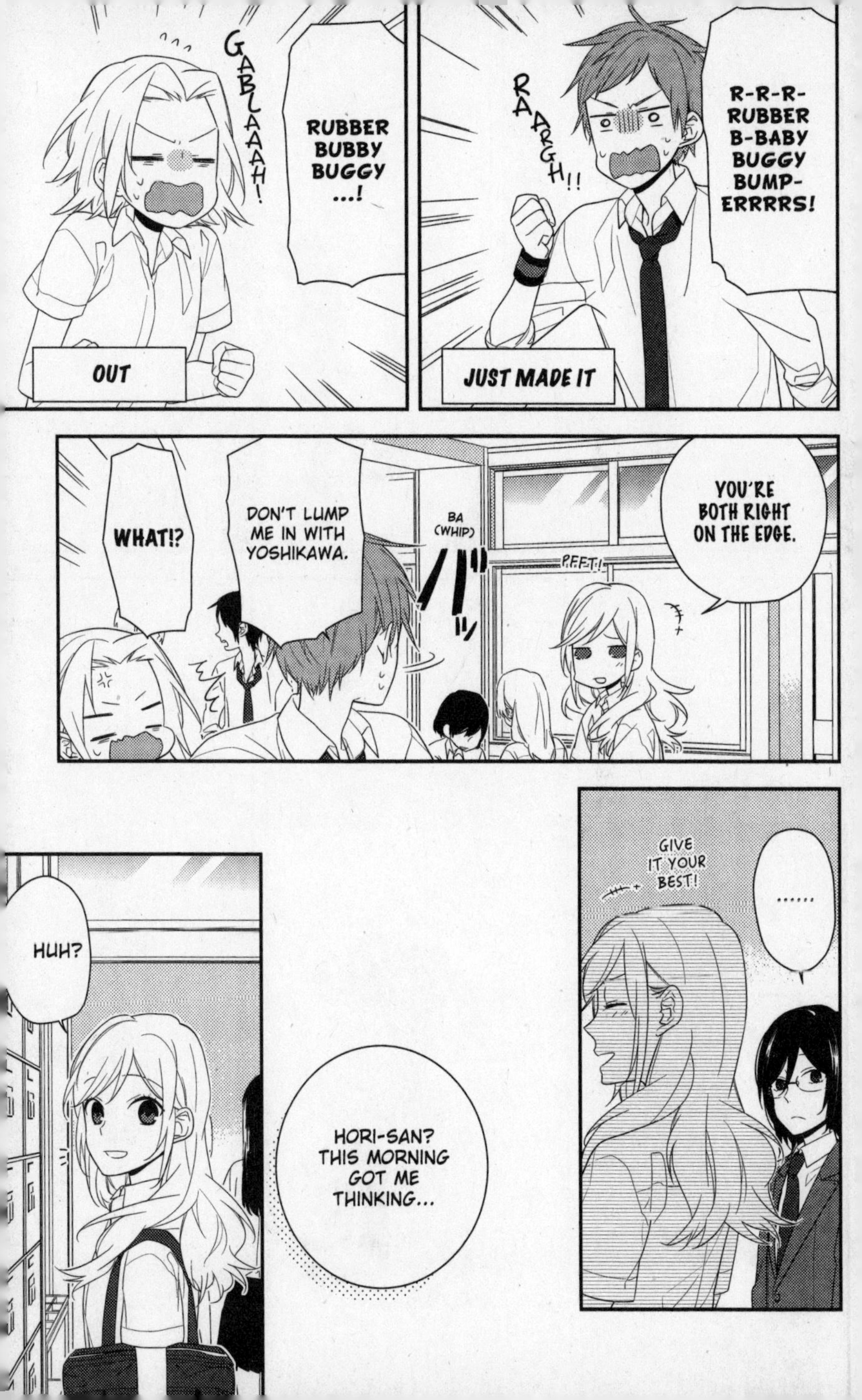
RAARGH!!
R-R-R-RUBBER B-BABY BUGGY BUMP-ERRRRS!
JUST MADE IT
RUBBER BUBBY BUGGY ...!
GABLAAAAH!
OUT
YOU'RE BOTH RIGHT ON THE EDGE.
P.F.F.T.!
BA (WHIP)
DON'T LUMP ME IN WITH YOSHIKAWA.
WHAT!?
......
GIVE IT YOUR BEST!
HORI-SAN? THIS MORNING GOT ME THINKING...
HUH?

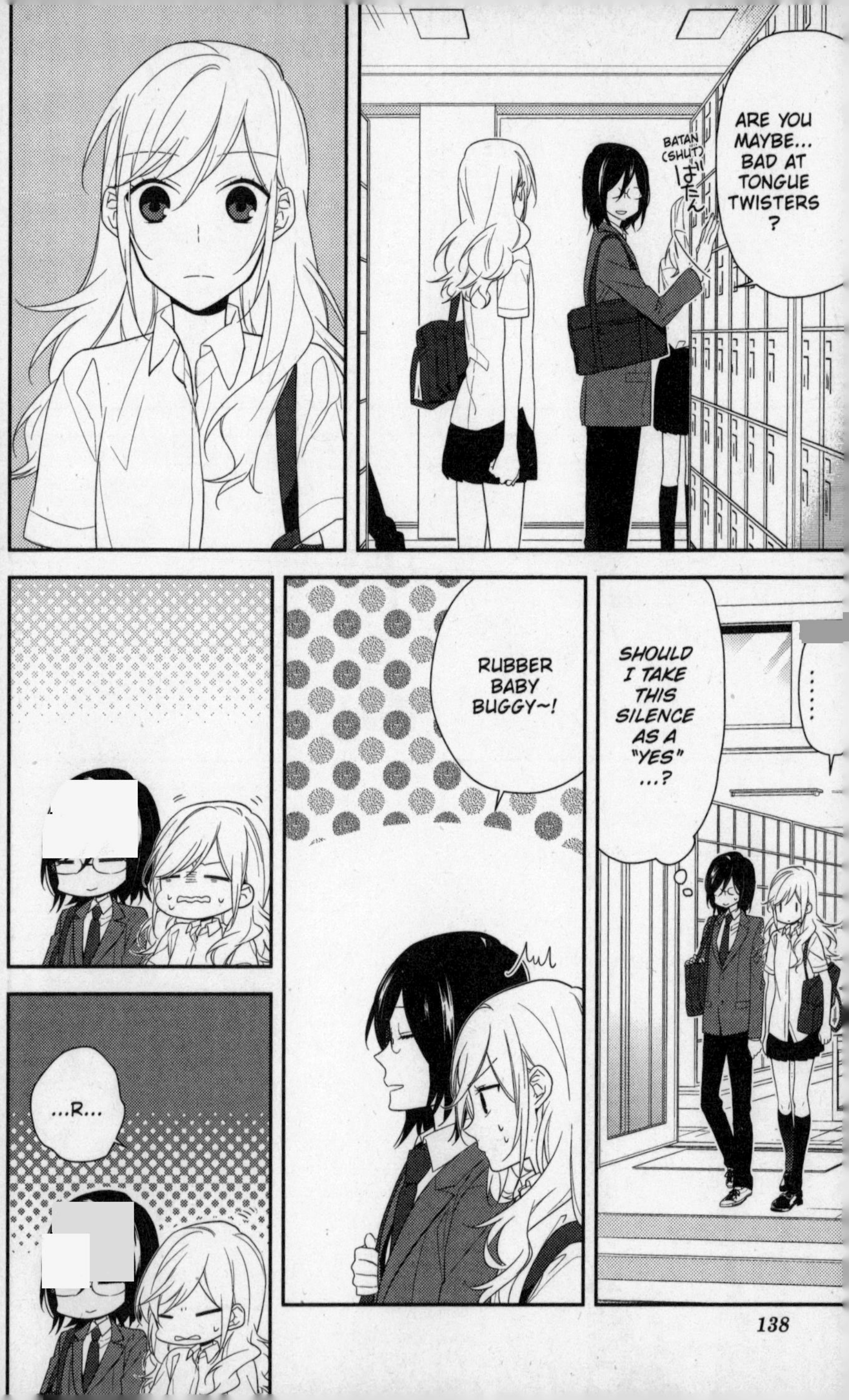
BATAN (SHUT)
ばたん
ARE YOU MAYBE... BAD AT TONGUE TWISTERS?
......
SHOULD I TAKE THIS SILENCE AS A "YES" ...?
RUBBER BABY BUGGY~!
...R...

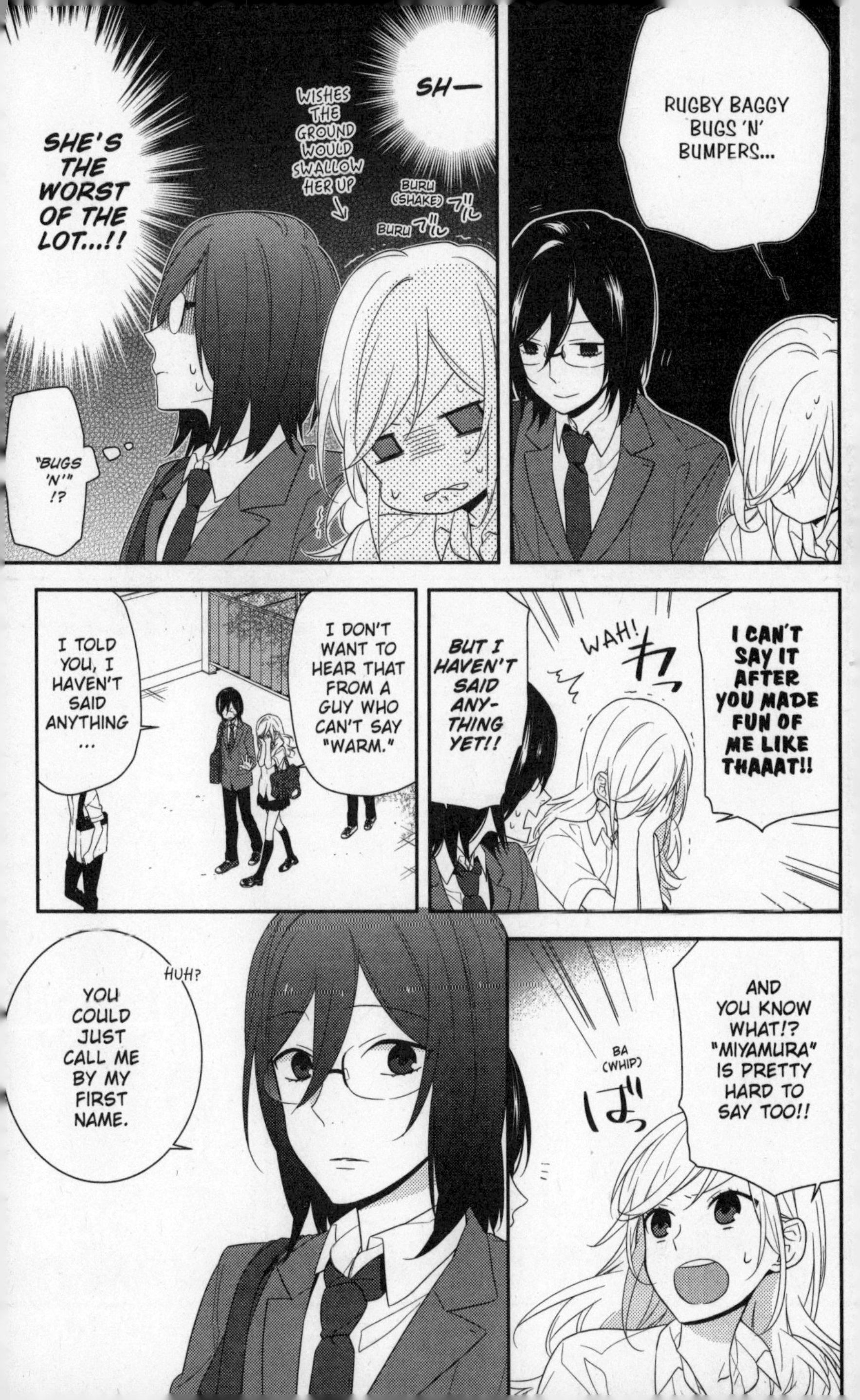
RUGBY BAGGY BUGS 'N' BUMPERS...
SH—
WISHES THE GROUND WOULD SWALLOW HER UP
BURU (SHAKE)
BURU
SHE'S THE WORST OF THE LOT...!!
"BUGS 'N'" !?
I CAN'T SAY IT AFTER YOU MADE FUN OF ME LIKE THAAAT!!
WAH!
BUT I HAVEN'T SAID ANY-THING YET!!
I DON'T WANT TO HEAR THAT FROM A GUY WHO CAN'T SAY "WARM."
I TOLD YOU, I HAVEN'T SAID ANYTHING ...
AND YOU KNOW WHAT!? "MIYAMURA" IS PRETTY HARD TO SAY TOO!!
BA (WHIP)
HUH?
YOU COULD JUST CALL ME BY MY FIRST NAME.

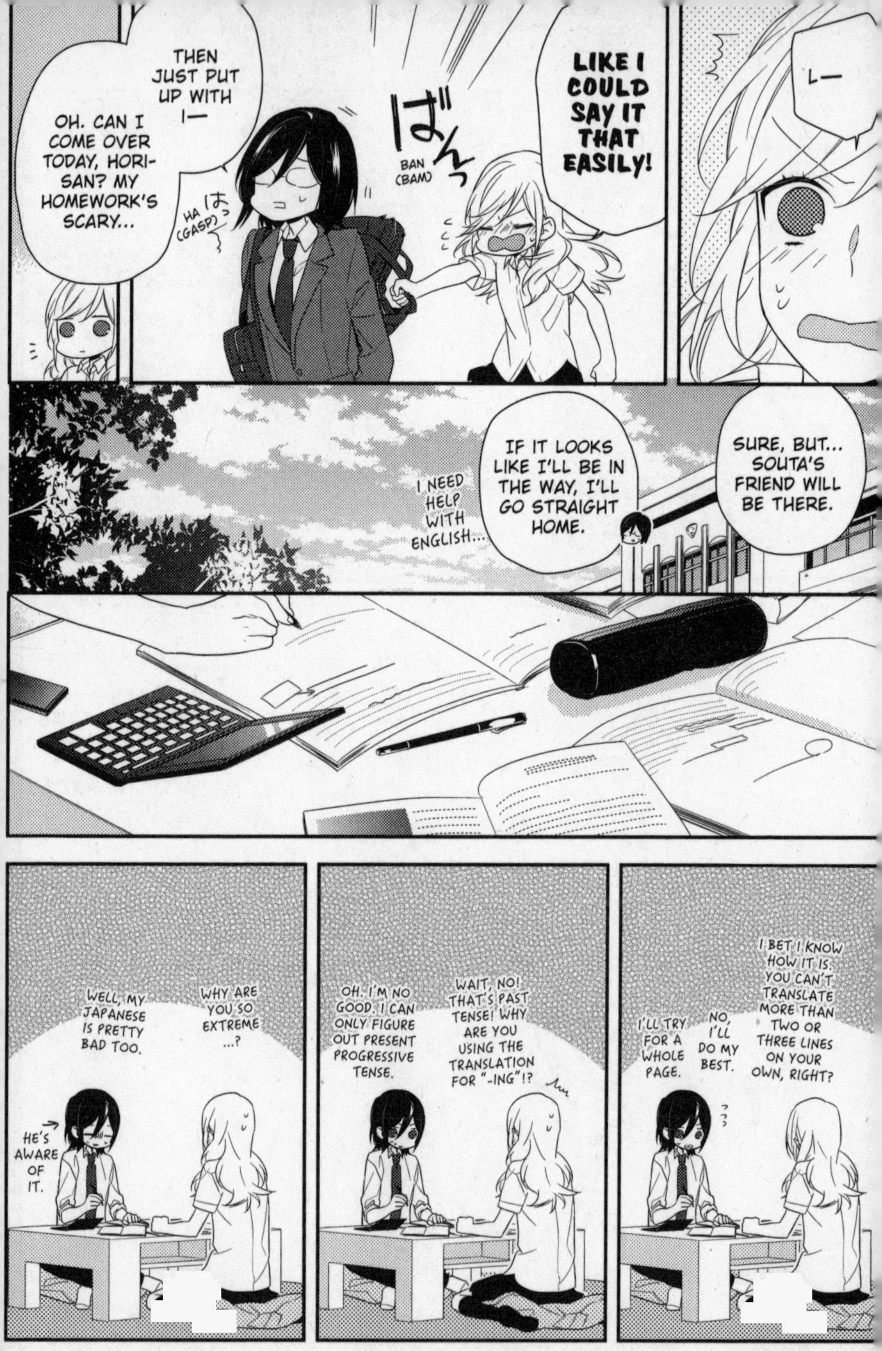
L—
LIKE I COULD SAY IT THAT EASILY!
ばん
BAN (BAM)
THEN JUST PUT UP WITH I—
は
HA (GASP)
OH. CAN I COME OVER TODAY, HORI-SAN? MY HOMEWORK'S SCARY...
SURE, BUT... SOUTA'S FRIEND WILL BE THERE.
IF IT LOOKS LIKE I'LL BE IN THE WAY, I'LL GO STRAIGHT HOME.
I NEED HELP WITH ENGLISH...
I BET I KNOW HOW IT IS. YOU CAN'T TRANSLATE MORE THAN TWO OR THREE LINES ON YOUR OWN, RIGHT?
NO, I'LL DO MY BEST.
I'LL TRY FOR A WHOLE PAGE.
WAIT, NO! THAT'S PAST TENSE! WHY ARE YOU USING THE TRANSLATION FOR "-ING"!?
OH. I'M NO GOOD. I CAN ONLY FIGURE OUT PRESENT PROGRESSIVE TENSE.
WHY ARE YOU SO EXTREME...?
WELL, MY JAPANESE IS PRETTY BAD TOO.
HE'S AWARE OF IT.

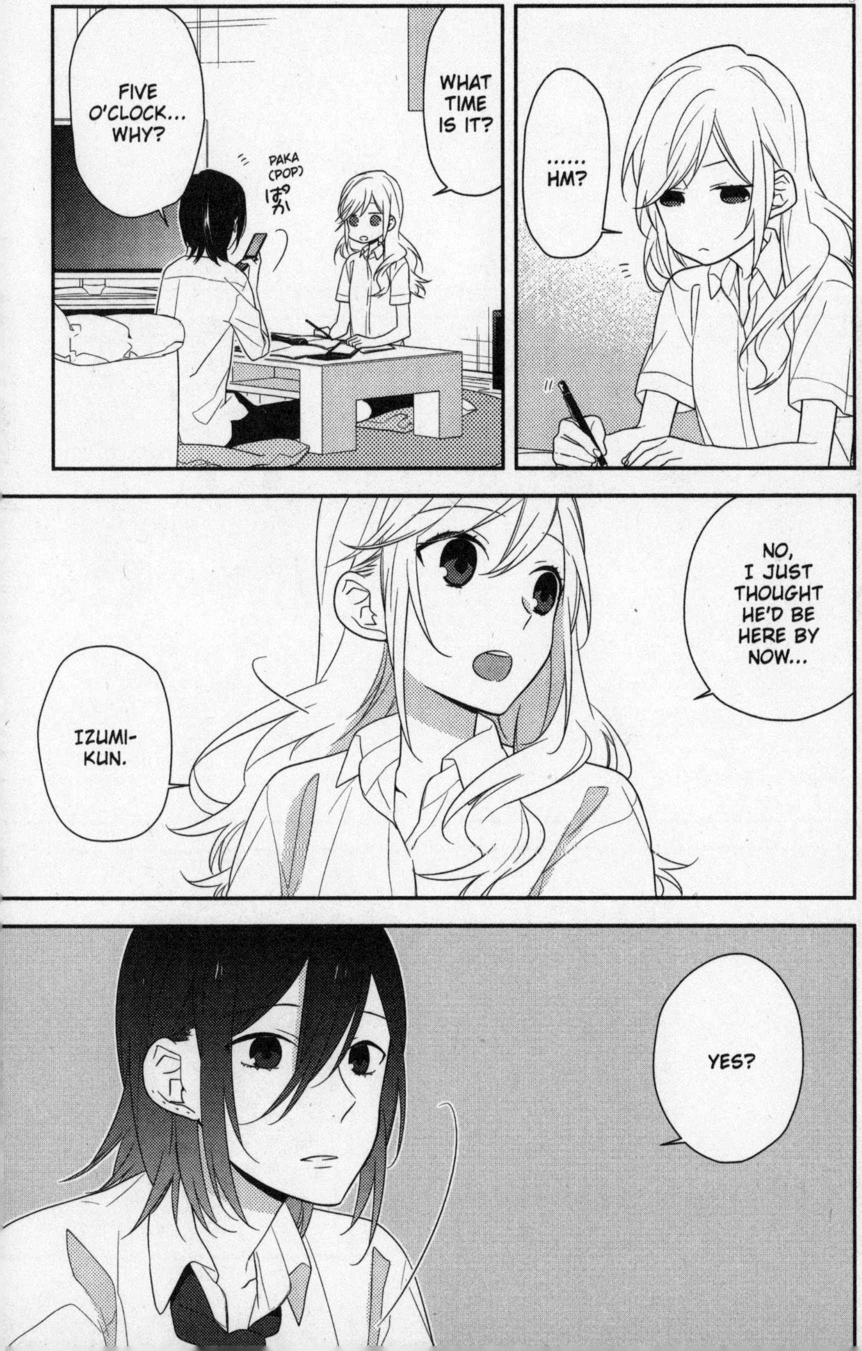
......
HM?
WHAT TIME IS IT?
PAKA (POP)
ぱか
FIVE O'CLOCK... WHY?
NO, I JUST THOUGHT HE'D BE HERE BY NOW...
IZUMI-KUN.
YES?

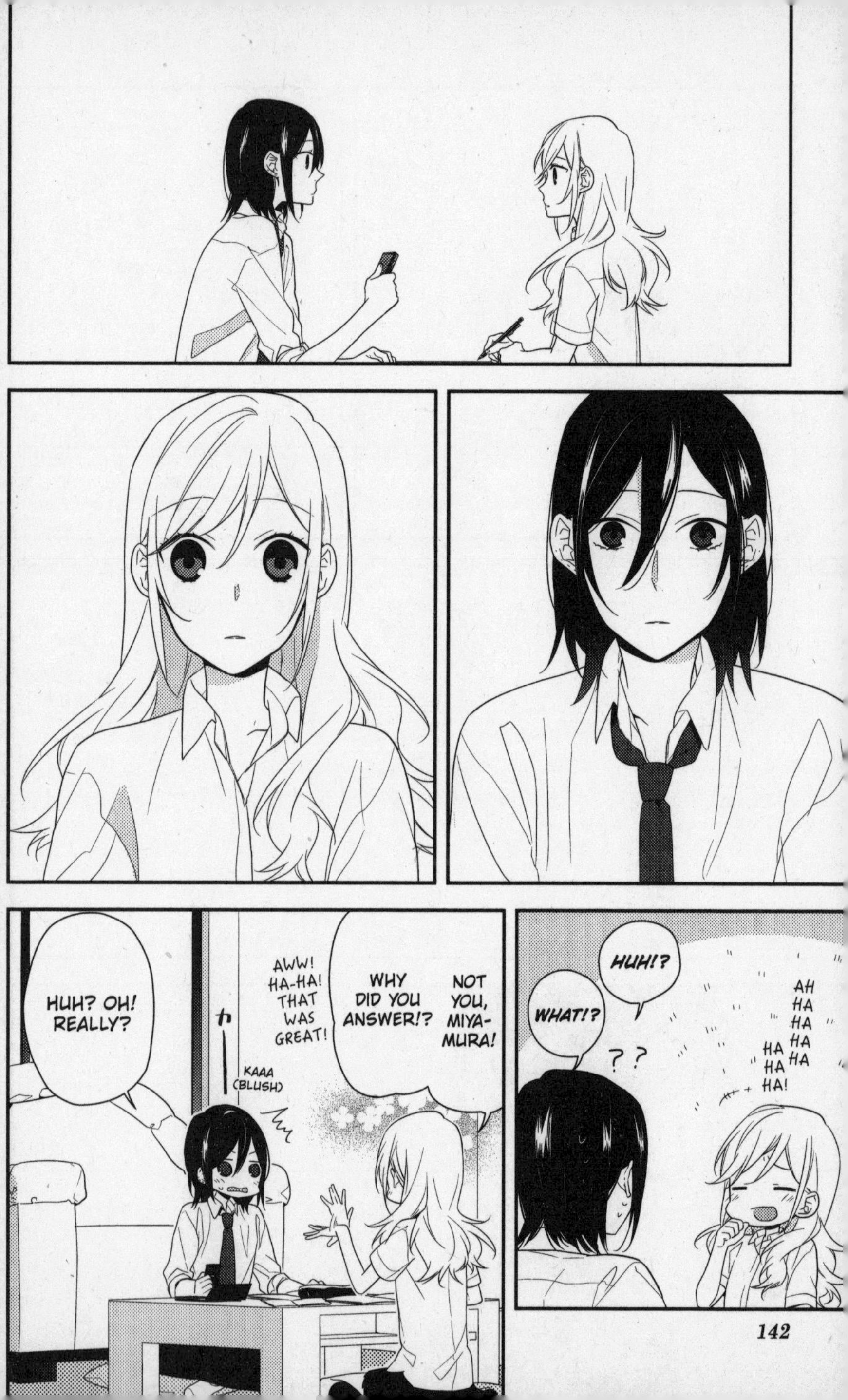
HUH!?
AH HA HA HA HA
HA HA HA!
WHAT!?
NOT YOU, MIYA-MURA!
WHY DID YOU ANSWER!?
AWW! HA-HA! THAT WAS GREAT!
KAAA (BLUSH)
HUH? OH! REALLY?

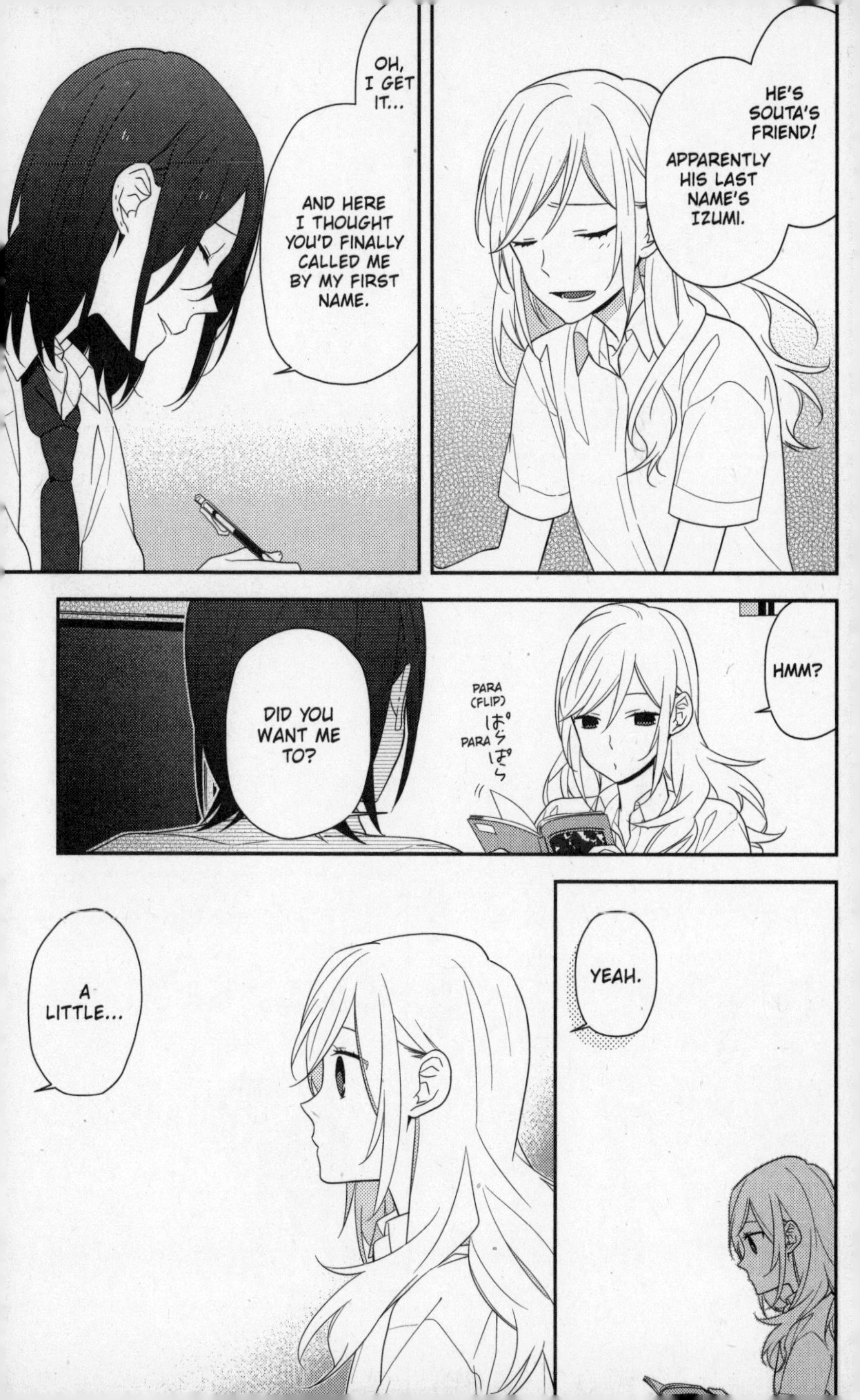
HE'S SOUTA'S FRIEND!
APPARENTLY HIS LAST NAME'S IZUMI.
OH, I GET IT...
AND HERE I THOUGHT YOU'D FINALLY CALLED ME BY MY FIRST NAME.
HMM?
PARA PARA (FLIP) ぱらぱら
DID YOU WANT ME TO?
YEAH.
A LITTLE...

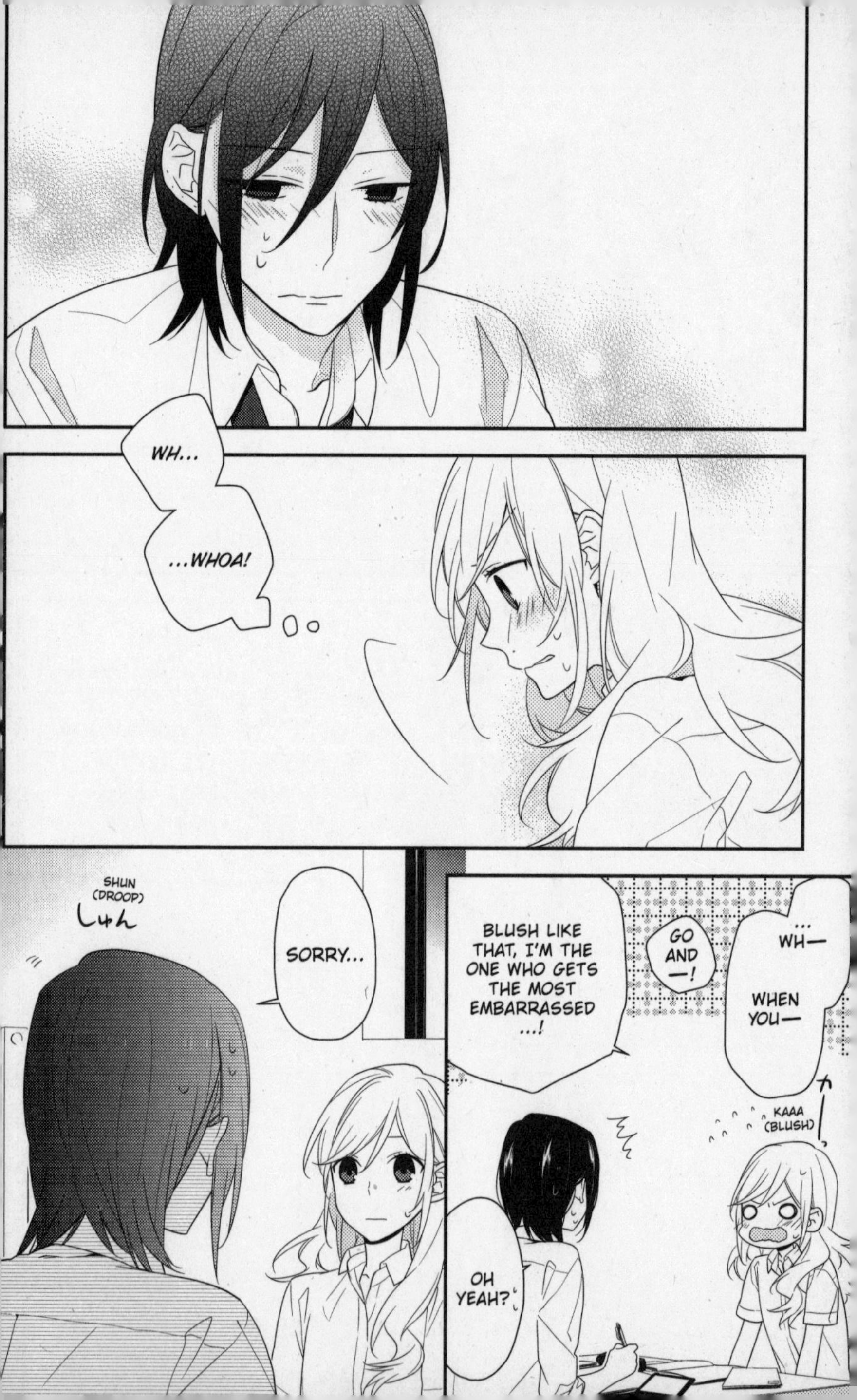
WH...
...WHOA!
...WH—
WHEN YOU—
GO AND—!
BLUSH LIKE THAT, I'M THE ONE WHO GETS THE MOST EMBARRASSED ...!
KAAA (BLUSH)
OH YEAH?
SORRY...
SHUN (DROOP)
しゅん

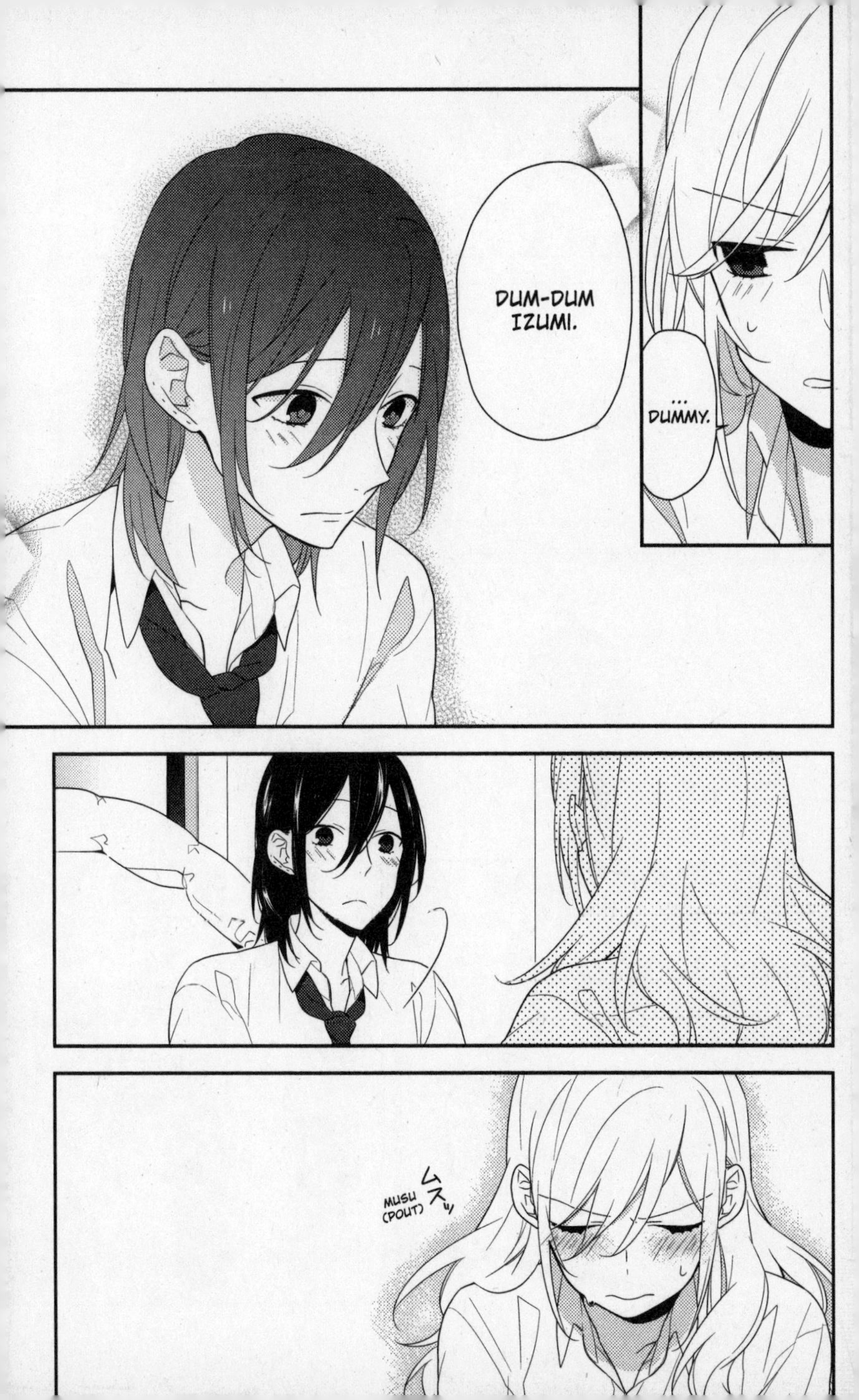
... DUMMY.
DUM-DUM IZUMI.
ムスッ
MUSU (POUT)

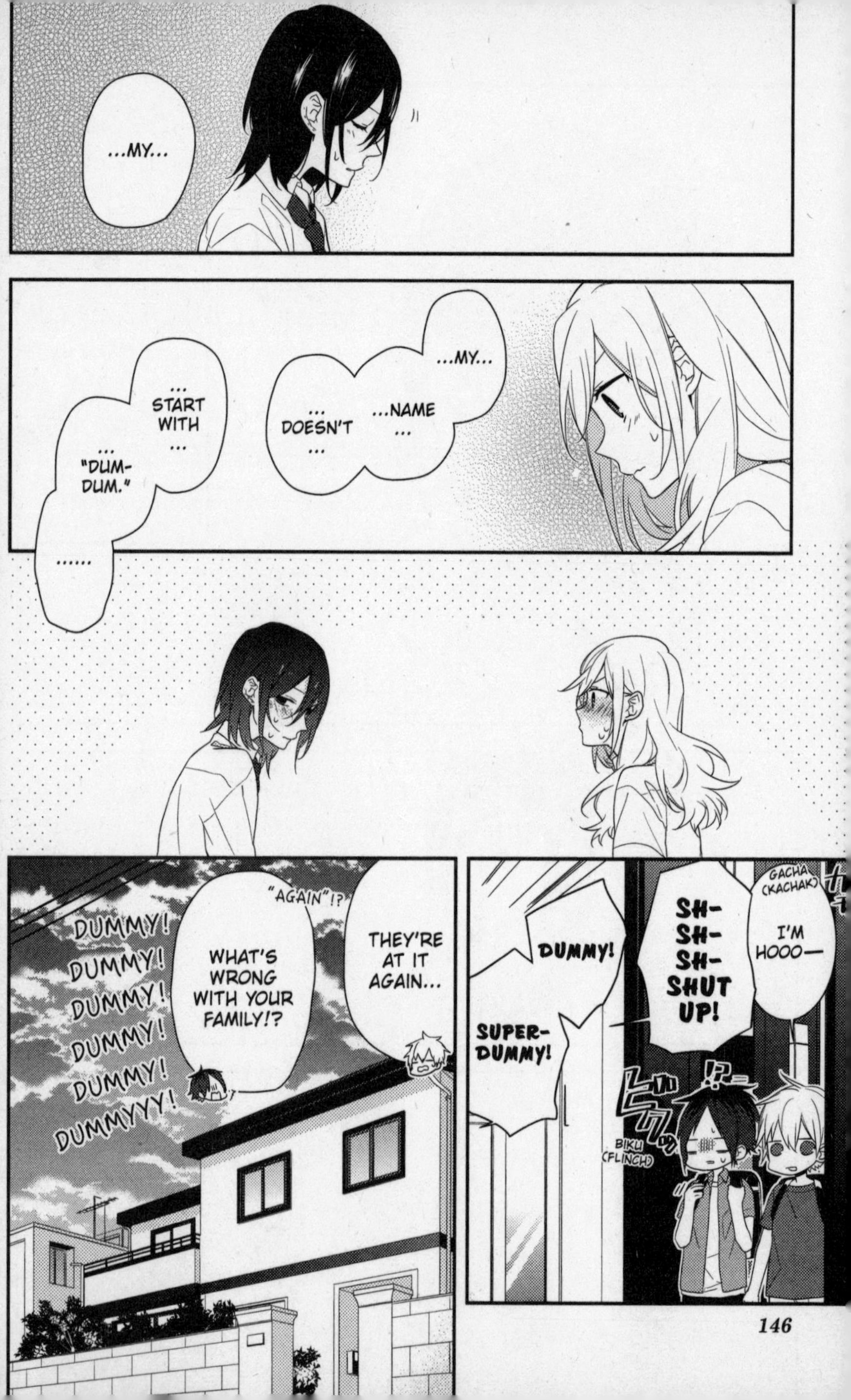
...MY...
...MY...
...NAME ...
... DOESN'T ...
... START WITH ...
... "DUM-DUM."
......
GACHA (KACHAK)
I'M HOOO—
SH-SH-SH-SHUT UP!
DUMMY!
SUPER-DUMMY!
!?
BIKU (FLINCH)
THEY'RE AT IT AGAIN...
"AGAIN"!?
WHAT'S WRONG WITH YOUR FAMILY!?
DUMMY! DUMMY! DUMMY! DUMMY! DUMMY! DUMMYY!

HORIMIYA

HORIMIYA

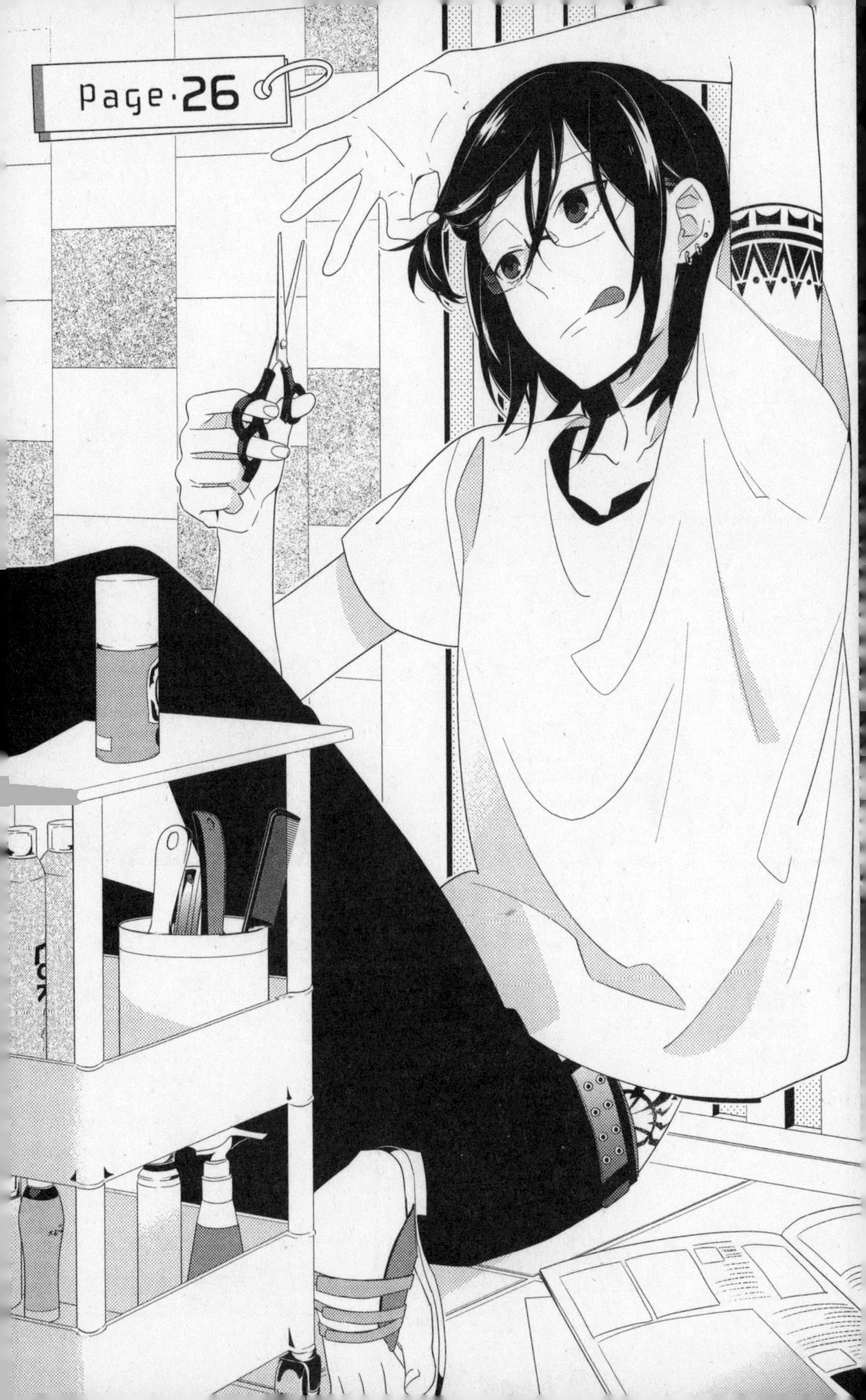
Page·26

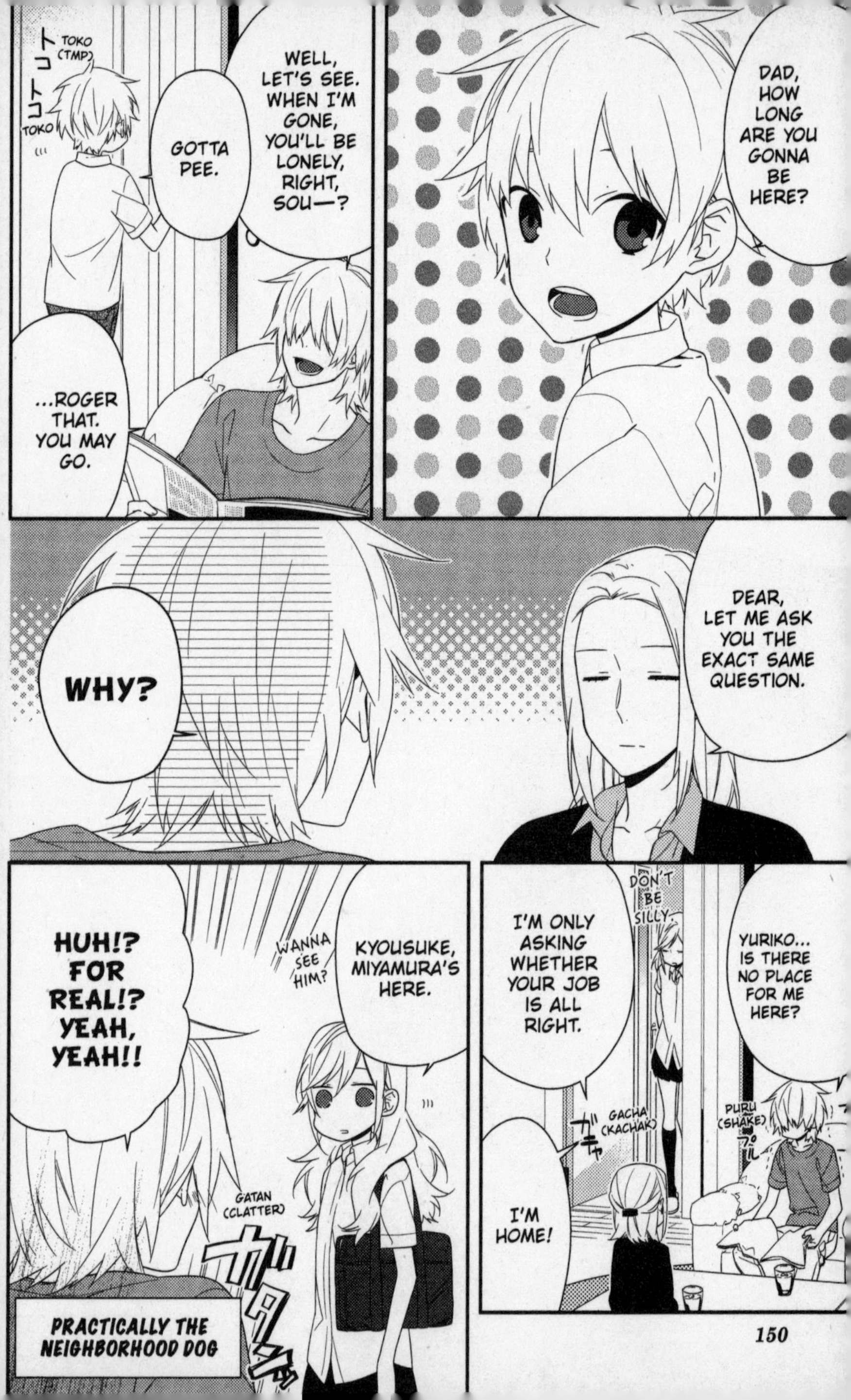
DAD, HOW LONG ARE YOU GONNA BE HERE?
WELL, LET'S SEE. WHEN I'M GONE, YOU'LL BE LONELY, RIGHT, SOU—?
GOTTA PEE.
TOKO (TMP) TOKO
...ROGER THAT. YOU MAY GO.
DEAR, LET ME ASK YOU THE EXACT SAME QUESTION.
WHY?
YURIKO... IS THERE NO PLACE FOR ME HERE?
PURU (SHAKE)
I'M ONLY ASKING WHETHER YOUR JOB IS ALL RIGHT.
DON'T BE SILLY.
GACHA (KACHAK)
I'M HOME!
KYOUSUKE, MIYAMURA'S HERE.
WANNA SEE HIM?
HUH!? FOR REAL!? YEAH, YEAH!!
GATAN (CLATTER)
PRACTICALLY THE NEIGHBORHOOD DOG

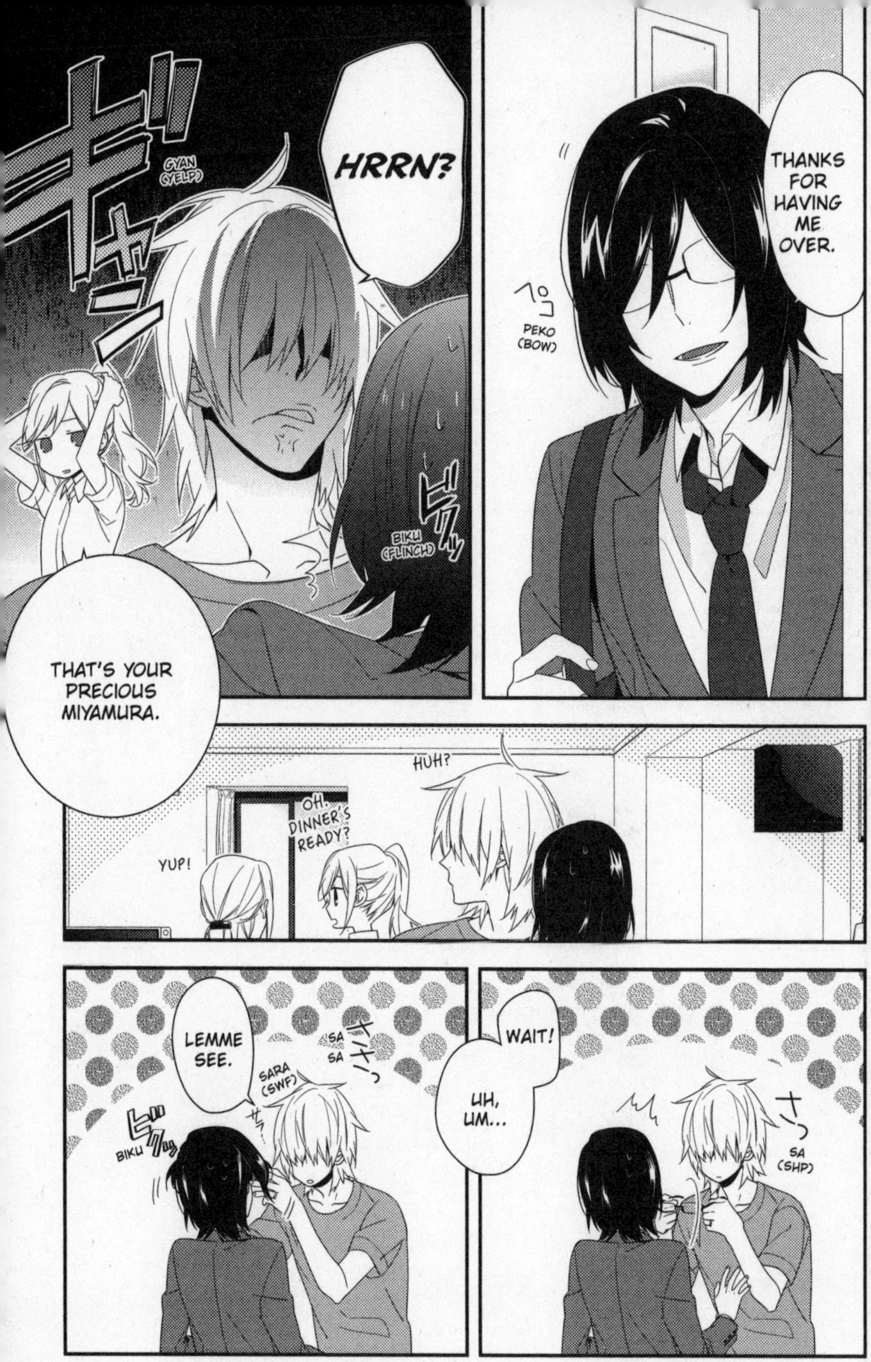
THANKS FOR HAVING ME OVER.
PEKO (BOW)
HRRN?
GYAN (YELP)
BIKU (FLINCH)
THAT'S YOUR PRECIOUS MIYAMURA.
HUH?
OH. DINNER'S READY?
YUP!
WAIT!
UH, UM...
SA (SHP)
LEMME SEE.
SA SA
SARA (SWF)
BIKU

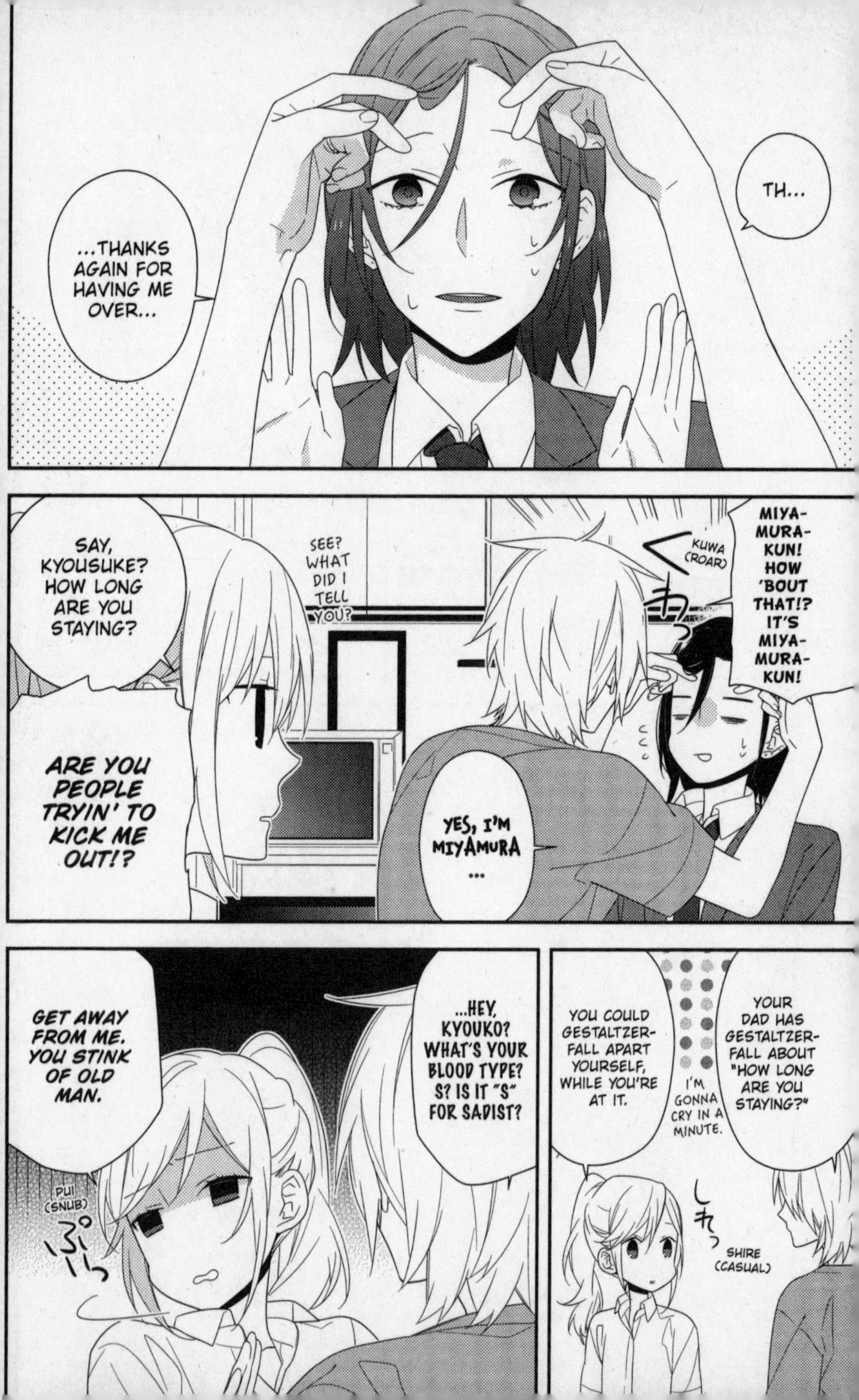
TH...
...THANKS AGAIN FOR HAVING ME OVER...
MIYA-MURA-KUN! HOW 'BOUT THAT!? IT'S MIYA-MURA-KUN!
KUWA (ROAR)
SEE? WHAT DID I TELL YOU?
YES, I'M MIYAMURA ...
SAY, KYOUSUKE? HOW LONG ARE YOU STAYING?
ARE YOU PEOPLE TRYIN' TO KICK ME OUT!?
YOUR DAD HAS GESTALTZER-FALL ABOUT "HOW LONG ARE YOU STAYING?"
I'M GONNA CRY IN A MINUTE.
YOU COULD GESTALTZER-FALL APART YOURSELF, WHILE YOU'RE AT IT.
SHIRE (CASUAL)
...HEY, KYOUKO? WHAT'S YOUR BLOOD TYPE? S? IS IT "S" FOR SADIST?
GET AWAY FROM ME. YOU STINK OF OLD MAN.
PUI (SNUB)

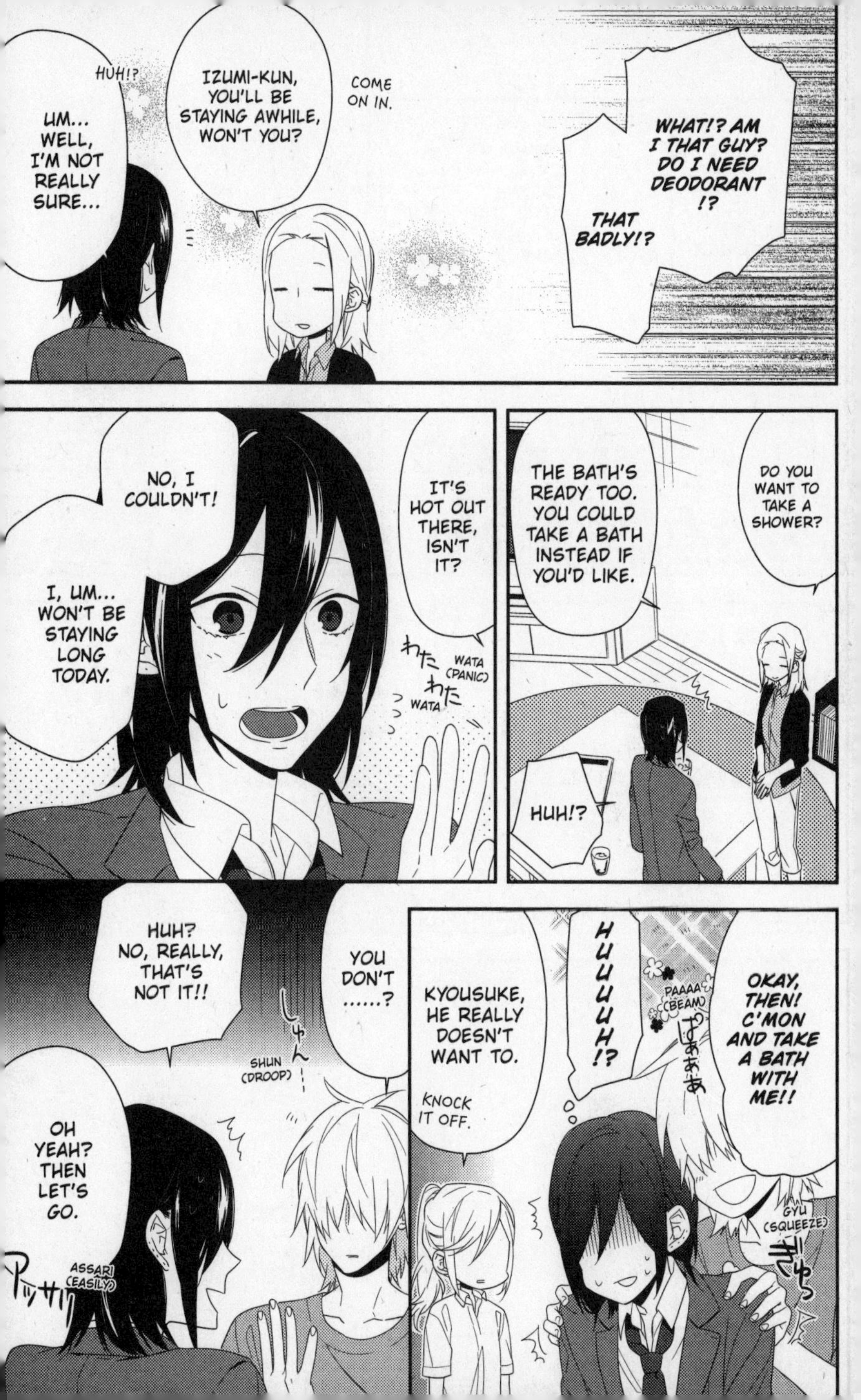
WHAT!? AM I THAT GUY? DO I NEED DEODORANT !?
THAT BADLY!?
COME ON IN.
IZUMI-KUN, YOU'LL BE STAYING AWHILE, WON'T YOU?
HUH!?
UM... WELL, I'M NOT REALLY SURE...
DO YOU WANT TO TAKE A SHOWER?
THE BATH'S READY TOO. YOU COULD TAKE A BATH INSTEAD IF YOU'D LIKE.
HUH!?
IT'S HOT OUT THERE, ISN'T IT?
わたわた
WATA (PANIC) WATA
NO, I COULDN'T!
I, UM... WON'T BE STAYING LONG TODAY.
OKAY, THEN! C'MON AND TAKE A BATH WITH ME!!
HUUUUH!?
ぱあああ
PAAAA (BEAM)
KYOUSUKE, HE REALLY DOESN'T WANT TO.
KNOCK IT OFF.
ぎゅっ
GYU (SQUEEZE)
YOU DON'T ......?
しゅん
SHUN (DROOP)
HUH? NO, REALLY, THAT'S NOT IT!!
OH YEAH? THEN LET'S GO.
アッサリ
ASSARI (EASILY)

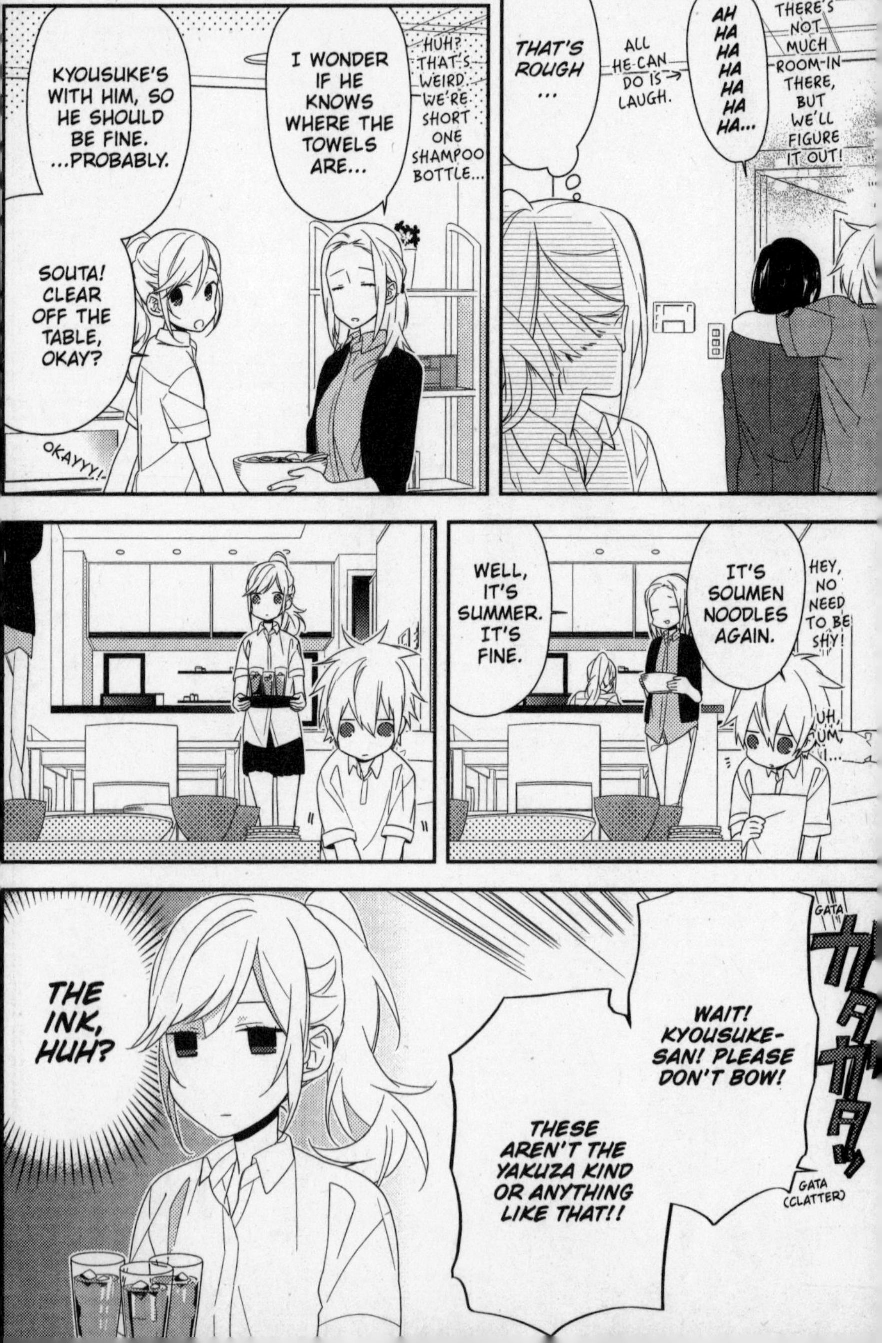
THERE'S NOT MUCH ROOM IN THERE, BUT WE'LL FIGURE IT OUT!
AH HA HA HA HA HA HA...
ALL HE CAN DO IS LAUGH.
THAT'S ROUGH...
HUH? THAT'S WEIRD. WE'RE SHORT ONE SHAMPOO BOTTLE...
I WONDER IF HE KNOWS WHERE THE TOWELS ARE...
KYOUSUKE'S WITH HIM, SO HE SHOULD BE FINE. ...PROBABLY.
SOUTA! CLEAR OFF THE TABLE, OKAY?
OKAYYY!
HEY, NO NEED TO BE SHY!
IT'S SOUMEN NOODLES AGAIN.
UH, UM, I...
WELL, IT'S SUMMER. IT'S FINE.
GATA
GATA (CLATTER)
WAIT! KYOUSUKE-SAN! PLEASE DON'T BOW!
THESE AREN'T THE YAKUZA KIND OR ANYTHING LIKE THAT!!
THE INK, HUH?

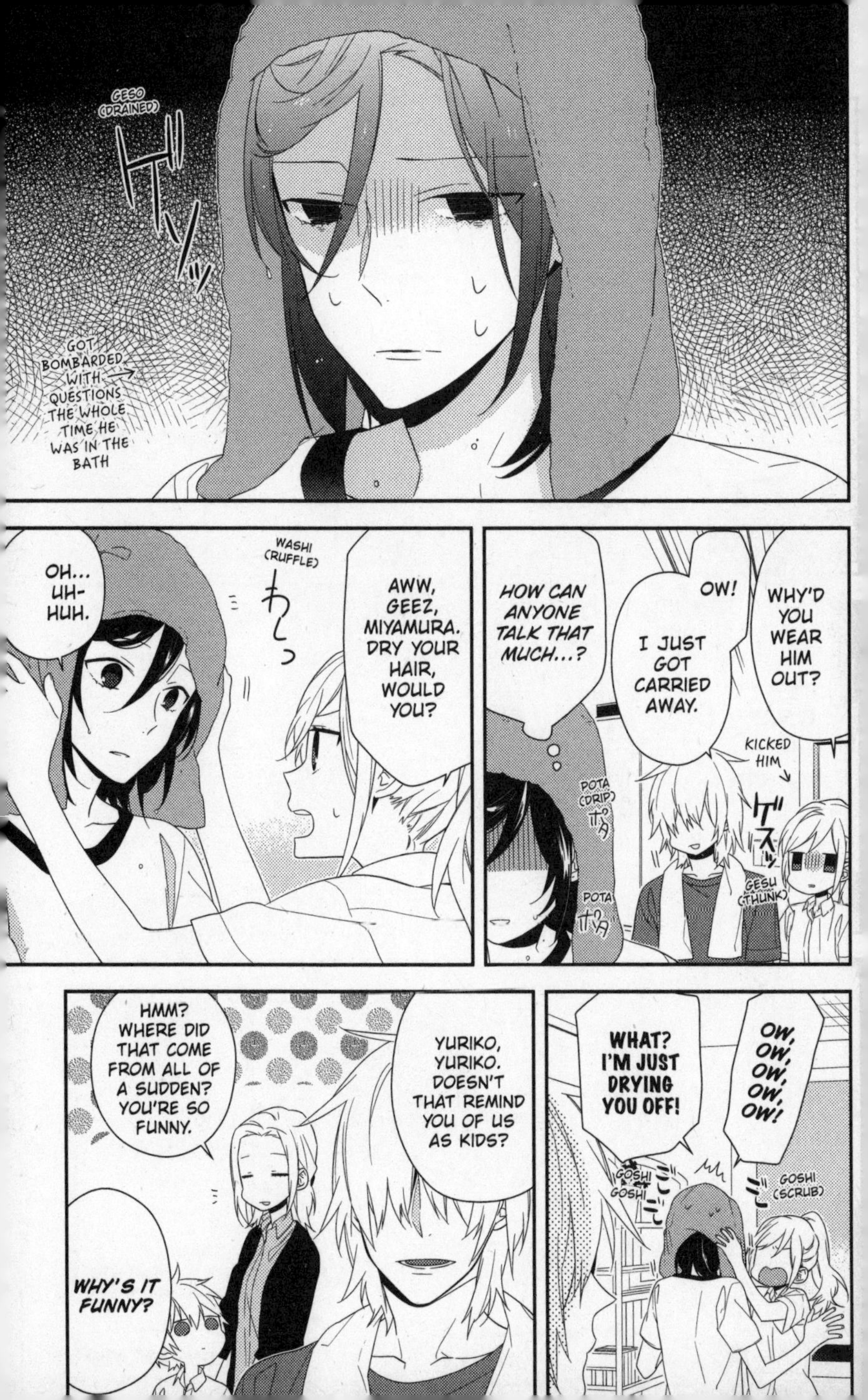
GESO (DRAINED)
GOT BOMBARDED WITH QUESTIONS THE WHOLE TIME HE WAS IN THE BATH
WHY'D YOU WEAR HIM OUT?
OW!
I JUST GOT CARRIED AWAY.
HOW CAN ANYONE TALK THAT MUCH...?
KICKED HIM
GESU (THUNK)
POTA (DRIP)
POTA
AWW, GEEZ, MIYAMURA. DRY YOUR HAIR, WOULD YOU?
WASHI (RUFFLE)
OH... UH-HUH.
OW, OW, OW, OW, OW!
WHAT? I'M JUST DRYING YOU OFF!
GOSHI (SCRUB)
GOSHI GOSHI
YURIKO, YURIKO. DOESN'T THAT REMIND YOU OF US AS KIDS?
HMM? WHERE DID THAT COME FROM ALL OF A SUDDEN? YOU'RE SO FUNNY.
WHY'S IT FUNNY?

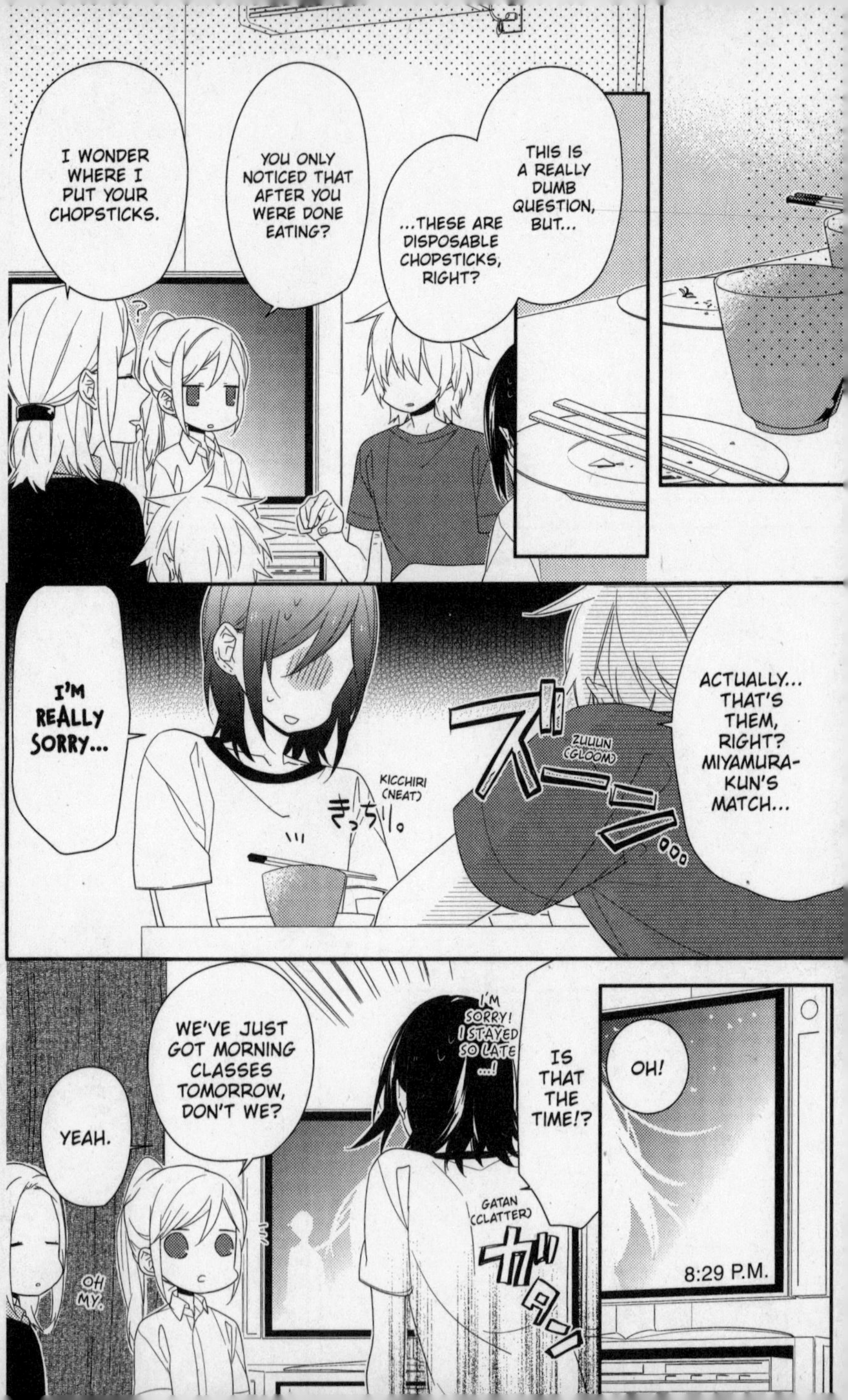
THIS IS A REALLY DUMB QUESTION, BUT...
...THESE ARE DISPOSABLE CHOPSTICKS, RIGHT?
YOU ONLY NOTICED THAT AFTER YOU WERE DONE EATING?
I WONDER WHERE I PUT YOUR CHOPSTICKS.
ACTUALLY... THAT'S THEM, RIGHT? MIYAMURA-KUN'S MATCH...
ZUUUN (GLOOM)
KICCHIRI (NEAT)
I'M REALLY SORRY...
OH!
8:29 P.M.
IS THAT THE TIME!?
I'M SORRY! I STAYED SO LATE...!
GATAN (CLATTER)
WE'VE JUST GOT MORNING CLASSES TOMORROW, DON'T WE?
YEAH.
OH MY.

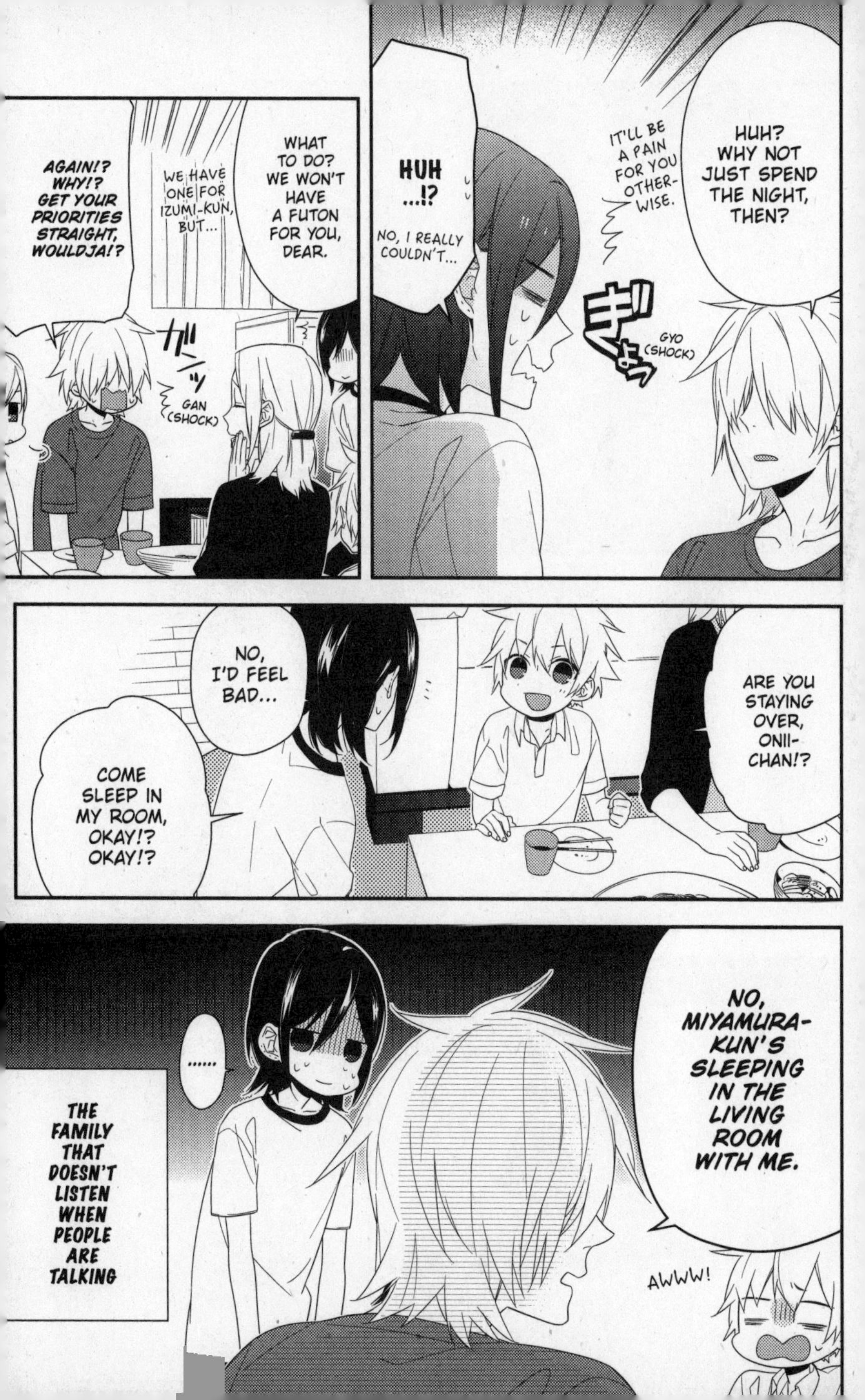
HUH? WHY NOT JUST SPEND THE NIGHT, THEN?
IT'LL BE A PAIN FOR YOU OTHERWISE.
GYO (SHOCK)
HUH ...!?
NO, I REALLY COULDN'T...
WHAT TO DO? WE WON'T HAVE A FUTON FOR YOU, DEAR.
WE HAVE ONE FOR IZUMI-KUN, BUT...
GAN (SHOCK)
AGAIN!? WHY!? GET YOUR PRIORITIES STRAIGHT, WOULDJA!?
ARE YOU STAYING OVER, ONII-CHAN!?
NO, I'D FEEL BAD...
COME SLEEP IN MY ROOM, OKAY!? OKAY!?
NO, MIYAMURA-KUN'S SLEEPING IN THE LIVING ROOM WITH ME.
AWWW!
......
THE FAMILY THAT DOESN'T LISTEN WHEN PEOPLE ARE TALKING

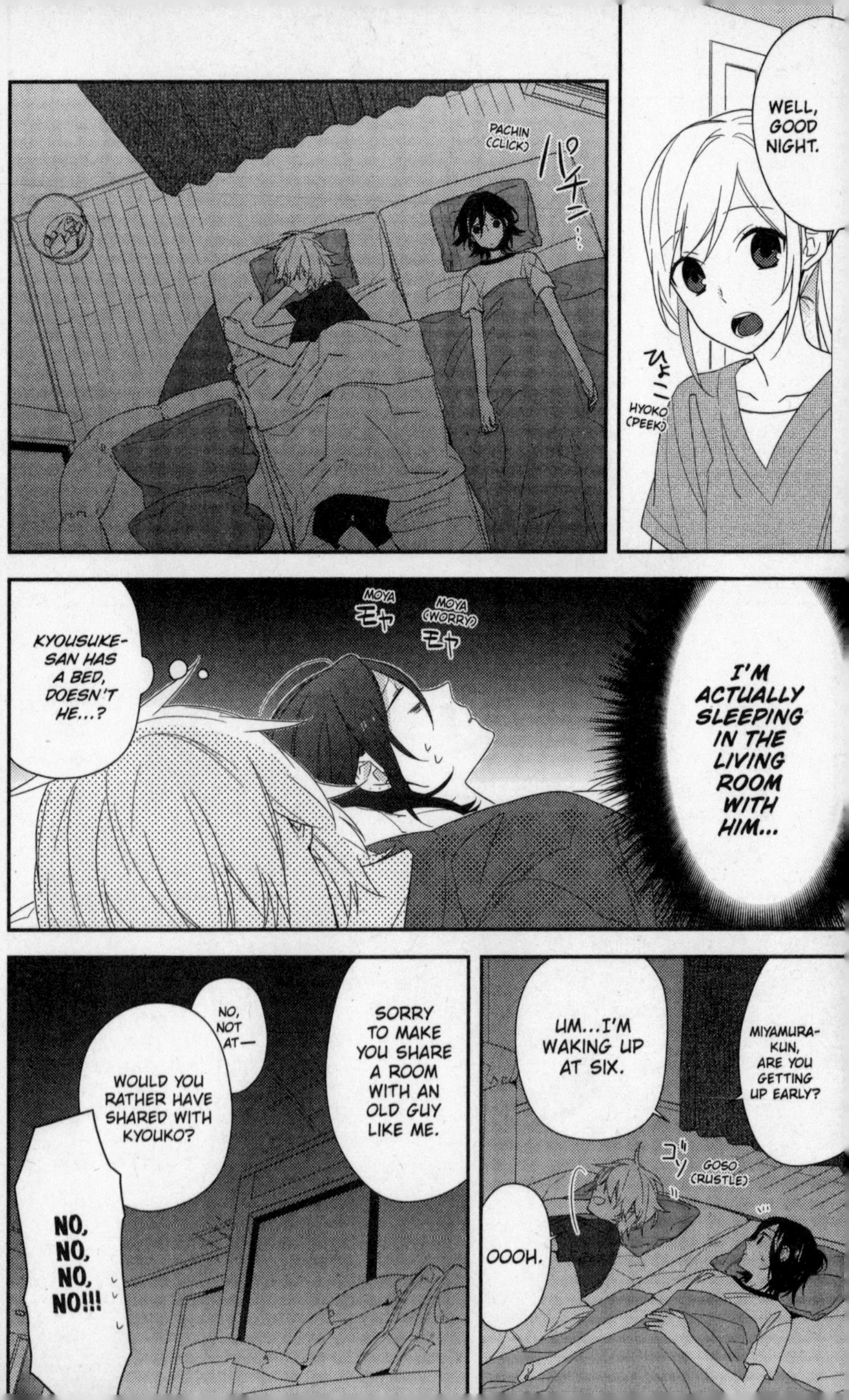

WELL, GOOD NIGHT.
ひょこ
HYOKO (PEEK)
パチン
PACHIN (CLICK)
I'M ACTUALLY SLEEPING IN THE LIVING ROOM WITH HIM...
モヤ
MOYA
モヤ
MOYA (WORRY)
KYOUSUKE-SAN HAS A BED, DOESN'T HE...?
MIYAMURA-KUN, ARE YOU GETTING UP EARLY?
UM...I'M WAKING UP AT SIX.
ゴソ
GOSO (RUSTLE)
OOOH.
SORRY TO MAKE YOU SHARE A ROOM WITH AN OLD GUY LIKE ME.
NO, NOT AT—
WOULD YOU RATHER HAVE SHARED WITH KYOUKO?
NO, NO, NO, NO!!!

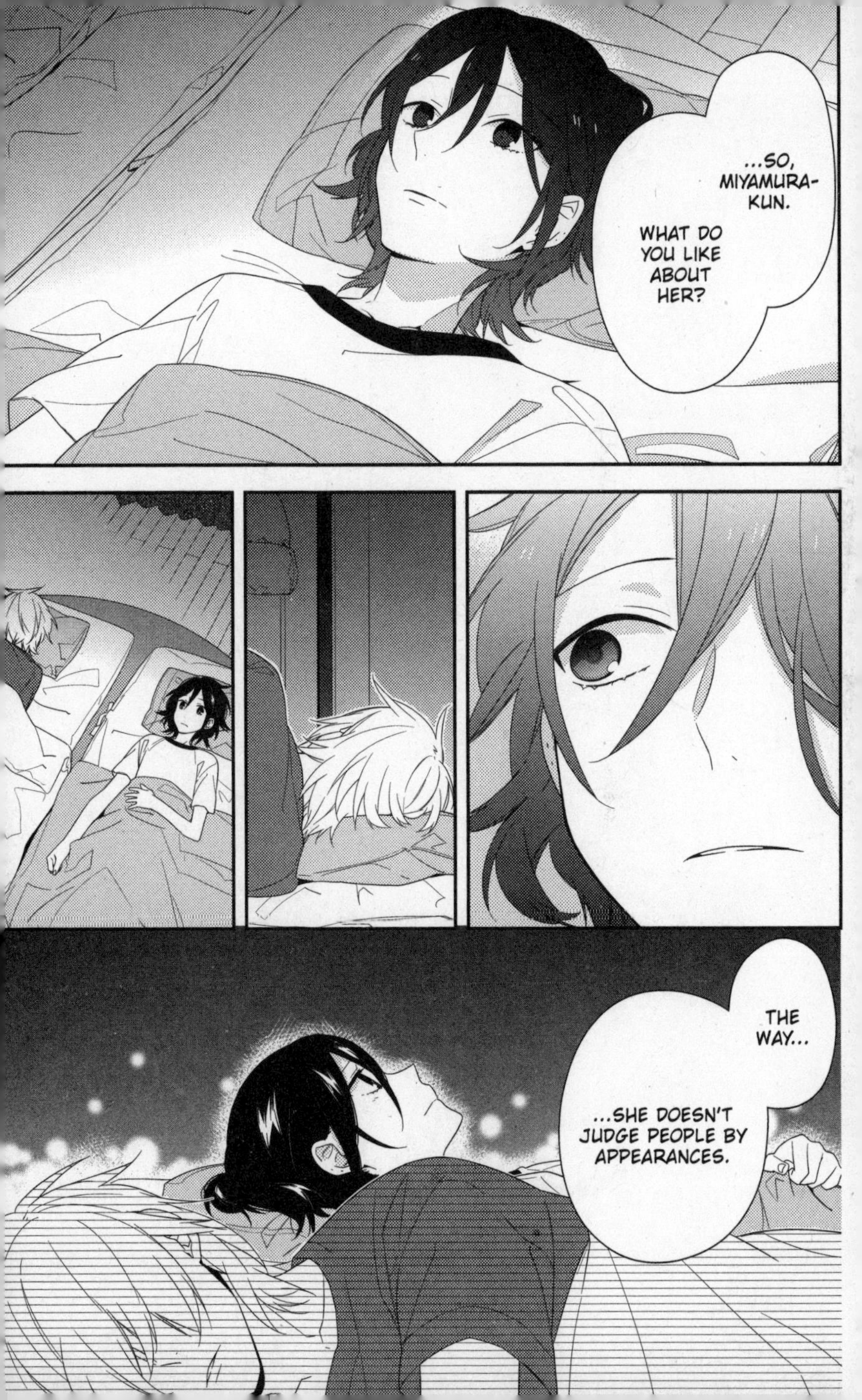
...SO, MIYAMURA-KUN.
WHAT DO YOU LIKE ABOUT HER?
THE WAY...
...SHE DOESN'T JUDGE PEOPLE BY APPEARANCES.

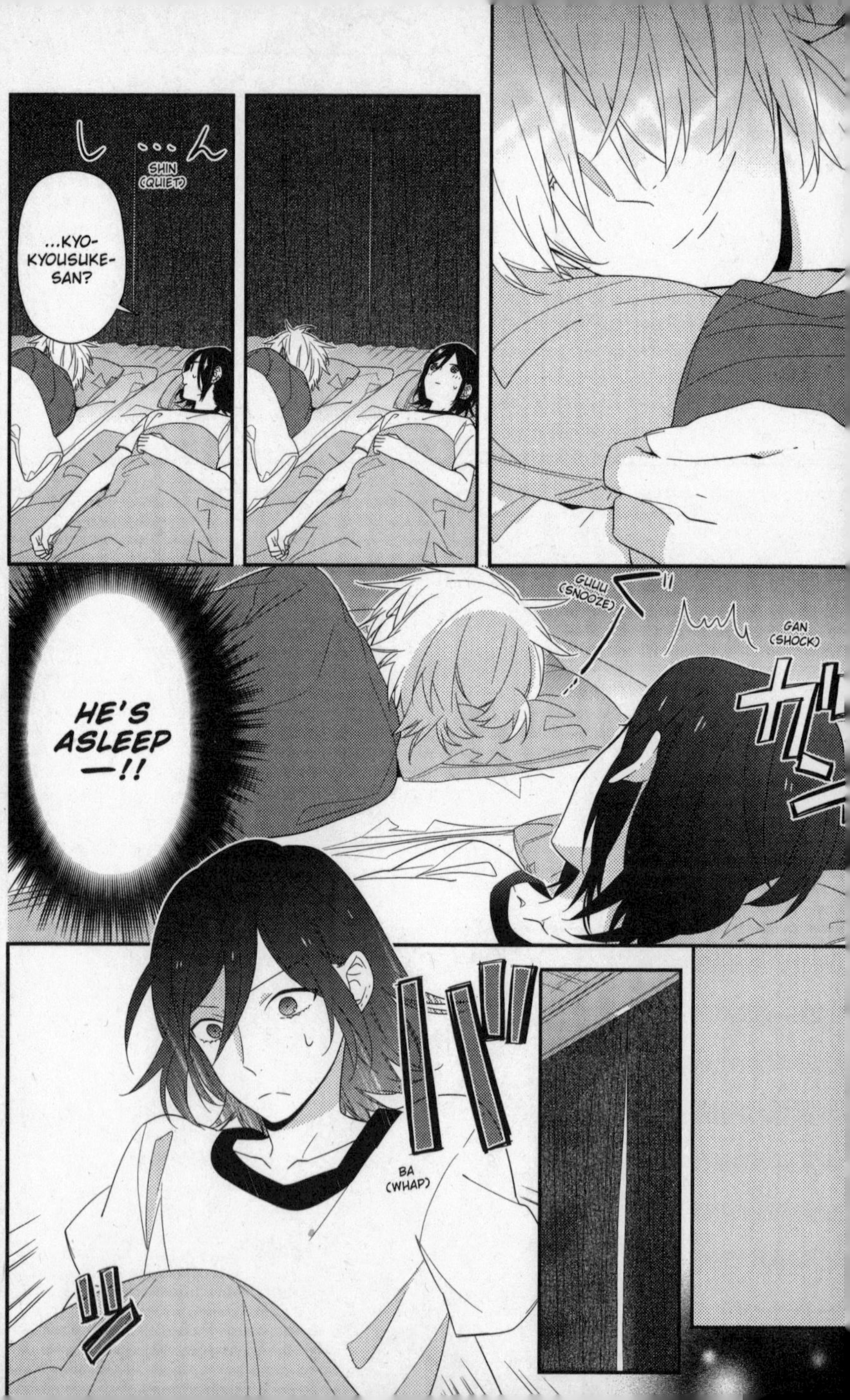

し…ん
SHIN (QUIET)
...KYO-KYOUSUKE-SAN?
GAN (SHOCK)
GUUU (SNOOZE)
HE'S ASLEEP—!!
BA (WHAP)

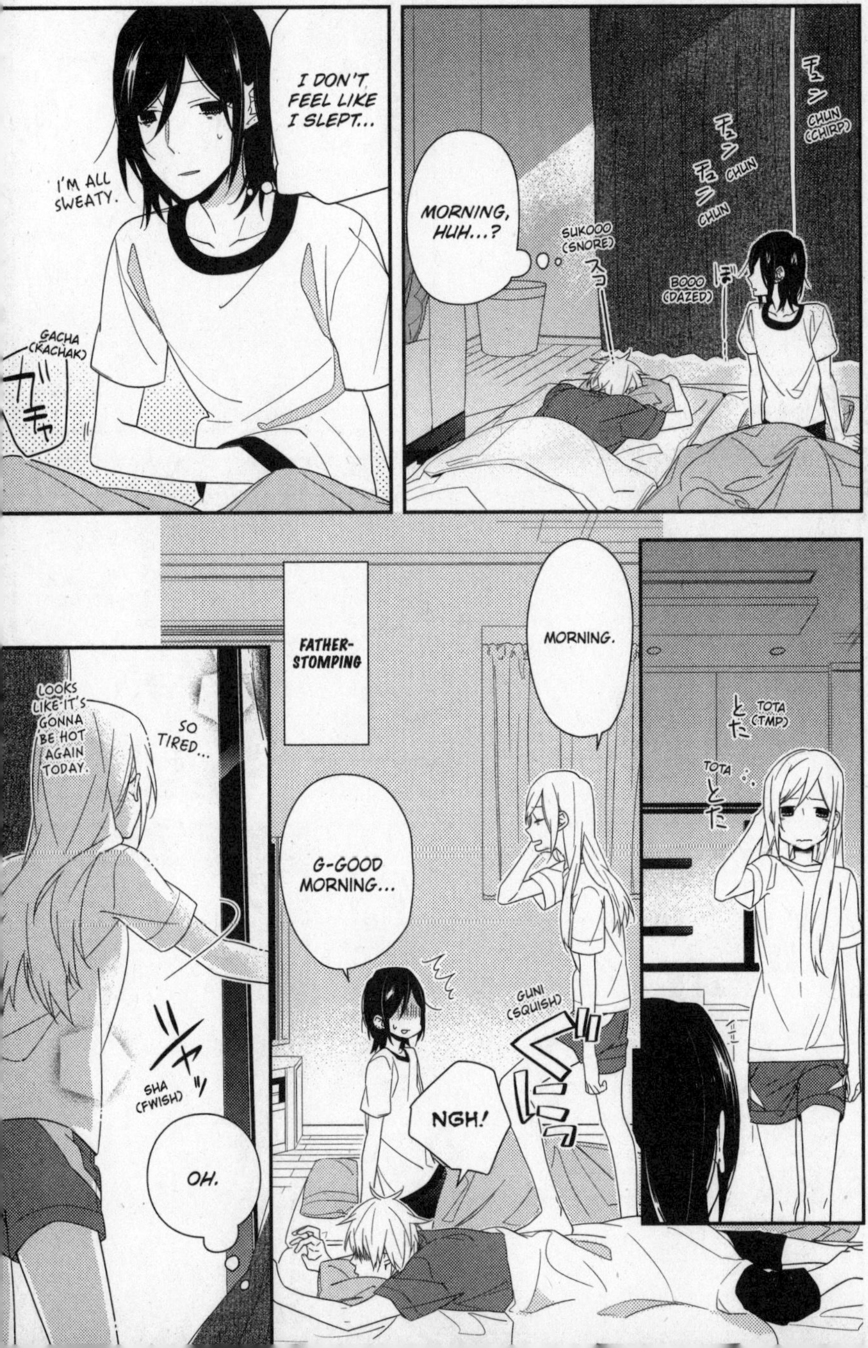
チュン
CHUN (CHIRP)
チュン
CHUN
チュン
CHUN
MORNING, HUH...?
SUKOOO (SNORE)
スコー
BOOO (DAZED)
ぼー
I DON'T FEEL LIKE I SLEPT...
I'M ALL SWEATY.
GACHA (KACHAK)
ガチャ
MORNING.
とた
TOTA (TMP)
TOTA
とた
G-GOOD MORNING...
GUNI (SQUISH)
ぐにっ
NGH!
FATHER-STOMPING
LOOKS LIKE IT'S GONNA BE HOT AGAIN TODAY.
SO TIRED...
シャッ
SHA (FWISH)
OH.

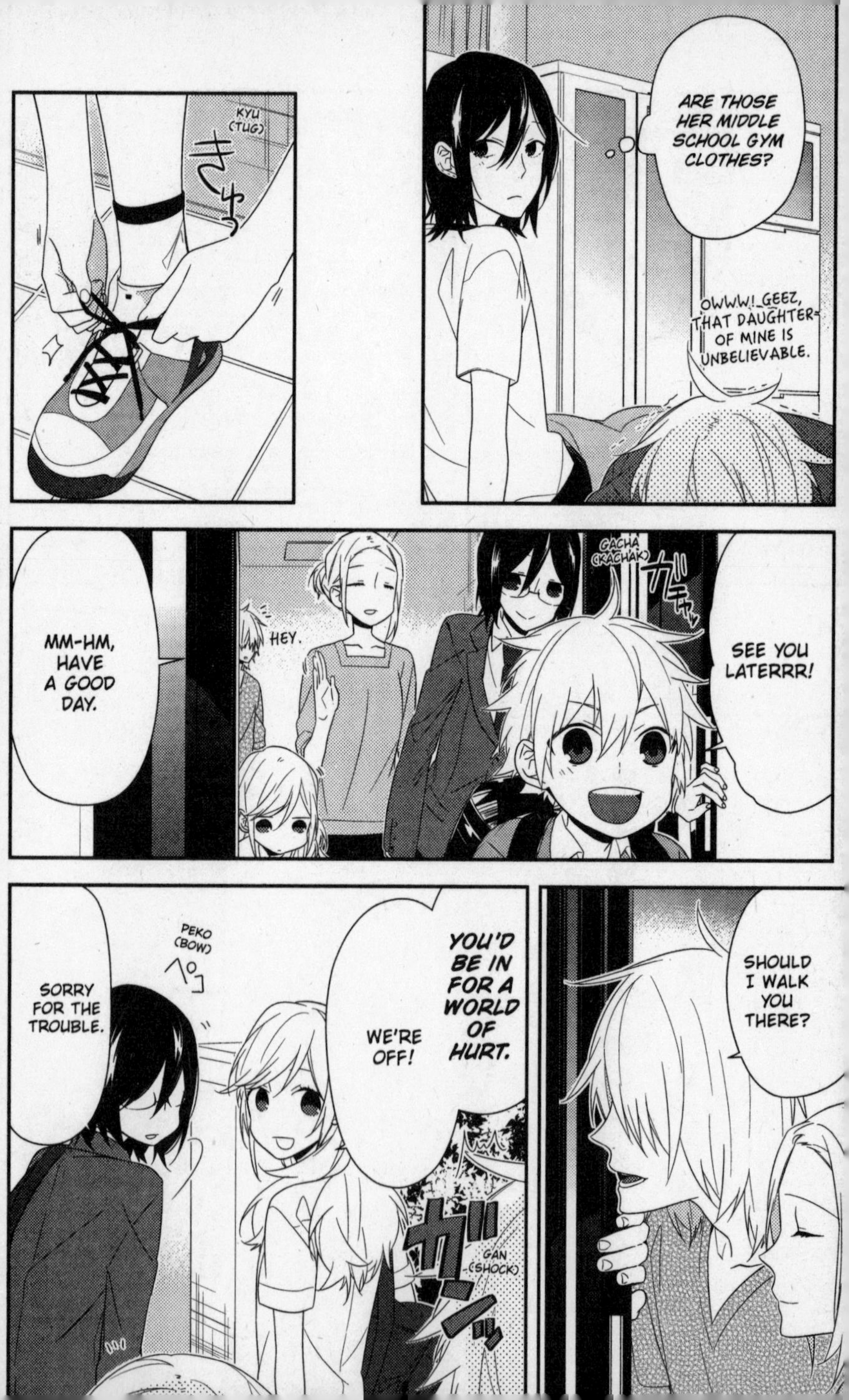
ARE THOSE HER MIDDLE SCHOOL GYM CLOTHES?
OWWW!_GEEZ, THAT DAUGHTER OF MINE IS UNBELIEVABLE.
KYU (TUG)
SEE YOU LATERRR!
GACHA (KACHAK)
HEY.
MM-HM, HAVE A GOOD DAY.
SHOULD I WALK YOU THERE?
YOU'D BE IN FOR A WORLD OF HURT.
GAN (SHOCK)
WE'RE OFF!
PEKO (BOW)
SORRY FOR THE TROUBLE.

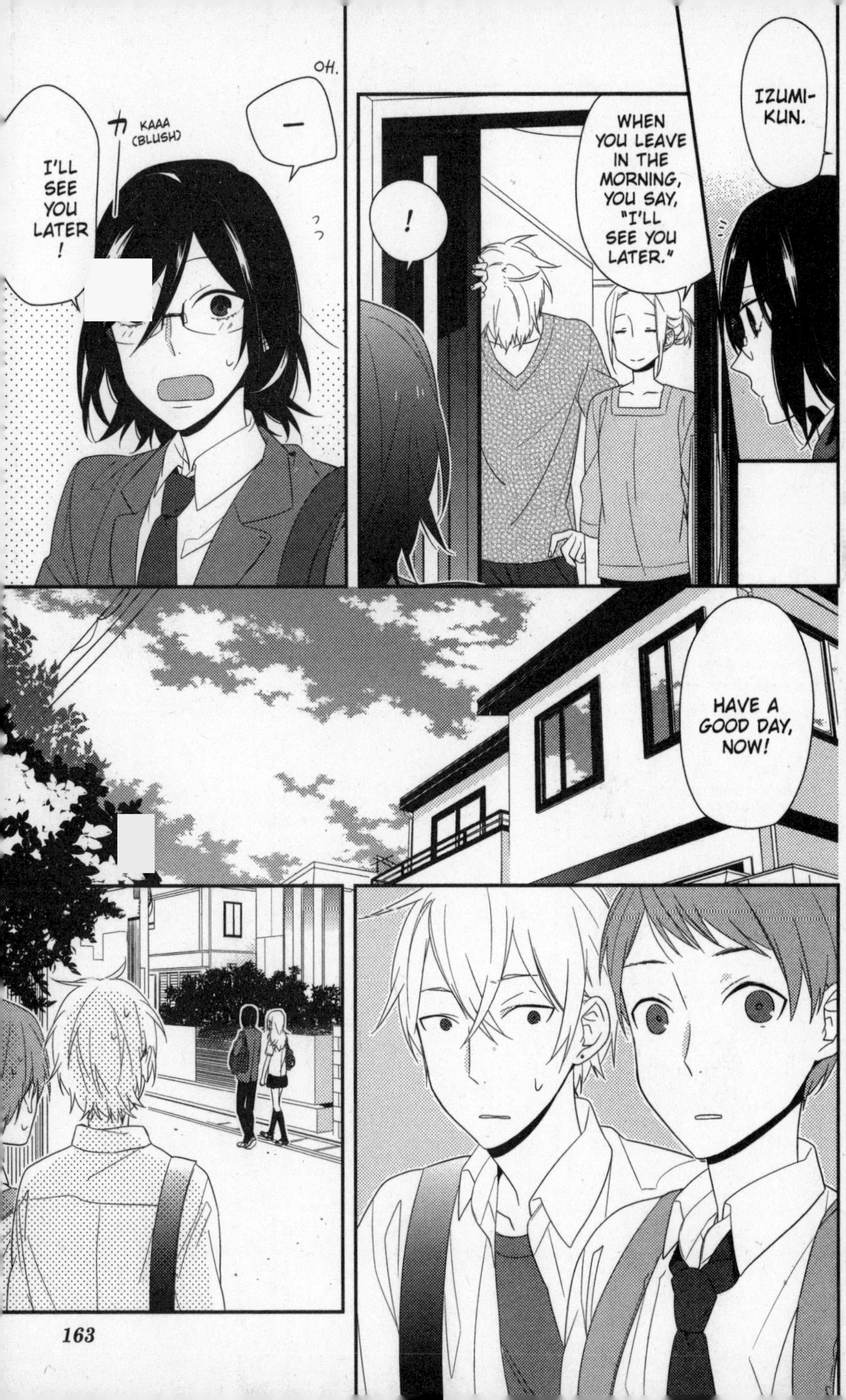
IZUMI-KUN.
WHEN YOU LEAVE IN THE MORNING, YOU SAY, "I'LL SEE YOU LATER."
!
OH.
—
カ
KAAA (BLUSH)
I'LL SEE YOU LATER!
HAVE A GOOD DAY, NOW!

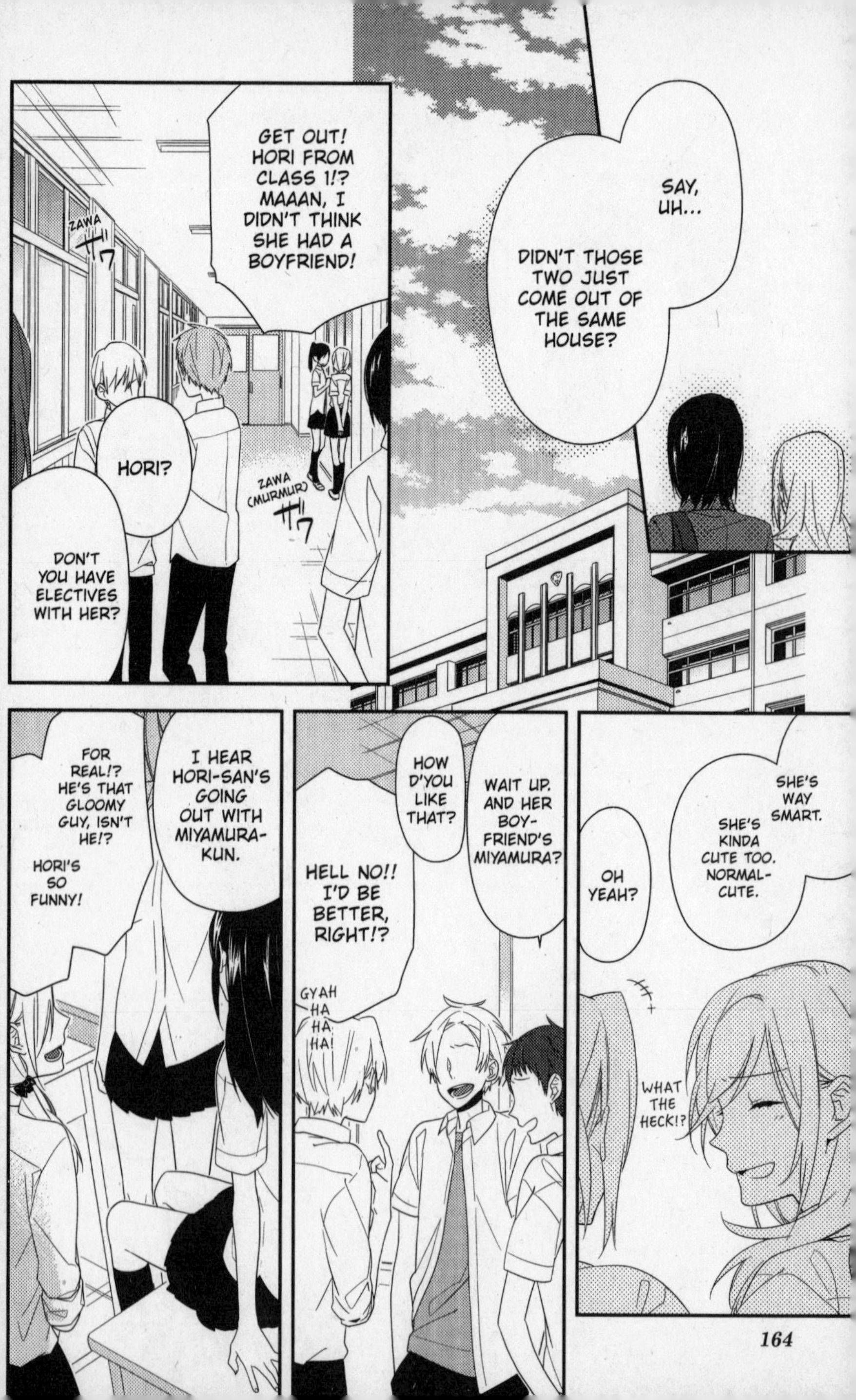
SAY, UH...
DIDN'T THOSE TWO JUST COME OUT OF THE SAME HOUSE?
GET OUT! HORI FROM CLASS 1!? MAAAN, I DIDN'T THINK SHE HAD A BOYFRIEND!
ZAWA
HORI?
ZAWA (MURMUR)
DON'T YOU HAVE ELECTIVES WITH HER?
SHE'S WAY SMART.
SHE'S KINDA CUTE TOO. NORMAL-CUTE.
OH YEAH?
WHAT THE HECK!?
WAIT UP. AND HER BOY-FRIEND'S MIYAMURA?
HOW D'YOU LIKE THAT?
HELL NO!! I'D BE BETTER, RIGHT!?
GYAH HA HA HA!
I HEAR HORI-SAN'S GOING OUT WITH MIYAMURA-KUN.
FOR REAL!? HE'S THAT GLOOMY GUY, ISN'T HE!?
HORI'S SO FUNNY!

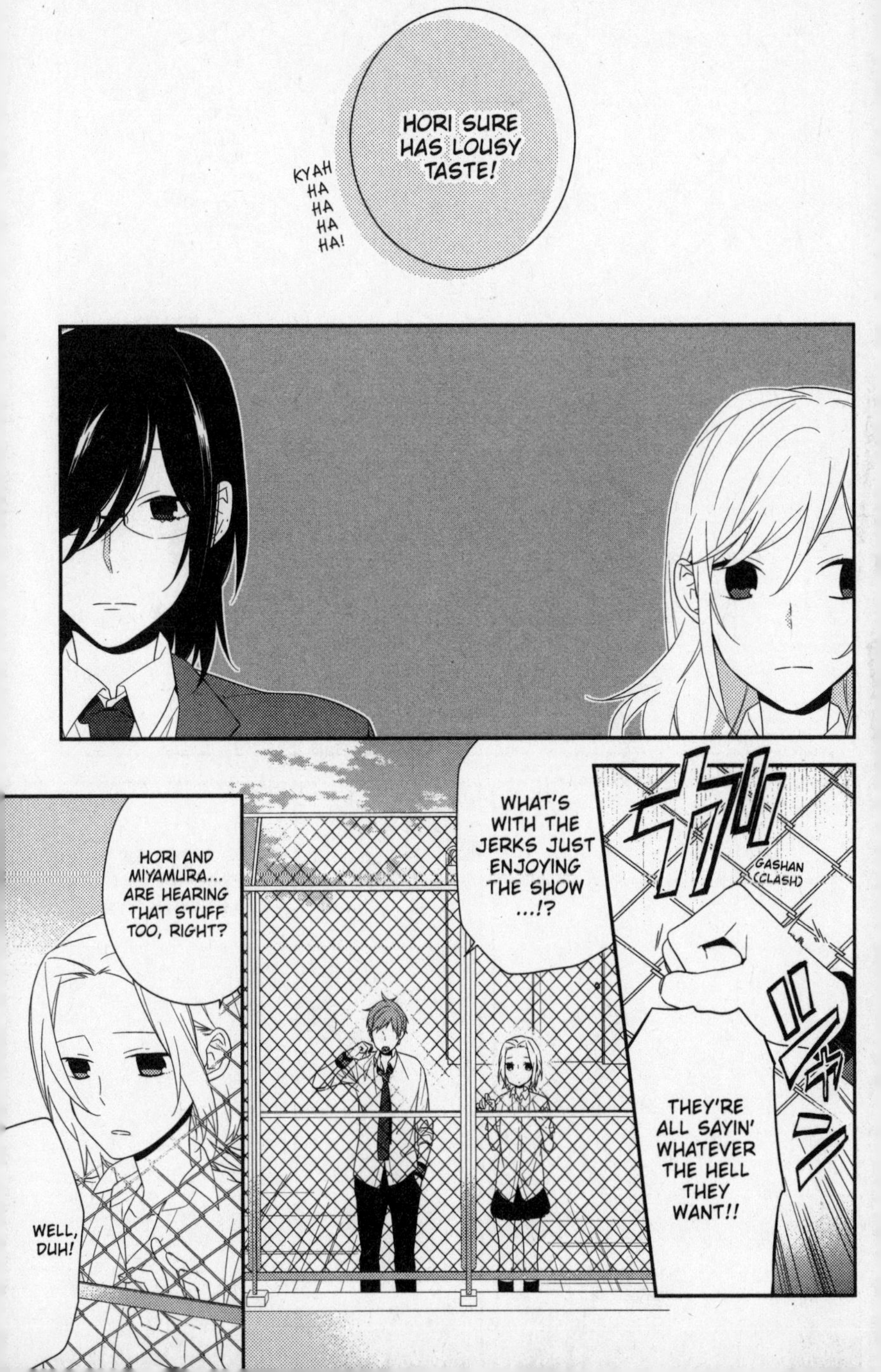
HORI SURE HAS LOUSY TASTE!
KYAH HA HA HA HA!
GASHAN (CLASH)
WHAT'S WITH THE JERKS JUST ENJOYING THE SHOW ...!?
THEY'RE ALL SAYIN' WHATEVER THE HELL THEY WANT!!
HORI AND MIYAMURA... ARE HEARING THAT STUFF TOO, RIGHT?
WELL, DUH!

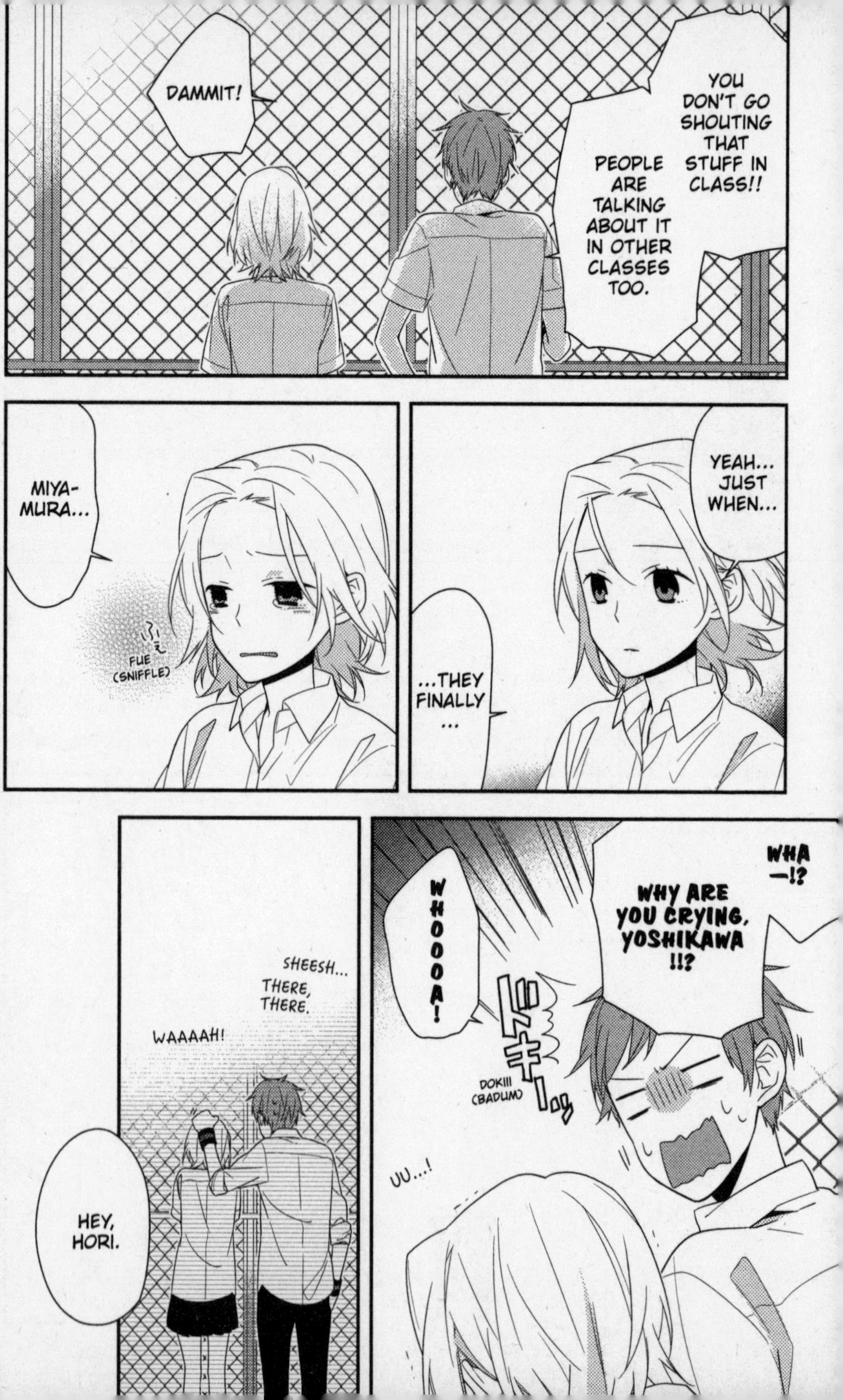
YOU DON'T GO SHOUTING THAT STUFF IN CLASS!!
PEOPLE ARE TALKING ABOUT IT IN OTHER CLASSES TOO.
DAMMIT!
YEAH... JUST WHEN...
...THEY FINALLY ...
MIYA-MURA...
ふぇ
FUE (SNIFFLE)
WHA—!?
WHY ARE YOU CRYING, YOSHIKAWA!!?
WHOOOOA!
ドキーッ
DOKIII (BADUM)
UU...!
SHEESH... THERE, THERE.
WAAAAH!
HEY, HORI.

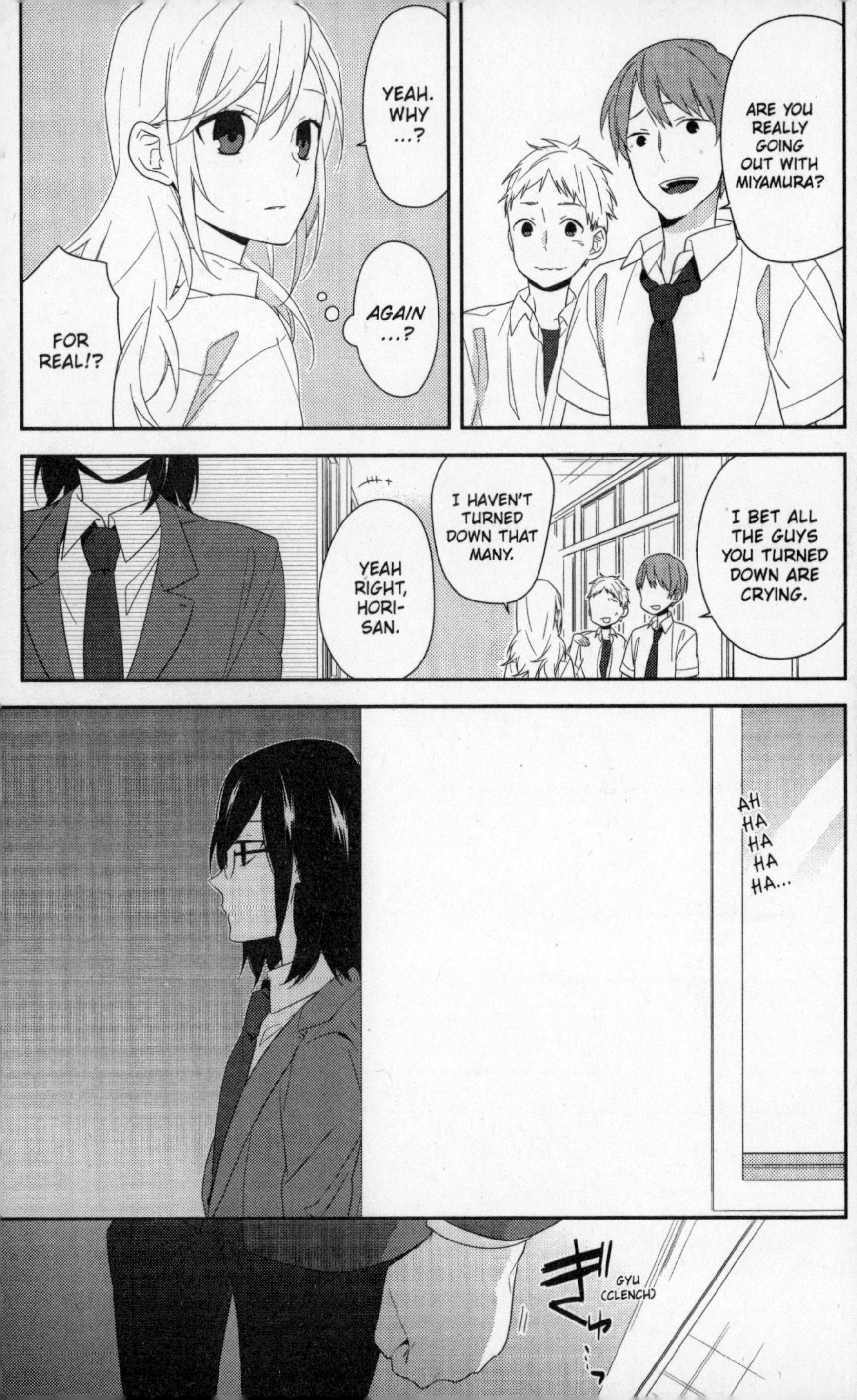
ARE YOU REALLY GOING OUT WITH MIYAMURA?
YEAH. WHY ...?
AGAIN ...?
FOR REAL!?
I BET ALL THE GUYS YOU TURNED DOWN ARE CRYING.
I HAVEN'T TURNED DOWN THAT MANY.
YEAH RIGHT, HORI-SAN.
AH HA HA HA HA...
GYU (CLENCH)

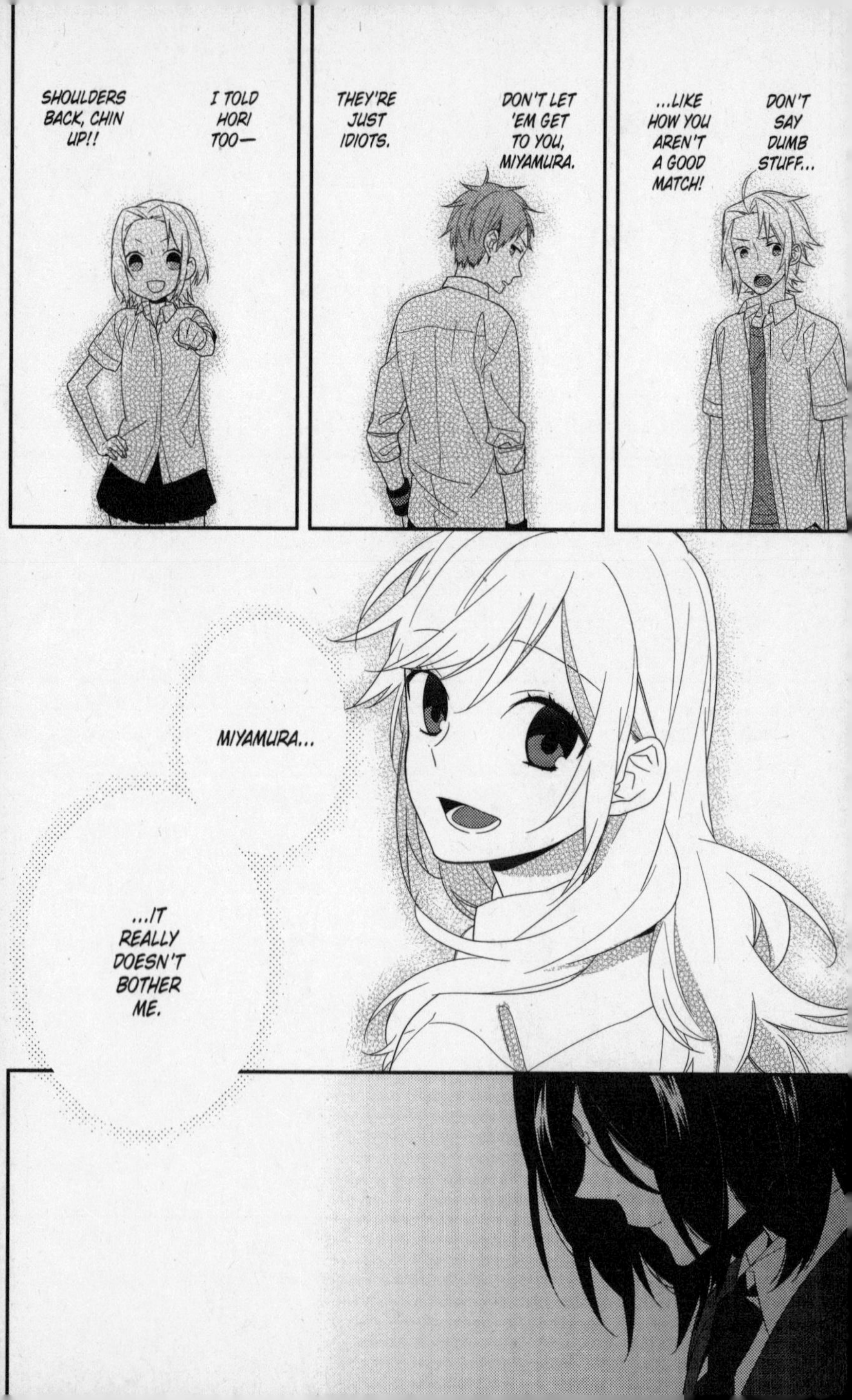
DON'T SAY DUMB STUFF...
...LIKE HOW YOU AREN'T A GOOD MATCH!
DON'T LET 'EM GET TO YOU, MIYAMURA.
THEY'RE JUST IDIOTS.
I TOLD HORI TOO—
SHOULDERS BACK, CHIN UP!!
MIYAMURA...
...IT REALLY DOESN'T BOTHER ME.

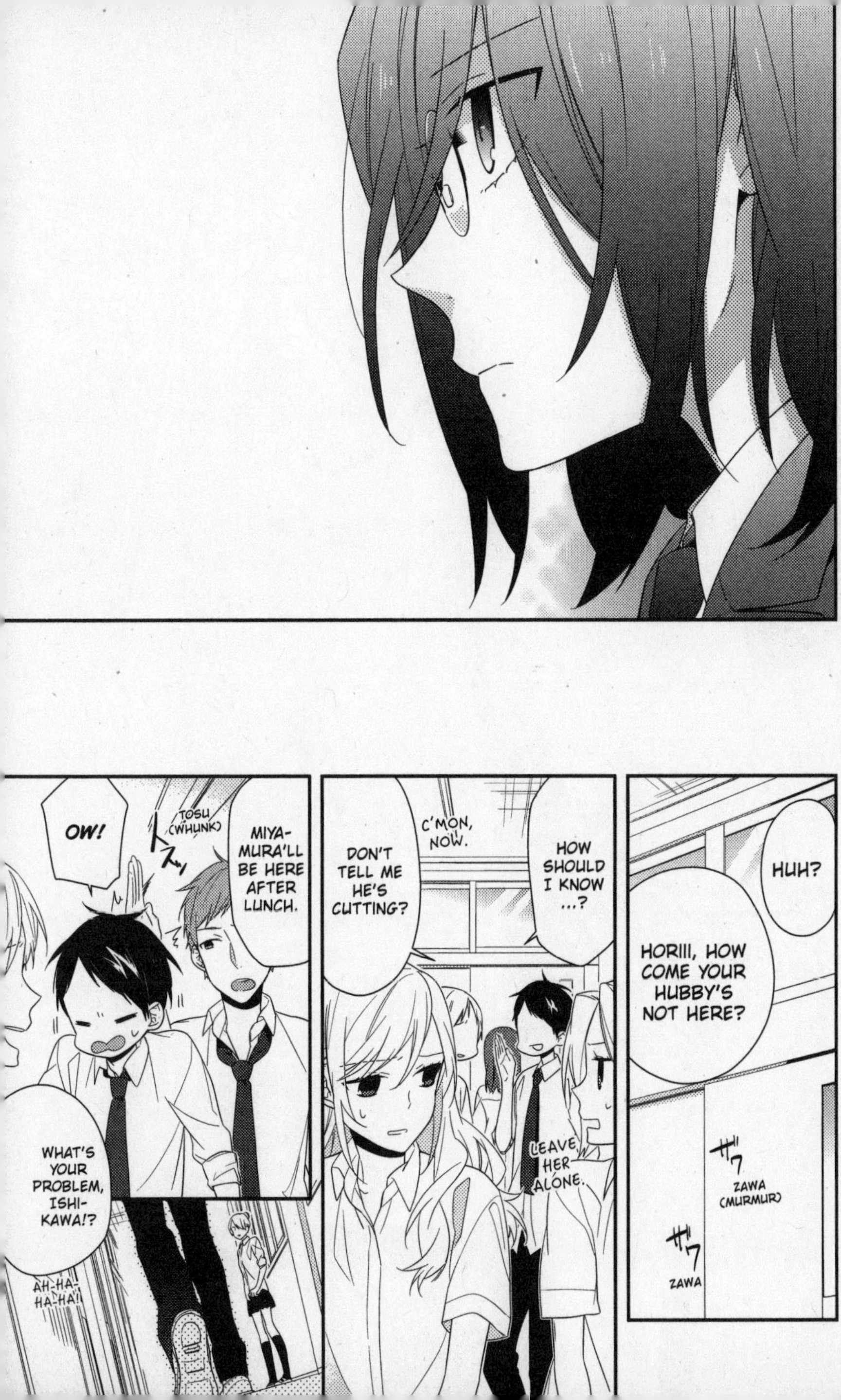
HUH?
HORIII, HOW COME YOUR HUBBY'S NOT HERE?
ZAWA (MURMUR)
ZAWA
HOW SHOULD I KNOW ...?
C'MON, NOW.
DON'T TELL ME HE'S CUTTING?
LEAVE HER ALONE.
MIYA-MURA'LL BE HERE AFTER LUNCH.
TOSU (WHUNK)
OW!
WHAT'S YOUR PROBLEM, ISHI-KAWA!?
AH-HA-HA-HA!!

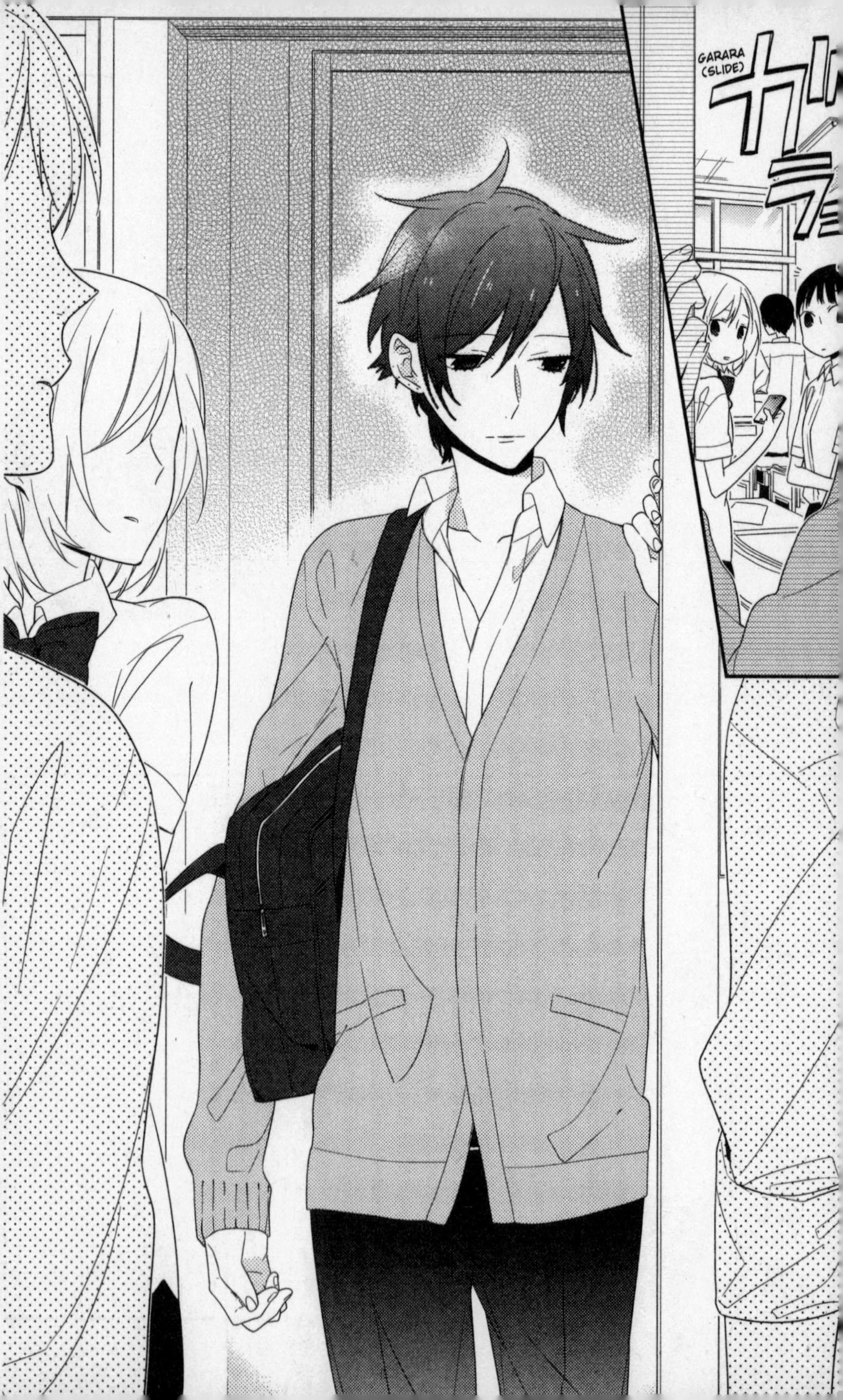
GARARA (SLIDE)

KYU
キュ
(SQUEAK)

キュ
KYU

KYU
キュ

ス...
スッ
(PASS)

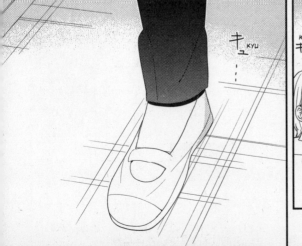

キュ
KYU
...

キュ
KYU

キュ
KYU

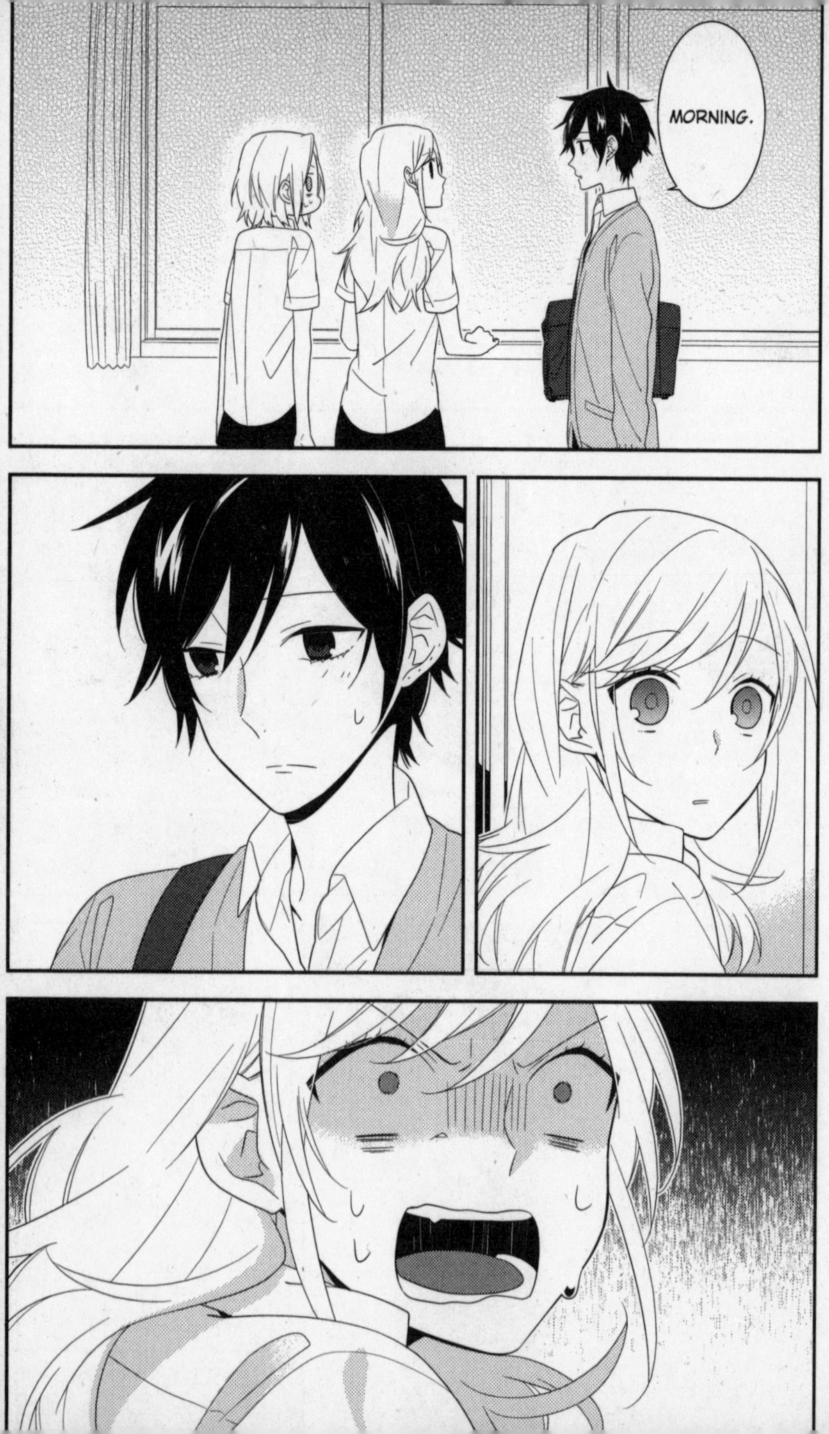
MORNING.